Spirit Possession and the Origins of Christianity

Also Available from Bardic Press

The Gnostic:
A Journal of Gnosticism, Western Esotericism and Spirituality

The Revolt of the Widows
Stevan Davies

The Gospel of Thomas and Christian Wisdom
Stevan Davies

Voices of Gnosticism: Interviews with Elaine Pagels, Marvin Meyer, Bart Ehrman, Stevan Davies and Other Leading Scholars
Miguel Conner

Planetary Types: The Science of Celestial Influence
Tony Cartledge

New Nightingale, New Rose: Poems From the Divan of Hafiz
translated by Richard Le Gallienne

The Quatrains of Omar Khayyam:
translated by Edward Fitzgerald, Justin McCarthy and Richard Le Gallienne

Door of the Beloved: Ghazals of Hafiz
translated by Justin McCarthy

The Four Branches of the Mabinogi
Will Parker

Christ In Islam
James Robson

My Dear Father Gurdjieff
Nikolai de Stjernvall

Visit our website at www.bardic-press.com
email us at info@bardic-press.com

SPIRIT POSSESSION AND THE ORIGINS OF CHRISTIANITY

Stevan Davies

Bardic Press
Dublin

Copyright © 2014 Bardic Press
Text of *Spirit Possession and the Origins of Christianity* Copyright © 2014 Stevan Davies

Printed on acid-free paper

Published by Bardic Press
71 Kenilworth Road
Dublin 6W
Ireland

http://www.bardic-press.com
info@bardic-press.com

ISBN 978-1-906834-19-7 (Paperback)
ISBN 978-1-906834-20-3 (Kindle)
ISBN 978-1-906834-28-9 (Hardcover)

Contents

Preface	1
Introduction:	
On the Pentecostal Origins of the Christian Movement	3
Jesus the Healer:	
1 The Quest for the Historical Jesus	41
2 Spirit Possession	57
3 Prophets and Prophecy	78
4 Baptism	87
5 Jesus' Healings	101
6 Demon Possession	113
7 Jesus' Exorcisms	125
8 Jesus and His Associates	140
9 The Function of Jesus' Parables	155
10 Jesus' Therapeutic Speech	172
11 The Sayings of the Spirit	186
12 The Christian Cult	204
13 Missionary Inductive Discourse	223
14 Conclusion	239
On the Odes of Solomon as Evidence For a Pre-Christianity	245
The Odes of Solomon	284
Afterword: The Two Most Important Events in Western History	312
Bibliography	318

Preface

This book consists of several investigations into the question: "How did Christianity begin?" Most of the book was written during a National Endowment for the Humanities Summer Seminar at Princeton University. The rest I wrote at Misericordia University. These investigations are united by my conviction that Christianity began as a movement based on the human potential for personality dissociation, explained intra-culturally as the entrance of a spirit-person into the body, which spirit-person takes over the body and the mind for a period of time. This is "spirit-possession," a category of religious experience recognized and studied by anthropologists for well over a century, but not a category of religious experience that scholars of early Christianity often seem to recognize or utilize. Their lack of interest is surprising and a bit perplexing because the foundational texts of the Christian movement, i.e. the New Testament, are replete with accounts of spirit possession as the root factor in formative Christian experience.

Perhaps the kind of spirit possession understood as the experience of the Holy Spirit entering into Christian people is regarded by Christian scholars as an entirely different sort of thing than spirit-possession understood as the experience of some other Spirit (African? Chinese? Cuban?) entering into some other non-Christian people. I suppose if you believe that there is a Christian Holy Spirit out there in the real world who does in actual fact enter people, and that all other supposedly divine Spirits do not exist in reality and so do not enter people, you would not want to discuss spirit-possession generically at all. Certainly one can find hundreds of books on the New Testament and the rise of Christianity and the career of the Historical Jesus that tacitly assume that when a Holy Spirit (aka Paraclete) is said to enter into people that this is a sui generis sort of experience unique to Christianity.

I will frequently discuss the experience of the Holy Spirit in the present book. It is, in my considered opinion, the single most important factor in the rise of the Christian religion, and I will show that the principal authors of the New Testament (Mark, Luke, Paul, John, etc.) thought so too. The beginning of the Gospel, according to Mark (whose account is the foundation for the later gospels of Matthew and Luke, and perhaps also that of John) is the event of Jesus experiencing what he believed to be a spirit entering into him. The beginning of the Acts of the Apostles describes the entry of a spirit into all Jesus' followers. Paul speaks of spirit experience as crucial to the experience of members of his churches. John has Jesus foretell the arrival of a spirit-paraclete that will function within the members of the nascent church. And so forth.

The essays in this book are several different investigations. They have in common the fact that the experience called "the spirit," is a central factor in New Testament accounts of the origin of Christianity. However, my different investigations are not intended to be one self-contained argument. They are approaches to similar questions, but they come from different angles of approach. It may be the custom among authors to make sure that their various approaches to a question are self-consistent and mutually reinforcing, but this book contains differing approaches, some that are not altogether consistent with one another. As such, they are suggestions, ideas, lines of thought, provocations to think differently about the origins of the Christian religion. If you find one part convincing but another not so, that is just as well. I hope readers will enjoy this book and find ideas in it that they can work with and improve upon.

Introduction: On The Pentecostal Origins of the Christian Movement

Jesus of Nazareth had very little to do with the initial foundation and spread of Christianity, or so I will argue. Further, I will maintain that the description of the importance of Jesus' career as an exorcist, provided and then rejected in the Gospel of Mark, and the vision of the originating Pentecostal impetus of the Christian movement presented in Luke's Acts of the Apostles, are generally correct and that those descriptions of the career of Jesus and the rise of the Christian movement do sufficiently account for the origin of Christianity.

Recently an intellectual movement called Mythicism has received considerable attention.[1] Mythicism argues that Jesus of Nazareth never existed at all. It claims that the Christian movement invented him as a founder figure, a mythical heavenly entity come down to earth. The reports of the sayings attributed to him, and the deeds supposedly performed by him, are entirely invented or mistaken according to Mythicism.

The Mythicists' argument is founded on the fact that our earliest

---

1 Cf. e.g., George A. Wells, *The Jesus Legend*, Open Court Publishing Company, 1996; Robert M. Price, *Deconstructing Jesus*, Prometheus, 2000; Earl Doherty, *Jesus: Neither God Nor Man - The Case for a Mythical Jesus*, Age of Reason Publications, 2009, For an attack on the mythicist position cf. Bart Ehrman, *Did Jesus Exist? The Historical Argument for Jesus of Nazareth*, HarperOne, 2013 and for counterattacks cf. Richard Carrier ed., *Bart Ehrman and the Quest of the Historical Jesus of Nazareth: An Evaluation of Ehrman's Did Jesus Exist?*, American Atheist Press, 2013.

surviving Christian texts, the New Testament epistles, show almost no interest in the life or teachings of Jesus. Except for his last week on earth, there is almost no such interest shown in the Acts of the Apostles. Interest in Jesus' life story was surprisingly late to develop, and when it developed it did so almost entirely through the reworking and creation of ahistorical legends and miracle stories and, in the case of the Gospel of John, accounts of a divinity come to earth. Indeed, there really are only two accounts, that of Mark and that of John, and the latter may be dependent on the former for its basic narrative. I will endeavor to explain why this was the case, and to show how Christianity first came into being, and why the historical Jesus was of little interest to the first Christians. I am not making a Mythicist argument here, but I do think that the Mythicists have discovered problems in the supposed common-sense of historical Jesus theories that deserve to be taken seriously.

What I will be discussing immediately below will not be surprising news to biblical scholars; it takes what scholars generally know and posits that what they know is correct, i.e. that we know very little about Jesus. And then, reasonably enough, I raise the question: why? If Jesus was the founder of the Christian movement, why did Christians care so little about his life and teachings that they failed to retain reasonably accurate records of them? And why, as time went on, did records of his life and teachings begin to be created out of imagination? What started the Christian movement if Jesus didn't? Or did he found it, but nevertheless his life story and program of teachings had little to do with it? I'll suggest answers to those questions shortly.

Faith that there was an historical Jesus begins with the fact that we have several biographical narratives about his life: the narrative Gospels of Matthew, Mark, Luke, and John, and James, at least two long lists of his sayings, the Gospel of Thomas and Q, and letters by foundational Christians, especially those of Paul and the pseudo-Pauls. Scholars today tend to presume that these materials, while certainly not accurate by the historical standards of the twenty-first century, are good enough for religion work, and as good as you have any reason to expect from people writing so very long ago. But they are not good sources at all for an historical Jesus. For well over a century now, scholars of the New Testament have found evidence that what appear to be biographical narratives about the life of Jesus are, with one possible exception, works of fiction. Let's begin with the last early Christian biographical gospel to be written, the culmination of the synoptic tradition: the Gospel of James.[2] It purports to give a biography of Jesus' mother Mary beginning with discussion of her parents Joachim and Anna and the events that led up to Mary's conception, then it describes the privileged environment wherein she was raised until such time as she could enter the Jerusalem temple and dwell there provisioned by angels. Then Joseph becomes her guardian, an angel announces her impregnation, and we read an interestingly revised amalgamation of Luke's and Matthew's accounts of Jesus' birth.[3] It's a fascinating story. Protestants know nothing of it. For Catholics the story once had quasi-canonical status. Great European churches (e.g. Santa Croce and Santa Maria Novella in Florence, the Cathedral of Orvieto, Giotto's Scrovegni Chapel) feature sanctuaries sumptuously decorated with huge paintings illustrating the story of Christ. On the right side one finds the story of Jesus as found in the canonical scriptures, on the left side the precedent story found in the Gospel of James. The Gospel of James is the alpha, the canonical scriptures the omega.

The Gospel of James is not part of the canon. Accordingly, scholars have no commitment to defend its historicity and most believe it to be fiction from start to finish except where it overlaps with canonical tales. There, of course, its miracles of virginal conception and stellar proclamation and angelic presence are defended by churchmen as factual. But the whole Gospel of James is as fictitious as the stories of the miracles of prenatal Buddha in the Jataka tales.

The Gospel of John's tales of an incarnate God walking about speaking of His descent from another world into this world of devil and death are fiction. As with the Gospel of James' accounts, scholars know perfectly well that the Gospel of John does not give us factual accounts of Jesus' life, deeds, discourse, and so forth. Only insofar as there are similarities to the accounts in the synoptic gospels is John's book defended as historically plausible. Otherwise, its miracles and many stun-

---

[2] The "synoptic" gospels are Mark and the expanded revisions of Mark: Luke and Matthew. James, which is an expanded revision of the first chapters of Luke and Matthew, is also thereby a "synoptic" gospel.

[3] The Gospel of James describes the cessation of time itself at the moment of Jesus' birth and then the resumption of time. This is the break between B.C.E. and C.E. The passage is one of the most remarkable in all of ancient literature.

ning paragraphs of unadulterated self-promotion by the Incarnate One are commonly acknowledged to be no more historical than are the stories of Krishna performing miracles on earth.

The dominant theory of New Testament scholarship for the past century and a half has been that the Gospels of Matthew and Luke are revised and expanded versions of the Gospel of Mark. Most scholars affirm that Matthew and Luke used Mark as a narrative framework, added independent accounts of his miraculous birth and miraculous resurrection, and incorporated, each in his or her own way,[4] a list of sayings attributed to Jesus that German scholarship of the mid nineteenth century called "die Quelle" or "the Source." Today the list is known as Q, an abbreviation of Quelle. [5]

Matthew and Luke principally add miracle stories, birth legends and narratives about resurrection appearances (Matthew's in Galilee, Luke's in and about Jerusalem), to Mark's gospel along with various sayings known from no other canonical sources (e.g. the Prodigal Son and the Good Samaritan). They add narrative settings necessary to incorporate the sayings list Q, which was nearly devoid of narrative, into the ongoing biographical narrative scheme developed by Mark. Matthew favors the idea that Jesus gave lectures and so we have a great many sayings from Q and from Mark and from Matthew's imagination and/or tradition incorporated into five or six principal speeches.[6] Luke pre-

---

[4] This is not the place to argue the case, but it is quite likely that the Gospel of Luke and the Acts of the Apostles were written by a woman, one who was similar to Lydia who is discussed in Acts chapter 16. For a good explication, cf. Randal Helms, *Who Wrote the Gospels*, Millenium Press, 1997 and also Stevan Davies, "Afterword" in *The Revolt of the Widows: The Social World of the Apocryphal Acts*, Second Edition, Bardic Press, 2012.

[5] A minority of scholars hold "the Farrer hypothesis" that Matthew revised Mark and then Luke revised Mark using Matthew as a source. Hence, for them, Q never existed. But since they do not hold that Matthew invented most of the sayings he added to Mark, the sayings said to be from Q were actually added by Matthew from somewhere unknown. It turns out that it does not really make much difference if there was a Non-Markan-Matthew source or a Q source for both hypothetical sources share the same basic set of sayings and one can reasonably presume that those sayings give us evidence of a pre-Matthean Christian point of view regarding Jesus' teachings.

[6] There are commonly said to be five speeches of Jesus in Matthew's gospel: the Sermon on the Mount (chapters 5-7); instructions to disciples (10); the Parables (13); the Discourse on the Church (18); a speech on the End Times (24-25). But chapter 23 too is a lengthy speech, one briefly confirming the divinely ordained authority of the Pharisees and then excoriating them at length for hypocrisy, and that makes six.

fers to represent Jesus' discourse as ongoing dialogues and occasional discussions frequently set during meals. The lectures and dialogues and narrative elements that Matthew and Luke use to embed Q into their gospels are their own creations. Possibly many of the isolated sayings that they used go back to Jesus himself, but it is not likely that a great many do.[7]

A moment's thought will reveal that you, gentle reader, know more of the life of Jesus than Matthew or James or Luke or John ever did. You have read all their works and the Gospel of Thomas besides, and the Gospel of Mark, and the reconstructed Q.[8] None of the sacred authors had as many written sources as you have. An appeal to their knowledge of unwritten sources is meaningless for, if any of them had a significant store of information that they did not incorporate in their writing, we know nothing whatsoever about it because they did not think it significant enough to use.

The biography of Jesus is really only transmitted by one narrative gospel, not five. The Gospels of John and James are fictitious, the revised versions of Mark, i.e. Gospels of Luke and Matthew, are fictitious narratives except insofar as they are following the Gospel of Mark if indeed Mark is a valid historical source. If a Gospel gives reliable information regarding the biography of Jesus it is only Mark's. But Mark's Gospel is far from reliable. I will now survey the contents and intentionality of the Markan account in some detail so that you can see how little interest Mark really had in the life of an historical Jesus.

Mark's story begins with a man, Jesus, who goes to John for baptism in respect to his sins and experiences a Spirit descend upon him, a state known to anthropology as "spirit possession." For a time he wanders in the desert being "tempted by Satan," which I suspect means that we are to think he was tempted to think himself possessed by Satan. But no, he is possessed by the Holy Spirit. Angels attended him and, after John is imprisoned "Jesus went into Galilee, proclaiming the good news of God. 'The time has come,' he said. 'The kingdom of God has come

---

[7] In a sense none of them do if we consider that Jesus spoke Aramaic and the sayings attributed to him in the Bible are recorded in Greek. For most of the Gospel of Thomas they have been translated from Greek to Coptic.

[8] John Kloppenborg, *Q, the Earliest Gospel: An Introduction to the Original Stories and Sayings of Jesus*, Westminster - John Knox Press, 2008, Stevan Davies, *The Gospel of Thomas Annotated and Explained*, Skylight Paths Press, 2002, Andrew Philip Smith, *The Gospel of Thomas*, Ulysses Books, 2002.

near. Repent and believe the good news!'" (Mark 1:14-15). Jesus immediately assembles four principal disciples, Simon and Andrew, James and John, professional fishermen who for no given reason leave their families and walk off with him.

Beginnning at 1:21, Jesus enters Capernaum and "begins to teach", although we do not hear anything of what the teaching is except that he exorcises a man whose demon recognizes Jesus as the holy one of God. The people then acknowledge that he teaches with authority because he provides, "'A new teaching—and with authority! He even gives orders to impure Spirits and they obey him.' News about him spread quickly over the whole region of Galilee." Jesus' authoritative "teaching" is his command of demons according to Mark. A few hours later Jesus says to his four disciples "'Let us go somewhere else—to the nearby villages—so I can preach there also. That is why I have come.' So he traveled throughout Galilee, preaching in their synagogues and driving out demons." By the end of the very first chapter of the Gospel of Mark, due to his extraordinary success in commanding and driving out demons "Jesus could no longer enter a town openly but stayed outside in lonely places. Yet the people still came to him from everywhere."

In chapter three, Mark constructs a complex attack on the family of Jesus. We hear again that Jesus attracts huge crowds due to his proficiency as an exorcist. He appoints twelve principal disciples (nowhere does Mark even hint that this has anything to do with the twelve tribes of ancient Israel). His family resolves to take charge of him; saying he is out of his mind, or outside himself, a phrase implying that some other being is in his mind since he is not. There follows a colloquy about whose spirit possesses Jesus. Is it Beelzebul's? Is it Satan's? Is it some unclean spirit (affirmation of which proposition is the unforgiveable sin)? No. He is possessed by the Holy Spirit as we have learned from chapter 1:10 on. He does not command demons because he is their king, but because he has a divine Spirit more powerful than the demons are. Fair enough. Here come the family, brothers and mother, to take charge of him. He is in a structure with a crowd of followers and, learning that his former family stands outside, asks "Who are my mother and my brothers?" Then he looks at those now seated in a circle around him and says, "Here are my mother and my brothers! Whoever does God's will is my brother and sister and mother," (3:31-35). And that is that. The mother, brothers and sisters of Jesus disappear forever after from the Gospel of Mark, having been dismissed by Jesus himself.

We move on to chapter four, a series of parables. The chapter as a whole is certainly not a transcript of a particular occasion, but a setting within which Mark assembles a collection of material. According to this Gospel, Jesus intends his parables to be incomprehensible. First Jesus gives a parable and provides an allegorical explanation of it. Then, "When he was alone, the Twelve and the others around him asked him about the parables. He told them, "The secret of the kingdom of God has been given to you. But to those on the outside everything is said in parables so that they may be ever seeing but never perceiving, and ever hearing but never understanding; otherwise they might turn and be forgiven," (4:10-12). People in general who are attentive to Jesus' teachings are given parables that he does not intend for them to understand. They are not at fault for failing to understand, they are being told parables that they cannot understand, for otherwise they might turn and be forgiven, which is, for whatever reason, something Jesus wants to avoid having happen. At the end of the sequence of parables in this chapter the narrator Mark remarks "With many similar parables Jesus spoke the word to them, as much as they could understand. He did not say anything to them without using a parable. But when he was alone with his own disciples, he explained everything."[9] According to Mark, Jesus taught in parables to most people but he did not intend them to understand him.

There are, however, a few others who are given special explanations: his disciples, the twelve and the others around him who include, Mark informs us, many women. One may easily make the mistake of assuming that, while the sympathetic masses were taught in parables so that they might be confused, the twelve and others who received explanations understood Jesus properly for, after all, Jesus gave them the secret of the Kingdom of God (4:11). But after eight chapters of instruction, special secrets, and explanations of everything, the disciples have no clue. In the middle of chapter 8 Jesus angrily turns on his followers and shouts "Do you still not see or understand? Are your hearts hardened? Do you have eyes but fail to see, and ears but fail to hear? And don't you remember?"[10] Soon thereafter we are given a famous colloquy between Peter and Jesus, at the end of which Jesus announces that Peter

---
9 Mark 4:33-34.
10 Mark 8:17-18.

thinks as people think, not as God thinks, and that to Jesus, Peter is Satan. Since Peter has managed to connect the word "Christ" to Jesus, Christians often assume that Peter has finally achieved proper understanding despite Jesus' anger at his disciples' ignorance shortly before. But one would be wise to assume that if Jesus calls Peter "Satan," Peter got it wrong.

We reach the word-count midpoint of the Gospel a few paragraphs later during the Transfiguration scene where, despite the appearance of Jesus and Elijah and Moses together, the disciples still have no idea what to make of Jesus. They are terrified. Later they discuss among themselves, not with Jesus, what "rising from the dead" might mean. The Gospel here is half over; the disciples still do not understand what is most significant.

According to Mark what is most significant is Jesus' death as "a ransom for many," (10:45) and Jesus four times spells that out to his disciples. In 8:31, he tells the disciples that 'the Son of Man must suffer many things and be rejected by the elders, the chief priests and the teachers of the law, and that he must be killed and after three days rise again. He spoke plainly about this." Jesus mentions his principal mission and purpose again in 9:12 at the Gospel's midpoint, and gives it once more at 9:31. The disciples, Mark informs us, "did not understand what he meant and were afraid to ask him about it. They came to Capernaum. When he was in the house, he asked them, 'What were you arguing about on the road?' But they kept quiet because on the way they had argued about who among them was the greatest," (9:32-34).

Jesus summarizes his mission one last time in 10:33-34 only to have the disciples immediately again maneuver among themselves for power. Their continued failure to understand Jesus concludes the central section of the Gospel, a section flanked by two symbolic miracle stories of blind men coming to see clearly (8:22-26 and 10:46-52).

Following two chapters of various teachings, observations and comments placed in and around the area of the Jerusalem Temple, and chapter 13, which is an extended discourse on the events that will accompany the arrival of the cosmic Son of Man[11], Mark's gospel con-

---

11 As Jesus refers to this cosmic and coming "Son of Man" in the third person (13:26-27), as he also does during his trial (14:62), and in lectures to his disciples (8:38) one cannot conclude from the Gospel of Mark that Jesus is always referring to himself by

cludes with the detailed story of the suffering, death and resurrection of Jesus in the "passion narrative."

The passion narrative begins with the actions of an anonymous woman who is the only person in the whole of the Gospel of Mark to be fulsomely praised. She understands that Jesus' body will not be present in the tomb after his death and so she anoints him for burial beforehand despite the disciples' wrongheaded liberal-Christian notion that the valuable oil should be sold for the benefit of the poor. Jesus has no interest in that (14:1-9).

The narrative continues with the story of the Last Supper and the failure of the principal disciples to stay awake in Gethsemene despite Jesus' repeated warning to "stay awake," the same warning that concludes the apocalyptic discourse of chapter 13. Quickly we hear of the betrayal by Judas, the desertion of Jesus by all of his disciples (14:50) and Peter's triple denial of knowing Jesus at all, which hearkens back to Jesus' warning in 8:38 "If anyone is ashamed of me and my words in this adulterous and sinful generation, the Son of Man will be ashamed of them when he comes in his Father's glory with the holy angels."

The story concludes with a "grand jury" inquiry before the Sanhedrin, a trial before Pilate, Jesus' crucifixion and his death. His male followers having all deserted him, his female followers keep watch and determine where his body is placed. They subsequently come to anoint his body for burial, although they should have known already that it would not be present for that purpose, which the praised woman of chapter 14 did know. The women are told to inform Jesus' disciples of his resurrection, but they do not do so. End of Gospel.

Mark wrote a complex book. It is not primarily intended to narrate the life story of Jesus. It is written as a weapon in an internal church-political struggle defending Mark's point of view that Jesus came to suffer die and rise again, against points of view held by his disciples and his family. [12] Mark constructs a narrative intended to demonstrate that the family of Jesus was estranged from him and that his disciples were power-hungry incompetents who eventually all deserted him and ran away. From Mark's account we can gather that they believed Jesus was an authoritative Holy Spirit possessed commander of demons, a successful exorcist and a worker of miracles, for that is what he is in the

---

the phrase. Sometimes he does, sometimes perhaps he does not.
12 Cf. Theodore Weeden, *Mark: Traditions in Conflict*, Augsburg, 1979.

first part of Mark's gospel up to chapter 8 wherein he begins to explain that he came to be arrested, suffer, die, and rise again, an explanation that his disciples do not understand.

Strange book, this Gospel of Mark, but it is what we can know about the life of the Historical Jesus. We learn nothing of historical value from the Gospel of James and virtually nothing from the Gospel of John and nothing much (apart from a considerable number of added sayings) from the revised versions of Mark composed by Matthew and Luke. All we really have is Mark.

The author of the Gospel of Mark is not particularly interested in relaying a coherent program of Jesus' teachings. Jesus is said to have mentioned a Kingdom of God and a coming Son of Man and certainly, in the opinion of Mark's Gospel, Jesus held a variety of strong opinions about how Christians in leadership positions should act humbly, like children, instead of arrogantly, like the disciples. But what primarily matters to the Jesus that Mark creates is that he will suffer, die and rise again. That is the point Jesus plainly taught that Mark then narrates in detail down to specifying precise hours of the day in chapters 14 – 16. But Mark's Gospel was not written in order to explain the purpose of Jesus' demise but rather to argue that his trusted disciples and intimate followers did not understand that purpose. Perhaps Mark's intended audience did believe they knew the special purpose of Jesus' death, (cf. 10:45) and how that would constitute a ransom (from what, paid to whom?) of many (who are who?); perhaps they did not.

What is one to make of the historicity of all this? Should one believe that Jesus of Nazareth's main ambition was really to go to Jerusalem, suffer, die and rise again? Of course not, that is a Markan fiction based on Pauline doctrine. Did Jesus' sundry "teachings" in Jerusalem in Mark's chapters 11 and 12 give rise to the Christian movement? Certainly not; read them, you'll agree they are not cult-forming principles. How about his predictions that the Son of Man (who as a cosmic being may well be somebody other than Jesus himself) is soon to come after days of disaster to gather his elect from the four corners of the earth, etc.? (13:7-30). Is that something we are to see at the foundation of the Christian movement? It is a motif rarely mentioned again in the textual tradition. And the Kingdom of God, which may or may not have anything to do with the story of Jesus' demise and resurrection, what of that? You will learn virtually nothing about it in Mark's Gospel save that in the first days of his life as a Spirit possessed healer he spoke favorably of it.[13]

Matthew and Luke are familiar with Mark's Gospel. Furthermore, both of them are familiar with the list of sayings attributed to Jesus that scholars call Q. Both thought that Jesus' sayings were coherent and that Jesus taught people in a fashion that led some of those people to understand what he was talking about. Both take the context-free material found in the Q sayings list and import it into the narrative world that Mark created, while subverting Mark's attack on Jesus' disciples and family so that those Christian founders and role-models are left looking reasonably capable and responsible.

According to John Kloppenborg's analysis, Q went through three stages of development.[14] The first stage contained fairly simple sayings called "wisdom" sayings, a great many of which are also to be found in the Gospel of Thomas. The second stage takes on a darker tone with the addition of many sayings suggesting that prophetic messengers from God, i.e., Jesus and John the Baptist and by implication the leaders of the Q community, have been rejected by the present generation and that in response God will wreak vengeance upon the earth. This material is generally labeled "apocalyptic." It seems quite likely that most of this material was created by the Q community in order to give some substance and ideology to the proverbial wisdom materials that were circulating under Jesus' name. The third and final stage of Q begins to organize the Q sayings list into a story by beginning with the baptism by John and the temptation sequence.

Our other major source for teachings ascribed to Jesus is the Gospel of Thomas, which contains well over one hundred short sayings most of which begin simply "Jesus said...." Scholarly convention counts 114 sayings and, while a few of them have brief narrative introductions such as "a woman in the crowd said to him... Jesus replied..." by and large the sayings in the Gospel of Thomas exist in a narrative vacuum. About half the sayings are recognizably similar to sayings found in the

---

13 If Chapter 13 describes the arrival of the Kingdom, then it is quite a bit like the arrival of thermonuclear war. How chapter 13 describes "good news" is difficult to understand, and so possibly that chapter is not discussing the arrival of the Kingdom at all. Similarly, Q/Luke 17:26-29 warn of the horrors of the "Days of the Son of Man."
14 John Kloppenborg, *Excavating Q: The History and Setting of the Sayings Gospel* Fortress Press, 2000.

synoptic gospels, but rarely with exactly the same wording and almost never in the same sequence. The Gospel of Thomas does not contain sayings found in John's Gospel. Evangelical scholarship has fought to relegate Thomas' gospel into irrelevance by arguing that its contents, when similar to the synoptic material, must have been taken from the canonical scriptures but there is little if any evidence that this was the case.[15]

The overlap between Thomas' material and Q material is almost, but not quite, confined to sayings that Kloppenborg's analysis places in the stage Q1. Thomas lacks the Q2 notion of the rejection of prophets and the coming apocalyptic horror of the Day of the Son of Man. About half of the sayings found in the Gospel of Thomas are found nowhere else in Christian tradition, and scholarship has concluded that, with only a couple exceptions, that material cannot traced back to the historical Jesus. This means, of course, that for the most part it was borrowed or invented as was, probably, most of the Q2 and Q3 material. One would therefore be left only with the residue, the earliest stratum shared by Q and Thomas. Those sayings have been called "wisdom" sayings and they consistently lack specific ideological foundation. Here are some examples:

QLk12:2 // GTh 6b. For nothing is hidden that shall not be revealed and nothing is covered that shall that shall remain without being revealed.

QLk12:3 // GTh 33a What you will hear in your ear, in the other ear proclaim from your rooftops.

QLk 11:33 // GTh 33b // Mark 4:21] No one kindles a lamp and puts it under a basket, nor does he put it in a hidden place, but he sets it on a lampstand so everyone who comes in and goes out will see its light

QLk6:39 // GTh 34 If a blind person leads a blind person, both of them will fall into a hole.

QLk 6:44-45 // GTh 45 Grapes are not harvested from thorn trees, nor are figs gathered from thistles, for they yield no fruit. Good persons produce good from what they've stored up; bad persons produce evil from the wickedness they've stored up in their hearts, and say evil

---

15 Cf. Stephen Patterson *The Gospel of Thomas and Christian Origins*, Brill 2013.

things. For from the overflow of the heart they produce evil.

Qlk16:13 // GTh 47b A slave cannot serve two masters, otherwise that slave will honor the one and offend the other.

There are many other such sayings. While they lack ideological content, they are sensible. It is hard to imagine anyone anywhere, from Confucianists to physicists, who would say these statements are wrong, or who would find them very interesting. For most of them a context is needed to make them meaningful in any way. "What are you talking about with 'nothing is hidden? What sort of "nothing?" "What kind of talk are we supposed to proclaim?" "What is 'lamp' a metaphor for here?" "OK, fair enough, blind people can't see well, we know that, and so?" "Good people are better than evil people, nobody disagrees, but what is your point?" "Right about slaves, that's for sure. So?" And so on and so forth. Without any answers to such common sense questions, the "wisdom" sayings are meaningless, pleasant but meaningless. Yet a significant number of the earliest Jesus sayings tradition is just such material. It was Mark's epochal decision to put such sayings into a biographical context so as to give them some meaning that founded the practice of Christians writing narrative gospels.

In order to generate some sort of ideological perspective for the sayings of Jesus, early Christians variously supplemented the early "wisdom" sayings material with apocalyptic Q sayings and mystical Thomas sayings. In the case of the Gospel of Thomas, at least, that didn't work very well. Whoever put that collection of material together wound up challenging his readers to fathom the seemingly incomprehensible sayings in his collection, writing "whoever discovers the interpretation of these sayings will not taste death." Evidently the compiler of these sayings didn't feel that his list of Jesus' sayings could be rationally understood as a whole. And frankly, as one who has published two books on the Gospel of Thomas and its sayings, I must say that I agree.[16] Scholars can select a subset of sayings, make sense of them, then interpret the remainder loosely in light of whatever subset they chose, but the list as a whole remains opaque and I am quite certain that it was opaque to

---

16 Cf. Stevan Davies, *The Gospel of Thomas and Christian Wisdom*, Second Edition, Bardic Press, 2004 and *The Gospel of Thomas Annotated and Explained*, Skylight Paths Press, 2002.

those who first put it together.[17]

As to the Teachings of Jesus, what we have of them are sayings found in the Gospel of Mark and the wisdom sayings of the Common Tradition (Q /Thomas overlaps or, if you prefer, Q 1) as our historical kernel, if we have a kernel at all. The apostles as portrayed in Acts, and the apostles as revealed through the letters of Paul, and the pseudo-Pauls, and the other early canonical epistleographers care little or nothing about Jesus' supposed teachings; they almost never quote them and they do not seem to depend on any tradition arising from them. From that day to this, the teachings of Jesus seem to depend almost entirely on what any individual, group, or church would like them to be. Even to this day we have, for example, the idea of Jesus the Prince of Peace, who was evidently said in the first Christian decades to be one committed to bringing Peace to the world except that, supposedly, he rejected the very idea very explicitly: "Do not suppose that I have come to bring peace to the earth. I did not come to bring peace, but a sword," (Mt. 10:34//Lk. 12:51 – Q). Or, for the billion Christians who are trained by the Church to ignore it, we have "And do not call anyone on earth 'father,' for you have one Father, and he is in heaven," (Mt. 23:9). The teachings of Jesus, if indeed there were any that survived into the age of the Greek-language church of the New Testament, were not crucial to the formation of the Christian religion.

Regarding the Resurrection

I learned in Sunday School that Christianity arose because Jesus' disciples spread the word of his resurrection, announcing as they did that Jesus' overcoming of death demonstrated that all people now are freed from that inevitability. The gospel, the good news, is said to be Jesus' resurrection. Therefore, subsequently, the rise of the Christian movement came about through the happy acceptance of this good news by considerable numbers of faithful people. Not only did people accept the news of Jesus' resurrection, but they confidently applied it to their own condition, thinking that Jesus was but the first of a host of people who would imitate his death and resurrection with their own, and that

---

17 If anyone ever did have the correct interpretation of the Gospel of Thomas we can assume from Saying 1 that he or she is still alive and, we can hope, will someday publish a definitive essay on the subject.

they too could confidently look forward to rising from the grave as Jesus did. Or something of that sort.

Many are still convinced that the good news of Jesus' resurrection was the principal content of the early Christian message and that this brought a sufficient number of people into the movement to make the movement an eventual success. Bart Ehrman has recently argued that assertions of Jesus' divinity did not arise during the lifetime of that preacher of apocalypse.[18] He concludes that such assertions arose postmortem, from visions of a risen Jesus variously beheld by his former disciples. But the idea that the message of Jesus' resurrection was a principal part of the earliest Christian teaching is problematical.

First, the story as given in our only source for Jesus' life, the Gospel of Mark, does not strongly support an argument that Jesus was raised from the dead at all. It does indicate that there were people who thought so, including Mark the author, but Mark's version of the story is weak. Supposedly some women associated with Jesus came to a tomb into which Jesus' body had been placed, found it empty, and heard "a young man dressed in a white robe" tell them that Jesus had risen and gone to Galilee and asked them to inform Jesus' disciples. They did not do so. That's the story (16:1-8). The other gospel writers found this story unsatisfactory and made substantial alterations. The young man becomes an angel in Matthew's story, two men in shining garments in Luke's, and in the Gospel of John he becomes two angels. Such embellishment is not surprising for it is just the sort of expansion and elaboration one would expect in a legend circulating within a religious movement.

However it is significantly surprising that the stories of Jesus' subsequent appearances to his followers are so utterly different from one account to the other. In Matthew's Gospel Jesus speaks briefly to disciples in Galilee. By Luke's account he appears in altered form on the road from Jerusalem to Emmaus to two disciples who don't recognize him at all. Subsequently, having spent forty days in and around Jerusalem, he and his disciples go to nearby Bethany and he is taken up into heaven. John's story has none of this. There Jesus appears to Mary Magdalene just after his resurrection, although she does not recognize him at first. Later that day he passes into a locked room and displays his hands and

---

18 Bart Ehrman, *How Jesus Became God: The Exaltation of a Jewish Preacher from Galilee*, HarperOne, 2014.

side. A week later he passes again into that same locked room and is touched by Thomas. The disciples having evidently returned to their fishing chores on the Sea of Galilee, Jesus appears there and orchestrates a miraculous catch of fish. We hear once of a time when five hundred people simultaneously envision a risen Jesus -- Paul writes that many of those folks are still alive (1 Cor. 15:6).

My point is not that these discrepancies disprove the claim that Jesus' corpse was miraculously re-animated, I'm taking it for granted that such a claim does not require disproof; it didn't happen. Rather, the great diversity in resurrection narratives shows that there was no established account of the resurrection in the early church. From the evidence, we have to assume that stories of all sorts were invented because no account had been passed on at an early time. The earliest recorded account we have is from Paul who, three years or so after Jesus' death, believes that he apprehended Jesus. But for Paul, Christ was revealed *in* him, he does not seem to think that he visually apprehended a resuscitated person walking on the earth (Galatians 1:16). And one must presume that he thinks that the other apostles had experiences of the risen Jesus cognate to his own. Obviously, various diverse stories of Jesus' resurrection came to flourish in the early Christian movement. But there does not seem to have been a story of Jesus' appearance from which all of the variations arose, which indicates that the retelling of such a story was not part of the earliest missionary effort.

In fact, Mark's account of what happened to Jesus' body is quite credible. Mark reports that Jesus was crucified at nine o'clock in the morning and that he died at about three o'clock in the afternoon (Mark 15:25,34). Crucifixion was intended to be a long torturous process and Jesus' early demise surprised even Pilate. Jesus died about four hours before the beginning of the Sabbath on Friday evening. As it would be unseemly to have a corpse hanging in the environs of Jerusalem, especially throughout the twenty four hours of a Passover Sabbath, one Joseph of Arimathea, a member of the Sanhedrin counsel who had presumably joined his fellow council members in arranging for Jesus to be handed over to the Romans, asked for Jesus' body.[19] With Pilate's

---

[19] According to Deuteronomy 21:23 "You must not leave the body hanging on the pole overnight. Be sure to bury it that same day, because anyone who is hung on a pole is under God's curse. You must not desecrate the land the Lord your God is giving you as an inheritance."

permission, Joseph's servants removed the body for temporary placement in an expensive tomb carved from solid rock. So far this is Mark's account and everything makes good sense. What would happen next? It would be most reasonable to assume that after the Sabbath ended on Saturday evening, around 7 PM, Joseph's servants removed Jesus' body from its temporary place in the rock-carved tomb and put it in a place appropriate for the burial of crucified Galileans. We do not know what place that might be, but Roman authorities would not have permitted the body's location to be shared with his immediate band of followers.[20] In any event, it is credible that when some of Jesus' women disciples came to the tomb Sunday morning the body was not there. From this beginning the stories of Jesus' resurrection increased in complexity and geographical dispersion until we have him on the shores of the Sea of Galilee in John's gospel, appearing to an assembly of five hundred followers according to Paul, dining in Emmaus in Luke's version, and so forth.[21]

Suppose that we imagine that Jesus' disciples came up to people in villages and towns and announced that their companion had risen from the dead and occasionally walked with them for a period of several days. What might the reaction to such a report be? Think about it. To what degree do people want other people to rise up from the grave and walk among us? In Mediterranean cultures, as in most other culture, it was thought possible for some people sometimes to come back from the dead. But people did not want the dead coming out of their tombs and returning to life.

The notion of a possible mass return of the dead from their graves was sufficiently familiar in ancient times that Matthew can casually mention that when Jesus died, "The earth shook, the rocks split and the tombs broke open. The bodies of many holy people who had died were raised to life. They came out of the tombs after Jesus' resurrection and went into the holy city and appeared to many people," 27:52-53.

---

20 Cf. Raymond E. Brown, "The Burial of Jesus (Mark 15:42-47)," *Catholic Biblical Quarterly* April, 1989.
21 In Matthew's account he appears in Galilee, but "some doubted." In Luke's version Jesus' disciples walk with the risen Christ but don't recognize him. Mary Magdalene in John's story does not recognize him and presumes that he is a gardener. In another Johannine account he passes through a locked door and must then demonstrate to doubting Thomas that he actually is who he says he is. Such stories could not have served as effective propaganda for cult formation.

That must have been quite a sight! Did the many people who saw this parade of the living dead run off in terror? The fact that Matthew presents Jesus' being raised to life as but one resurrection among many is generally overlooked in Christian circles.

What society or what culture has ever wanted the dead to rise and walk among us? Cinematic folklore of the "horror" genre is filled with the living dead: vampires, Frankenstein-monsters, ghosts and many other fictional characters. No society encourages ghosts; there are no accounts of the dead climbing out of their graves and everyone excitedly shouting "Hooray! Welcome back!"

On the other hand, there can be legendary reports of men with the miraculous power of raising the dead. Jesus raises the son of a widow in Nain back to life, he raises Lazarus and he raises the daughter of Jairus. According to the Acts of the Apostles, Peter raised Tabitha from the dead (9:36-42) and Paul raised Eutychus from the dead (20:7-12). While there is no hint in these stories that people fear the risen dead after they miraculously return, the point of the stories is not the resurrections themselves but that Jesus and Peter and Paul thereby demonstrate their miracle-working power. Such stories show that legends of the time were open to the possibility of the dead returning to life, given proper divine intervention. Accordingly, it seems unlikely that a story of Jesus returning to life thanks to divine intervention would be taken to be uniquely an astounding event.[22] No one claims that there ever was a resurrection-based gospel of Lazarus.

The initial impetus for the Christian movement could not have been people telling other people that a dead man rose from the grave and walked among them. That would not have constituted uniquely "good news". Certainly it became the "good news" in the Christian culture, but there must have been an established Christian culture already. Everyone raised in a Christian culture has heard from childhood that the resurrection message led people in the initial decades of Christian times to join the Christian movement. But that message will be joyful and convincing only to those already sealed in their faithful membership.[23]

---

[22] Some scholars try to distinguish resuscitation from resurrection from revivification from reanimation and so forth, with the preferred term applying uniquely to Jesus, as if such fine distinctions in the manner of the dead rising would have been of interest to ordinary Aramaic speaking people two thousand years ago.

[23] Similarly, the problem of "original sin" that Christianity solves is considered to be

On the Pentecostal Origins   21

What got them involved in the first place, if not the message that a dead man came back to life? What did the Christian movement's salesmen sell that people eagerly bought and found well worth the price? That's the question (and a good 1930's American metaphorical question it is, if I do say so myself).

Let's begin with what it wasn't. It was not the message of Jesus or his teachings or his prophetic words. We do not know what those teachings were. Our sources are as confused as we are and two of them, Mark and Thomas, indicate that they thought his public teachings basically incomprehensible. Paul shows no interest in them, nor do the other letter writers of the New Testament, and Jesus' teachings play no role in the spread of the Christian movement according to the Acts of the Apostles. John freely makes up teachings for Jesus to teach.

Jesus' life story as we know it was an invention of the author of the Gospel of Mark. Mark may have had some factual historical knowledge to work with beyond a list of sayings, a variety of fictitious miracle stories and a passion narrative, but it is not likely that he knew much more than that Jesus was from Nazareth in Galilee, that various of his followers were fishermen from Capernaum, that he was considered exceptionally capable as an exorcist and that he was crucified by Pilate. From that story no movement of significance could have arisen. The story of Jesus' resurrection presumably developed from the fact that women went to an expensive stone-cut tomb owned by Joseph of Arimathea where Jesus' body had been placed just before the beginning of the Sabbath and found, when they arrived in the morning, half a day after the Sabbath ended, that the body no longer was there.

Stories of Jesus' appearances to his disciples after death are obviously invented by various sources not in communication with each other. In any event, the idea that Jesus arose from the grave and walked among his disciples would not have been taken to be a piece of ambiguously good news. People in every culture prefer the dead to stay in their tombs.

Christianity did not begin with apostles successfully founding a movement by spreading teachings, biography, or accounts of Jesus ris-

---

a problem by no one on earth but members of the Christian religion; the solution of the problem and the recognition of the problem are two sides of the same coin. I doubt that anyone has ever lived who has thought "I have a problem of original sin and I don't know of any solution for it." The solution causes the problem.

en from the grave. Those things were developed as a consequence of the foundation of the Christian movement. The question is not what was it about the life of Jesus that gave rise to the Christian movement, but what was it about the Christian movement that gave rise to narratives of the life of Jesus.

If Jesus was not the immediate cause of the rise and spread of the Christian movement, and yet that movement did rise and did spread and did become the dominant cultural force in the western world, what was its initial impetus? Luke, in the Acts of the Apostles, offers a credible and convincing theory. Luke's theory of Christian origins has a modern day exemplar that provides indirect analogical evidence for what seems to have happened in the middle of the first century. Further, it is supported by eye-witness evidence from Paul's letters. Luke's theory allows one to see how it might be that, although Jesus and his life and teachings and so forth had nothing very much to do with the initiation of Christianity in its first years, nevertheless many were motivated to focus particular attention on Jesus.

In the Acts of the Apostles, Luke advances the theory that the Christian movement was pentecostal in nature, i.e., that Christians experienced and shared what they believed to be the Holy Spirit coming into them and giving them divine powers.[24] In other words, Christianity rose and spread because of an experience that was highly desirable, that was transmissible from one person to other people, and that was effective as a community-creating focal element, and that provided free medical care. The experience came first and, to answer my own question "What did the Christian movement's salesmen sell that people eagerly bought and found well worth the price?" it was the experience of spirit possession, which they came to understand to be the experience of God's Holy Spirit.

The Holy Spirit is a form of experience that falls under the general category of spirit possession. It is a form of experience that is probably available to any human being given the right cultural setting. The

---

[24] I will be using the term "Pentecostal" in two ways. One way is generic, (lower case "pentecostal") to denote a style of religion that is strongly focused on dissociative experience presumed to be caused by the Holy Spirit. The other use is specific, (upper case "Pentecostal") to denote the modern form of Pentecostal Christianity. The claim by present day Pentecostals that their experiences are essentially the same sort of experiences as those that took place on the day of Pentecost described in the second chapter of the book of the Acts of the Apostles is, I believe, correct.

experience can be described in various ways, but it can include a loss of some physical control with concomitant jerking about, staggering, swaying or passing out. It may involve uncontrolled verbal utterances. With increased experience there may be considerable physical control, and with increased verbal control, a propensity to prophesize articulately. The experience is pleasurable, calming (when concluded), and results in heightened self-esteem. It may be in some ways psychologically cognate to the negative, unpleasant, socially unacceptable experience called "demonic possession" but it is not the same thing.

The Holy Spirit is an explanatory paradigm for a particular form of dissociative human experience now practiced by hundreds of millions of Pentecostal Christians, practiced in past centuries by small numbers of Christians on the margins of the established religion, and practiced by the Christians at the foundations of the faith in the period described by Luke and experienced by Paul.[25] Since the Holy Spirit is a form of experience its existence cannot reasonably be denied. You can videotape or otherwise record the experience or, to be precise, you can record the physical manifestations of the experience and thereby evaluate the statements made by those experiencing. Indeed, you can hook the faithful up to an EEG or a similar device and see what is going on in their neuronal regions whilst the possession experience takes place.[26]

Since the Holy Spirit is an observable, measurable, experienced phenomenon, people do try to explain it. There are two possible explanations. From the perspective of the people within the Christian movement, the Holy Spirit is an external person of a Spiritual nature who comes into a human body and to a considerable degree temporarily takes over the mental and physical functioning of that body. This is standard spirit possession theory found virtually everywhere on earth, from the traditional cultures of China to the traditional cultures of sub-Saharan Africa. From an outsider perspective the Holy Spirit is a name given to a particular dissociative psychological experience that arises wholly from the internal mental functioning of an individual within a particular cultic setting. One can believe in the reality of the Holy Spirit as a form of human experience without any need to affirm its external or theological reality.

---

25 Cf. e.g. 1 Corinthians 12.
26 E.g. Persinger, M.A., *Perceptual and Motor Skills*, 1984, 58(1) "Striking EEG profiles from single episodes of glossolalia and transcendental meditation" 127-33.

The nature of the pentecostal experience is that one feels that the power of one's ordinary ego has been replaced, to a greater or lesser degree, by another ego. The alternative ego is believed to have divine powers, knowledge, abilities, that are distinct from one's original ego. Accordingly, in various cultures such as, e.g., the Yoruba, there are people who occasionally become gods (orisha) and, during the time of the possession experience, others in the cultic setting interact with them as if they were gods, asking for their advice or intervention. In the Christian formative Christian setting it was understood that the Holy Spirit also was Christ and as the Holy Spirit was of God, the Holy Spirit was God. These terminological and theological factors were subsequently sorted out into a Trinitarian formulation whereby Christ was a person, the Holy Spirit was a person, and God the Father Almighty was a person and those three persons, theologically One, were kept conceptually separate. But one need only turn to Chapter 8 of Paul's Letter to the Romans to see that the Holy Spirit, the Spirit of Christ, and the Spirit "of the one who raised Jesus from the dead" are used synonymously. In 1st Corinthians 12 Paul stresses his conviction that there can be but one Spirit of God in the Christian church. That this Spirit is also the Spirit of Christ and the Spirit of the Son of God complicates matters for people who think in a Trinitarian fashion, but Paul lived well before anyone thought that way.

As far as Mark is concerned, Jesus' relevant activity began when he came to John for baptism and the Holy Spirit descended upon him or, we might say, he had an experience of an alternative ego emerging within him. After an understandable period of confusion denoted as wandering in the desert, Jesus concluded that he had become possessed by the Holy Spirit and he discovered himself empowered by his experience, by the Spirit, and able to teach authoritatively by casting out demons, forgiving sins, and otherwise functioning as a successful ancient physician. I know of no reason to disbelieve this account in general, and neither did Matthew or Luke.

Luke tells us that Jesus' female followers were drawn from the ranks of women who were experienced in demonic possession experience and I do not doubt that the same was true for most of his male followers as well (Lk. 8:2). According to Mark, Jesus' fame as an effective exorcist spread rapidly and widely and he was thronged by demon possessed people eager to have his Spirit cast out theirs. This is the scene Mark establishes through his first chapters,(1:1-8:21) only to insist in his subsequent narrative that Jesus in fact was intent on suffering, dying and rising again rather than on continuing to pursue a successful medical practice (8:22-16:8). If Jesus linked the notion of a coming Kingdom of God with his sudden power to exorcise through an indwelling Spirit, there would be a connection between his crucifixion as a seemingly anti-Roman prophet predicting the imminent arrival of a non-Roman Kingdom in Judea and Galilee and his career as a Spirit possessed exorcist. Such a connection is nicely summarized in a statement Matthew attributes to Jesus: "if it is by the Spirit of God that I drive out demons, then the Kingdom of God has come upon you," (Mt. 12:28)

In the Acts of the Apostles, Luke briefly summarizes Jesus' life up to the time of his trial and crucifixion as follows: "Jesus of Nazareth was a man accredited by God to you by miracles, wonders and signs, which God did among you through him," (Acts 2:22). And again, "Beginning in Galilee after the baptism that John preached— how God anointed Jesus of Nazareth with the Holy Spirit and power, and how he went around doing good and healing all who were under the power of the devil, because God was with him," (Acts 10:37-38). I suspect that this was the life story of Jesus as Christians knew it for the first decades of the Christian movement. Jesus was understood to have been a Spirit possessed exorcist and healer with exceptionally effective powers. I doubt that Luke knew very much else about him at the time he wrote Acts, apart from a story of his death and resurrection. After writing Acts, Luke became cognizant of Mark's gospel and of Q, and so, from those sources, he learned more. Later, having heard Matthew's Gospel read aloud once, Luke recognized that Matthew had combined Mark and Q and determined to do the same thing, but to do it better. Hence she wrote the Gospel of Luke (including a new segue into the first pages of the Acts of the Apostles). At a later time Luke wrote an introductory two chapter account of Jesus' conception and birth featuring his mother Mary. The fact that virtually nothing of the pre-passion life and teachings of Jesus as found in the Gospel of Luke is discernible in Luke's Acts of the Apostles means that Acts was written first; the fact that nothing of the virgin-birth narrative or appreciation of Mary as found in the first two chapters of Luke appears elsewhere in either the Gospel of Luke or in Acts means that the birth narrative was written after the other parts were completed, as does the fact that the first sentences of chapter three are clearly a book's beginning paragraph.

The literary evolution of Luke's story of the origins of the Christian movement replicates the history and evolution of the movement itself as it related to Jesus. At first (as in Luke's Acts) Jesus was regarded as a Spirit possessed exorcist and healer whose special status began at his baptism; his death and resurrection were separately of great importance. Then decades later Jesus was regarded as one whose life story and whose teachings were of significant interest apart from his exorcisms, his death and his resurrection (Luke's Gospel 3:1 ff.). Then, finally, in the early second century (as in Luke's and then James' birth narrative) Jesus was conceived to have been a man whose miraculous birth and exemplary mother proved that he had supernatural excellence well prior to his baptism.

Christianity Begins

Jesus died. Whether or not some of his followers believed that they had seen him for a few weeks after his death, Luke's story has it that Jesus no longer lived among them after his ascension. At this point there was no Spirit-empowered personage in their movement; their erstwhile leader had gone. For no known reason, fifty days after Passover all of the followers of Jesus remaining in Jerusalem had the experience called the Holy Spirit. They had a model for this: Jesus himself. Further, it is likely that not only the women but also the men who accompanied Jesus had had dissociative psychological experiences understood to be demonic possession and were already familiar with the experience of dissociative episodes. In any event, Luke contends that they all did come to experience positive dissociative episodes they understood to have been caused by the Holy Spirit. Further, they found that they could transmit such experiences to outsiders and, based on their common experiences, establish family-like communities. The Holy Spirit experience was the defining mandatory element in the Christian movement, as Luke's account in Acts makes clear, and as Paul makes clear as well (cf. e.g. Romans 8, 1 Corinthians 12, Galatians 2-3.)

While it seems impossible that a movement of Spirit possessed people could erupt from a single nuclear event and spread rapidly through many cultures in a few years, the rise of contemporary Pentecostal Christianity happened just that way. Beginning in Azusa Street in Los

Angeles in 1906 under the ministerial supervision of William Seymour, the Pentecostal movement of Spirit possessed Christians spread rapidly throughout the United States and into Latin America, Southern Africa, and East Asia with tremendous success. There are today, by some estimates, hundreds of millions of Pentecostal Christians in the world.[27] So it can happen. And, while pushing an historical analogy too far always leads to sorrow, the successful spread of Pentecostal Christianity in the twentieth can confirm the possibility of the successful spread of pentecostal Christianity in the first century.

The experience of Spirit possession has many positive features. It is, for example, self-confirming, i.e. the experience confirms the reality of the experience. If the experience is preceded by dogmatic affirmations, e.g., "if you receive the Spirit of God it will confirm that my message about Christ is correct," then doctrinal conviction can follow experience. Experience confirms doctrine, as Paul argues in Galatians 3:2-5

> I would like to learn just one thing from you: Did you receive the Spirit by the works of the law, or by believing what you heard? Are you so foolish? After beginning by means of the Spirit, are you now trying to finish by means of the flesh? Have you experienced so much in vain—if it really was in vain? So again I ask, does God give you his Spirit and work miracles among you by the works of the law, or by your believing what you heard?

Here the experience that is the Holy Spirit occurs and, in Paul's opinion, thereby the experience confirms Paul's doctrine. If the Spirit experience is the sine qua non of membership in the Christian movement, as Paul says it is, then everyone in the movement will have shared the experience and be united in a unique community. As Paul puts it in Romans 8:9-11

> You, however, are not in the realm of the flesh but are in the realm of the Spirit, if indeed the Spirit of God lives in you. And if anyone does not have the Spirit of Christ, they do not belong to Christ. But if Christ is in you, then even though your body

---

27 According to the Pew Forum, "At least a quarter of the world's 2 billion Christians are thought to be members" of Pentecostal or related charismatic forms of Christianity. http://www.pewforum.org/2006/10/05/pentecostal-resource-page/

is subject to death because of sin, the Spirit gives life because of righteousness. And if the Spirit of him who raised Jesus from the dead is living in you, he who raised Jesus from the dead will also give life to your mortal bodies because of his Spirit who lives in you.

We are assured that everyone properly belonging to a church community has the Spirit living in them; this has been proven by their having had the experience called the Spirit. In many spirit possession groups the possessing entity is said to enter at the outset of the experience and leave at its termination; in the Christian communities of Paul and others, the Spirit having entered remains quiescently within the individual, erupting into experience sporadically thereafter.

The experience of Spirit possession, as understood in the Christian movement of ancient times, gave access to free and effective medical care. Each Christian community would have its exorcists, via the Spirit, and each community would have access to other supernatural benefits through the various gifts that the Spirit experience manifested in various people (cf. 1 Corinthians 12). On the one hand individuals would be benefitted by the supernatural powers of their fellow church adherents, on the other hand individuals would themselves take pride in the particular divine powers manifested through the Holy Spirit dwelling within them. This is the case today in the tens of thousands of churches in the Pentecostal movement.

People became divine through Spirit possession; that is the defining nature of possession, that people supposedly become the person by whom they are possessed. If one is possessed by a divinity, one becomes a divinity. If one is possessed by the Spirit of Christ, one becomes Christ (Gal. 2:20), if one is possessed by the Spirit of the Son of God, one becomes the Son of God (Gal. 4:6, Rom 8:14-16), and so forth. This is all quite logical within the parameters of Spirit possession theory in human cultures all over the world. If people believed that the Spirit of God possessed Jesus, as Mark assures us that they did, then affirming Jesus (for that reason and in that sense) to be God or Son of God would not be unexpected.

In the canonical texts of Judaism there are prophets who are Spirit possessed individuals, but they are exceptional personages and few in number. Even if one goes back centuries to a time when there were bands of prophets, there were still few such people. In the ancient world generally, while oracles and exorcists and prophets were not terribly rare, they were certainly not present in substantial numbers nor did they constitute whole communities of men and women. But within the earliest Christian movement every member was a prophet, an oracle, a Christ and a Son of God. Jesus was no exception.

Something new had happened, something that could not be found in Jewish scriptures or in Judean religion. The question had to arise, what had happened such that previously the Holy Spirit of the Judean God did not come to people in general, especially not to Gentiles, and now it came to people in significant numbers, especially to Gentiles.

Since the Christian movement was the spread of a kind of experience, and no large-scale spread of that kind of experience had been known before, there must have been an event that could account for the onset of the new situation. According to Luke, in a speech written for Peter, the onset of pentecostal experiences was the following: "God has raised Jesus to life, and we are all witnesses of it. Exalted to the right hand of God, he has received from the Father the promised Holy Spirit and has poured out what you now see and hear," (Acts 2:32).

Evidently the newly available Spirit experience was accounted for by the hypothesis that instead of God sending his Holy Spirit to a few extraordinary Judean prophets, God had delegated the Holy Spirit to Jesus, who was now able and willing to send it to virtually anyone. In heaven Jesus receives and sends the Spirit, first to his own followers and then subsequently to their followers. If Jesus can now send God's Spirit, then necessarily that recently deceased Galilean must have risen from the dead in order to ascend into heaven. If the Spirit experience was the center of this pentecostal movement, and if the idea of Jesus sending the Spirit was the explanation of that novel possibility, then faith that Jesus was risen and ascended would be entailed in the belief that the Spirit now came forth from him.

So, what has the historical Jesus to do with any of this? Nothing much. What, one might ask, does William Seymour have to do with the manifested experiences of Pentecostal Christians throughout the world today? Nothing much.

Evidently Jesus was thought to be the continuing source of the possession experience enjoyed by the members of the movement. Such present activity, proven by the self-confirming fact of the possession experience, logically entailed his survival of death. If we know that there is a Spirit experience because we have it, and we are given to understand that this experience derives from Jesus as it was delegated to him by God, then Jesus certainly lives in heaven with God. This is a very strange sort of notion, as the Spirit of God would be under the control of a deceased human being who is certainly not God and not even Judean. The dispensing of the Spirit of God would no longer be God's work but the work of a recently deceased Galilean. Such an irrational set of ideas could not prevail. Rather, it would inevitably generate the logically consequential notion that Jesus must not be just a Galilean exorcist, but that Jesus must in some way be and have been God.

So the initial "gospel" would not have been that Jesus rose from the dead. Nor did it have anything to do with some program of teachings. Nor did it really have anything crucial to do with Jesus as a Spirit possessed exorcist, nor with his travels in Galilee or with his final travails in Jerusalem. The initial "gospel" featured the present availability of the experience called the Holy Spirit and Jesus' role was to account for its arrival within all interested persons. Jesus' followers after his death had the pentecostal Spirit experience that they presumed that Jesus had also had, and they found that they could facilitate others into having the pentecostal experience as well. How they did that I don't know, but there are tens of thousands of Pentecostal ministers and missionaries active today who do know how it can be done and they are doing it.

The Historical Jesus was not a supremely important factor in the foundation of the Christian movement in the sense normally understood. He gathered followers from among persons whom he had exorcised; he functioned as a role model and example to his followers who later found themselves to be spirit possessed; he inspired those followers to form a community that persisted after his death. It is no accident that his ideological intentions and message and his supposed teachings are insignificant in the book of Acts and in the canonical epistles, for they were also insignificant in the creation of the Christian movement.

Logically, and in accord with the Scriptures (to a degree), here is what happened:

1. Jesus spontaneously experienced what he took to be Holy Spirit possession and discovered that he thereby had an exceptional talent for exorcism. Some of those he exorcised became followers, perhaps because in his absence they feared they would revert to their previous

condition, perhaps because their families had had enough of them already and encouraged them to go. Jesus may have connected his Spirit experiences with the idea of a coming Kingdom of God. This is the story that Mark tells in the first half of his Gospel.

2. Jesus suffered and died, perhaps because the Roman authorities correctly understood any predictive use of Kingdom of God terminology to be inherently anti-Roman. His body did not remain in the tomb where Jesus' women followers had seen it placed. When they arrived at that tomb they were surprised to find it gone.

3. Jesus' followers, estranged from their families, remained in Jerusalem until, a few weeks after his death, they spontaneously experienced what they understood to be Holy Spirit possession like his. They discovered themselves able to facilitate the experience in others as well. These events are analogous to the origin and spread of Pentecostalism in the twentieth century.

4. In order to explain to themselves what had changed in the divine dispensation such that instead of a few ornery bearded prophets howling in the wilderness, now ordinary people in significant numbers, both male and female, Jew and gentile, slave and free, were experiencing the Spirit of God. The idea came into being that Jesus was sending the Spirit to them; therefore he must have risen from the dead, ascended to Heaven, and received the divine role of "pouring-out" the Spirit.

5. It would follow that Jesus was divine now and, presumably, in some sense or other, he had been divine from the beginning. If the key initiative postulate of the movement was that the Spirit of God now was distributed by Jesus, it would follow that Jesus must have been in some sense God or Son of God, for it is an absurdity to think that an ordinary human Galilean could send down God's Spirit. Certainly the notion of Jesus' divinity appears startlingly early in the Christian movement.

6. Further speculations were made: that Jesus was the Messiah, the Christ, that Jesus was Son of God. The Spirit sent by Jesus was God's divine Spirit in one sense, but also it was Jesus' Spirit and, insofar as Jesus was Christ or Son of God, so those who received his Spirit received the Spirit of Christ and of the Son of God and could thereby be identified as Christ or Son. Because one who receives a possessing Spirit can be identified with that Spirit, Christians began to identify as ones who had become Christs and Sons of God (cf. Paul's Letter to

the Galatians). Some, receiving Jesus' spirit, may have identified themselves with Jesus.[28]

7. The initial pentecostal impetus of the Christian movement began to fade away over time. Jesus Christ began to be understood to have been uniquely Christ and Son of God. His death and resurrection came to be understood to be the principal salvific point of the Christian movement and Mark wrote to insist on that point. Narratives were written to explain his divinity, i.e., the Gospel of John.

8. It was thought reasonable to conclude that while on earth Jesus must have preached a divinely initiated profound and significant program of teachings, and various programs came into being for him to have taught (e.g. those of the Gospel of Matthew, or the Gospel of Thomas, or the sayings list Q). But as the sayings of an Aramaic speaking Galilean exorcist were probably not preserved, the development of a program of teachings for Jesus to have taught was carried out by Greek speaking Christians sharing various wisdom sayings that came to be associated with Jesus.

9. Eventually early pentecostal Christianity was suppressed by the organized non-charismatic church exemplified in the Pastoral Epistles. Jesus was elevated to the status of the Second Person in the Trinitarian Godhead. The idea of Christians possessed became anathema, except for rare exceptional outbreaks, until the work of William Seymour initiated the enormous successes of modern Pentecostal Christianity.

The idea that Jesus had a successful career as an exorcist and the idea that Christianity arose as a rapidly spreading pentecostal movement theorizing that its Spirit experiences were sent from an ascended Jesus are in accord with the reports in the first half of Mark's Gospel and in Luke's Acts of the Apostles. None of this has anything much to do with the teachings of an historical Jesus or with any ancient theorizing about the soteriological implications of his rising from the dead, or with the various visionary sightings of Jesus that conclude the canonical gospels. The teachings of an historical Jesus had little to do with the initial rise of the Christian movement, and Luke's Acts of the Apostles, along with the New Testament Epistles, do not imply that they did. The disinter-

---

[28] Mark has Jesus say: "Many will come in my name saying, 'I am he" and they will lead many astray," (13:6, and cf. 13:21-22). . Similarly we are told that Herod identified Jesus with John the Baptist, presumably because he believed that Jesus had received the spirit of John from John (Mark 6:14-16).

est in the life and times of Jesus found in Paul's letters and the other early New Testament letters, and their concomitant lack of interest in Jesus' supposed teachings support the idea that the ongoing pentecostal experiences were the primary initiating factor.

The group who had traveled with Jesus remembered him as their group's initiator and as the role model for spirit possession, and regarded him as the initiator of their Spirit experiences. Speculations as to Jesus' role and nature expanded from there. Pneumatological theory accompanied such speculation and merged with it. The Spirit of God who is the Spirit of Jesus Christ and who is the Spirit of the Son of God evidently began to possess people within the Gentile world. Subsequently Mark invented an Historical Jesus for his own intra-Christian political purposes and then Matthew and Luke re-invented versions of Mark's Jesus to serve their own purposes. Jesus Christ and the Paraclete/Spirit came to be equivalent modes of operation of the same power as the Gospel of John's narrative presents it. Eventually the first Mythicists came into being, people who affirmed their experiences of the Spirit of Jesus but denied that there ever was an historical Jesus. The conflict between such Mythicists and their rival Historicists is described, from the latter's point of view, in the Johannine epistles.

The Mythicists are mistaken. Those questing for Jesus' message are wasting their time. The teachings of the Churches are fantasies based on fictions. By and large the Scriptures have it right, at least insofar as Luke's Acts of the Apostles has it right. The Acts of the Apostles gives an account of a pentecostal religious cult spontaneously beginning and then spreading rapidly without any concern whatsoever for any program of Jesus' teachings or any interest in Jesus' life story prior to his last week on earth. We think it all began with Jesus and it did, just as modern Pentecostalism with its hundreds of millions of adherents began with William Seymour. But the life and teachings of William Seymour had virtually nothing to do with the success of twentieth century Pentecostalism, and the life and teachings of Jesus of Nazareth had virtually nothing to do with the success of mid-first century pentecostal Christianity.

James Crossley, in a recent article in the *Journal for the Study of the*

Historical Jesus[29] declares that it is obvious that "the study of the historical Jesus is overwhelmingly concerned with fact finding, description and descriptive interpretation in its various forms, with little concern for questions such as why the Jesus movement emerged when and where it did and why this movement subsequently led to a new religion."[30] Insofar as that sort of thing has been attempted, he does not think much success has been achieved. I think he is quite right. And I think he is right to question the progress made in quests for the historical Jesus resulting in "countless portraits of Jesus that have become famous: the Cynic-like figure, the revolutionary, the charismatic, the eschatological prophet, the sage, the rabbi, the social critic and so on."[31] It is quite likely that the quest for the significance of the historical Jesus through the quest for an understanding of his teachings has been misguided. In fact Jesus' significance for history may lie elsewhere, mainly in his gathering together of people once possessed by demons (as they understood it) and his modeling for them the state of a person possessed by a holy spirit (as he understood it). That would mean that scholars of the New Testament and of Christian origins must become much more knowledgeable about the anthropology of spirit-possession in societies, more understanding of the role of altered states of consciousness in religious formation, and more sympathetic to the styles of religion now practiced by Pentecostal Christians throughout the world.

Crossley wants to understand the historical socio-economic conditions that led to the presence of such a large number of women in the Christian movement. He adduces the role women have played in various revolutionary social movements as analogous to their probable interest in the revolutionary movement led by Jesus, although I think he would admit that he doesn't think there is clear evidence that there ever was such a movement. More significant is the fact that in most spirit possession movements throughout the world women predominate. There are almost always men and women together, but the headcount will go to the women. If you want to experiment, attend your local Pentecostal church wherever you are and count. If you find more men

---

29 "Writing about the Historical Jesus: Historical Explanation and 'the Big *Why* Questions', or Antiquarian Empiricism and Victorian Tomes?" [sic] in the *Journal for the Study of the Historical Jesus* 7, 2009, 63-90.
30 Ibid. 68.
31 Ibid. 65.

than women, write me and astonish me. Why exactly women tend to predominate in spirit possession oriented cults is not a topic I plan to investigate further here, but they do.[32]

Professor Crossley is also concerned about why it is that there is such a preponderance of Torah-free Gentiles in the Christian movement. The spirit experience, once it begins to spread, tends to alarm people who think that it should be confined to a particular population. The experience does not distinguish, as Paul wrote, between Jew and Greek, slave and free, male and female. The Azusa Street revival led by William Seymour (an African-American) attracted black and white, poor and not as poor, women and men, and the admixture of those classes in the shared experience was alarming to the authorities in 1906 California. Jesus and his followers were Galileans, and Galileans were not Judeans. Galileans had never been Judeans except in the fantasies of Judean rulers (cf. the Deuteronomic History). Some Galileans may have been forced to follow Judean law during the time of the Maccabees, but surely the Idumean Herods under Roman domination did not strive with enthusiasm to impose Judean law on that foreign population. A Galilean-founded pentecostal movement surely never had any commitment to Judean legalities. Accordingly, in the pentecostal movement that arose first among a movement of Galileans there presumably would not have been any particular interest in study or observance of Torah. When the spirit experience that defined their movement began to occur among Gentiles the original Galilean Christians would not think that therefore those Gentiles should become obedient to Judean laws. It's more puzzling to try and figure out why anybody did think that way (e.g. Paul's opponents in Galatia, Matthew the evangelist) than why so many did not. In any event, the logic of the situation was that God's Spirit came to people wholly apart from their observance of or knowledge of the Torah. Accordingly, the religious centrality of Torah was moot. It's interesting that in terms of textual history descriptions of Jesus' life and teachings become ever more concerned with Torah observance, from Paul and Thomas, to Mark, and then to Matthew

---

32 Cf. e.g., I. M. Lewis *Ecstatic Religion: A Study of Shamanism and Spirit Possession* 1971; Maria Cruz, "Causes of Spirit Possession in African Women," http://web.wm.edu/so/monitor/issues/07-1/3-cruz.htm; Alice Kehoe, and Dody Giletti, "Women's Preponderance in Possession Cults: The Calcium Deficiency Hypothesis Extended," *American Anthropologist* 83, 1981.

at which point Jesus has become a full-fledged defender of Pharisaic Judaism (although not of the Pharisees themselves).[33]

The theory I have advanced in this essay, that Jesus was an exorcist presumed to be possessed by the Spirit who thereby attracted a group of associates who experienced, after Jesus' death, what they believed that he had experienced previously, and that they believed he was sending God's Spirit down to them such that they could now spread the experience to others, is a theory I find in the beginning of Mark's Gospel and in the book of Acts. It is supported by the eyewitness testimony of Paul, and by the propensity of John's gospel (and the Johnanine letters) to emphasize Spirit/Paraclete experience as being the continuation of the experience of Jesus. In the historical development of the Christian religion in the first century, first there was spirit experience, then came interest in Jesus as a mytho-historical founder and a dying/rising savior. Then lists of sayings arose to constitute his recorded teachings.[34] Then came interest in his divine nature and, finally, attention came increasingly to be paid to his blessed mother.[35]

The Jesus of history, apart from modeling the spirit experience and assembling a cohort of people prone to dissociative possession experiences, had little to do with the origin of Christianity. That religious movement began as a pentecostal religion that assumed Jesus was the proximate cause of the new mass availability of spirit experience to all and sundry and so he must have survived death, (cf. Acts of the Apostles *passim*). Speculations as to his divine status followed from his role as pourer-out of God's Spirit. Interest in ascribing teachings to him came later still, followed by efforts to construct a biography for him so as to put teachings into a context. Christianity came first; both the divine and the didactic roles of Jesus followed after.

The motivation for people to join the Christian movement was initially to experience the dissociative state called the Holy Spirit, not to engage in any activities political or social, apocalyptic or mystical, that had been advocated by Jesus. The reason for the incredible range of ideologies that emerge with the early Christian movement is that the movement had no single foundational ideology and thus was open to almost unlimited inventiveness in that regard. And, since the historical

---

33 Matthew 23:2-3 and then Matthew 23 *passim*.
34 E.g. Q, the Gospel of Thomas, Mark's chapter 4.
35 E.g. the Gospel of John, Luke 1:1-3:1, the Gospel of James.

Jesus had no initial importance to the movement (although the sacrificed, risen and ascended Jesus did have importance), the initial quests for the historical Jesus carried out by Mark and subsequent revisers of Mark's work discovered little more reliable historical material regarding Jesus' supposed teaching program than we have. They were free to use Jesus to advocate their own agendas, as we do. It is interesting to note that Mark's book was principally designed to repudiate claims to leadership by Jesus' disciples. Among their failings, as Mark presents them, was that they were overly impressed by Jesus' career as a spirit possessed exorcist (Mark 1:1 – 8:21) and not sufficiently dedicated to Jesus' (i.e. Mark's) idea that Jesus principally intended to suffer, die and rise again (8:22 – 16:8). The point of view Mark ascribed to Jesus' disciples more closely reflects the reality of the career of the historical Jesus than Mark's revisionist view does, and this should not be a surprise.

Professor Crossley's "Big Why questions" include "why the Jesus movement emerged when and where it did and why this movement subsequently led to a new religion."[36] Both can be answered without difficulty using my paradigm. It emerged when and where it did because of the unusual circumstance that a group of exorcised people alienated from their familial and geographical origins had come together into a surrogate family and, upon the death of their spirit possessed leader, all spontaneously experienced positive possession for which he was their model. The rise of a spontaneous and highly successful cult of this type can be studied analogously in the spread of Pentecostalism from 1906 on. Further, why the movement led to a new religion is a question that answers itself, for the movement was a new religion as soon as the "Pentecost Event" of spirit possession transpired and was discovered to be transferable to others. There were no communal associations of gentile and female spirit possessed prophets of the Judean God before this beginning. The manifest pleasures and powers and associational values of a community based on mutual spirit possession by the spirit of the Judean God led to immediate success and expansion. Why this should have been the case can, again, be understood by consideration of the global success of modern Pentecostalism.

The teachings of the historical Jesus had little if anything to do with the origins of Christianity; neither did the teachings of William

---

36 Crossley, 68.

Seymour have anything to do with the rise of the modern Pentecostal religion. The social and political situation in Galilee had little if anything to do with the origin of the Christian movement; neither did the social and political conditions of Southern California in 1906 have anything significant to do with the emergence of modern Pentecostalism. Searching for the origins of the Christian religion in events that took place prior to the Pentecost event, be those events teachings, manifestations of Jesus' charismatic character, or visionary resurrection appearances, all miss the crucial point, that Christianity began on the day of Pentecost.

Jesus the Healer

1

THE QUEST FOR THE HISTORICAL JESUS

From the time that Albert Schweitzer's *Von Reimarus zu Wrede* (1906) received an English title, *The Quest of the Historical Jesus* (1910), researchers inquiring about the historically valid facts concerning Jesus have conceived their enterprise to be a quest akin to romantic medieval quests for the Holy Grail.[1] Few Jesus researchers are displeased by this notion, for it correctly attributes a special kind of importance to their work.

The quest for the historical Jesus has been going on now for over a century.[2] Recently we have had presented to us Jesus the Magician,[3] the Zealot,[4] the Galilean Charismatic,[5] the Pharisee,[6] the socially radical

---

1 Schweitzer, Albert, *The Quest of the Historical Jesus: A Critical Study of Its Progress from Reimarus to Wrede*, transl. William Montgomery (New York: Macmillan, 1968, first published 1906); Robinson, James, *A New Quest of the Historical Jesus and Other Essays* (Philadelphia: Fortress, 1983); Hamilton, William, *A Quest for the Post-Historical Jesus* (New York: Continuum, 1994).
2 Cf. Evans, Craig, *Life of Jesus Research: An Annotated Bibliography* (Leiden: Brill, 1989). Evan's 1,300 entries of books and articles are far from being exhaustive.
3 Smith, Morton, *Jesus the Magician* (San Francisco: Harper and Row, 1978).
4 Brandon, S. G. F., *Jesus and the Zealots* (Manchester: Manchester University Press, 1967).
5 Vermes, Geza, *Jesus the Jew* (Philadelphia: Fortress, 1973) and similarly Borg, Marcus, *Jesus: A New Vision* (San Francisco: Harper, 1987).
6 Falk, Harvey, *Jesus the Pharisee* (New York: Paulist Press, 1985).

Wisdom Sage,[7] the advocate of antipatriarchal peasant communes,[8] the eschatological prophet,[9] and the peasant Jewish Cynic[10]; more, doubtless, are to come. It is not my intention to prove those theories wrong. Rather, I shall present a comprehensive thesis more in accord with the evidence and let readers draw their own conclusions.

The apocryphal Acts of John contains a hymn wherein Jesus says: "A mirror am I to those who know me." Scholars engaged in Jesus research not infrequently find a Jesus with whom they are in very substantial agreement, but when this happens they should beware.

One might think that this problem, discussed at length by Albert Schweitzer in his classic survey of the history of Jesus research up to his time, and a problem of which all Jesus researchers are consciously aware, would no longer cause difficulty.[11] Schweitzer devastatingly criticized attempts to interpret the teachings and career of the historical Jesus, discovering that scholars tended to present a Jesus congenial to them, who taught what they thought should be taught, a Jesus who was, at the time of Schweitzer's survey, a good European liberal Christian. Today Jesus is not uncommonly found to have been a good American liberal Democrat.

In Helmut Koester's 1991 presidential address to the Society of Biblical Literature, he noted that since the portraits of Jesus in ancient Christian materials are the result of theologizing by early Christian churches it follows that scholars seek to isolate units of tradition that are not completely altered, or indeed created, by eschatological and other theological interpretations put forward later by the early church.[12] Many scholars believe, he said, "What must be stripped away

---

7 Patterson, Stephen, *The Gospel of Thomas and Jesus* (Sonoma, California: Polebridge, 1993).
8 Horsley, Richard, *Jesus and the Spiral of Violence* (San Francisco: Harper and Row, 1987).
9 Sanders E. P., *Jesus and Judaism* (Fortress: Philadelphia, 1985), and Fredriksen, Paula, *From Jesus to Christ* (New Haven: Yale University Press, 1988).
10 Crossan, John Dominic, *The Historical Jesus* (San Francisco: Harper and Row, 1991) and similarly Downing, F. Gerald, *Christ and the Cynics* (Sheffield: Sheffield Academic Press, 1988). A historical survey and a critique of the Cynic Jesus hypothesis may be found in Betz, Hans Dieter, "Jesus and the Cynics: Survey and Analysis of a Hypothesis," *The Journal of Religion*, Vol. 74, No. 4, October, 1994.
11 Schweitzer, *The Quest of the Historical Jesus*.
12 Koester, Helmut, "Jesus the Victim," *Journal of Biblical Literature*, Vol. 111, 1992: 6.

are early attempts at gnosticizing or catholicizing Jesus' message, adherence to patriarchal, antifeminist, and hierarchical structures of society, the desire to establish rule and order in religious communities with their worship, liturgy, creeds, and systems of subordination."[13] Koester argued that when this set of presuppositions is combined with a supposed scholarly "consensus" that Jesus' preaching was not eschatological in regard to the kingdom of God, and with "the terms of our own view of the world which leaves little room for reckoning with supernatural powers such as God and Satan," scholars almost inevitably will discover an intellectually modern and socially contemporary "historical" Jesus."[14] Accordingly, Koester observed that "we are again on the way toward a human Jesus who is just like one of us, one who holds values that are very close to our ideological commitments, a Jesus who is a social reformer and who attacks patriarchal orders, a Jesus who, as a real human person, can stand as an example and inspiration for worthy causes."[15]

Koester's remarks stand firmly in the tradition of Schweitzer and of Henry J. Cadbury, who wrote in 1937 of *The Peril of Modernizing Jesus:*

> The unconscious process behind our claiming Jesus as one of ourselves is easily understood. There is usually even in the most emancipated minds a feeling that Jesus was probably right. . . . The gospels are books with varied content and permit of even more varied construction. Without effort, without dishonesty, and even without realizing what is happening, one can read into them and out of them one's own ideas. In fact such a process is almost unavoidable if one has any respect for the person of Jesus. We so easily assume that our own approach is the right one, and therefore that a person of Jesus' insight must have shared it.[16]

We should be suspicious when we read today of Jesus' affinities to feminism, of his advocacy of personal freedom in the face of political oppression, and of his desire to restructure his society to permit greater

---

13 Ibid.
14 Ibid., 7.
15 Ibid.
16 Cadbury, Henry J., *The Peril of Modernizing Jesus* (New York: Macmillan, 1937), 37-38.

egalitarianism.

The Problem of Jesus the Teacher

Practically all historical scholars engaged in Jesus research presuppose consciously or unconsciously that Jesus was a teacher. E. P. Sanders writes, for example, "I do not doubt that those who find the teaching attributed to Jesus in the synoptics to be rich, nuanced, subtle, challenging, and evocative are finding something which is really there. Further, in view of the apparent inability of early Christians to create such material, I do not doubt that the teaching of Jesus contained some or all of these attributes. In short I do not doubt that he was a great and challenging teacher."[17] And so, it should follow, we know what Jesus taught. But we don't.

Every scholar engaged in Jesus research is by profession a teacher and so every construction of Jesus the Teacher is formulated by a teacher. These teachers, professors by trade, should wonder if there is not a bit of a Jesus-Like-Us in their constructions.

The paradigm of Jesus the Teacher usually leads the scholars who adopt it to regard all of Jesus' activities as teachings. The incident of "cleansing the Temple" is a teaching about the Temple's invalidity; Jesus' activities as a healer and exorcist are teachings about the power of the kingdom of God; Jesus' tendencies to be casual about Sabbath observance and to dine with the sinners who invite him are teachings about the Torah; Jesus' decision to go to Jerusalem for Passover is a teaching about self-sacrifice, and so on. From the "Jesus the Teacher" perspective everything he is supposed to have said and most of what he is supposed to have done constitute one or another sort of teaching.

Although he writes admiringly of Jesus' teaching, Sanders admits, "I regard most of the exegetical efforts of the last decades as proving a negative: analysis of the sayings material does not succeed in giving us a picture of Jesus which is convincing and which answers historically important questions."[18] It would appear that earnest efforts to find out what Jesus taught do not, in the end, produce a comprehensive and credible picture. The plethora of historical Jesus books presenting

---

17 Sanders, *Jesus and Judaism*, 129. Sanders is, however, very critical of "one-sided" views

18 Sanders, *Jesus and Judaism*, 133.

us with a Cynic or rabbinic or socially radical teacher who affirmed the presence of a Kingdom of God or, rather, insisted on its arrival in the future, whose ethos was one of unbounded love, yet who required mandatory hatred toward one's family, who sought the reformation of Israel or rather, predicted its immediate destruction, and on and on. . . means one of several things. Perhaps we have not yet found the single correct modality for understanding his teachings (we have found a dozen, mutually inconsistent modalities); perhaps there never was a single correct modality, and his teachings were simply incoherent; perhaps he was not primarily a teacher at all.

Jesus the Teacher in the New Testament

Because we are millennia removed from his time it may be that while the teachings of Jesus were relatively clear to his near contemporaries they are obscure to us because we do not understand clearly enough the social setting within which Jesus spoke. Perhaps then, if we can just learn enough about the social, religious, cultural, and political environment of early first-century Galilee we can understand Jesus' teachings in a way approximating the way his contemporaries understood them. John Dominic Crossan recently made a thorough effort to do just that, an effort that may be misguided, for it presupposes that Jesus' contemporaries *did* understand him.[19] It is by no means certain that they did.

Two of our principal sources of information about Jesus did not believe in Jesus the Teacher at all. Paul refers on occasion to teachings, generally as proof-text support for his own opinions, but Jesus the Teacher is otherwise of no interest to him. Paul swears to the Galatians "Before God I am not lying!" that he made no effort to learn about Jesus and his teachings from the eyewitnesses easily accessible to him (Gal. 1:1-2:15). John's gospel, similarly does not contain the teachings of Jesus as that phrase is understood in contemporary scholarship.

The sayings lists Q and Thomas seem to convey teachings, and overlap to a considerable degree, but they disagree profoundly as to what Jesus' teachings were about. The former emphasizes the imminent apocalyptic arrival of the Kingdom of God and the Son of Man, the latter stresses the present reality of the Kingdom, with the term "son of man" being of no significance. If one abstracts from Q and Thomas

---

19 Crossan, *Historical Jesus*, passim.

their common sayings one obtains a list of sayings very much in accord with the lists of sayings that many scholars separately (e.g., Crossan)[20] or collectively (i.e., the Jesus Seminar participants) believe to be authentic.[21] But this list conveys no program, has no ideology and, to put it bluntly, makes no clear sense.

Mark writes that Jesus' parables and proverbs were essentially incomprehensible and that Jesus must have intended them to be so (Mark 4:10-12, 33-34). But when Jesus does speak "clearly" and not "in parables" we hear Mark's voice, not Jesus' (Mark 8:31-32). Mark also informs us that Jesus' disciples, to whom his teachings were delivered, failed to understand them. The idea that Jesus' contemporaries did understand him, even though later generations do not, is a point of view Mark very explicitly denies (8:17-21).

Matthew and Luke disagree considerably about what Jesus taught and the constructions of his teachings in both gospels are made by the evangelists themselves, as is well known. It may be less well known that when Luke summarizes Jesus' mission in Acts' apostolic speeches, e.g. 2:22-36, 10:36-43, Jesus the Teacher is nowhere to be found; nor do Acts' apostles have the slightest interest in communicating the teachings of Jesus.

It might be argued that Jesus was a great teacher but, thanks to radical changes in his followers' view of him after his death, his teachings were no longer relevant to their enterprise. But Q, Thomas, Matthew, Mark, and Luke (in the Gospel) do give us teachings; indeed, *it may well be that the very idea that Jesus was primarily a teacher came into being only after his death.* Perhaps it was not the case that Jesus' coherent "message" was distorted after his death and thus we have several very different views of it. It seems more likely that Jesus was thought to have a coherent "message" only after his death and so we have several different creations of it.

It is universally agreed, I believe, that both Q and Thomas contain inauthentic sayings that supplement a corpus of authentic sayings; the purpose of the former was to impose meaning on the latter. Similarly, Mark and Matthew and Luke contextualize and supplement sayings to

---

20 Ibid.
21 The Jesus Seminar's conclusions in regard to the authenticity of purported sayings of Jesus may he found in Funk, Robert, et al. (eds.), *The Five Gospels* (Sonoma: Polebridge, 1994).

impose meaning. All five of these sources construct different meanings. It follows: either Q, Thomas, Matthew, Mark, Luke, and, for that matter, John did not know clearly what Jesus' teachings were; or they didn't care; or that they did know but disagreed with him so that they revised what he taught into something else; or that they did know what were said to be his teachings, did not trust those reports, and revised accordingly. Something odd is going on here.

Jesus the Teacher in Scholarship

It should not be this hard. When Sanders, standing in here for nearly all Jesus research scholars, says, "I do not doubt that he was a great and challenging teacher," I am baffled. Mark doubts it (4:10-12, 8:17-21), neither Paul nor John pay any significant attention to those teachings, Luke cares little about the matter (taking Acts as representative of Luke's bottom-line assessment).[22] Scholarship, theological and historical both, is in a state of near conceptual chaos regarding the message of Jesus the Teacher: countercultural wisdom sage, peasant Jewish Cynic, Pharisaic rabbi, antipatriarchal communalist, eschatological preacher? If he had a coherent message and neither we nor his known near contemporaries know for sure what it was, he ought not to be thought, first and foremost, to have been a great and challenging teacher.

It is possible to suppose that since so many of his teachings were lost in transmission we cannot reconstruct his program with any certainty. However, to assert that we would know him to have been a great teacher *if* we knew the program of his teachings simply begs the question. Everybody gives advice, holds opinions, argues points, disagrees with other points of view, and shares information. Jesus did too. But not everybody is, first and foremost, a teacher, and neither was Jesus.

Cadbury observed that the "eschatological school" of Schweitzer is akin to the "social school" of those who regard Jesus as a "social re-

---

[22] This judgment in regard to Luke is, of course, questionable. Luke did write a lengthy biography incorporating the sayings of Jesus. However, unlike Matthew and Mark where the reader must make his or her own assessment of Matthew and Mark's understanding of their own texts (with the usual hermeneutical difficulties) in some of Acts' speeches Luke assesses Jesus' principal purposes and accomplishments and so gives us his own understanding of his previous biographical text. Jesus' teachings play no significant part whatsoever in his assessments.

former, a propagandist with a program.[23] Both "wish to relate Jesus' action to a definite policy or program.... They assume that his own life was shaped by the same purpose—a Purpose with a capital P—unwavering, conscious, absorbing, glorifying."[24] The idea of an overriding Purpose arises logically from the "Jesus the Teacher" model since a teacher would normally be expected to have a conscious program to teach about. Cadbury wrote however,

> What I wish to propose is that Jesus probably had no definite, unified, conscious purpose, that an absence of such a program is a priori likely and that it suits well the historical evidence. Further I think that this explains some of the phenomena connected with his teaching. The sense of purpose, objective, etc., as necessary for every good life is more modern than we commonly imagine.... My impression is that Jesus was largely casual. He reacted to situations as they arose but probably he had hardly a program or a plan.[25]

The present book evolves out of a point of view similar to Cadbury's.

The quest for the historical Jesus has primarily been conducted under the umbrella of a single ruling metaphor: Jesus the Teacher. If that paradigm is not the best one to apply, then we must supplement it with another ruling metaphor. Further inquiries into Jesus' "teachings" on society, Torah, cynic philosophy, peasant hierarchies, theories of the kingdom of God, morality, political structures, and so forth are not likely to generate much more progress than has been achieved to date. The problem that has brought historical Jesus studies into some disrepute, the problem that has led to conceptual diversity if not chaos in that field of endeavor, is not with the sources or with the scholars. Scholars look for a teacher and analyze his teachings and end up with something, every time, but something different, every one. The texts are rich, the scholars are learned, but the paradigm Jesus the Teacher has proven itself to be very problematic.

The ruling metaphor, or paradigm, that does work, that does reveal

---

23 Cadbury, *Peril of Modernizing Jesus*, 128. These schools are alive and well and their adherents do very much what their predecessors did in the thirties. Admittedly, they do so with greater social-scientific and literary-critical sophistication.
24 Ibid., 128-29.
25 Ibid., 141.

an historical Jesus who did pretty much what the New Testament says he did, and who is *not* a social type never before or since heard of in the world (e.g., a peasant Jewish Cynic) is the metaphor of Jesus the Healer. Start with the question "how did he heal" rather than the question "what did he teach" and many things become clear. Because the paradigm Jesus the Healer is practically unheard of in historical Jesus studies, while the paradigm Jesus the Teacher is almost universal, the contents of the present book will seem very strange to many readers. Bear with me. A shift of ruling metaphor, a change in paradigm, is no small thing and it does take some getting used to.[26]

The Jesus of History and Theology

Jacob Neusner well summarized the philosophy of evidence current in Jesus research:

> From the beginnings of the quest for the historical Jesus, before the middle of the last century, to the present day, intense historical study has addressed to the Gospels a secular agendum grounded in three premises. These have been [1] historical facts, unmediated by tradition, themselves bear historical consequence, the gift of the Reformation (show me as fact in the sources, for example, Scripture); [2] historical facts must undergo a rigorous test of skepticism, the donation of the Enlightenment (How could a whale swallow Jonah, and what else did he have for lunch that day?); and [3] historical facts cannot comprise supernatural events, the present of nineteenth-century German historical learning (exactly how things were cannot

---

[26] In *Jesus the Magician,* Morton Smith sought to explicate the practices of Jesus the Healer. However, the analogies to Jesus' practices that Smith found in the magical papyri seem forced, and have convinced few if any scholars. Even those who find the magical papyri interesting and indicative of common and not-to-be-despised religious practices [I am one such person] have a hard time seeing where evidence exists that Jesus in fact did any of the things the practitioners of ancient magic did.

Geza Vermes's *Jesus the Jew* likens Jesus to the Galilean "charismatics" Honi the Circle Drawer and Hanina ben Dosa. But the slight and fragmentary evidence for their activities is drawn only from considerably later rabbinic sources and their reported activities (e.g., causing and stilling rainstorms) are more akin to reports of Jesus' supposed nature miracles than to the New Testament's reports of his healings. Nevertheless, the idea of Jesus as a Galilean charismatic may have affinities to the thesis advanced in this book.

include rising from the dead).[27]

All of this is perfectly true. Later traditions and interpretations do not determine the meaning of prior historical facts. Skepticism is always appropriate. Yet skepticism must be tempered by the fact that historians seek not ultimate truth but highest probability. One must avoid the extreme of skepticism whereby one can find cause to doubt the unquestioned veracity of every supposed historical fact and, in the end, know nothing whatsoever.[28] The last of Neusner's three premises, "historical facts cannot comprise supernatural events," has led, in my judgment, to the present chaos in Jesus research. As it stands it is a premise I accept absolutely. Yet it begs the question: what count as supernatural events? In answering that question wrongly scholarship on Jesus has gone adrift.

Let me begin with Neusner's example: "how things were cannot include rising from the dead." That is so. Still, "how things were" can certainly include as potential historical fact that people claimed they saw Jesus after he had died. We may say they saw something that they took to be Jesus, perhaps a gardener or a ghost, but the historical experience of such seeing cannot be denied by Neusner's third premise. Hence, *a supernatural event can be a historical event with a supernatural explanation attached to it.*

One may, of course, repudiate the supernaturalistic explanation: Jesus rose, and substitute for it a naturalistic explanation: given that Jesus was seen after his death, what was seen was a gardener or a ghost. One may be able to discuss intelligently the social and psychological conditions of those who saw (grief, fear, breakdown of their social unit, absence of their former leadership) in order to account for their seeing and one may make valid analogies to a wide variety of reports of people

---

27 Neusner, Jacob, "Who Needs 'the Historical Jesus'? Two Elegant Works Rehabilitate a Field Disgraced by Fraud," in his *Ancient Judaism: Debates and Disputes*, Third Series, Number 83, (Atlanta: Scholars Press, 1993), 171.
28 Burton Mack approaches this null point by reading virtually all of Mark (and, even more, the other biographies of Jesus) as a myth of origins, a historically false invention of events designed to justify then contemporary rituals and beliefs. He believes Jesus himself to have been like a Cynic philosopher. Cf. Mack, Burton, *A Myth of Innocence* (Philadelphia: Fortress, 1988), and his *The Lost Gospel: The Book of Q and Christian Origins* (San Francisco: Harper, 1993).

seeing individuals after they had died. If the supernatural is quickly rejected as a category of acceptable historical event, it is all too easy then to reject reports of supernatural events lock, stock, and barrel. *In the case of reported supernatural events one must always be clear as to what the reported event was as distinguished from what the reported supernatural explanation of the event was.* Often one may affirm the historicity of an event but wish to deny the supernatural explanation of it.

"How things were" can also include the *belief* that people rise from the dead. Jesus research, and New Testament research generally, dismisses claims to supernatural events per se, but tends not to dismiss claims to belief in supernatural events. The field quite correctly acknowledges that beliefs have powerful historical consequences. So, one may affirm both the historicity of "they saw Jesus after he had died" and the historicity of "they believed Jesus had risen from the dead." "They saw" is not the same as "they believed." The former is a historical claim of visual hallucination (or misinterpretation) reasonably explicable on psychological grounds. The latter is an explanatory paradigm for the supposed seeing by eyewitnesses, or a statement of conviction by other chronologically later persons that such seeing would have been possible.[29] Systematic errors have been made by Jesus researchers by virtue of the fact that crucial supernatural events reported of Jesus in our earliest biographical sources have been construed only to have been chronologically later statements of belief.

Of course, there are cases where later beliefs were written into gospel accounts. For example, it is highly unlikely that people thought that Jesus would rise from the dead prior to his having, in fact, died. It follows that when such claims appear in the four canonical biographies[30] of Jesus, they are retrojections into the period ca. 28-30 C.E. of ideas current only during the period ca. 30-100 C.E.[31] Similarly, the legends that arose in the decades after Jesus' death emphasizing his divine power over nature, legends that spoke of his walking on water, feeding mobs

---

[29] Why this would have been important to other persons is another question and will be addressed below. *Seeing a ghost is not, ipso facto, an important event to anyone but those who saw it.*

[30] The gospels are written to convey the ideas and defend the interests of those who wrote them. Be that as it may, they are still biographies.

[31] John Meier's dates Jesus' "mission" from quite early in 28 C.E. to April 7, 30 C.E. Cf. Meier, John P, *A Marginal Jew: Rethinking the Historical Jesus*, (New York. Doubleday, 1991), 372-409.

with a few loaves and fishes, turning water into wine, were later incorporated into the evangelists' biographies.

Spirit Christology

The idea that Jesus was the embodiment[32] of the spirit of God arose not from pious belief alone but from a series of historical events: repeated occurrences of alterations in ego identity, to be classified anthropologically as possession-trance. This set of historical events received a supernatural explanation during his lifetime: that Jesus was possessed by the spirit of God.

I will argue that the historical Jesus became the embodiment of the spirit of God and that this fact, in part, answers the question "how did Jesus heal?" To phrase it differently, Jesus had explicable psychological experiences of a sort that were understood by himself and others to be experiences such that, on occasion, he should not be identified as himself, Jesus of Nazareth, but as another person, the spirit of God. And I will argue that this is *not* in the category of a "supernatural event" but is in the category of a verifiable historical event, understanding "verifiable" in the usual sense of being evidenced by ancient sources appropriate to the time under discussion (ca. 28-30 C.E.), and in keeping with valid reasoning based on those sources, and in accord with the present state of knowledge in such fields of study as contemporary anthropology and psychology. I will argue that the historical fact that Jesus was understood to be possessed by the spirit of God was caused by understandable historical factors and that his spirit-possession led, during his life, to understandable consequences in accord with reliable elements of the biographies we have.

Perhaps I will bring closer together the two continents of Jesus research: historical scholarship and theological reflection. I will not do this in the usual way, by pretending that theological reflection is historical scholarship, but by insisting that historical scholarship has misunderstood certain historical events by assuming that they are supernatural events and then dismissing them from consideration. In other

---

32 I use "embodiment" in preference to "incarnation" because the latter term is so heavily weighted in theological discourse. Many readers will be better able than I am to judge whether or not the idea of "incarnation" is applicable to the thesis advanced in this hook.

words, historical scholarship has taken a supernatural explanation to be all there is to a historical fact when, rather, the fact was first and the explanation followed.

Gerald O'Collins observes that contemporary secular scholarship has found no place for the "incarnation of the divine person" in reference to the historical Jesus:

> Some revisionist Christologies (if one may call them Christologies rather than "Jesuologies") have been chipping away at the central belief that is very closely connected with Christ's preexistence—namely, the incarnation of his divine person. The objections are manifold: (a) During his ministry Jesus did not teach this about himself. (b) The doctrine of the incarnation gradually evolved—in a kind of apotheosis of Jesus. (c) This was promoted by common thought-forms in the ancient world and reached its climax in 325 when the Council of Nicea declared him to be "of one being" with God the Father. (d) It is logically incoherent for one person to be simultaneously divine and human. (e) The traditional doctrine of the two natures, besides being inexplicable, leaves Christ's humanity depersonalized and turns Jesus the man into a nonperson. (f) The revisionists encourage us to talk of the incarnation as "merely" metaphorical and accept Jesus simply as someone through whom God acted decisively and who embodied the divine purposes and ideals for us.[33]

Throughout the course of his essay O'Collins responds to these objections through lines of thought informed by Catholic theology.

I too will respond to them, but in a very different way. Throughout the course of this book I argue that it does make secular historical sense to conclude, in reference to O'Collins's list of objections that: (a) Jesus did teach this about himself. (b) and (c) The evolution of the doctrine of the incarnation began from understandable circumstances in the life of the historical Jesus. (d) It is not only coherent but it is widely attested in the world's cultures that one man or woman may be both divine and human. (e) Jesus the man is not less human if he was understood

---

33 O'Collins, Gerald, "What They Are Saying about Jesus Now," *America*, Vol. 171, August 27, 1994: 10-11.

during his lifetime to have sometimes been divine. (f) The incarnation was not conceived to be "merely" metaphorical either during Jesus' life or during the formative period of the Christian church.

I do not pretend to have even amateur expertise in theology, so I shall not pass on my own reflections but shall relate certain pertinent ideas of the Cambridge theologian Geoffrey W. H. Lampe:

> The category of Spirit-possession was used to some extent in early Christian thought to interpret not only Christ's present relationship to believers but also his relationship to God. If believers are sons of God through the indwelling of God's Spirit, possessing their souls and reshaping their lives according to the pattern of Christ, can Christ's own sonship be interpreted in the same terms? The gospels suggest this possibility. In the synoptists Spirit-possession and messianic sonship are linked together in the narrative of Christ's baptism. The Spirit descends upon him and he receives the divine assurance that he is Son of God.[34]

Spirit-possession is the category I shall be using throughout this book to discuss the origin and development of both Jesus' career and the later expansion of the Christian movement. It is also the principal category needed to explain and to understand the origin of some of the principal ideas of Paul and John. I will discuss spirit-possession in ways informed by cross-cultural anthropological study and contemporary psychological theory. I will also point out that Lampe is right, in the historical context of the first century, to say

> The early church felt constrained to interpret Jesus in terms of deity "coming down" to the human sphere in his person. It might be expected that the most appropriate concept for the expression of this image would be Spirit-possession.[35]

---

[34] Lampe, G. W. H., "The Holy Spirit and the Person of Christ," in Sykes, S. W., and J. P. Clayton (eds.), *Christ, Faith and History: Cambridge Studies in Christology* (Cambridge: Cambridge University Press, 1972), 117.
[35] Ibid.

Indeed, I will argue that this was not only an interpretation of the early church but also the interpretation of Jesus' followers and of Jesus himself. The idea that Jesus was spirit-possessed is not, in other words, a later christological speculation; it was an interpretation made by Jesus himself of a definable psychological state. In a state of spirit-possession Jesus of Nazareth was no longer who he had been but he became, as it was then understood, the spirit of God:

> This union might be envisaged as "indwelling", or as the descent of "Spirit" from heaven and its incarnation as a man. Had the church developed this concept it might have been able to work out a highly valuable christology. One of its merits is the use of the same term "Spirit", to denote both "deity" as such, that is, God in his own being, and also God as present and manifested in the historical person of Jesus. This could have been a good foundation for the Nicene assertion that the deity that we recognize in Christ is the deity of God in his own being, and nothing less. A developed Spirit-christology lends itself readily, on the other hand, to a full appreciation of the truth that Christ is the "proper man". If the relation of Spirit to manhood in Christ is conceived of in terms of possession rather than incarnation it becomes possible to assert that Christ reveals both the nature of God and also the perfection of man. God's creative Spirit does not diminish the completeness of a human personality by taking total possession of it.[36]

My job is not to argue for Lampe's Spirit-christology nor to elucidate it in my own words. Rather, I will show that *Spirit-christology in crucial aspects is not only a theological theory but a historical fact;* it is a set of historical events that were given a supernatural explanation. I will show this with arguments and lines of reasoning that I suspect the late Professor Lampe might have found disagreeable. In the end, however, I will show that Jesus "the embodiment of the spirit of God" or, to put it differently, Jesus as a spirit-possessed healer, is the best modality through which to understand the *historical* Jesus.

It will not be until a later section of the book that I will again refer to possible implications of my argument for present day christology

---

36 Ibid., 118.

and then only briefly. I am not a christological theologian; I may be of service to christological theologians should they wish to take advantage of the arguments I make.

2

Spirit Possession

Professor Lampe found "Spirit-possession" to be an appropriate and significant category for his christological theology. I will be using the term "spirit-possession" (and a related but not synonymous term "demon-possession") throughout the course of this book. What I mean by spirit-possession is perhaps not the same thing Professor Lampe meant. So I will explain my terminology and provide examples of how the terms are used. Then I will survey anthropological and psychological theories of possession in some detail.

First, however, I will acknowledge what many readers may already have noticed. I am not using the standard phraseologies of either historical or theological Jesus study where one finds all manner of ill-defined acknowledgments that Jesus, individual Christians, and formative Christians generally had some sort of relationship with spirit. We hear of their "receiving the spirit," "experiencing the spirit," "being empowered by the spirit," "having the spirit," "possessing the spirit," "being possessed *of* the spirit," and so forth. Not only are these usages ill-defined, they do not occur in anthropological or psychological scholarship and so they allow the study of a crucial element of formative Christianity to remain in an intellectual cocoon. These usages seem to be conscious or unconscious attempts to avoid using the one phrase that has definable anthropological and psychological meaning: "possessed *by* the spirit."¹

In every case the terminologies of present-day historical and theological usage implicitly give individual human egos control and power over the spirit. Those who possess or who are empowered by the spirit maintain supremacy over the "spirit" they experience. Current terminology does not imply "not I but the spirit," but, rather, I possess or I have or I experience or I am empowered by the spirit and so "I" am ultimately in charge. Thus, an individual's preaching (Peter's or Jesus') is said to be inspired or empowered by the spirit, but the preaching remains the self-created property of the individual.² By and large, the idea of inspiration in New Testament scholarship is more of a romantic theory of artistic and poetic inspiration than a pre-modern idea of spirit-possession.

To be possessed "by" the spirit means that "I" am not only not in charge but that "I" temporarily do not exist. "I"—the individual—does not receive, or have, or find himself or herself possessed *of*, a spirit. Rather, "I" the individual gives way and another "I: the spirit" comes to be. Standard metaphors for this are dramatic: I die, I am passing away. But the consequence is worth the price; "I" rise, "I" am born again. As Paul put it, "It is no longer I who live but Christ who lives in me" (Gal. 2:20).

In the words of the anthropologist Vincent Crapanzano, "spirit possession may be defined . . . as *any altered state of consciousness indigenously interpreted in terms of the influence of an alien spirit."*³ In anthropological parlance possession is a form of trance state and, as Crapanzano points out, "Certainly most trance states are associated with a removal

---

1 For an immensely learned and comprehensive book on the views of the spirit in New Testament scholarship, see James D. G. Dunn, *Jesus and the Spirit* (Philadelphia: Westminster, 1975).
2 This is probably how Luke viewed the situation, but we are not, at this point, discussing Luke's particular pneumatology. To anticipate discussion in Chapter Twelve, below, a cult of possession may well shift over the course of a few generations from a modality of "possession by spirit" to a modality of "spirit inspiration" meaning empowerment, assistance, good-feeling, peace and good works, etc. This is roughly the shift from the time of Jesus and Paul, to the time of Luke. Similar processes of change occurred also among the Methodists and the Quakers, to name just two of many instances. And, as Wesley's Methodism reemerged as Pentecostal Holiness, so spirit-possession reemerged in the second century with Montanism.
3 Crapanzano, Vincent, "Introduction" in his and Vivian Garrison (eds.), *Case Studies in Spirit Possession* (New York: John Wiley and Sons, 1977), 7 (emphasis in original).

from the normal cues and rules of sociability; the trancer is lost from his socially constructed self."[4] The anthropologist M. J. Field, looking at possession from a more psychological point of view, writes that

> The possessed person is in a state of dissociated personality whereby a split-off part of the mind possesses the whole field of consciousness, the rest being in complete abeyance. Splitting of the stream of consciousness into parallel streams is familiar to anyone who can "do two things at once," such as playing the piano and simultaneously planning a summer holiday . . . . It is the total banishment of all but one stream which is the essential feature of dissociation.[5]

Possession, then, is the substitution of an altered form of consciousness for an individual's normal form of consciousness, with the consequence that the identity of the individual is believed to have been replaced with the consciousness and identity of a possessing spirit. Accordingly, the social roles and expectations of the individual are replaced by social roles and expectations appropriate to the possessing spirit.

Everyone understands the concept of possession in the sense the term is used in popular culture. A person is possessed when he or she ceases being himself or herself and begins, temporarily, to be someone else altogether, to think and act and speak as a different being. American popular culture assumes knowledge of possession on the part of general audiences. Movies such as *The Exorcist* concern demonic possession; the movie *Sibyl* depicts the secular analog labeled "multiple personality disorder." *Ghost* features the possession of an actress by the spirit of a man recently deceased; the movie *Wolf* is based on the assumption that humans may be possessed by and ultimately transformed into wolves. The idea of the Incredible Hulk or Spiderman is not possession per se, but derives from the same pattern of thought, that an ordinary indi-

---

4 Ibid., 9.
5 Ibid. 8, from Field, M. J. "Spirit Possession in Ghana," in Beattie, John and J. Middleton, (eds.), *Spirit Mediumship and Society in Africa* (London: Routledge, 1969) 3. Crapanzano observes, however, that there are cases where a possessed individual will be conscious of his or her altered state and for such individuals the usual stream of consciousness has not been not totally banished.

vidual can on occasion function as a superpowered individual.[6] While use of the possession motif in popular culture makes it well known, it also tends to make the phenomenon seem entirely fictional. There are no such things as wolfmen and ghosts, after all. Because "possession" in common American parlance almost always refers to "demon-possession" one must be on guard not to confuse that socially and personally deleterious condition with the intrasocially and personally advantageous condition of spirit-possession.

Possession is not a fiction, not a pretense, not a kind of folk belief. Possession is a powerful psychophysiological experience that is so widespread in human cultures that the potential for the possession experience is part of the genetic inheritance of all people. To put it bluntly, if you do not occasionally become possessed it is because you have not placed yourself in circumstances where the achievement of the possession state is possible. Similarly, the potential to have an LSD experience is genetic, but if you do not take LSD you will not have the experience.

Possession Belief—Possession Trance

The anthropologist Erika Bourguignon distinguishes between "possession belief" and "possession trance," and her terminology has been widely accepted. "Possession belief" occurs when a state of affairs in regard to a human being is explained as having been caused by the presence of a spirit or demon *without* any change in the integrity of the ego-identity of that person. Most commonly, possession belief is used to account for diseases. In the New Testament, for example, we hear that Jesus cast out a demon that caused muteness (Mt. 9:32-34) and that Jesus "rebuked" a fever (Mk. 1:2932) to cause it to leave Peter's mother-in-law. In such cases the possessing "demon" is an explanatory paradigm for physiological symptoms.[7]

"Possession trance," Bourguignon insists, is also an explanatory para-

---

6 For other examples see Bourguignon, Erika, *Possession* (San Francisco: Chandler and Sharp, 1976), 1-3.

7 The apocryphal *Testament of Solomon*, a fascinating, funny, Disney cartoon of a document, states repeatedly that demons cause human physical problems. A text included in it as its chapter 18 provides an index of physical disorders, the names of demons that cause them,and angelic beings that can control the demons and eliminate the physical disorders. Similar lists appear in the long version of the *Apocryphon of John*.

digm, "an idea, a concept, a belief, which serves to interpret behavior."[8] She distinguishes possession belief from possession trance as follows: "we shall say that a *belief in possession* exists, when the people in question hold that a given person is changed in some way [muteness, fever, etc.] through the presence in or on him of a spirit entity or power, other than his own personality, soul, self, or the like. We shall say that *possession trance* exists in a given society when we find that there is such a belief in possession *and that it is used to account for alterations or discontinuity in consciousness, awareness, personality, or other aspects of psychological functioning.*"[9]

Possession trance is an altered state of consciousness wherein an individual experiences a change in personal identity so that he or she feels himself or herself to be, and is socially defined to be, some other person altogether. That other person can be a god, a divine spirit, a demon, or a deceased human being. The possessed individual will experience that his or her ego/persona is temporarily replaced by the ego/persona of another person who dwells in him or her and acts through his or her body controlling both physical movements and, most importantly, controlling speech.

A note on vocabulary is in order here. I assume that normally one person has one *persona*, his or her identity, or self, or personality, which are terms I will use synonymously, but for the most part I will use the term *persona*. I include therein implications both of "ego" as a mental faculty and "personality" as a social self-presentation. I do not in any way mean to imply a Jungian or any other technical psychological understanding of the term *persona*. My term *persona* is synonymous with *ego* as that term is used in common parlance; however, as the term *ego* has technical meanings in psychological theory that I do not intend to imply, it seems better not to use it here. To avoid repetitiousness, however, I will sometimes use *ego*, in its naive sense, synonymously with *persona*.

In the experience of possession a mind generates alternatively (not simultaneously) more than one persona. These personae are called *alter-personae* in literature on Multiple Personality Disorder.[10] I will

---

8 Bourguignon, *Possession*, 7.
9 Ibid., 8-9 (emphasis added).
10 Theories of Multiple Personality Disorder provide a useful etiology for some cases of demon-possession (cf. Chapter Six below), but those theories are not relevant to

sometimes call them *alter-personae* but I do not intend any implication that they are necessarily a form of disorder. I will sometimes call a possessed individual's persona prior to or apart from his or her possession persona, his or her *primary persona*.

The psychologist and theorist of possession states Traugott Oesterreich concluded

> the most important thing is to see clearly that we are dealing with a state in which the [possessed] subject possesses a single personality and a defined character, even if this is not the erstwhile one. The subject retains the memory of . . . past states, but he can no longer be conscious that this other personality has normally been his. He considers himself as the new person, the "demon," and envisages his former being as quite strange, as if it were another's. . . . As applied to this form of possession, which seems to have been very frequent, in fact, more so than any other, the statement that possession is a state in which side by side with the first personality another has made its way into consciousness is very inaccurate. Much more simply, it is the first personality which has been replaced by a second.[11]

One individual may have several alter-personae, especially in cases of demon-possession (Mary Magdalene had seven, cf. Luke 8:2-3).

I have no interest in the niceties of professional personality theory, which argues that from various perspectives (e.g., age, social role) a primary persona may be quite variable. When speaking of possession we are not discussing "variable" but "radically different" personae. Further, religious possession is to be distinguished from ritual or dramatic enactments where, although the individual may be socially defined as another person, the sense of personal identity remains unaltered.

Within a possession-oriented group, a second personality will be identified as a different person altogether and if asked "who are you?" it will respond with some form of self-identification, "I am so and so" (one or another named spiritual being). Thus possession assumes a body—mind dichotomy; the body remains the same; the persona is

---

cases of spirit-possession.
11 Oesterreich, Traugott, *Possession: Demoniacal and Other* (London: Kegan Paul, 1930), 39.

considered to have changed. The definition of the persona is dependent on the identity ascribed to it, not to the body it inhabits. For the period of the possession experience, it is not I but another in me who does and says what my body does and my voice says.

Possession experience is almost universally attested. Alex Wayman observes that "certain individuals, by idiosyncrasy or artificial stimulation of the psychic constitution become 'possessed.' Since it is a matter of persons, such possession states have a worldwide distribution; have taken place in the past, do so in the present, and will again in the future."[12] Erika Bourguignon surveyed 488 cultures that anthropologists have examined in some detail, and concluded that in 90 percent of those cultures forms of religious trance and/or religious possession took place with some regularity.[13] "Trance" states are altered states of consciousness achieved deliberately and interpreted to have religious significance but which are *not* accompanied by any belief in possessing spirits. Bourguignon discovered that 437 of the 488 separate societies she surveyed had belief in trance, or possession trance, or both. Trance experiences alone were found in 186, or 38 percent; both trance and possession trance in 116, or 24 percent; possession trance, which I term spirit or demon possession, in 251 or 52 percent. There were only 51 of the 488 societies without trance or possession belief and it should be noted that in some of these cases such beliefs may be held but for one reason or another were not reported in the ethnographic materials available to Bourguignon. Her data demonstrate that religiously defined altered states of consciousness, specifically possession trance, are to be found in essentially all areas of the world and within essentially all types and developmental stages of human society.

---

12 Wayman, Alex, "The Religious Meaning of Possession States," in Prince, Raymond (ed.), *Dance and Possession States* (Montreal: R. M. Bucke Memorial Society, 1966), 167.
13 Bourguignon, Erika, *Religion, Altered States of Consciousness, and Social Change* (Colum-htiks Ohio State University Press, 1973), 9-24; Bourguignon, "World Distribution and Patterns of Possession States," in Prince, *Trance and Possession States*, 3-32; Bourguignon, *Possession*, 31.

Holy Spirit-Possession

The idea of holy spirit-possession has both a universal and a particular dimension. Insofar as it is a form of psycho-physiological *experience* it is universally available and will be found to occur in a great many regions of the world. Insofar as it is a particular *explanation* for that state it is only to be found where Christian people have adopted that paradigm.

Before surveying anthropological and psychological theories of possession I shall illustrate the basic factors of the experience of spirit-possession as they are implicit in a single sentence drawn from the Gospel of Mark 13:11: "[When they lead you away and deliver you up, do not worry beforehand about what you are to say. But say whatever will be given to you at that time.] *It will not be you who speak but the holy spirit.*" This one sentence reveals the essence of the experience. The formulation "not you but spirit" affirms that a primary persona has been temporarily eliminated or subordinated and another persona, "the spirit," is temporarily dominant and functional within the body and mind of the former person. The claim made is in the first place essentially psychological. What is the status of the persona "you" when the spirit is speaking? That persona does not control the speech; it is absent or subordinated. What is the nature of the spirit that speaks? It is an alternative to the subordinated persona of the individual, and, hence, it is a type of persona.

Mark's Christian explanatory paradigm presents us with the idea that the holy spirit is an external independent person who temporarily comes to inhabit and function through a subordinated human being. If we grant the reality of the experience, and bracket the Christian paradigm for it, the assertion "not you but spirit" describes the activation of an alternative persona from the existing psychological potential of a particular human being. The experience "not you but spirit" is an altered state of consciousness. I. M. Lewis suggests that

> Possession ... is a condition where problem-solving processes result in an unusual dramatization of a certain part of the "me" aspect of the self, that part being constituted by forced and urgent identification with another personality credited with transcendental power. The nature of the possessing personality, or agency, can be under-

stood psychologically—and we have reviewed abundant examples of this—in light of the subject's own personality needs, his life situation, and cultural background which determine the normality or otherwise of the condition.[14]

The idea that other people should interact with the individual experiencing an altered state of consciousness *as if* the individual were another known person (i.e., holy spirit) requires the acceptance of a particular paradigm on the part of both the individual and the audience. The individual has learned to some degree how to behave so as to comport with the expected behavior of the holy spirit, and the audience has learned how to respond correctly to that behavior. Possession entails a change in social behavior. Because social behavior depends on the social statuses of those involved, the status of an individual experiencing the altered state of consciousness called spirit possession will shift radically upward if it is understood that his or her former social status has been temporarily replaced with the social status of the holy spirit.

In reference to the example in question (Mark 13:11) *only* Christians would have heard the holy spirit speak although the others would have heard speech. To whom they would have attributed that speech would depend upon their own paradigms for the individual's altered state of consciousness should they recognize it as such (e.g., here is a lunatic, Apollo speaks, we hear Beelzebul, etc.).

If we look at the particular social interaction Mark 13:11 discusses, speech, other implications may be drawn. In theory, what is said by the spirit is drawn from what is known by the spirit and not from what is known by the possessed individual. Accordingly, the idea of spirit speech entails the idea of spirit knowledge and it follows that the spirit is not simply a source of verbal formulations but a source of information.

The spirit speaks about what it knows. If we move from the judicial context of Mark 13:11 to a purely intra-Christian context, an individual who speaks in an altered state of consciousness and is heard as the holy spirit will have exceptional authority, enjoy radically elevated

---

14 Lewis, 1. M., *Ecstatic Religion: Second Edition* (London: Routledge, 1989), 179; following Yap, P. M., "The Possession Syndrome—A Comparison of Hong Kong and French Findings," *Journal of Mental Science*, 106, 1960.

social status, and function as a source of reliable information. All this is entailed in the idea "it will not be you who speak but the holy spirit."

The holy spirit is not a "reality" in the sense of being a condition of the world *apart from* human experience. Rather, the holy spirit is a culturally conditioned explanatory paradigm for a *type* of human experience, one that often includes the delivery of speech or the reception of information or an acknowledged capability of healing, which does not seem to derive from the individual.

Possession Phenomena

Possession occurs in two contrasting forms, and cultures may have either or both. One I shall call "demon" possession: i.e., those instances of possession where an individual is believed to have had his or her persona occasionally replaced by a malevolent alternate ego causing him or her to act in socially unacceptable ways, sometimes with deleterious effects upon his or her own person. I shall call "spirit" possession those instances of possession where an individual is believed to have had his or her persona replaced by a benevolent and/or useful alternate-ego causing him or her to act in ways beneficial to, or at least acceptable to, his or her immediate society. The question of whether a person's possession status is to be labeled "demon" or "spirit" depends on the perspective of the observer. I adopt the perspective of Jesus and his entourage that he was spirit-possessed, but note that some representatives of the established social order disagreed (Mk. 3:22-30). In cases of this sort the debate is not in regard to an individual's experience of possession but in regard to whether that possession is or is not beneficial or acceptable to society. Jesus' entourage defined the situation one way; some authorities defined it the other way, saying "he has an unclean spirit" (Mk. 3:30).

I. M. Lewis, working cross-culturally and seeking to make broad categorizations, distinguishes between "central possession religions," and "peripheral possession cults."[15] From the point of view of the elite in a given society, the former are approved, the latter disapproved; the former are "moralistic" and uphold the value systems of the elite, the latter may challenge elite values and so be regarded, by the elite, as amoral. Context matters; Yoruba possession religion in Nigeria fits the

---
15 Ibid., 29.

category of "central possession religion," but when it appears in the form of Santeria in southern Florida it might be regarded as a "peripheral possession cult."

Chandra Shekar and Colleen Ward prefer more neutral terminology, extending Lewis's original distinctions.

> Ritual possession is said to be generally voluntary, reversible, and short-term. It is supported and encouraged by cultural beliefs and induced in ritual ceremonies. It often functions as a defense mechanism and is irrelevant to cultural concepts of illness. No curatives are sought.
>
> Peripheral possession is involuntary, long-term, and evaluated negatively by the host culture. It is generally induced by an individual's stress and constitutes a pathological reaction. It is connected with physical and mental illness and curatives are sought.[16]

It is entirely possible that within a particular culture there will be disagreement about the status of particular cases of possession. While within a particular subculture possession may be categorized as "ritual possession" by a benevolent spirit, from the point of view of those outside the subculture it might be categorized as "peripheral possession" by an inimical demon or, in modern societies, as evidence of mental pathology.

Shekar testifies to the ubiquity of possession in India:

> The phenomenon of possession is very common in India, especially in rural areas. Every person believes in possession, and in every village one or two persons are said to experience possession by either spirits or God. There are many shrines where the priests become possessed by God for the benefit of the masses. Large numbers of people gather on that day and seek advice, guidance, solutions for their problems, and treatment for their

---

16 Shekar, C. R. Chandra, "Possession Syndrome in India," in Ward, Colleen, *Altered States of Consciousness and Mental Health: A Cross-Cultural Perspective* (Newbury Park: Sage Publications, 1989), 83. He follows Ward, Colleen, "Spirit Possession and Mental Health: A Psycho-Anthropological Perspective," in *Human Relations* 33, 1980, 149-63.

ailments.[17]

Similar comments may be made in regard to cultures of China. Of voodoo religion in Haiti, which counts among its adherents the vast majority of Haitian people, Ari Kiev informs us

> Possession is a central feature of Voodoo. It is the means by which the loa, or deities, interact with mankind. Through possession of congregants the loas enter the Haitians' world to punish or reward them and to treat their ills and worries.[18]

The same could be said for the subcultures of Puerto Rico, Cuba, and the United States where Santeria and Vodun are practiced, and for the widespread and rapidly growing numbers of Brazilian Umbanda, Macumba, and Candomblé practitioners.[19]

Because cultures where possession trance occurs are so common and widespread, one cannot avoid the conclusion that the capacity to experience possession and trance is a normal psychobiological capability of the human species. Whether or not the capacity to experience possession trance is actualized depends mainly on cultural expectations: where it is expected it occurs frequently; where it is not expected it occurs rarely. Possession trance is not a pathological condition. It is not, for example, a form of schizophrenia, or epilepsy, or hysteria, although where possession trance is culturally expected some persons who are diagnosable as mentally ill may be counted among those possessed.

Physiological aspects of the possession experience tend to be similar wherever the experience occurs. Those possessed usually have considerable muscle rigidity and loss of control of gross motor movements. In the initial phases of the possession experience, people often move jerkily, shake uncontrollably, fall and have difficulty rising. The labels "shakers," "quakers," and "holy rollers" for Christian charismatic groups arose from observation of those behaviors by outsiders. They

---

17 Ibid., 86-87.
18 Kiev, Ari, "The Psychotherapeutic Value of Spirit-Possession in Haiti," in Prince, *Trance and Possession States*, 143.
19 Karen McCarthy Brown's research into Vodun in New York City leads her to conclude that "there is no Vodou ritual, small or large, individual or communal, which is not a healing rite." Brown, Karen McCarthy, *Mama Lola: A Vodou Priestess in Brooklyn* (Berkeley: University of California Press, 1991), 10.

will often speak in a babbling "abbabahab" fashion (Gal 4:16), or, with practice, in the more rhythmic cadences of glossolalia (1 Cor 14:18), or they might utter powerful groans, shouts, barks and other inarticulate sounds (Rom 8:26). Shekar reports that throughout India "mediums" may be found. He gives this general description:

> ... in the morning after bathing, he or she worships the deity, often in a ceremonial context; then, suddenly, the God descends. The individual exhibits an altered state of consciousness, with trembling movements, and may shout, abuse, curse, and bless, according to the mood. Overall, the state is characterized by restlessness and hyperactivity; the audience reacts with fear and deference, seeks the medium's predictions, and carries out orders faithfully.[20]

The ritual possession terminates abruptly when the individual falls to the ground, exhausted.

The explanatory paradigm serving to account for spirit-possession receives experiential justification and validation from the experience. The explanatory loop is this: if the experience occurs as we say it will, then the explanation of the experience we offer is validated by the fact of the experience itself. As Kiev puts it:

> Experiencing the unusual psychic state of possession which is associated with the reduction of usual defenses, induces the individual to seek to understand an experience which cannot readily be understood in common-sense terms. The cognitive dissonance engendered in the possessed, and in others witnessing their neighbors genuinely behaving as if in the control of outside forces, cannot fail to impress everyone with the validity of whatever theory is immediately at hand to explain the phenomenon.[21]

While it is not universally the case, it is not uncommon for possessed people to be amnesiac to a greater or lesser degree regarding their exploits while possessed, because their normal memory-forming ego was absent during the time of the experience. As Lambek reports

---
20 Shekar, ibid., 89.
21 Kiev, "Psychotherapeutic Value of Spirit-Possession," 145-46.

in reference to Mayotte in the Camoros Islands, "The spirit speaks and acts while the host is 'absent' during trance, and there is consistency and continuity from one appearance of a given spirit to the next. Hosts by and large do not remember what occurred while they were in trance (since they were not present, how could they?) but they are often told by others what happened."[22] But Felicitas Goodman remarks about possession more generally that "Whether people remember the content of the ecstasy is not left to individual choice, but rather depends on what is expected in their religious community. In other words, amnesia, i.e., forgetting, is not an inherent quality of the religious trance. Amnesia will set in only if there is an express instruction demanding it."[23]

At its conclusion, a possession experience usually leaves the individual in a state of extreme, but pleasurable, exhaustion. Viewed from the outside the experience looks arduous and unpleasant, but reports by participants often describe it as pleasurable and declare that at least at its conclusion the experience brings joy and peace and relaxation. Felicitas Goodman, who has studied trance experience in considerable detail, reports that

> the trancers are rewarded with a feeling of an overwhelmingly sweet joy, an intense euphoria, that comes upon them after the conclusion of the trance. Especially during an early experience, this tends to linger. Later on it becomes less pronounced. Together with the perception of heat during the trance, it is this euphoria that is most often mentioned by participants in a religious trance ritual.[24]

The practice of spirit-possession is essentially social in nature. Rarely do individuals enter a possession state in solitude for their own personal benefit. People who become possessed do so in the presence of others and communicate with others. As E. M. Pattison writes, possession trance is "an interpersonal event, in which there is possession by, or entranced impersonation of, another being, in the context of com-

---

[22] Lambek, Michael, "From Disease to Discourse," in Ward, *Altered States of Consciousness*, 40.
[23] Goodman, Felicitas, *Ecstasy, Ritual, and Alternate Reality* (Bloomington: Indiana University Press, 1988), 39-40.
[24] Ibid., 38.

munal activity and witness to the behavior.[25] Possession is a communication medium that in theory allows human beings to communicate with gods, but which in fact allows a transformed manner of communication between human beings and other human beings.

Michael Lambek observed that typically three sorts of message may be transmitted by spirit-possessed persons:

> First, one must consider the period of the emergence of a spirit in a particular host, during which messages concerning its individual status and immediate and prospective social relationships predominate. . . . For society the emergence process is a matter of accepting and validating the difference between host and spirit and affirming the relationship between them and the identity and power of the latter.
>
> Second, we can distinguish the play or performance activities that take place mostly among the spirits (i.e., the possessed hosts) themselves, but also between spirits and nonpossessed humans. . .
>
> Third, then, there are the substantive conversations held between established spirits and their human consociates, including the "internal" conversations maintained by adepts, but also the conversations established between curers and clients, and within families, especially between the spirit and the host's spouse or among the spirit and two generations of hosts?[26]

When a possessed individual speaks, he or she is socially defined as a divine, deceased, or demonic person. Accordingly, the normal persona, the normal social person, cannot be held accountable for the communication and, indeed, in theory has nothing to do with the communication. The possessed person has changed in a psycho-physiological sense and he or she has become a different social entity.

---

25 Pattison, E. M., "Trance Possession States," in Wolman, Benjamin and Montague Ullman (eds.), *Handbook of States of Consciousness* (New York: Van Nostrand, 1986), 288.
26 Lambek, "From Disease to Discourse," 43-45.

Social Uses of Possession Phenomena

In instances of demonic possession, the speech and behavior of a person possessed is understood to be the speech and behavior of a demon. Accordingly, he or she is freed to act out otherwise repressed aggressions and resentments without fear of retaliation. The American phrase "the devil made me do it" applies here.

The social construction of a demon-possession paradigm allows aggressive reaction and reprisal by possessed persons against other people who cannot in turn retaliate. To retaliate against a demon would be to risk supernatural attack; to retaliate against the possessed person's normal self would be unjust and would imply rejection of the possession paradigm itself. Freedom of action and speech is considerably enhanced when a person becomes possessed. They may, however, be subjected to exorcism. In American law a somewhat similar principle applies to individuals judged "not guilty by reason of insanity"; they are not subjected to punitive incarceration, but they will most probably be committed to a psychiatric institution for rehabilitation.

Instances of demon-possession are to be found much more commonly among classes and kinds of persons who are otherwise unable aggressively to respond to oppression and insult. Demon-possession is more often than not a coping mechanism, an attempt to solve problems resulting from unsatisfactory personal relationships by those whose social status is so subordinate that they have no other effective recourse. Children may use this means to act out aggressions toward parents; wives may discover that a demon can express to husbands, or mothers-in-law, feelings and demands that could not otherwise be expressed.

In accounts of demon-possession one must inquire, or at least wonder, why that particular method of communication was adopted, why it was necessary for a demon to speak instead of the individual. In the absence of psychopathology, it will often be found that the possessed individual had no other recourse. Because it is socially and physically problematic to be in a state of negative alter-persona possession or, to put it another way, to be considered one who occasionally turns into a demon, anyone adopting that option will have few or no other options available. An exorcism, to have any lasting effect, will *necessarily* have to be accompanied by a shift in the social or family relationship system which gave rise to the coping mechanism of demon-possession in the first place.

One underlying principle crucial to understanding of affirmative (spirit) or negative (demon) possession, and found across cultures, is that a possessing entity, the alternative persona that arises in the possession experience, has a higher social status than ordinary people do. Ghosts are more powerful and dangerous than mothers; deities are more powerful and knowledgeable than chieftains. Any possession experience immediately alters the status relationships within the relevant social group. I. M. Lewis has observed that, from a sociological perspective,

> possession plays a significant part in the enhancement of status. One result of possession by those spirits which we have classified as "peripheral" is to enable people who lack other means of protection and self-promotion to advance their interests and improve their lot by escaping, if only temporarily, from the confining bonds of their allotted stations in society.[27]

Except in cases where clear psychopathology exists, and they are comparatively rare, individuals who experience possession do so (consciously or unconsciously) for their own benefit and for the benefit of their local social groups.[28] Possession is not, per se, a pathological disorder.

In most instances of possession, an individual will enact one of several alternative roles in the guise of one of several alternative forms of spiritual being. If there is a plurality of possible gods, as is often the case, to be possessed by a goddess of love, a god of war, a god of healing, a goddess of streams and so forth requires the possessed individual to act out differential roles and often to don symbolic garb, carry symbolic devices and to speak in different tones of voice depending on the nature of the deity by which he or she is possessed.

The different potential roles and powers of people in the state of possession are explained by the hypothesis of different possessing entities. To say, for example, "when she is possessed she is aggressive and violent," or "when he is possessed he knows the secrets of the healing

---

27 Lewis, *Ecstatic Religion*, 114.
28 How demon possession can seem beneficial to individuals will be discussed in more detail in Chapter Six below.

herbs," identifies her, let us say, as a god of lightning and him as goddess of healing. As a general rule the distinctions of sex among human beings does not carry over to the distinctions of sex among possessing deities. A woman may be possessed by a male god and enact the role of a male; a man may become a goddess and act the role of a woman.

Prince summarizes the principal social therapeutic effects of possession as follows:

(1) the attainment of high status through a cult role,
(2) the acting out of aggressive and sexual behavior,
(3) the reversal of sexual roles,
(4) the temporary freedom from responsibility for actions.[29]

He believes that there are wider social therapeutic effects as well, especially that instances of possession supply occasions for the tightening of the social structure of the society in question.[30]

Gods, spirits, or benevolent ancestral ghosts often provide information and give advice. They predict the future and interpret the past, advise the performance of established rituals, announce the design of new rituals, specify charms and medicines to solve problems of health, or explain how best to go about winning the favors of persons of the opposite sex. A person possessed has immediate claim to temporary group leadership, a state of affairs that causes no difficulty in established cults. In groups still in the process of hierarchical stratification, however, the elevated statuses accorded to spirit-possessed persons will usually lead to conflict between possessed persons and persons intent upon asserting personal or titular authority.

Because possessed persons enjoy an upward alteration in social status during the period of their possession, more often people of relatively low social status, marginal people, people in a condition of social oppression, choose to join possession-oriented groups. People whose opinions normally are received with respect and whose resentments normally can be effectively expressed will be less likely to experience and act out the roles of possession. But they can do so; no one has as

---

29 Mischel, W., and F. Mischel, "Psychological Aspects of Spirit Possession" *American Anthropologist* 60, 1958, 249-60, cited in Prince, Raymond, "Possession Cults and Social Cybernetics," in *Trance and Possession States*, 157.
30 Prince, *Trance and Possession States*, 161.

high a status as a god and the experience of possession is not purely social in nature; it has its inherent euphoric rewards and, as in Christian communities, it may be ascribed soteriological benefits.

Following the analysis of Leonora Greenbaum, who examined possession phenomena in sub-Saharan Africa, Bourguignon concludes

> possession trance, by offering a decision-making authority in the person of a medium, revealing the presumed will of the spirits, allows persons oppressed by rigid societies some degree of leeway and some elbow room. As such, possession trance may be said to represent a safety valve, of sorts, for societies whose rigid social structures causes certain stresses.[31]

She believes that possession trance is often a "search for compensation and self-respect among men humiliated in their daily lives."[32]

The kind of society most prone to give rise to the practice of possession trance is sedentary and dependent on agriculture and/or animal husbandry.[33] It has local groups larger than 1,000 and an overall population greater than 100,000, with a jurisdictional hierarchy extending beyond the local level, and a rigid hierarchical system often including a form of slavery. Spirit-possession is often a way that certain individuals work around restrictions imposed by their economic, sexual, or social status, and so it will most often be found in societies where those restrictions are rather clearly defined. The society of first-century Palestine meets these criteria.

Possession and Revealed Knowledge

Information transmitted by persons in a possession state may be information unavailable to them in their normal persona state. That is not to say such information comes from supernatural sources. Rather, both religious trance and religious possession assist individuals in gaining access to otherwise unavailable unconscious potentials.

Unconscious potentials are unconscious because the normal persona

---

31 Bourguignon, *Possession*, 31; cf. Leonora Greenbaum, "Social Correlates of Possession Trance in Sub-Saharan Africa," in Bourguignon, *Reli;gion, Altered States of Consciousness*.
32 Bourguignon, *Possession*, 33.
33 Ibid., 43-44.

cannot access them, but an alternative ego structure will not have the same repressions and inhibitions as the normal ego. Thus an alternative ego structure can, as it were, go around the normal ego's defense mechanisms and tap into the unconscious. The presumption that a possessed person has had an alternative persona emerge requires the corollary that the alternative persona's interaction with the unconscious will be different from the normal persona's interaction.

Because alternative ego/persona access to the unconscious allows individuals to attain knowledge and insight into personal and social circumstances that they cannot attain in a normal persona state, their critiques, advice, and insights may be surprisingly apt and, when accompanied by the general placebo effect to be expected when individuals believe themselves to have had the benefit of divine advice and assistance, the advice given by those possessed will often have real value. In addition, access to unconscious insights and information interpreted as knowledge derived from divine wisdom (i.e. the spirit informs me, I do not inform myself), provides an individual the feeling that he or she has come to know mystic and secret things, things revealed by the gods.

There is more to the experience of access to unconscious knowledge than just the socially constructed notion that such information is divine in origin. Arnold Ludwig emphasizes that one of the most intriguing features of almost all altered states of consciousness is

> the predilection of persons in these states to attach an increased meaning or significance to their subjective experiences, ideas, or perceptions. At times, it appears as though the person is undergoing an attenuated "eureka" experience, during which feelings of profound insight, illumination, and truth frequently occur. . . . I would surmise that this "raw" sense of significance, which lends import and conviction to the "revelations" attained during mystical consciousness or religious possession states, has been a major factor in the stabilization of many religions, sects, and cults.[34]

From this it follows that the experience of possession, with its concomitant alter-persona access to unconscious knowledge and learning,

---

34 Ludwig, Arnold, "Altered States of Consciousness" in Prince, *Trance and Possession States*, 79, 81.

carries with it an inherent propensity to find that knowledge to be of extraordinary significance. That propensity, coupled with the social definition of the possession state as one giving direct access to the supernatural, means that information transmitted by persons in the possession state will be held in the highest regard.

Before I turn from general discussion of spirit-possession to analysis of New Testament materials, I must stress that we have perhaps 1 percent, more likely .001 percent, of the information available to us in our texts that an anthropologist has who has done even a modicum of field-work in a particular culture. My analysis must of necessity be of a general sort and draw rather general conclusions because there are not enough data available to do more.

3

Prophets and Prophecy

In regard to Jesus research E. P. Sanders correctly observes, "There is, as is usual in dealing with historical questions, no opening which does not involve one in a circle of interpretation, that is, which does not depend on points which in turn require us to understand other [points]," and he insists that "one must be careful to enter the circle at the right point, that is, to choose the best starting place."[1] The best starting place, it follows, is one that is historically secure with a meaning that can be known somewhat independently from the rest of the evidence. It further follows, as he rightly says, that one should *"found the study on bedrock,* and especially to begin at the right point."[2]

In the field of Jesus research, however, one person's bedrock is another person's sand. I cannot honestly think of a single supposed bedrock event or interpretive stance that somebody has not denied.[3] Nor, to my knowledge, are there any two constructions of the "authentic" sayings of Jesus that are identical. One might compile a short set of parables, proverbs, and aphorisms that are universally conceded to be from Jesus, but they will be that set that conveys the *least* inherent meaning (e.g., neither those featuring a future kingdom nor those featuring a present kingdom) and where one can go from there I am not at all sure.

---

1 Sanders, *Jesus and Judaism*, 10.
2 Ibid. (emphasis added).
3 For example, it is the position of conservative Islamic scholarship that Jesus was not crucified.

Still, there do appear to be two *bedrock* facts on which we can rely: scholars agree almost unanimously that during his lifetime Jesus was regarded by some people as a prophet, and they almost all agree that he worked effectively as a healer and exorcist. Eugene Boring writes that "Christian scholars of the most varied theological positions have generally agreed that *the New Testament's picture of Jesus as prophet is historical bedrock.*"[4] According to John Meier, "*Nothing is more certain about Jesus than that he was viewed by his contemporaries as an exorcist and a healer.*"[5] If we can understand the implications of these two foundations then we will understand the nature and career of the historical Jesus. I will begin by examining the idea of Jesus as an early first-century Jewish prophet, proceed in my next chapter to the "right point" at which to start, Jesus' baptism, and discuss in subsequent chapters how the ideas of prophet, exorcist, and healer cohere in the reports of Jesus' activities.

Spirit and Prophet

Throughout the gospels Jesus is said to be a prophet. His near associates believe this of him, as do the crowds who come to him (Lk. 7:16, 24:19, Mt. 21:11, Jn. 4:19). He seems sometimes to have used the term self-referentially (Mt. 13:57, Lk. 13:33). His enemies call him a prophet sarcastically (Mk. 14:65). David Hill summarizes the prevailing view of present day scholarship when he writes

> Within the Judaism of the time, the possession of [sic] the holy Spirit, the Spirit of God, was regarded as *the* mark of prophecy: therefore Jesus' inspiration and equipping for ministry by the Spirit of God signifies that he was (and probably regarded himself as) a prophet. His claim to possess [sic] the Spirit is quite explicit if "the blasphemy against the Holy Spirit" (Mark 3:29) is rightly interpreted as the denial of the *divine* source of the spiritual power with which Jesus casts out demons.[6]

David Aune also concludes that Jesus believed himself to be a proph-

---
[4] Boring, Eugene, *The Continuing Voice of Jesus* (Louisville: John Knox Press, 1991), 57 (emphasis added).
[5] Meier, John, "Jesus" in the *Jerome Biblical Commentary (Revised)* (New York: Doubleday, 1986), 1321 (emphasis added).
[6] Hill, David, *New Testament Prophecy* (Atlanta : John Knox, 1979), 58.

et: "the conclusion that Jesus closely identified his own mission with that of the prophets of ancient Israel is very probable."[7] In a similar vein Richard Horsley observes that in at least two separate movements, reflected in pre-Q and pre-Markan materials respectively, Jesus was understood in prophetic terms. He writes that "it is far more likely that Jesus was understood as a prophetic figure from the outset than that he was 'reimagined' as a prophet only later, but virtually simultaneously in two separate movements."[8]

I am not concerned with the theological interpretation of the meaning of the prophetic phenomenon, nor with the content and ideology of Hebrew canonical prophecy. I am interested only in the nature of the prophetic experience in Judaisms current at Jesus' time and in terms of the life of Jesus himself. We have much less descriptive information about the prophetic experience than we have records of prophetic utterances. Nevertheless, in the words of R. R. Wright,

> enough clues have been preserved in the OT to suggest that Israelites thought of the prophetic experience as one that occurred when people were possessed by the spirit of God. "The hand of the Lord" fell upon them (1. Kings 18:46; 2 Kings 3:15; Jer. 15:17; Ezek. 1:30); the spirit of God "rested on them" (Num. 11:25-26) or "clothed itself" with them (Judg. 6:34). In this situation they were no longer in control of their own actions and words but were completely dominated by God. They felt compelled to speak the divine message that had been given to them (Amos 3:8; Jer. 20:9).[9]

Wright's observations are completely in keeping with our common-knowledge concept of prophecy. The point and purpose of a prophet is to speak the words of God. The prophet is, therefore, not speaking his own words but words that supposedly originate from a supernatural

---

[7] Aune, David, *Prophecy in Early Christianity and the Mediterranean World* (Grand Rapids: Eerdmans, 1983), 157.
[8] "Horsley, Richard, "Q and Jesus: Assumptions, Approaches, and Analyses," in *Semeia Volume 55: Early Christianity, Q, and Jesus* (Atlanta: Scholars Press, 1991), 208.
[9] Wilson, R. R., "Prophet" in *Harper's Bible Dictionary* (San Francisco: Harper, 1985); also *see* his "Prophecy and Ecstasy: A Reexamination" *Journal of Biblical Literature*, Vol. 98, 1979: 323.

person external to himself. The prophet does not select or determine the words, they just come forth from him and are, accordingly, attributed to another. Therefore, when written down, they may be introduced not by "thus saith Jeremiah" but by "thus saith the Lord." The Lord supposedly formulated ideas in certain modes of expression and used Jeremiah's mouth to communicate them.

The hypothesis that such words originate externally to the mind of the person uttering them (the prophet) is a culturally established explanation for a state of affairs; psychologically speaking, the words originate from an alter-persona of the original person. In either case the statement that the persona, e.g., "Jeremiah," is not speaking but the persona "spirit of God" is speaking is true. The difference between the culture's explanation and a psychological explanation comes in whether "the spirit of God" is conceived to be a feature of the mind that generated the persona Jeremiah or to be a feature of the mind of God.

By many ancient definitions prophets are people who are dissociated from the origination of their own ideas and from the origination of their own words and often from the usual tone of their own voices; through their voices gods speak. In all cases this dissociation is psychological. Prophecy is an unusual psychological state, an altered state of consciousness. Not *this* persona had these ideas, words, utterance, but *that other* persona. The author of Second Peter put it very well: "No prophecy ever came by the impulse of man, but men moved by the Holy Spirit spoke from God" (1:21).

It is practically tautological to assert that Hebrew Bible prophets were spirit-possessed, for alter-persona spirit speech is a defining characteristic of a prophet. The only alternative is that some of the Hebrew Bible prophets acted in conscious imitation of Jewish people who were spirit-possessed. This would be the case if there were "literary" prophets who, while in their own right minds (primary personae), dictated or wrote carefully constructed poetic materials that they instructed their scribes to attribute to God. Such a procedure could occur only in a culture that accepts the existence of possessed prophets, people whose primary personae were on occasion replaced by the persona of the spirit of God. It will do absolutely no good to attribute one's literary productions to the persona of God unless such attribution is already an acknowledged possibility in the culture.

The New Testament materials report virtually nothing about the physical manifestations of possession.[10] Although one might argue from reports of the physical correlates of the general phenomenon of possession experience attested in hundreds of cultures to the specific instance of New Testament persons, nothing is gained thereby. No New Testament evidence exists concerning the physical side of possession experiences.[11] Peter Michaelsen writes, "The theory affirming the existence of ecstasy among prophets in ancient Israel does not only seem extremely likely but also rather banal and hackneyed, considering that such states of consciousness occur among all other well-known prophets, shamans and intermediaries everywhere and at all times."[12] Similarly, in the absence of New Testament evidence, if an assumption is to be made, it would be more reasonable to assume that "ecstatic" physical correlates occurred in instances of possession trance than that they did not.

Jewish Prophets of the First Century

It is sometimes argued that there could have been no prophets in the first century because Judaism had concluded that the prophets "ceased from Israel" several centuries earlier. This line of thought is false. It stems from a passage found in Tosephta Sotah 13.2, Yoma 9b: "From the death of Haggai, Zechariah, and Malachi, the latter prophets, the Holy Spirit ceased from Israel." However, that passage was composed at least two centuries later than the time of Jesus and it is contradicted by good first-century evidence from the New Testament, Josephus, and Philo. Even in respect to its own time, a passage of this sort would have reflected the opinion of members of the rabbinic elite and not necessarily the opinion of the peasantry. In any event it makes a claim regarding a certain type of prophecy, the sort recorded in the books of Haggai, Zechariah, and Malachi; it would be grossly anachronistic to presume

---

10 The report that Christians once seemed drunk to outsiders is all there is to go on (Acts 2:13-15). Peter's response that they would not be that drunk quite so early in the day is an interesting one.
11 There exist scholarly polemics against the "excesses of the Corinthian ecstatics" based on 1 Corinthians. But everything the Corinthian Christians do in the spirit Paul does too. Paul is not opposed to "ecstatics" per se; he is interested only in the regulation of spirit-inspired behavior during community gatherings.
12 Michaelsen, Peter, "Ecstasy and Possession in Ancient Israel: A Review of Some Recent Contributions," *Scandinavian Journal of the Old Testament*, No. 2, 1989: 37.

that if Jesus was an early first-century prophet he must have spoken in ways characteristic of prophetic individuals who lived several centuries before and, of course, there is no reason to think that he did so.

Our three principal sources for early first-century theories of prophetic experience are the New Testament, and the works of two individuals: Josephus and Philo of Alexandria.

Josephus's views of prophecy are knowable to some extent, and I will discuss them immediately below. But they are marginally relevant to the case of Jesus. Josephus is not sympathetic to, nor is he very interested in, the ideas of prophecy held by peasants. He writes political-historical tracts and so he is particularly interested in the canonical prophets as historians and predictors of political events.[13] Fair enough, and one can find references in his books to the supposed prophets of the first century whom he mentions in passing, although he does not ever call them prophets. However, one comes away from Josephus with very little evidence as to what early first-century peasant Jews expected from prophets.

Robert Webb sought to categorize the Jewish prophets of the first century, using Josephus's writings for his principal evidence.[14] He finds the types "clerical prophet," "sapiential prophet," and "popular prophet."[15] By Webb's classification Jesus was a "popular prophet." Webb derives this type partly from Josephus's discussion of circumstances during the siege of Jerusalem by Herod in 37 B. C E.

> throughout the city the agitation of the Jewish populace showed itself in various forms. The feebler folk, congregating round the temple, indulged in transports of frenzy *(edaimonia,* "experienced spirit or divine possession") and fabricated oracular utterances *(theiodesteron)* to fit the crisis.[16]

---

[13] Josephus's views have been thoroughly and well analyzed by rebecca Gray in her *Prophetic Figures in Late Second Century Palestine: The Evidence from Josephus* (New York: Oxford University Press, 1993).
[14] Webb, Robert, *John the Baptizer and Prophet: A Socio-Historical Study, Journal for the Study of the New Testament Supplement Series Number 62* (Sheffield: JSOT Press, 1991); cf. Richard Horsley, "'Like One of the Prophets of Old': Two Types of Popular Prophets at the Time of Jesus," *Catholic Biblical Quarterly*, Vol. 47, 1985: 435-63.
[15] Ibid., 346.
[16] Ibid., 399; quoting Josephus, *War*, 1.347.

Webb concludes that "their method of prophecy according to Josephus was possession by a spirit—possibly evil—though those who participated would not take this view."[17] We learn little from this except the fact that spirit-possessed popular prophets were known in Israel at about the time of Jesus.

From Josephus's minimal evidence we know there were individuals whom other individuals believed to be prophets during the first century. Yet there does not seem to have been any standardized early first-century view that a prophet must do this, speak this way, perform these actions, and so forth. An early first-century Jewish prophet did not have to fit any established pattern. He might have led people in pathetic religio-political revolt as did Theudas; he might have shouted "Woe Unto Jerusalem!" as did Jesus ben Hananiah. A person might be labeled a prophet metaphorically if he interpreted scripture intellectually so as to find its application to the present day as did the "sapiential" Qumran exegete-prophets, or perhaps if he used political acumen to predict forthcoming politico-military events as did Josephus himself. He might have announced the imminent arrival of a time of judgment and the necessity of repentance, as did John the Baptist.

Philo of Alexandria and Jesus were alive at the same time. Philo, however, was an Egyptian Jew, a member of one of the wealthiest families in all the ancient world, and a prolific author of Hellenistic philosophical midrash. I take advantage of Philo's writings to support just one point: Philo insists emphatically and repeatedly that a prophet is a person whose primary persona is on occasion replaced wholly by another persona; in the language I am using, Philo believed that prophets are, by definition, spirit-possessed. His view of the matter is completely in keeping with anthropological theory of spirit-possession, psychological theory of spirit-possession, and with the conclusions of many scholars of Hebrew Bible prophecy.

This, then, is Philo's understanding of prophecy: "divine possession of the speaker is manifest, in virtue of which he is above all and in the strict sense considered a prophet" *(Mos. 2:191).*[18] "The prophet utters nothing that is his own, but his utterances are of alien derivation, the

---
17 Ibid.
18 Unless otherwise indicated passages from Philo's writings are taken from Winston, David, *Philo of Alexandria: The Contemplative Life, the Giants, and Selections* (New York: Paulist Press, 1981).

prompting of another . . . . All, at any rate, who are recorded by Moses as just are introduced as possessed and prophesying" *(Her. 259)*. For Philo that sort of experience is not only an interpretation of past scriptural events. He himself has been "frenzied with divine possession and unconscious of the place, the company, myself, and spoken and written words" *(De Migr. Abr. 34-35)*. In a passage that seems to reflect his own experience, Philo writes:

> So long as our own mind, pouring as it were noonday light into the whole soul, shines about us and encompasses us, we are in ourselves (en *heauktois* as opposed to *en theo)*, and are not possessed. But when this light reaches its setting then, as might be expected, ecstasy and divine possession and madness fall upon us. For when the divine light shines, the human sets, and when it sets, then the other rises and shines. And this is wont to happen to the prophetic kind. The mind that is in us is banished at the coming of the divine spirit, and at its departure returns home. . . . For the prophet, even when he appears to speak, is in truth silent, and Another uses his organs of speech, his mouth and tongue, to declare whatsoever he wills. *(Quis Rer. 264-66)*[19]

C. H. Dodd writes of this passage that "Philo uses the term *pneuma* (spirit) because he understands the experience in terms of prophecy as described in the Hebrew Bible. Philo reads Genesis 12:1 to advocate that people should 'escape also your own self and stand aside from yourself, like persons possessed and corybants seized by Bacchic frenzy and carried away by some kind of prophetic inspiration. For it is the mind that is filled with the Deity and no longer in itself.'" *(Her. 69)*.[20] Philo unequivocally claims that prophecy is a form of spirit-possession and that spirit-possession involves the replacement of a primary persona with a supposedly divine alter-persona. Philo believes that the prophetic state is desirable, that it is intermittent, and the prophet is sometimes himself and sometimes the Deity. He believes this state can be attained in his own day as it was formerly attained in the days of the

---

19 C. H. Dodd's translation in his *The Interpretation of the Fourth Gospel* (Cambridge: Cambridge University Press, 1953), 191.
20 Ibid.

canonical prophets.

The idea of prophetic spirit-possession in Judaism is attested both in Hebrew Bible texts and in documents written in the first century. Given that Jesus was thought during his lifetime to have been a prophet, then we can only determine what manner of prophet he was from information presented in the New Testament itself. Philo's ideas are no more than supporting evidence; Josephus's accounts are sketchy at best. The New Testament evidence, as will be discussed at length below, shows that Jesus presented himself as one who, on occasion, spoke and acted as the persona spirit of God rather than as the persona Jesus of Nazareth. Centuries earlier, and in very different ways, Elijah, Isaiah, Malachi, etc. also spoke as the persona spirit of God.

The account of Jesus' baptism relates the foundational event of his life as it is known to history. It was then that the spirit of God first came to him. He presented himself to people in Galilee as a spirit-possessed prophet from that point on, as we shall see by beginning, as E. P. Sanders suggests, "at the right point"; at the baptism of Jesus.

4

Baptism

One day in or about the year 28 C.E. Jesus of Nazareth came to the Jordan River along with scores of other people. There, having repented of his sins, he was baptized by John, son of Zechariah. He saw the heavens torn open and the spirit descend upon him like a dove and he heard a voice from heaven say, "You are my beloved son; with you I am well pleased." Then the spirit drove him out into the desert where he was tempted by the devil.

Did something like this happen or was it a fiction invented to serve the needs of the Christian movement? The latter position is held by at least one scholar, the former by nearly all the rest.[1] Yes, they affirm, something like this happened. The picture of a repentant Jesus humbling himself before John was modified by each evangelist to support the belief that John recognized Jesus as his superior, but their need to modify the story testifies both to the fact that the story was embarrassing to them and that there was something so important about the story that none of the evangelists could simply leave it out. In fact, each placed it in a position of greatest prominence, the beginning of Jesus' career. At this point, they say in effect, it all began.

The evangelists believed Jesus was sinless and that John was Jesus' inferior. Yet those who came for John's baptism were both repentant

---

1 Burton Mack, in *A Myth of Innocence*, argues that Jesus' baptism, along with nearly all the other events in Mark's gospel, was invented to serve mythic purposes. And cf. his *The Lost Gospel*, 155.

of sin and subordinate to the one baptizing. Accordingly, the baptism story does not fit with the ideology of early Christianity and so it meets the "Criterion of Embarrassment."

John Meier lists ten criteria by which the historicity of sayings or events in the gospels may be evaluated. Five criteria he believes to be primary. Of these five primary factors the first is the Criterion of Embarrassment, which is nothing more than the reasonable presumption that Jesus' followers would not have invented sayings or events that undercut their claims regarding Jesus and so give evidence to those who oppose such claims.[2] Meier declares Jesus' baptism by John to be "a prime example" of an event with a solid claim to historicity by virtue of the application of this criterion.

The baptism story also meets the Criterion of Multiple Attestation (Matthew, Mark, Luke, and by implication, John and Q), and it is in accord with the Criterion of Dissimilarity, for nowhere else in Judaism or early Christianity is it attested that the Holy Spirit descends during a Johannine baptism (Luke specifically denies this in Acts 19:1-6), or during any other Jewish immersion ritual. Insofar as the Criterion of Coherence is anything more than circular reasoning, the story of Jesus' baptism meets that criterion too, as I shall argue at length below. The fact that Jesus experienced reception of the spirit at his baptism by John is as historically certain as the fact of Jesus' crucifixion.

Matthew and Luke and John understood the derogatory implications of the Baptism story and worked to explain them away. As Meier puts it,

> Matthew introduces a dialogue between the Baptist and Jesus prior to the baptism; the Baptist openly confesses his unworthiness to baptize his superior and gives way only when Jesus

---

2 Meier, *Marginal Jew*, 168-84. The other primary criteria are the Criterion of Discontinuity, words or deeds of Jesus that cannot be derived either from Judaism at the time of Jesus or from the early Church; the Criterion of Multiple Attestation, the presumption that the more numerous the independent sources that contain an account of a deed or saying of Jesus the more likely it is to be an authentic account; the Criterion of Coherence, that if a saying or deed is coherent with an established set of authentic sayings or deeds it is also likely to be authentic; the Criterion of Rejection and Execution, that an account of Jesus' career must account for, or at least allow for, the fact of his execution. These criteria are not Meier's own invention and he is not uncritical of them.

commands him to do so in order that God's saving plan may be revealed (Matt. 3:13-17, a passage marked by language typical of the evangelist). Luke finds a striking solution to the problem by narrating the Baptist's imprisonment by Herod before relating the baptism of Jesus: Luke's version never tells us who baptized Jesus (Luke 3:19-22). The radical Fourth Evangelist, John, locked as he is in a struggle with latter-day disciples of the Baptist who refuse to recognize Jesus as the Messiah, takes the radical expedient of suppressing the baptism of Jesus by the Baptist altogether; the event simply never occurs in John's Gospel. We still hear of the Father's witness to Jesus and the Spirit's descent upon Jesus, but we are never told when this theophany occurs (John 1:29-34). Quite plainly, the early Church was "stuck with" an event in Jesus' life that it found increasingly embarrassing, that it tried to explain away by various means, and that John the Evangelist finally erased from his Gospel. It is highly unlikely that the Church went out of its way to create the cause of its own embarrassment.[3]

The stated or implied account of Jesus' baptism in all four gospels initiates his career.[4] In Mark this is unmistakable, for no sooner are we told that we are at "the beginning of the gospel of Jesus Christ. . . ." (1:1) than we are introduced to John and the baptism of Jesus takes place.

Beginning With the Baptism

Luke's account is preceded by a fairly lengthy birth narrative, but it is likely that an earlier edition of Luke's gospel began at 3:1, which is Luke's careful historical dating of the baptism (most probably early 28 C.E. according to Meier's detailed argument).[5] The birth narratives introduce, in detail, characters never again mentioned in Luke's two-volume work, emphasize a virgin birth that also is never again mentioned, and distribute the spirit cavalierly in a way contrary to Luke's caution in the remainder of his works. Ideas and persons emphasized

---
3 Meier, *Marginal Jew*, 169.
4 I use "career" in preference to the more common, but theologically tendentious terms, "mission," and "ministry."
5 Ibid., 372-407.

in Luke 1:1-2:52 are ignored in Luke's summaries of Jesus' career (Acts 2:22-36, 10:37-42). Significantly, the latter summary follows Mark in placing the inception of Jesus' career at his baptism, for Luke writes, "Beginning with the baptism of John. . . ." It is likely that Theophilus's edition of the Gospel and Acts was expanded from an earlier edition that began with 3:1.[6]

All four evangelists began Jesus' career with an account of, or an account presupposing, Jesus' baptism and it is probable that Q did so as well. In modern reconstructions of Q, the preaching of John the Baptist is followed by the story of the Temptation. Q began, then, as follows: Q/Lk 3:2, Q/Lk 3:7-9, Q/Lk: 3:16b-17, Q/Lk 4:1-13.[7] The reconstruction of the Q version of Jesus' baptism per se is not possible because for that event both Luke and Matthew follow Mark. The Q material listed above moves from the teachings of John the Baptist (i.e., the events preceding and in a respect "causing" Jesus' baptism), to the Temptation story (i.e., the events following and so an "effect" of Jesus' baptism) thus leaving us a clear line to presume that the intervening event between causal factors and factors of effect was also recorded in Q. This gives us five sources for the baptism story, three of them independent (Q, Mark, John).

Although we have information from Q about John the Baptist's preaching and about the Temptation, and information from the Gospel of John that some of Jesus' followers were previously followers of John the Baptist (1:35-42) and that the Baptism took place near Bethany (1:28), for most of our information about the Baptism we must turn to the Gospel of Mark. Mark reports a set of events combining both human actions (John preaches, Jesus arrives) and supernatural actions (a spirit descends, a voice from heaven is heard, Satan tempts Jesus). Secular scholarship tends to accept human actions and deny or prescind from supernatural actions. But narrated supernatural actions may also be human actions: a voice from heaven is the human expe-

---

[6] Modern authors, for whom the production of an "expanded edition" entails more than a year of work may forget that in the ancient world an expanded edition could be produced any time a work was copied by a scribe. Rather than to imagine ancient "publishing" as analogous to modern publishing, we would be wise to think of it as analogous to word-processing whereby one may print out an expanded edition of any stored text at any time.

[7] Following the reconstruction in Kloppenborg, John, et al., (eds.), *Q Thomas Reader*, (Sonoma: Polebridge, 1990).

rience of hearing a voice, a spirit descending is a human experience of psychological dissociation, and so forth. I will argue here that the events given and implied in Mark's account, including various "supernatural" events, happened pretty much as Mark says they happened.

Psychological Causality

A preacher of repentance will normally combine threat and promise as did John. From Q we learn of threats (Lk. 3:7-9): "He said therefore to the multitudes that came out to be baptized by him, 'You brood of vipers! Who warned you to flee from the wrath to come?' Bear fruits that befit repentance, and do not begin to say to yourselves, 'We have Abraham as our father;' for I tell you, God is able from these stones to raise up children to Abraham. Even now the axe is laid to the root of the trees: every tree therefore that does not bear good fruit is cut down and thrown into the fire." Similarly, from Q (Lk. 3:16-17) "I baptize you with water; but he who is mightier than I is coming, the thong of whose sandals I am not worthy to untie; he will baptize you with the Holy Spirit and with fire. His winnowing fork is in his hand, to clear his threshing floor, and to gather the wheat into his granary, but the chaff he will burn with unquenchable fire." John likens his unrepentant audience to a brood of vipers, to barren trees that will be cut down and thrown into the fire, to chaff that will be burned with unquenchable fire. And he offers that audience a baptism that will bring them into a contrary affirmative state.

John, then, encourages psychological change, works to cause such a change, and insists on its necessity. He says, in effect, "change from regarding yourselves as acceptable and begin to regard yourselves as damnable vipers, barren trees, chaff" and then, "change from regarding yourselves as damnable vipers, barren trees, chaff, and regard yourselves as repentant and forgiven and acceptable to God." To put it more simply, "cease from accepting yourself and begin despising yourself," then "cease from despising yourself and begin accepting yourself as transformed."[8]

Given that Jesus came for baptism by John it follows that Jesus accepted John's appraisal of Jesus; a sinner who should regard himself as

---

[8] I am not adopting "pop psychology"; I am trying to reify metaphors in as simple a way as possible.

a viper, a barren tree, as chaff and so deserving of destruction. In other words, Jesus began to despise himself as he was and to accept the premise that he should be and could be in another condition. Here I am just reasoning that in the presence of a known cause and a known effect, the known cause produced the effect rather than that an unknown cause produced the effect. That Jesus came for baptism due to some cause other than the cause given in our evidence, the preaching of John designed to adduce repentance among sinners, is incompetent reasoning.

The reader may recall that Jesus is reported in the gospels to have happily dined and otherwise affiliated with tax collectors and sinners and not to have been given to pious practices such as fasting and strict sabbath observance. Accordingly, it is likely, indeed I would think certain, that these traits are indications of his general mode of life prior to his baptism. This is supported by the report that Jesus was not well respected in Nazareth prior to his baptism (Mark 6:1-6). To put it more strongly, it is historical nonsense to think that it was only *after* his baptism for repentance of his sins that Jesus *began* to be the sort of person who might be accused of being "a glutton and a drunkard, a friend of tax collectors and sinners."[9] (Matt. 11:19)

John the Baptist is strikingly similar to contemporary revival preachers both in his requirement for psychological change [i.e., *metanoia*, repentance] and in the rhetoric he used to effect such a change in members of his audience. A revival preacher insists on the denigration of the self-concept of his or her audience members by emphasizing their sinfulness, their inevitable damnation should they remain as they are, and then offers a way out, possession by the Holy Spirit and, accordingly, forgiveness of sins. Or, "cease from accepting yourself and begin despising yourself," then "cease from despising yourself and begin accepting yourself as forgiven, transformed into one who has received the Holy Spirit."

The same general dissociative psychological process occurs when individuals first begin to speak in tongues. "An experience invariably concomitant with the onset of speaking in tongues and described by every tongue-speaker interviewed, usually in the same way, was a sense of worthlessness. . . . Their feeling of worthlessness lifted and was replaced by a tremendous euphoria as soon as they learned to speak in

---

9 That he was accused of being such a person is likely by virtue of the Criterion of Embarrassment.

tongues. . . . It was considered a tangible indication that one was indeed a different person—an outward and visible sign of receipt of a spiritual gift."[10] Many, perhaps most, individuals who generate alternative personae in religious contexts are people who have first self-denigrated their primary personae.

The revival preacher, like the preacher who encourages glossolalia, is powerfully assisted by the factors of expectation and modeling. When spirit-possession is considered possible and desirable, when it is modeled by others (the preacher or members of the audience) who attest to the benefits of the state, then uninitiated individuals are quite prone spontaneously to achieve the state.

Raymond Prince has discussed such experiences in considerable detail:

> Under some circumstances of life stress and artificially induced hyperstress, the threatened individual may suddenly experience a profound sense of tranquillity. This flip-over from terror to euphoria is commonly linked with the idea of supernatural intervention . . . because the tranquillity arises for no externally visible reason, as a kind of deus ex machina. . . . In the context of highly stressful life circumstances, the response may be ego disintegration. The phenomenology of these states is well known and includes feelings of panic and world destruction and a loss of ego boundaries. Reality testing is grossly impaired. In the midst of this *Gotterdammerung* there emerges a feeling of revelation and mastery associated with the delusion of ego omnipotence.[11]

He finds this set of responses to occur in spontaneous religious experiences in circumstances, again, of heightened life stress: "The subject is visited by a brief ecstatic state with loss of ego boundaries, sometimes hallucinatory experience, a certainty that the experience contains valid truths, and often the belief that the state is a manifestation of the divine."[12] Among the forms of hyperstress that he believes can lead to

---

10 Kildahl, John, *The Psychology of Speaking in Tongues* (New York: Harper and Row, 1972), 64.
11 Prince, Raymond, "Shamans and Endorphins," *Ethos*, Vol. 10, 1982: 418.
12 Ibid., 419.

this kind of experience are "evangelical preaching and cult initiations that evoke strong feelings of sinfulness and unworthiness, followed by conversion experiences."[13] Such experiences arise often "in circumstances of self-perceptions of impotence and serious losses of esteem."[14] The religious experience of the denigration of the primary ego and the spontaneous emergence of what seems to the individual to be a new divine persona is not something difficult to account for.

In the Palestinian culture of Jesus' time possession was considered possible, as is attested by spirit-inspired prophets abroad in the land, and spirit-possessed oracles in neighboring lands, and by the idea that there were numerous demon-possessed people. The modality of possession, then, was commonly accepted.

The story of Jesus' baptism is more than the story of Jesus' repentance and immersion, it is the story of his initial spirit-possession experience. As the gospels say or imply, Jesus' baptism initiated all that followed and so it could not be ignored.

It is thoroughly reasonable, historically and psychologically, that a spirit-possession experience would occur under the circumstances described in Mark's gospel, especially as supplemented by Q's information about the Baptist's preaching. Jesus' culture accepted possession as a possibility, the "revivalistic" psychological shift between a self-denigrated and despised self to an immediately changed self-affirmed forgiven self is the principal point of John's preaching. Therefore it follows that the psychological conditions that engender spirit-possession were in effect for Jesus and the cultural conditions that permit spirit-possession were also in effect.

It might be thought that the lines of reasoning I am using here are unacceptable psychologizing; in other words, that I am simply inventing moods, thoughts, emotions for Jesus that go far beyond any available evidence. On the contrary, I am taking the evidence itself and pointing out that it is coherent, consistent and explicable. Evidence reporting *metanoia,* repentance, and visionary and auditory experience on the order of hallucination, and spirit experience and demonic temptation is, first and foremost, evidence concerned with psychological states and events. What I am doing, therefore, is *not* of the same order as are the modern accounts one reads of what Jesus "must have"

---
13 Ibid., 419-20.
14 Ibid., 420.

thought about this, or what he "surely" felt about that.

The Prophet John

According to the evidence we have, John the Baptist was thought to have been a prophet. This is the perspective of Q (Matt. 11:7-11; Luke 7:24-28). Mark reports that "all held that John was in fact a prophet" (11:32), and in this he is followed by Matthew (21:26) and Luke (20:6). John evidently dressed "in a rough coat of camel's hair, with a leather belt round his waist" (Mark 1:6), a sort of hairy garment that had been a prophetic badge of office from at least the time of Elijah.[15] He looked like a prophet, he spoke like a prophet, people evidently thought of him as a prophet and so, by the logic of the duck, he was a prophet. In John the Baptist, a prophet, hence a spirit-inspired person, Jesus had a model for the possibility of affirmative spirit-inspiration.[16]

It is possible, but not certain, that John predicted the arrival of One to Come who would baptize with spirit. Charles Scobie argues at some length that the prediction of a future "outpouring" of God's spirit is quite in accord with John's other eschatological teachings and that it is also in accord with some Jewish thought of the time. He concludes that "there is thus nothing improbable in supposing that John did in fact speak of God's 'holy spirit'" and that "there is little reason to doubt that John did speak of a Messiah who would baptize, not with water as John himself did, but with both fire and holy spirit."[17]

If we assume that Scobie is correct, then we can surmise the origin of an important theme of Jesus' own proclamation. John's time frame for the arrival of baptism with spirit was the eschatological future. It should follow that if the spirit arrived, then in some sense the eschatological future arrived. Jesus received the spirit in the present. Accordingly, if he received the eschatological spirit in the present he could but conclude that the eschatological future was in fact present insofar as his reception of the spirit was concerned. This may answer the question of how it came to be that Jesus believed that his own spirit-inspired activities were the proleptic in-breaking of the future Kingdom to the

---

15 Scobie, Charles H. H., *John the Baptist* (Philadelphia: Fortress Press, 1964), 128.
16 I use "spirit inspired" in preference to "possessed" because 1 have no evidence of John's sociopsychological status.
17 Ibid., 71, 73.

present world. But this answer is far from being certainly true; it is possible to eliminate John's supposed prediction of the eschatological spirit from the equation and to assume that Jesus on his own account came to the conclusion that the future Kingdom was becoming present in his spirit-directed activities.

Jesus' Reception of the Spirit

We hear that Jesus saw the heavens torn open and the spirit descend in the form of a dove. Although it is of no consequence to the case I am making, I will point out that during an initial possession experience visual hallucinations are not uncommon. Further, there is little precedent or consequence to the spirit of the Jewish God appearing in the form of a dove. By the Criterion of Dissimilarity (and also perhaps the Criterion of Embarrassment, for opponents of the Christian movement may well have said contemptuously, as did Morton Smith, that "No Hebrew Bible prophets had birds roost on them") this probably happened.[18] Most likely, Christians believed Jesus saw the spirit descend in the form of a dove because that was what Jesus saw and he told them about it; why someone would make this up I cannot imagine.

What is of more consequence is the supposed *bat kol* ("daughter of the voice" of God) announcing "You are my beloved Son; with you I am well pleased" (Mark 1:11). John 1:33-34 indicates that Johannine tradition knew of an association between the descent of the spirit upon Jesus and immediate witness that he was Son of God. It is therefore unlikely that Mark simply invented the *bat kol.* I shall argue that Jesus did regard himself as the Son of God, or, to put it exactly, that Jesus believed that the spirit of God was such that when the spirit was active in him he was transformed into the Son of God. I know of no precedent for such an equation of spirit with Son but, like most people, Jesus was surely capable of thought and speech that was not simply derivative but his own.[19] Apart from a line of reasoning that is certainly unacceptable psychologizing [i.e., that Jesus' illegitimacy led him to hypothesize a Father to whom he could be a Son], and in the absence of any prec-

---

18 Smith, *Jesus the Magician*, 97. Embarrassment is also implied by the fact that John's gospel attributes the vision of the dove to John the Baptist, 1:32, rather than to Jesus.
19 The Criterion of Dissimilarity is predicated on this fact.

edent, it seems to me quite possible that Jesus identified the spirit by which he was possessed as the Son because, in psychological circumstances where auditory hallucinations are nearly normative, Jesus heard a voice saying something to the effect "this [the spirit] is my beloved Son." But I do not think this is certain. *That* Jesus identified the spirit with Son is more than likely, as I shall discuss in Chapter Eleven below. *How* he came to do this is uncertain. But a *bat kol* (here, an auditory hallucination occurring to a radically dissociated person) is, in context, perhaps the single most likely hypothesis for Jesus' evidently unique terminology and it is a hypothesis advanced by our earliest biographical sources.

In the absence of a supportive set of cultural expectations, there is no reason why Jesus would immediately have defined his alternative persona experience as being "the holy spirit." Even if John predicted an outpouring of spirit in the eschatological age, he did not predict it would happen to individuals when he baptized them. The prediction "spirit will come" would not have immediately defined the experience "spirit has come." The prediction of a holy spirit is not the same thing as the experience of an alter-persona assumed to be a spirit of some sort or other. The experience was: I am not who I was but another person; another persona is in me. Jesus' culture presented him with two basic options. Either he had the experience of the holy spirit of prophecy replacing his primary persona or he had the experience of a demon replacing his primary persona. In the former case there existed the culturally established label of prophet, in the latter case the culturally established label of demon.

The experience of radical dissociation is not immediately self-defining. We hear that immediately after his baptism Jesus was driven by his alternative persona into the desert where he was tempted by the devil (Mark 1:12-13). He had to fathom which cultural paradigm he would adopt. A demon paradigm was common (following New Testament evidence); a prophet paradigm was rare (but alive among the peasantry). Was he one of the hundreds of the demon-possessed or, perhaps, a new peasant prophet?

Cross-cultural statistical analysis shows that spirit-possessed healers commonly are

> selected for their roles through spontaneous spirit-possession

experiences which involve culturally defined episodes of possession by spirits in which the personality of the practitioner is believed to be replaced by that of a spirit entity. Mediums [i.e., spirit-possessed healers] differ from other shamanistic practitioners in that the *initial* ASC [Altered State of Consciousness] episodes leading to the need for training for the practitioner status are thought to be spontaneously induced and outside of the control or intention of the practitioner to be; the status is not viewed as being sought in a voluntary fashion.[20]

The experience of radical dissociation, of the emergence of an alternate persona, is one that by its very definition is outside of the control of the primary persona. Accordingly, when we read that Jesus was "driven" into the desert by the spirit (and the Greek word Mark uses has connotations of being violently driven against one's will) we should not be at all surprised. That is just what one would expect to happen if someone experienced possession outside of an established cultic context designed to moderate and define the experience. The "temptation" by the devil, in context, would have been the temptation to regard the emergent alternative persona as the persona of the devil, i.e., demon-possession, which seems to have been the most common explanatory paradigm available at the time. Jesus did not accept this alternative.

Reports of Jesus' temptation experience are in accord with cross-cultural evidence regarding initial possession experiences. Crapanzano reports that "almost all reports of spirit-possession stress the fact that the novice is unusually clumsy and must learn to be a good carrier for his spirit.[21] Appropriate behavior and understanding are learned by spirit-possessed persons, they are not self-evident by virtue of the experience itself. Further, he informs us that

> The movement from initial illness to final incorporation within a cult is often accompanied by an indeterminate period in which the possessed resists the call of the spirit and suffers depression, extreme alienation, dissociation, and even fugues. Such a period, analogous in many respects to what mystics

---

20 Winkelman, Michael, *Shamans, Priests and Witches: A Cross-Cultural Study of Magico-Religious Practitioners* (Tempe: Arizona State University, 1992), 61.
21 Crapanzano, *Case Studies in Spirit Possession*, 15.

refer to as the dark night of the soul, may be symbolized as a period of wandering.[22]

Mark tells us that Jesus was "driven" by the spirit in him out into the desert where Jesus, now in the power of the spirit, communicated with demons. This, again, is a case where historically reasonable events are interpreted in terms of supernatural explanations. Throughout the story of Jesus' baptism, the events related fit remarkably well with what one might predict in regard to an individual who came to baptism for repentance and who then received a spontaneous possession experience.

Summary

It is all very well to affirm that the story of Jesus' baptism is, in general, historically reliable, most scholars agree that it is. But what does it mean and why is it there at all? It is there, at the beginning of the gospels, because that is the beginning of the time when Jesus was possessed by the spirit of God. Prior to that time he was not possessed by the spirit of God. Accordingly, in the story of Jesus' baptism the crucial factor is not what John does but what happens to Jesus. The story is, then, fundamentally *psychological* in nature; *this* psychological event (spirit-possession) happened under *those* psychologically facilitating circumstances (John's baptism).

John's preaching was designed to convince hearers that they were sinful and so to denigrate their existing self-concepts. He also sought to convince hearers that, if they would repent, his baptism would facilitate a change in their self-concepts so that they might attain an affirmative state of forgiveness. John, then, advocated and brought about a psychological change. Those hearers who showed up for baptism *must* be supposed to have appropriately denigrated their existing self-concepts and to have been prepared to accomplish the sort of psychological change John advocated.

John, believed to be a prophet, modeled the possibility of "prophet," which is to say he modeled the potentiality of humans to be inspired by the spirit of God. John may also have predicted the arrival of a time when the spirit of God would inspire or possess all repentant people.

---

22 Ibid., 16.

Jesus was baptized under circumstances where psychological change, *metanoia* (repentance), was a sine qua non for attendance. John, a model for spirit-inspiration, was present and, perhaps, announced the potential imitability of his state by saying that the repentant would someday receive the spirit. The reports that Jesus, under such circumstances, entered into a state of alter-persona consciousness, which he came to define as possession by God's spirit, are based on reliable historical fact.

The story of the baptism of Jesus is not about what happened (John baptized Jesus) or what Jesus believed (he presumably believed what John said), but about the origin of a dissociative psychological transformation. The reason the story is told as "the beginning of the gospel. . . ." is that the story of Jesus for formative Christianity was the story of a spirit-possessed man whose new social role resulted from that specific status.

The evangelists do not frequently make the forthright claim that Jesus was possessed by the spirit of God. Instead, they use, or imply, the story of Jesus' reception of the spirit at his baptism as the prolegomenon to all that follows. Thus they do not often reiterate what has already been established. Rather, they proceed to report on the consequences of the baptismal experience.[23] What Jesus of Nazareth formerly could not do, the spirit of God subsequently could do. And what the spirit of God did, acting through Jesus' body, is some of what the historical Jesus did. Or so he and those associated with him believed.

---

23 In *The Holy Spirit and the Gospel Tradition* (London: S.P.C.K, 1947, reprinted 1966) C. K. Barrett presents a complex theory to explain, as he puts it in the title to his final chapter, "Why Do the Gospels Say So Little about the Spirit?" But I think the answer is simple: Mark especially, and the evangelists who use his account, presuppose that their audiences are fully familiar with Jesus' relationship to the spirit. Having introduced the subject with reference to Jesus' initial reception of the spirit, they do not feel constrained often again to address the subject directly. That Mark presupposes sophisticated Christian knowledge on the part of his audience is evident, e.g. from his passing reference to complex soteriological theory in 10:45b. John, I will argue, *does* say a great deal about the spirit; see Chapter Eleven, below.

5

JESUS' HEALINGS

I mentioned in an earlier chapter that one of my two "bedrock" facts about Jesus is that, in John Meier's words, *"Nothing is more certain about Jesus than that he was viewed by his contemporaries as an exorcist and a healer."*[1] In this chapter I will discuss Jesus' activities as a healer. I will then proceed, in a subsequent chapter, to discuss more specifically his activities as an exorcist. But I will try to make clear that the distinction between those two modes of behavior, and between the corresponding two kinds of diagnosis, was not then and is not now clearly demarcated.

No fact about Jesus of Nazareth is so widely and repeatedly attested in the New Testament gospels as the fact that he was a healer of people in mental and physical distress. From the synoptic tradition we hear that: "They brought to him all who were ill or possessed by devils; and the whole town was there, gathered at the door. He healed many who suffered from various diseases and drove out many devils. . . . All through Galilee he went, preaching in the synagogues and casting out the devils. . . . He cured so many that sick people of all kinds came crowding in upon him to touch him. The unclean spirits too, when they saw him, would fall at his feet and cry aloud, 'You are the Son of God" (Mark 1:32-34, 39, 3:10-11). Luke and Matthew echo many of

---

[1] Meier, John, "Jesus," 1321, (emphasis added). (The other was that it is "historical bedrock" that Jesus was thought to be a prophet.)

these reports and add others to the same effect. John reports that he healed a crippled man (5:1-9), a blind man (9:1-7) and, more generally, that "Jesus withdrew to the farther shore of the Sea of Galilee and a crowd of people followed who had seen the signs he performed in healing the sick" (6:1-2). Luke summarizes Jesus' life's work as "doing good and healing all who were oppressed by the devil" (Acts 10:38).

It is entirely possible that Jesus thought of himself as a physician. Three times he is reported to have used the term physician self-referentially, in each case by citing a proverb. Mark reports that when he was criticized for dining with tax collectors and sinners he responded "It is not the healthy who need a physician but the sick" (2:17). Luke claims that when Jesus came to his hometown he said to his compatriots "No doubt you will quote the proverb to me: 'Physician heal yourself'" (Luke 4:23). The Gospel of Thomas contains a proverb attributed to Jesus which Mark evidently knew and revised into a narrative: "A prophet is not accepted in his own village; a physician does not heal those who know him" (Thomas 31 cf. Mark 6: 1-6).

Whom Jesus Healed

Today, accounts of Jesus as a healer and an exorcist are conflated in the popular imagination with accounts of occasions when he is said to have overcome natural law; this conflation leads to a tendency to discuss the "miracles" of Jesus as though healings and walking on water were in any way related. I regard all reports that Jesus overcame natural law as legends that arose after Jesus' lifetime and I have nothing new to say about them.

It can be argued that instances of "raising the dead" that are found in the Gospels and Acts are historically credible if they report on times that persons who were unconscious or comatose were brought back to consciousness. It is certain that unconsciousness and comatose states have sometimes been taken to be death (although the Lazarus case is not explicable by this means). But this is not a matter that one can consider in any detail except through the a priori reasoning that if individuals rose "from the dead" then they were not dead or (to concede a point to near-death-experience theory) they hadn't been dead for long. I note that the story of Jairus' daughter (Mk 5:22-24, 35-43), which is often taken to be a raising-of-the-dead story, is a story of Jesus' insight into her condition, that she was in fact asleep and only seemed dead: "The child is not dead but sleeping," Jesus said (Mk. 5:39).

Jesus is said to have healed paralysis (Mk 2:1-12, Jn. 5:1-9), a withered hand (Mk. 3:1-6), curvature of the spine (Lk 13:10-17), dropsy (Lk 14:1-6), excessive menstrual bleeding (Mk. 5:24-34), fever (Mk. 1:29-32), deafness (Mk. 7:31-37), aphonia [dumbness] (9:32-34), blindness (Mk. 8:22-26, 10:46-52, Mt. 9:27-31, Jn. 9:112), and psoriasis, "leprosy" (Mk. 1:40-45, Jn. 17:11-19).

The gospels contain accounts of Jesus "healing lepers," or so translations make it appear. The common understanding of his "healing lepers" is incorrect.[2] What we normally think of as "leprosy" is more properly known as "Hansen's disease"; it is produced by the bacillus *Mycobacterium leprae;* it is not very infectious and, most significantly, it did not exist in the Mediterranean area much before the time of Jesus. Perhaps native to India, it seems to have been brought into the Mediterranean region by returning troops after the time of Alexander the Great, perhaps no sooner than 62 B.C.E. when Pompey returned from his campaign against Mithridates of Pontus. Despite plentiful skeletal remains that would evidence Hansen's disease if it had existed, no evidence of that disease has been found in Egypt prior to the second or third century C.E. When Hansen's disease is mentioned by ancient medical writers they use the term *elephas* or *elephantiasis* for it.[3] Further, "Hansen's disease" does not have the characteristics of "leprosy" that can be inferred from Hebrew Bible evidence.

The disorder that is termed *leprosy* in the Hebrew Bible is characterized by flaking skin (white flakes that fall "like snow") and redness beneath the skin. From these, and other considerations, biblical "leprosy" is certainly psoriasis. However, biblical "leprosy" might have been diagnosed for individuals suffering from favus, a severe fungus infection, and perhaps also seborrhoeic dermatitis, patchy eczema, and other flaking skin disorders.

---

2 In what follows I am summarizing E. V. Hulse, "The Nature of Biblical 'Leprosy' and the Use of Alternative Medical Terms in Modern Translations of the Bible," *Palestine Exploration Quarterly* Vol. 107, 1975: 87-105.
3 To make matters even more complicated, "elephantiasis" today in medical terminology refers not to leprosy but to the massive swelling of body parts and is most frequently mentioned in its form "filarial elephantiasis," an African disorder caused by a species of round worm spread by mosquitoes.

We do not hear from New Testament reports that Jesus cured psoriasis or any other form of biblical "leprosy" so much as we hear that he "cleansed" people who were "leprous." Cleansing is not a medical intervention of any natural or supernatural sort. Cleansing is the act of declaring an individual formally clean in a ritual sense; it is the prerogative of Jerusalem temple priests. Cleansing is not a cure but a positive diagnosis. We hear that Jesus cleansed lepers and then ordered them to show themselves to a priest (Mk 1:40-44, Lk 17:11-14). The puzzling thing about this is what role Jesus is thought to have played. It is not said that he cured the lepers and it was not in his purview to pronounce them ritually clean; appropriately, he sent them to the proper authorities.

The simplest explanation may be the best one. Jesus had a considerable reputation as a healer. People who were said to be lepers came to him and asked his opinion whether or not their condition remained leprous or not. He said sometimes that they were clean of leprosy; they rejoiced to hear his opinion and subsequently they journeyed to Jerusalem to have his opinion formally verified.

At first glance the evidence regarding Jesus' career as a healer divides neatly into two categories: healings of somatic disorders and exorcisms of supposedly possessing demons. Demons and deafness do not, to us, have any relationship at all. But to peasant Galileans these two categories blended together. And, oddly enough, the peasant Galilean view of the matter is more in accord with psychological theory than is our commonsense dualism.

My analysis begins with the proposition that Jesus did heal cases of the sort reported in our texts by the means reported in our texts: acknowledgment of his power to heal. If so, then those cases were of a certain sort, not just any disorders but disorders of the kind that can be healed, on the spot, by the words or self-presentation of the healer. The term "faith healer" applies in such cases, for faith the power of the healer and the healer's self-presentation is the key factor involved, as it is a key factor in the clinical practice of modern physicians. Cases alleviated or cured by faith healing are usually, but not invariably, psychosomatic in nature.

To use more precise terminology than "psychosomatic," faith healers can be expected to cure problems produced by "conversion disorders." Conversion disorders, known in earlier years as conversion hysteria and then as conversion neurosis, are a recognized category in psychiatric medicine. A conversion disorder can occur when an individual because of actions for which he feels guilt, refuses to accept the guilt, and interiorizes it. That interiorized guilt is then manifested by self-punishment such as blindness, or paralysis, or dermatitis. It is assumed in psychoanalytic theory that the manner of the displayed conversion disorder will correlate in some way with the nature of the event that gave rise to the guilt in the first place. Similarly, traumatic experiences can give rise to conversion disorder when they are repressed and reemerge as physical symptoms.

Conversion disorder is technically defined as follows:

> The essential feature of this disorder is an alteration or loss of physical functioning that suggests physical disorder, but that instead is apparently an expression of a psychological conflict or need.[4]

Two coordinate mechanisms have been suggested to account for conversion disorder:

> In one mechanism, the person achieves "primary gain" by keeping an internal conflict or need out of awareness. In such cases there is a temporal relationship between an environmental stimulus that is apparently related to a psychological conflict or need and initiation or exacerbation of the symptom. For example, after an argument, inner conflict about the expression of rage may be expressed as "aphonia" [dumbness] or as a "paralysis" of the arm; or if a person views a traumatic event, a conflict about acknowledging that event may be expressed as "blindness." In such cases the symptom has a symbolic value that is a representation and particular solution of the underlying psychological conflict.
>
> In the other mechanism, the person achieves "secondary gain" by avoiding a particular activity that is noxious to him or her and getting support from the environment that otherwise might not be forthcoming. For example, with a "paralyzed"

---

4 DSM-III-R: *Diagnostic and Statistical Manual of Mental Disorders, Revised Edition*, (Washington, D.C.: American Psychiatric Association, 1987), 257. Standard notation for this is DSM-III-R.

hand, a soldier can avoid firing a gun.[5]

The usual age of onset for conversion disorder is adolescence or early adulthood and it is usually of short duration, with abrupt onset and resolution. Predisposing factors include "extreme psychosocial stress (e.g., warfare or the recent death of a significant figure)."[6]

"Somatization disorder" is a related syndrome. It has as its essential features: recurrent and multiple somatic complaints, of several years' duration, for which medical attention has been sought, but that apparently are not due to any physical disorder. Symptoms usually begin in the teen years or, rarely, in the twenties. Somatization disorder has conversion or pseudoneurologic symptoms which include loss of voice, deafness, blindness, paralysis, or muscle weakness and excessive menstrual bleeding.[7] Somatization disorder is, in essence, a form of conversion disorder that takes place over a longer period of time.

Dumbness, deafness, blindness, paralysis (full or partial), and excessive menstrual bleeding constitute the majority of the cases of healing Jesus is reported to have performed. The sort of people who were successfully cured by Jesus probably had the kinds of disorder discussed above. The characteristics of such people were probably the same then as they are now. According to R. A. Depue, there are

> four major subgroups of individuals who are likely to exhibit elevated scores on nonspecific measures of somatic symptoms in the absence of physical illness: (a) individuals with elevated scores on personality dimensions such as neuroticism or frankly diagnosable personality disorders (b) individuals with chronic psychopathological disorders (e.g., depressive disorders), (c) individuals experiencing chronic life difficulties such as prolonged unemployment, chronic marital conflict, or an unsafe neighborhood, and (d) individuals experiencing an acute episode of stress-related psychological symptomotology (e.g., grief reaction following death of a loved one).[8]

---

5 *DSM-III-R*, 257.
6 *DSM-III-R*, 258.
7 *DSM-III-R*, 261-62.
8 Depue, R. A., and S. M. Monroe, "Conceptualization and Measurement of Human Disorder in Life Stress Research: The Problem of Chronic Disturbance," *Psychological Bulletin*, Vol. 99, 1986, 36.

Conversion disorders are fundamentally dissociative in nature. While an individual normally has an integrated consciousness including sight, hearing, limb mobility, etc., in cases of conversion disorder these functions are shut off, dissociated from the individual. Demonic possession trance is an explanatory paradigm, similarly constructed within literally hundreds of separate cultures, for a state of dissociative consciousness. Formally defined, dissociation has as essential features:

> alteration in the normally integrative functions of identity, memory, or consciousness. The disturbance or alteration may be sudden or gradual, and transient or chronic. If it occurs primarily in identity, the person's customary identity is temporarily forgotten, and a new identity may be assumed or imposed, or the customary feeling of one's own reality is lost and is replaced by a feeling of unreality.[9]

In the case of conversion or somatizing disorders, the disintegration of the self is manifested by somatic or sensory disorders or nonfunctioning. In the case of demonic-possession trance the disturbance is within the function of identity so that alternative identities emerge and "possess" the person involved.

One can construct, then, a scale of dissociative phenomena ranging from the somatic (fever, excessive menstrual bleeding, aphonia) to the sensory (deafness, blindness) to radical changes in individual self-identity. On a contemporary scale radical dissociation in personal identity is labeled multiple personality disorder, our secular analog to demon-possession, a matter discussed in more detail in Chapter Six below.

The New Testament contains sufficient information for us provisionally to construct a dissociative scale for peasant Galilee:

Fever rebuked as a demon (Lk. 4:38-39)
Limb immobility (Mk. 2:1-12)
Curvature of the Spine caused by a demon (Lk. 13:10-12)
Blindness (Mk. 8:22-27)
Deafness (Mk. 7:31-37)
Blindness and Deafness caused by a demon (Mt. 12:22)
Demonic possession (Mk. 1:21-28)

---

9 *DSM-III-R, 269.*

What we find here are explanatory paradigms wherein somatic, sensory, and identity dissociation are linked to and explained by the co-ordinated hypotheses of demon belief and demon-possession. It is not clear that disorders were always understood to be induced by demonic interference, but it does seem clear that all forms of disorder might have been so understood.

The difference between our contemporary appraisal of such cases and the appraisals evident in the New Testament is the difference between a "realist" view of the situation, that the problems arise from forces external to the individuals concerned, and an "idealist" view of the situation, which is our view, that the problems arise from forces internal to the individuals concerned. Precisely the same dichotomy governs any discussion of whether to accept the paradigm "Jesus was possessed by the spirit of God" or the paradigm "Jesus developed an affirmative dissociative alter-persona." *The facts of the situations are the same one way or the other; it is the culture's explanatory paradigm that varies.*

How Jesus Healed

It stands to reason that if acceptance of Jesus' power to cure led to essentially immediate cures (i.e., the "faith in him" modality) then the problems that were cured were mainly psychogenic and not purely somatic in origin. During Jesus' time, explanations for the origin of the problems he cured were "realist" in their presuppositions. The problems were thought to arise either from divine or demonic interference, not from psychological factors. Those problems that were thought to arise from God were explained to be the result of the sin of the individual, more precisely, God's punishment of the sin of individuals. The resolution of a problem understood to be the result of sin would be alleviated on the occasion of the forgiveness of sin by God. Problems that were thought to arise from the presence of demons would be resolved when the demons were overpowered by a more powerful supernatural force, the power of God.

From the peasant Galilean perspective, then, healing as reported in the New Testament involves the presence of an individual who can act as God. And so I return to the proposition that Jesus presented himself as one whose alter-persona was the spirit of God.

Mark 2:1-12 is the locus classicus of the healing modality "forgiveness:"

> And when he returned to Capernaum after some days, it was reported that he was at home. And many were gathered together, so that there was no longer room for them, not even about the door; and he was preaching the word to them. And they came, bringing to him a paralytic carried by four men. And when they could not get near him because of the crowd, they removed the roof above him; and when they had made an opening, they let down the pallet on which the paralytic lay. And when Jesus saw their faith, he said to the paralytic, "My son, your sins are forgiven." Now some of the scribes were sitting there, questioning in their hearts. "Why does this man speak thus? It is blasphemy! Who can forgive sins but God alone?" And immediately Jesus said to them, "Why do you question thus in your hearts? 'Which is easier, to say to the paralytic, "your sins are forgiven;" or to say, "Rise, take up your pallet and walk?" But that you may know that the son of man has authority on earth to forgive sins'—he said to the paralytic—"I say to you, rise, take up your pallet and go home." And he rose, and immediately took up the pallet and went out before them all so that they were all amazed and glorified God, saying, "We never saw anything like this."

The question asked by the scribes is exactly what would be expected from persons representative of the established religious hierarchy. Given the presumption that God forgives sin (both in cases of individual repentance and in respect to formal sacrificial ritual at the Jerusalem temple) it should follow that a human being who forgives acts as God. Priests may act on *behalf* of God and, from their own point of view as regards Torah, so perhaps did Pharisees act on *behalf* of God (cf. Mt. 23:2 "The scribes and the Pharisees sit on Moses' seat; so practice and observe whatever they tell you."). But acting on *behalf* of God is quite another thing from acting *as* God. So Mark's account gets it right; a son of man who forgives sins acts *as* God, to the surprise and dismay of religious authorities.

If we assume the psychological theory that sin is guilt or trauma projected out onto a god figure, then the elimination of sin is, psychologically speaking, formal permission to forgive oneself. That is to say, moving from a "realist" explanatory system to an "idealist" explanatory system, when forgiveness is granted by God or, in this case, Jesus presenting himself as the spirit of God, then what happens is that an individual has "divine" permission to forgive himself or herself. So forgiveness happens and, with it, the conversion symptomatology that guilt or trauma brought about fades away.

Thus, the first answer to the question of how it was that Jesus could heal is that he could present himself as the manifestation of God on earth (through spirit-possession), announce forgiveness and set in motion a comprehensible set of psychological factors that would lead to the elimination of the presenting symptoms. This is an example of how "supernatural events" can be understood to be historical events with added supernatural explanations.

The fact should not be overlooked that Jesus' initial spontaneous experience of spirit-possession took place in the context of a baptismal ritual for forgiveness of sins. If the bottom-line point of John's ritual was to affirm individuals' forgiveness by God, then Jesus' reception of the spirit occurred simultaneously with an experience of forgiveness. That he should have subsequently affiliated his possession by the spirit with the power to forgive does not follow necessarily, but it does fit neatly with the reports we have. If subsequent to his baptism Jesus presented himself to Galileans as the vehicle for God's spirit and announced forgiveness, it does follow necessarily (I should think) that many of those who accepted his claim to be such a vehicle, and who suffered from conversion disorders as understood within their own explanatory system, would find themselves cured. From that point Jesus' career as healer would have begun.

A standard understanding of the situation, that Jesus himself claimed power to forgive sins, begs the question (unanswerable, in my opinion) of why anyone would believe this. But a spirit-possession self-presentation, in a culture that accepts this modality as possible (and the prophetic tradition affirmed that modality) will enable people to bifurcate their understanding of Jesus into Jesus of Nazareth and, in an alter-persona, the spirit of God. The latter, it would be conceded, would be able to forgive sins. The question one should ask concerning Jesus as a healer is not the theological question of his "nature" but the anthropological question of his self-presentation. Various anthropologists have "emphasized that the native therapist's self-presentation as powerful, self-confident, omnipotent, and authoritarian energizes the therapeutic process, transforming the patient's hope for cure into a concrete reality."[10]

Thus, when we hear that "faith in Jesus" was a necessary or at least strongly contributory factor in his ability to heal (Mark 6:5-6), we hear nothing but plain common sense. Those who denied that Jesus was on occasion possessed by the spirit of God would rarely be healed; those who affirmed it would often be healed. The modifiers "rarely" and "often" are necessary here, the former because what one consciously denies may be what one unconsciously accepts, the latter because forgiveness and faith-healing will have limited effect in cases of viral and bacterial infection, etc.

But to say there will be limited effect is not to say that there can be no effect. A spirit-possessed healer may have considerable beneficial effect in such cases, for the optimism engendered by confidence that one has been supernaturally aided can be very beneficial to an immune system that has been suppressed by the stresses of fear or despair, stresses that may arise from the circumstances of disease itself. As there are cases where psychogenic illnesses arise through the dissociative power of the mind, so there are cases where the immune system is suppressed because the mind is anxious, concerned with guilt, and so forth. Faith in a healer who promises forgiveness and access to the power of God can immediately alleviate anxiety, stress, guilt and so permit the full functioning of the somatic immune system that may, in turn, eliminate diseases of viral, bacterial, etc., origins. The full range of "psychosomatic healing" is only now being comprehensively studied by the medical profession, but sophisticated analysis indicates that faith in physicians, faith in the medical paradigms of one's culture, plays an important role in all healing systems.

Jesus healed somatic disorders using two correlated mechanisms of which we know. He presented himself as possessed by the spirit of God and in that persona forgave sins and otherwise encouraged his clientele to believe that God had acted to cure them. And, of course, those who

---

10 Ward, Colleen, "Possession and Exorcism," 135-36 in her edited *Altered States of Consciousness and Mental Health: A Cross-Cultural Perspective*, (Newbury lark: Sage, 1989).

came to him to be healed were self-selected to have faith in him. He also used primitive techniques such as touching, spitting, and mud application, and recommended that individuals bathe in supposedly medicinally effective pools. The latter means seem to fall into the category of the placebo, a highly effective healing modality that also requires "faith" on the part of the client. As is well known, a placebo will be of benefit most of the time when a client believes the placebo to have spiritual or pharmacological effectiveness. The key element is the belief, the faith, of the client. The placebo effect is not a way of discounting curative techniques; it is highly effective but it raises the question of why individuals would have the necessary faith in the placebo; and the answer will be that faith in the placebo follows from faith in the healer who prescribes or makes use of it.

We have very, very little to go on in analyzing Jesus' healing techniques, and only a little more to go on in regard to Jesus' techniques of exorcism. But we can draw surprisingly informative general conclusions about his clientele and his techniques from cross-cultural anthropological reports. Before I look into these matters I must take a moment to examine certain views that threaten to become normative in Jesus research.

6

DEMON POSSESSION

Basing his analysis on the story of the Gerasene demoniac (Mk 5:1-19), Paul Hollenbach draws the conclusion that Jesus interpreted exorcisms differently from the Pharisees.

> Jesus' interpretation constituted a radical transformation of the values held by the Pharisees. They were conservatives who focused narrowly on doing God's will in everyday life. This permitted them to escape confronting directly the terrifying social conditions and issues of their day. They were ready to pay not only taxes but total allegiance to Caesar in exchange for maintaining their privileged place in Galilean society. They were willing, naturally, to practice a kind of genteel medicine that included intermittent exorcising. But to focus on exorcising (as well as other kinds of healing) as a major form of action was not within their purview, probably because they recognized, even if they refused to face up to, the connection between the illness of their time and the unjust colonial social system of which they were an integral privileged part. Thus, Jesus' exorcising activity must have appeared to them as an independent countercultural move which would ultimately be a threat to their social position. If a fair number of healed demoniacs were like the Gerasene demoniac, this would have exacerbated the relation

between Jesus and the Pharisees. So they moved against him.[1]

He believes that the demoniac "brought the man's and the neighborhood's hatred of the Romans out into the open, where the result could be disaster for the community."[2] In this sort of analysis he is followed by John Dominic Crossan.[3] The same line of reasoning underlies Richard Horsley's analysis of demonic possession.[4]

This line of thought is preposterous. But it seems to be a state-of-the-art regarding the exorcism texts in the New Testament. The cause of demonic possession is said to be Roman domination of Galilee and the resulting extraordinarily excessive taxation and indebtedness of Galileans; the act of exorcism is assumed then to be a political act with anti-Roman overtones that would have been clear to any who witnessed it. It is hard to know where to start in rejecting this interpretation. First, E. P. Sanders has shown repeatedly and unquestionably correctly that characterizations of the Pharisees as "conservatives who focused narrowly on doing God's will in everyday life" are Christian polemical constructions that should never be viewed as correct historical analysis by contemporary scholarship.[5] Second, the alleged political privileges of the pharisees, their resulting total allegiance to Caesar, the attribution to them of thoughts connecting colonial social systems with the illnesses of their time, and the assumption that during Jesus' lifetime Pharisees were a (or the) principal political power group—all are based on nothing more than pure imagination, and a polemical antipharisaic imagination at that. Third, while the story of the Gerasene demoniac is an anti-Roman allegory as it stands in Mark, as such it is a literary construction. *It is an imaginative allegory, not a historical reminiscence.* There never were 3,000 demons placed into 3,000 pigs who then ran quite a few miles to the sea of Galilee and jumped in and were drowned.

---

1 Hollenbach, Paul, "Help for Interpreting Jesus' Exorcisms," *SBL Seminar Papers* (Scholars Press: Atlanta, 1993)
2 Ibid., 124.
3 Crossan, Historical Jesus, 317, citing Hollenbach, Paul, "Jesus, Demoniacs and Public Authorities: A Socio-Historical Study," *Journal of the American Academy of Religion*, Vol. 99, 1981: 573.
4 Horsley, *Jesus and the Spiral of Violence*, 187-88.
5 Sanders, *Jesus and Judaism*, 23-58; cf. Neusner, Jacob *From Politics to Piety: The Emergence of Pharisaic Judaism* (New York: KTAV, 1979).

In the same volume as Hollenbach's essay quoted above, John Rousseau concludes that there probably once was an account of an exorcism in Gerasa of a demon-possessed man who broke chains, bruised himself with stones, cried out and lived among the tombs.[6] Rousseau notices, however, that there are several features in the latter part of the story that appear nowhere else in reports of Jesus' exorcisms, and that the idea that the demons fled to water contradicts Near-Eastern theory that evil spirits were afraid of water. He concludes that while there was an original exorcism story, "the initial account was embellished in 66 C.E. when told to Jewish insurgents just after the legions of Vespasian arrived at Ptolemais.[7] Yes, Mark 5:1-19 is an anti-Roman literary allegory, but as it stands it is not useful information in regard to the theory and practice of exorcism in ca. 29 C.E. nor is it significant information regarding the causality of demon-possession during that period.

In an article strongly disagreeing with trends in contemporary Jesus research, E. P. Sanders undermines the fundamental presuppositions that underlie the analyses of Hollenbach, Crossan, and Horsley, etc. The latter focus on the supposed psychological trauma that resulted in Galilee from Roman occupation and the concomitant extraordinary taxation of the Galilean peasantry. Sanders does not demonstrate so much as simply point out that *there were no Roman troops stationed in Galilee, nor were any stationed anywhere in the domain of Herod Antipas during the time of Jesus.*[8] Further, while it was the sorry situation of peasantry throughout the Roman Empire to be heavily taxed, and indeed this is the lot of such folk pretty much anywhere in the world, there is no evidence that the peasantry of Galilee were taxed more than peasantry elsewhere.[9] Indeed, because of the good relations between Herod and Rome it is likely that the tribute owed by Herod to Rome was relatively little and, therefore, that taxation of the peasantry by Herod was *less* than it might otherwise have been.[10]

For these reasons, and for others I shall turn to immediately, it is not possible to presume that nonexistent Roman occupying troops

---

6 Rousseau, John J., "Jesus, an Exorcist of a Kind," *SBL Seminar Papers* (Scholars Press: Atlanta, 1993), 129-53.
7 Ibid., 144-45.
8 Sanders, E. P., "Jesus in Historical Context," *Theology Today*, Vol. 50, 1993: 439.
9 Ibid., 446-47; cf. his *Judaism: Practice and Belief 63 BCE-66 CE* (Philadelphia: Trinity Press International, 1992) for a full discussion of these and related matters.
10 Ibid.

and their oppression were at the root of Galilean peasant possession experiences. If Judeans found it annoying that roughly 3,000(X) Roman troops were located in Judea, mainly in the city of Caesarea, it is preposterous to think that this annoyance manifested itself in possession phenomena.[11] Further, to put it mildly, demon-possession is not at all widely attested as a likely, understandable, or useful mode of response to taxation and indebtedness. Excessive indebtedness might lead to interpersonal conflicts that in turn lead to possession, one can imagine such things happening, but "might" is about as far as one can go. Whatever was happening to cause demon-possession in Galilee it was *not* discontent with the Roman mops in Judea, nor was it a form of response to indebtedness and taxation.

Possession as an Intra-Family Coping Mechanism

Many cross-cultural studies have made it abundantly clear that demon-possession is usually a means by which an individual in a socially subordinate role can respond to and cope with circumstances that cannot be effectively dealt with otherwise—most of he time, those circumstances arise from intrafamily conflicts. Accordingly, instances of demon-possession are found to occur most commonly among individuals who are the most subordinate members within family structures: wives and children. I. M. Lewis summarizes the situation this way:

> we are concerned here with a widespread use of spirit-possession, by means of which women and other depressed categories exert mystical pressures on their superiors in circumstances of deprivation and frustration when few other sanctions are available to them. Of course, spirit-possession is only one possible mystical mode.... Witchcraft and sorcery are from this point of view other, more direct processes of retaliation and attack.... One specific characteristic of spirit-possession is that, unlike at least some forms of witchcraft and sorcery, it appears usually to offer an explanation only of illness. It does not generally explain external misfortunes [e.g., taxation and indebtedness], at least not directly, and this seems to follow logically from the

---

11 Ibid., 442. It should be recalled that Jesus' activities took place about thirty five years before the beginnings of the Jewish War.

specific nature of possession as an invasion of the person.[12]

In many and perhaps all cases, demon-possession is brought about by interpersonal conflict and such interpersonal conflict is to be located usually within families.

Shekar gives examples of such cases of possessions from his experience in India:

> In most of the cases, the victim is a young woman who suffers severe psychosocial problems. . . . Because of conflicts in interpersonal relationships, sexual matters, and her status in the family, the victim suffers from severe anxiety, which is relieved through demon-possession (primary gain). After being possessed, she receives attention, sympathy, and concern from others, as well as relief from responsibilities (secondary gains).[13]

He cites the example of Sita, a twenty-year-old woman whose husband had no status in the family and who was treated like a servant by others, including her mother-in-law.

> One day Sita became possessed by her grandmother's spirit. She spoke in a different tone that was very authoritative. The spirit blamed those who were ill-treating Sita and warned them that if they did not change they would be punished. Family members became alarmed and talked about the demon-possession. Attention was given to Sita and she was taken to temples and healers.[14]

In another example, Gowri, a twenty-eight-year-old housewife whose husband drank and visited prostitutes became possessed by her mother's spirit when there was a ceremonial function at home.

> She declared openly that her son-in-law was purposefully neglecting her daughter, behavior for which he would pay dearly. Gowri's husband became panicky and assured the spirit in front

---

12 Lewis, I. M., *Religion in Context* (Cambridge: Cambridge University Press, 1985), 39.
13 Shekar, Chandra, "Possession Syndrome in India," in Colleen Ward, *Altered States of Consciousness and Mental Health* (Newbury Park: Sage, 1989), 87.
14 Ibid., 88.

of relatives that from then onward he would look after Gowri properly.... Once in a while [subsequently] the mother's spirit descends on Gowri and talks about protecting her due rights and warns the son-in-law.[15]

Stanley and Ruth Freed summarize their observations of possession as follows:

> One tentative inference from the Shanti Nagar data is that events precipitating spirit-possession are likely to be difficulties involving relatives of the nuclear or joint family and that the victim is often in a position where he can expect little support. These conditions pertain much more frequently to married women than to males or unmarried girls, and this is reflected in the preponderance of married women among those suffering possession. Spirit-possession may be thought of as a means of controlling relatives.[16]

The Freeds note particularly that "disputes or lawsuits over land, and financial reverses such as crop failure, theft, and the death of valuable animals," do not seem to cause possession.[17] They conclude more generally in regard to possession that

> Precipitating conditions have two general characteristics: (1) the victim of spirit-possession is involved in difficulties with relatives of the nuclear or joint family, and (2) he is often in a situation where his expectations of mutual aid and support are low.[18]

Our vocabulary is becoming muddled here. Readers should recall that I use "spirit-possession" for an affirmative state of alter-persona consciousness that is found to be beneficial by a social group, and "demon-possession" for a negative state of alter-persona consciousness that is not found to be beneficial. In the cases cited above benefits accruing

---

15 Ibid.
16 Freed, Stanley and Ruth Freed, "Spirit Possession as Illness in a North Indian Village," in Middleton, John, *Magic, Witchcraft, and Curing* (Garden City: The Natural History Press, 1967), 317 (emphasis added).
17 Ibid.
18 Ibid., 320.

to the individuals concerned are understandable but, nevertheless, the possession state is culturally disvalued and in many such cases exorcistic treatments are sought. Accordingly, I would label such cases "demon-possession."[19] Authors whom I am citing in this section are using "spirit-possession" and "demon-possession" interchangeably. I do not.

Demon-possession can work to the advantage of the possessed individual. In the words of Nicholas Spanos,

> The role of demoniac was most commonly adopted by individuals with little social power or status, [who had] few sanctioned avenues for protesting the dissatisfactions that stemmed from their lowly status. For such people the demonic role offered numerous advantages. Frequently, its adoption led to a dramatic rise in social status. On the one hand, demoniacs were viewed as helpless victims of satanic influence and consequently received sympathetic attention and a lightened work load. On the other hand, they were often treated as awesome seers whose affliction placed them in direct contact with the supernatural and whose performances commanded fearful respect and attention. Demoniacs often became the star attractions in what the community considered a deadly serious combat between the forces of Heaven and Hell. In short, adoption of the demonic role was often associated with increases in social position, power, and respect that would have been unavailable in other ways.[20]

Vincent Crapanzano and Vivian Garrison include in their book *Case Studies in Spirit-possession* essays from Egypt and Morocco inferring causalities for possession similar to those cited above; also in that volume Clive Kessler reports Malayan examples of

> the use of the possession idiom by women of three different statuses: (1) newlyweds who escape from an arranged marriage; older married women who wish to preserve their marriages;

---

19 I use "demon" as a term that can include spiritual beings considered to be ancestors, ghosts, devils, etc.
20 Spanos, Nicholas, "Hypnosis, Demonic Possession, and Multiple Personality," in Ward, *Altered States of Consciousness*, 106.

widows and divorcees of middle age.[21]

I. M. Lewis's theories of possession are in accord with the analyses discussed above. He writes that

> In peripheral cults [of possession, i.e., those not sanctioned by the dominant culture] the catchment area of possession is so circumscribed that those who occupy marginal social positions are strongly at risk. . . . Of course, the extent to which different individuals of subordinate status are actively involved will depend upon their particular life circumstances, and especially upon the severity and magnitude of the stresses to which they are subject. The happily married wife who is content with her lot is much less likely to resort to possession than her harassed sister whose married life is fraught with difficulty. . . . The keenest recruits and the most committed enthusiasts are women who, for one reason or another, do not make a success of their marital roles, react against new domestic confinement or who, having fulfilled these roles, seek a new career in which they can give free rein to the desire to manage and dominate others.[22]

In light of such anthropological analyses, which could be multiplied considerably, it is almost certain that the majority of the "demon-possessed" individuals whom Jesus exorcised found themselves to be in intolerable circumstances of social subordination *within their family groups* and it is likely that many and perhaps most of these were women (as Luke indicates in 8:1-3). Joanna Dewey, noting "the increased attribution of demon-possession to females" in Luke's books, asks whether this "is an idiosyncracy of Luke, or is it characteristic of literate men's views of women?"[23] This false dichotomy resting on anthropological ignorance is not entirely untypical of the writing of New Testament

---

21 Crapanzano, Vincent, "Introduction," in Crapanzano and Vivian Garrison (eds.) *Case Studies in Spirit Possession* (New York: Wiley, 1977), 29. Also see therein, C. Kessler, "Conflict and Sovereignty in *Kelatanese Malay Spirit Seances*," E. Saunders, "Variants in Zar Experience in an Egyptian Village," V. Crapanzano, "Mohammed and Dawia: Possession in Morocco."
22 Lewis, *Ecstatic Religion*, 171.
23 Dewey, Joanna, "Jesus' Healings of Women: Conformity and Non-Conformity to I),mutant Cultural Values as Clues for Historical Reconstruction," *SBL Seminar Papers* 1993, (Scholars' Press: Atlanta, 19)3), 181-82.

scholars on the subject of possession.

Men too might find themselves in intolerable socially subordinate family-group relationships in reference to their fathers, elder brothers, or other family patriarchs, and men who were slaves or servants might find themselves in intolerable, but unavoidable, patron-client relationships. Our New Testament evidence is so extremely sketchy that we cannot do much more than generalize that Jesus' clientele who came (or were brought) for exorcism were probably, more than anything else, victims of abusive family relationships.

We might wonder, then, what it was about the Syrophoenician woman that led her daughter to respond by being occasionally possessed by a demon (Mk 7:25-30), but we shall never know. What we can know is that becoming a demon is normally a mode of response, a coping mechanism, and not a supernatural event per se.

Demon-Possession as Multiple Personality Disorder

The phenomenon of multiple personality disorder [MPD] can allow another model to be used for the analysis of demonic possession. David Spiegel and Etzel Cardena formally propose criteria for a diagnosis of MPD for DSM-IV as follows:

> A. The existence within the person of two or more distinct personalities or personality states (each with its own relatively enduring pattern of perceiving, relating to, and thinking about the environment and self).
> B. At least two of these personalities or personality states recurrently take control of the person's behavior.
> C. There is an inability to recall important personal information that is too extensive to be explained by ordinary forgetfulness or by an organic mental disorder (e.g., blackout during alcohol intoxication).[24]

---

[24] Spiegel, David, and Etzel Cardena, "Disintegrated Experience: The Dissociative Disorders Revisited," Journal of Abnormal Psychology, Vol. 100, No. 3, 1991: 372. "Multiple Personality Disorder" is no longer the formal technical term to be used in psychiatric diagnosis; it has been replaced by "Dissociative Identity Disorder". However, as essentially all literature on the subject uses the term Multiple Personality Disorder I will use it here.

In accordance with growing cross-cultural sophistication in the field of psychiatry they note that

> it must be observed that many religious experiences labeled as *possession* ought not be considered pathological. They may have individual and social value, whereas other types of possession, particularly outside of a ritual context, are dysfunctional and may resemble to a greater or lesser degree what is known in Western psychiatric nosology as MPD, although with major differences in clinical profiles.[25]

Psychiatrists in India have observed that while MPD is very rarely diagnosed in India,

> other dissociative disorders, such as possession syndrome, have been reported very commonly in India but not at all in the West. The condition occurs almost exclusively among women and generally in the lower levels of literacy and socioeconomic class. . . . Such behavior focuses the attention of the family on the individual, valuable time is gained, and the resulting structural realignment of forces within the family often improves the precipitating condition.[26]

They conclude,

> *It can be hypothesized that possession syndrome in India and multiple personality disorder in the West represent parallel dissociative disorders with similar etiologies despite some major differences in clinical profiles.* The pathoplastic influence of the prevailing culture may be important in causing these differences. With the increasing Westernization of Indian society, the rate of possession syndrome is likely to fall. Such a decrease may, of course, be duly compensated for by an increase in the diagnosis of multiple personality disorder.[27]

---

25 Ibid., 374.
26 Adityanjee, G. S. P. Raju, and S. K. Khandelwal, "Current Status of Multiple Personality Disorder in India," *American Journal of Psychiatry*, Vol. 146, No. 12, 1989: 1609.
27 Ibid., 1610 (emphasis added).

By considering *some* cases of demonic possession perhaps to be MPD one does more than simply relabel the phenomenon. Psychiatric studies of MPD cases give a different etiology for the disorder than do anthropological studies of demonic possession. The latt find that cause of the disorder is predominantly a *present* situation of intolerable social stress, usually familial, encountered by a socially subordinate individual. The former find that MPD is almost always caused by specific traumatic instances in the *past,* usually during childhood, and that those instances are more often than not instances of sexual abuse.

Some psychiatrists report that most MPD patients reveal themselves to have been victims of child abuse.[28] There may be other etiologies: "exposure to the death of a loved one, accidents, and the carnage of war, as well as severe pain, illness, near death experience, cultural dislocation, and family chaos."[29] But, primarily, according to the preponderance of evidence and discussion, MPD is most frequently caused by childhood abuse, usually sexual abuse.

Psychiatric theory of the origin of MPD runs as follows:[30] a child with the capacity to dissociate (e.g., one who has an imaginary companion) is brutalized or molested. He or she then develops a personality to encapsulate the experience so that it is dissociated, separated from the child's primary personality. The child might then develop an intropunative personality based on the abuser, a protector personality, and perhaps other personalities. Over a period of time, anger over the abuse and any sexual stimulation experienced with it might also become organized into alter-personalities. With the beginning of adolescence, the MPD that developed to cope with intolerable childhood circumstances will often achieve some secondary autonomy and be increasingly maladaptive. As the individual approaches maturity, the independent activities of the personalities have fewer external restraints and so the condition becomes more overt and may begin to effect the individual's social relationships. Thus, although MPD begins in childhood, it is rarely diagnosed before late adolescence.

One might, therefore, expect to find that some people presumed to be demon-possessed in premodern cultures are subject to the influence

---

[28] Kluft, Richard P., "An Update on Multiple Personality Disorder," *Hospital and Community Psychiatry*, Vol. 38, No. 4, 1987: 366.
[29] Ibid.
[30] 'I am here summarizing Kluft, "Update," 366.

of alter-personae developed as a result of childhood abuse or trauma. The only way to guess which "demon-possessed" persons reported in the New Testament were victims of MPD would be to take seriously the observation that MPD individuals normally have a multiplicity of alter-personae and that persons using demon-possession as a coping mechanism normally have few, usually only one.

It appears, then, that the etiology of the cases of demon-possession reported in the New Testament may have been of two sorts. By analogy to cross-cultural anthropological studies we can presume that most of Jesus' clients were presently in situations of social, mainly familial stress, and that for them demon-possession was a somewhat effective, but socially unacceptable, coping mechanism. Other clients, based on analogy to MPD theory, may have been under the influence of alter-personae that originated in the past, during childhood, as defense mechanisms resulting from abuse. These two etiologies are not by any means mutually exclusive; occasions of abuse in childhood that resulted in MPD would indicate an oppressive family situation that might well continue into adolescence or adulthood and call forth a demon-possession coping mechanism. We might suspect that Mary Magdalene, exorcised of seven demons (Lk 8:2-3) was a victim of MPD, for a multiplicity of alter-personae is common for MPD victims but rare in instances of demon-possession as a social coping mechanism.

But such extremely speculative diagnoses are of no consequence to my argument.

I have, at some length, suggested possible etiologies for New Testament reports of Galileans reported to have been demon-possessed for two reasons. First, to show how it can be that what look like purely supernatural events, e.g., that Jesus cast out demons, are, within the bounds of our very slim evidence, accounts of historical events that can rationally be understood through cross-cultural or psychiatric analogy. Second, to show that reports of demon-possession are best understood to originate from family circumstances either in the past (for MPD) or in the present (for the demon-coping mechanism) or both. I will show that this etiological inference has very significant consequences for our understanding of the career of the historical Jesus. First, however, I will shift levels of analysis and move to "native exegesis," i.e., what do we know About the way "exorcism" was conceived in Galilee in ca. 29 C.E.

7

JESUS' EXORCISMS

Exorcism is neither a form of superstition nor a form of incompetent therapeutic practice. As Colleen Ward puts it,

> exorcism may be assessed as other therapies, with reference to dynamic processes in the therapeutic session, client-therapist relationship, and effectiveness of the technique. Viewed from a more global perspective, the dynamics of possession and exorcism may reflect a cycle of sickness behavior, help seeking, and cure displayed universally but patterned by cultural constraints and cosmologies.[1]

Our knowledge of Jesus' exorcisms comes primarily from the synoptic gospels, particularly the Gospel of Mark. We do not have a considerable body of evidence concerning other contemporary Galilean exorcism techniques.[2] While we have a few indications of exorcistic practice from the Greco-Egyptian magical papyri that might give clues to Galilean practice, they are of later date, from a different language area, and may not be applicable to Jesus at all.

Morton Smith's argument in *Jesus the Magician* that such texts are good evidence for knowledge of the historical Jesus seems forced. What may have led Professor Smith astray was that he fell into the standard

---
1 Ward, Colleen, "Possession and Exorcism," 128.
2 Cf. Graham Twelftree, *Jesus the Exorcist* (Peabody: Hendrickson, 1994).

line of thought that Jesus of Nazareth was "possessed of" the spirit, that he "had the power of" the spirit, and so forth. It should follow, then, that the many Greco-Egyptian magical texts that provide techniques for gaining possession of spirits, or attaining power over spirits, might explain how Jesus came to possess a spirit or to have acquired the power of a spirit.[3] Smith tried to do what I am trying to do, to explain how it can be that Jesus' supposed relationship with spirit can be understood historically rather than simply by virtue of axiomatic theological statements. However, from my point of view, Smith misunderstood that relationship. It was not the relationship: "possession *of*," but the relationship: "possession *by*," the fundamental difference being whether the identity Jesus of Nazareth was thought to be in control of a spirit entity, or whether the identity of Jesus of Nazareth was sometimes thought to have been replaced by a spirit entity. And that makes all the difference in the world.

Two exorcism accounts from the ancient world are commonly cited as potential parallels to Jesus' practice. Josephus provides an eyewitness account of an exorcism by a man named Eleazar:

> He put to the nose of the possessed man a ring which had under its seal one of the roots prescribed by Solomon, and then, as the man smelled it, drew out the demon through his nostrils, and, when the man at once fell down, adjured the demon never to come back into him, speaking Solomon's name and reciting the incantations that he had composed.[4]

We have a first century report from the Satirist Lucian of Samosata who tells this story:

> Everyone knows about the Syrian from Palestine, the adept in [exorcism], how many he takes in hand who fall down in the light of the moon and roll their eyes and fill their mouths with foam; nevertheless, he restores them to health and sends them away normal in mind, delivering them from their straits for a large fee. When he stands beside them as they lie there and says:

---

[3] Interestingly, the magical papyri are much more concerned with how an individual might acquire a spirit than how spirits are to be exorcised.
[4] Antiquities 8.47, translation taken from Rebecca Gray, *Prophetic Figures in Late Second Temple Palestine*, 5.

Whence came you into his body? The patient himself is silent, but the spirit answers in Greek or in the language of whatever foreign country he comes from, telling how and whence he entered into the man; whereupon by adjuring the spirit and if he does not obey, threatening him, he drives him out.[5]

I see nothing in New Testament reports of Jesus' exorcism technique that leads me to think that he practiced in the manner of Eleazar or the Syrian. He may have, it cannot be ruled out, but our reports of Eleazar and the Syrian are themselves quite sketchy and no reports have come down to us of Jesus' use of the name Solomon, or of roots and incantations that Solomon is thought to have recommended. We have one report that Jesus questioned a demon to find out its name, but it occurs in the allegorical section of the story of the Gerasene demoniac, Mk. 5:8. Still and all, it is evidence of a sort and fits with exorcistic practices attested elsewhere, and so Jesus may well have asked demons' names. To gain the name of the possessing entity would, it was commonly believed in the ancient world, give one controlling power over that entity.

Our reports of Jesus' exorcisms are very simple. Jesus seems to have credited his power to exorcise to the spirit of God. According to Matthew 12:28, Jesus said, "If it is by spirit of God that I cast out demons, then the kingdom of God has come upon you." The parallel version in Luke 11:20 substitutes "finger of God" for "spirit of God." Those are virtually synonymous phrases; the idea of the "hand of God" in prophetic texts is used synonymously with "spirit of God" to describe the initiation of prophetic experience. Scholarship is divided as to whether Luke or Matthew altered the Q original. Arguing, among other things, that Luke's conception of the spirit is as a power to effect speech, and not to perform miracles, Jean-Marie Van Cangh makes a strong case affirming that the original Q saying is preserved better in the Matthean

---

5 Harmon, A. M., *Lucian*, Loeb Classical Library, (New York: MacMillan, 1921), "Lover of Lies," 16.
6 Van Cangh, Jean-Marie, "Par L'Esprit De Dieu—Par Le Doigt De Dieu," 337-42, in Delobel, Joel, (ed.), *Logia: Le Paroles De Jesus—The Sayings of Jesus* (Leuven: Leuven University Press, 1982);
cf. also Rodd, C. S., "Spirit or Finger," Expository Times 72, 1961: 157-58;
and Hamerton-Kelly, Robert, "Note on Matthew 12:28 par. Luke 11:20," *New Testament Studies* 11, 1965: 167-69.

version, and I shall make use of that version with the understanding that Luke's version is essentially synonymous.[6]

Jesus' exorcisms took place in the context of a culture that maintained a strongly dichotomous view of the supernatural. On the one hand supreme power resided in God, God's spirit, God's angels. On the other hand God had allowed demons, led it seems by Satan, to have considerable power and influence over the earth. In apocalyptic theory there would come a time when God would reestablish authority over all of the earth and Satan and his minions would be eliminated.

To cast out a demon, then, perhaps heralded the arrival of the authority of God over all of the earth, or at least the beginning of that arrival. This authority of God, the reign of God, is translated somewhat misleadingly (i.e., with inappropriate geographical overtones) as "the kingdom of God." I will use that established term, but readers should keep in mind that the kingdom of God is a perceived condition of God's rule and authority and not a place. Accordingly, the saying, "If it is by spirit of God that I cast out demons, then the kingdom of God has come upon you," reflects both the conflict between the spirit of God and demons and the presumption that the spirit of God's victory over demons signifies the present activity of the Kingdom of God among individuals.[7]

Who is Jesus?

Mark reports that Jesus cast out a demon who recognized him:

> There was in their synagogue a man with an unclean spirit; and he cried out, "What have you to do with us, Jesus of Nazareth? *I know who you are, the Holy One of God.*" But Jesus rebuked him, saying, "Be silent, and come out of him." And the unclean spirit, convulsing him and crying with a loud voice, came out of him. (1:23-26)

---

7 In Romans chapters six through eight Paul gives detailed and fascinating testimony to the fact that for him the process of exorcism by the spirit has been interiorized. No longer a struggle between a person possessed by Spirit and persons possessed by Satan, exorcism has become a struggle between Spirit and sin within the psyche of a single individual. For Paul one must exorcise oneself.

Mark tells us that "whenever the unclean spirits beheld him, they fell down before him and cried out *You are the Son of God*" (3:11), and that a demon said "'What have you do with me, Jesus, *Son of the Most High God?* I adjure you by God, do not torment me.' For he had said to him, 'Come out of the man, you unclean spirit" (5:7-8).[8] Jesus' exorcisms are connected with Jesus' identity. The unclean spirits knew who Jesus was (1:33).

I think it is somewhat rarely observed to what a remarkable extent the question of Jesus' identity is raised in Mark, and in other ancient Christian texts. It should not be a question at all. The question is not one of category as one might expect (i.e., how should Jesus of Nazareth be classified), for which answers might be that he is a prophet or he is a son of God understood in the sense of a magician or wonder worker. No, the question raised concerns his personal identity; one would expect anyone's answer to have been that Jesus was Jesus.

However, according to Mark, Jesus asks his disciples the curious question, "Who do men say that I am?" and receives the even stranger answer, "John the Baptist; and others say Elijah; and ethers one of the prophets" (8:27-28), answers we are to think are wrong (8:33). The assumption of the question is that Jesus is not thought to be Jesus but that he is thought to be some other person entirely. Herod supposedly thought that Jesus was John the Baptist raised from the dead and "that is why these powers are at work in him" (6:14-16). One can but presume that because "powers are at work in him," he was thought no longer to be himself but someone else. The reasoning at work here is this: an individual who is possessed by the spirit of another individual, by the logic of possession, has assumed the identity of that other individual.

In 2 Kings 2:4-18 we find the story of Elijah who, having parted the waters of the Jordan, walked across with his companion Elisha. Elisha requested a double share of Elijah's spirit and subsequently received it so that the "sons of the prophets who were at Jericho saw him over against them, they said, 'The spirit of Elijah rests upon Elisha'" (2:18). The story of Jesus' baptism is reminiscent of this story. John the Baptist baptized Jesus in the Jordan and the spirit came upon Jesus. John the Baptist is unambiguously identified with Elijah in Matthew's gospel

---

8 This is the Gerasene demoniac story; note that the unclean spirit speaks of itself at this point in the story in the singular.

(17:13) and is usually thought to be identified with Elijah in Mark's gospel too (9:11-13). The following pattern follows from this:

Elisha received Elijah's spirit near the Jordan
Jesus received John's spirit in the Jordan
    Or, if John is Elijah
Jesus received Elijah's spirit in the Jordan

By the logic of possession, then, if Jesus received John's spirit he had therefore become possessed by John and so sometimes had John's identity. Or, if possessed by Elijah's spirit, he therefore sometimes had Elijah's identity.[9]

I have briefly considered this complicated case because, while it is certain that Mark disagrees that Jesus was John or Elijah, the logic by which those identifications were supposedly made derives from spirit-possession. The question that repeatedly arises in Mark's gospel is not *whether* Jesus was possessed but *by whom* is Jesus possessed and so, what is Jesus' identity.

Jesus' family are reported to have believed that Jesus was "outside himself" (3:21). In the context of that culture this is not just an example of the phrase we use for insanity "he is out of his mind," it is an example of a possession paradigm that assumes: given Jesus is out of his mind, another entity is in his mind. He is, in other words, not himself but another. He is possessed. Having reported Jesus' family's opinion that he is outside himself, Mark moves to offer explanations of what entity is inside him: "the scribes who came down from Jerusalem said, 'He is possessed by Beelzebul, and by the prince of demons he casts out the demons' (3:22). Immediately Jesus responds, "How can Satan cast out Satan?" (3:23) and so concedes that while he exorcises through a possessing entity, it is not Satan. He says, consistently with this, "Truly, I say to you, all sins will be forgiven the sons of men, and whatever blasphemies they utter; but whoever blasphemes against the

---

9 By a logic of metaphoric identification it might have been thought that, as Elisha was to Elijah, so Jesus was to John the Baptist. And so, if John was Elijah, Jesus was Elisha. This line of thought seems to have appealed to some in primitive Christianity, as is evident from the expansion of the miracle story of Elisha feeding one hundred men with a small amount of food (2 Kings 4:42-44) into the stories of Jesus' miracles of the loaves and fishes.

Holy Spirit never has forgiveness, but is guilty of an eternal sin;' for they had said, 'He has an unclean spirit" (3:28-30).

Mark, then, provides two quite different and unacceptable kinds of answers to the question of by what was Jesus possessed: it is not the case that Jesus having received the spirit from John (Elijah) should be identified with John (Elijah) and it is not the case that Jesus is possessed by Beelzebul, Satan, or any other unclean spirit. Rather, it is the case that Jesus was possessed by the Holy Spirit; to deny this and offer instead the demon-possession hypothesis is an unforgiveable sin.

Principal questions raised in Mark's first eight chapters concern the question of Jesus' identity. If he is sometimes not Jesus of Nazareth, then who is he? If this were only a polemical perspective of Mark's then perhaps it could be put aside as a later Christian problem. But the two authors who revised Mark's gospel, Matthew and Luke, both accept Mark's perspective, although they disagree with Mark on other matters. More significantly, Mark's first eight chapters were probably written to discuss the views of Mark's opponents. Mark does not disagree with the perspective that Jesus' identity is a crucial question, but his own agenda is emphatically to insist that Jesus, the son of man, came to be delivered up, to suffer, to die, and to rise again. For Mark, "Son of Man" signifies Jesus of Nazareth's own persona.

Mark's view of Jesus as a spirit-possessed healer and exorcist is not the view he wrote his gospel to affirm. Rather it is a view that has been passed down to him which he accepts, but which he takes pains to indicate should not predominate over his own, chronologically later, view of Jesus the suffering, dying, and rising son of man.

The question of Jesus' identity also occurs in the Gospel of John where "the Jews" say to him, "Is this not Jesus, the 'son of Joseph, whose father and mother we know? How does he now say, 'I have come down from heaven?" (Jn. 6:42). And here, as we see ubiquitously in the Gospel of John, unless one understands that Jesus is not the persona Jesus of Nazareth but the spirit of God come down from heaven, one fails to understand the situation at all.

John, like Mark, believes that people would have assumed that if Jesus is possessed he is demon-possessed: Jesus said, "'He who is of God hears the words of God; the reason why you do not hear them is that you are not of God.' The Jews answered him, 'Are we not right in saying that you are a Samaritan and are possessed by a demon?' Jesus answered, 'I am not possessed by a demon but I honor my Father, and you dishonor me" (Jn. 8:47-49). And also, "Many of them said, 'He has a demon and he is mad; why listen to him?' Others said, 'These are not the sayings of one who has a demon. Can a demon open the eyes of the blind?" (Jn. 10:20-21). To understand Jesus' words is to understand that it was not a human being who spoke but the spirit of God. Those who do not hear the spirit of God speak, and so hear the words of God, might well define an alter-persona differently, as a demon speaking. Such people would accept the possession paradigm but interpret it differently, as do Mark's scribes who came down from Jerusalem and declare that Jesus was possessed by Beelzebul.

Even the Gospel of Thomas raises the issue of Jesus' identity, presuming that "who Jesus is" would have been a reasonable question to ask: Thomas 43a, "His disciples said to him, '*Who are you* that you say these things to us?' [Jesus replied] 'By what I say to you, *you do not know who I* am, but you have become as the Jews." And Thomas 91: "They said to him, '*Tell us who you are* so that we can believe in you.' He said to them, 'you examine the face of the heavens and the earth, and (yet) *you have not known him who is in front of your face,* nor do you know how to examine this time." Whoever Jesus is, it seems from passages in Mark (and Matthew and Luke) and John and Thomas he is not (always) Jesus of Nazareth.

The Casting Out of Demons

Mark's exorcism stories tell us plainly that there were people who knew who Jesus really was and they were people who were possessed by demons: "Whenever the unclean spirits beheld him, they fell down before him and cried out, 'You are the Son of God'" (3:11).

The demons knew; but what does this mean? Jesus' exorcism technique was to cast out demons by the spirit of God. He did not *use* the spirit of God, he had the identity of the spirit of God which, as discussed in Chapter Eleven, below, he seems to have equated with the term "Son of God." Through that identity he forgave sins. A text from the Dead Sea Scrolls testifies to the fact that the connection between exorcism and forgiveness was not unique to Jesus. Called "The Prayer of Nabonidus (4QprNab)," it is a late second or early first century B.C.E. story of the recovery of the last king of Babylon. He writes "I was afflicted [with an evil ulcer] for seven years . . . *and an exorcist pardoned my sins*. He was a Jew from among the [children of the exile of Judah, and he said] 'Recount this in writing to [glorify and exalt] the name of the Most High God.'"[10] Unfortunately, from this short account we cannot learn very much.

Jesus' exorcistic technique took advantage of the culturally accepted fact that God is more powerful than Satan. God, acting through God's spirit, could command a demon to leave and the demon would leave. The logic of this is clear and complete, although process may have been much more dramatic. As James Robinson summarizes Mark on the subject:

> The clear-cut antithesis between the personages in the exorcism narratives is accentuated by the hostile attitude in which their discussions take place. We do not find calm conversations, but shouts and orders. The demons "shout" at Jesus: 1.23; 3.11; (5.5); 5:7; 9:26. In 5:7 the demon "adjures" Jesus. Jesus "orders" the demons (1:27; 9:25), or "reproaches" them with an order (1:25; 3:12; 9:25). The only passage approaching normal conversation is in 5:9-13, after the struggle is over and the authoritative word of exorcism had been uttered (v.8).[11]

Significantly, as many scholars have noticed, in exorcising demons Jesus does nothing but speak. The point is, of course, that roots, and rings, invocations, and other Solomonic magical techniques would not have been necessary if it were understood that a "demon" were confronted face to face with "the Holy One of God," for by cultural definition the spirit of God would be more powerful than any demon of Satan.

The drama of exorcism was played out on two levels. On the human level a person, let us say Mary of Magdala[12] was confronted by a person, Jesus of Nazareth and they spoke. But the human level was practically irrelevant to the issue, as the culture understood it. On the supernatu-

---

[10] Vermes, Geza, *The Dead Sea Scrolls in English* (Sheffield: JSOT Press, 1987), translation number 30.
[11] Robinson, James M., *The Problem of History in Mark* (Philadelphia: Fortress, 1982), 84.
[12] I will use her as a known example of an exorcised person, but will not press the point of her having, supposedly, "seven" demons.

ral level Mary of Magdala was possessed by demons and so, when she spoke, she was a demon who would be quoted as such. Mark writes, "the demons said," which is not the same thing as if he had written "people possessed by demons said"; Mark accepts the possession paradigm completely.

Mary, recognized as a demon, was confronted by another possessed person, she/demon recognized to be the Son of the Most High. The Son of the Most High drove out the demon. Subsequently, Mary of Magdala resumed the identity of Mary of Magdala and Jesus of Nazareth resumed the identity of Jesus of Nazareth.

One must bear in mind that such an exorcism, in its simplest process, is the act of transforming demon into Mary of Magdala. The act of exorcism was a drama played by two alter-personae, each recognizing the alter-persona state of the other. The demons knew who Jesus was, the Son of the Most High, and the Son of the Most High knew who the demons were (and so Jesus, like Lucian's Syrian and other known ancient exorcists, may well have demanded to know each demon's name and origin). When one recognizes that Jesus' exorcisms were carried out not by him but by the spirit/son/holy-one of God, just as one should recognize that he carried them out in regard to demons and not in regard to Mary or Joanna or Matthias, then one understands the situation. Morton Smith was wrong to assume that the spirit was an entity Jesus *had,* just as he would have been wrong to assume that a demon was an entity Mary of Magdala *had.* Rather, the spirit of God was an identity Jesus *became,* just as a demon was an identity Mary *became.*

The phenomena of conversion disorder and demon-possession are now and, in a sense, also were then understood to be different Forms of psychological dissociation (then, of demonic intervention). Jesus the healer and Jesus the exorcist should be understood to have played a social role based on one underlying paradigm. The spirit of God alleviated conversion disorders by forgiveness and the spirit of God alleviated radical negative dissociation by casting out demons.

Jesus' Social Healing Role Defined

Michael Winkelman has recently analyzed the techniques of religious healing in forty seven premodern cultures, both ancient and contemporary [he includes no form of Christian or Jewish or Palestinian culture].[13] By his analysis there are five types of healer. The *shaman* who heals through ASC [Altered States of Consciousness] techniques particularly involving soul flight and journey into supernatural realms; the *shaman/healer* who uses physical and empirical medicine, along with charms, exorcisms and spells and sometimes ASC; the *healer* who uses only charms, spells, propitiation of spirits but has little or no use of ASC; the *medium* who acts primarily through the ASC of possession; the *priest* who acts through propitiation and collective rites with limited or no ASC; the *sorcerer/witch* who is exclusively immoral, may use ASC, and is normally credited with the power of flight and animal transformation.[14]

Two observations follow from his analysis. One, Jesus is reported to have had few or none of the traits of the shaman, the shaman/healer, the healer, the priest, or the sorcerer/witch. Second, Jesus has almost all of the traits of the "medium" (or, in my vocabulary, the spirit-possessed healer). I will quote Winkelman extensively on the subject to demonstrate this point:[15]

> Magico-religious Activities. The primary activities of the Mediums [practitioners of spirit-possession] are healing and divination [prophecy]; they also provide protection [exorcism] against spirits [demons] and malevolent magical practitioners. Divination [prophecy] is accomplished through the use of ASC. Propitiation and worship of spirits [God] is another primary activity of the Mediums, frequently done in conjunction with agricultural rituals. Malevolent activities are essentially lacking in the Medium group.

It should be quite obvious that these characteristics are reported of Jesus. I have put in brackets terminology particular to the discussion of Jesus and to Palestinian circumstances. John reports three occasions on which Jesus attended the agricultural festival of Tabernacles; but this is

---

13 Winkelman, Michael, *Shamans, Priests and Witches: A Cross-Cultural Study of Magico Religious Practitioners*, Anthropological Research Papers: Number 44 (Tempe: Arizona State University, 1992).
14 Ibid., 30-33. I am summarizing his detailed and organized discussion of these categories.
15 Ibid., 61-62.

weak evidence of a particular interest on his part in agricultural rituals.

Sociopolitical Characteristics. Mediums are predominantly women and are generally of low social and economic status. Although there are a few societies in which practitioners of this type are largely male, they are generally found in this role infrequently. The Mediums are generally evaluated by the members of their culture [Palestinian peasant culture, to be differentiated from elite culture] as being exclusively moral and benevolent in their activities, and generally not associated with the negative use of magical power for harm of others.

With one exception this set of comments applies to the reports we have of Jesus and his clientele. Judaism retained a few records of ancient female prophets but certainly the vast preponderance of reports in canonical texts, coupled with the skimpy reports we have of first century Palestinian prophetic activity, indicate that in Palestine prophet-Mediums were male.

Professional Characteristics. Mediums are generally part-time practitioners, engaging in normal subsistence activities in addition to their activities as practitioners. Mediums frequently do not receive remuneration for their professional activities. There is little specialization among the Mediums. . . . Spontaneously induced ASC [is] typical of the selection for all of the Mediums. . . . These spontaneously induced ASC experiences which apparently occur outside of the control or intention of the toile practitioner no longer occur once the Medium undergoes a period of training. Subsequently, the possession episodes are no longer induced spontaneously, but occur only when there is a deliberate intention on the part of the Medium to enter an ASC.

The sections I have deleted from Winkelman's comments are reports of the typical, but abnormal, motor behaviors of spirit-possessed mediums. They are irrelevant to an account of Jesus' healing techniques because we have absolutely no evidence of those behaviors in the case of Jesus. In this matter an argument from silence (i.e., we have no reports because he exhibited no abnormal behavior) is unreliable due to the high probability that if there ever were such reports, they would not have been transmitted to us by the evangelists. The question is moot. Jesus seems to have been a full-time practitioner, but for a very short period of time. We have no reports of his receiving remuneration; Crossan takes this standard practice to be a fact of considerable significance, but it is evidently commonplace.[16]

> *Selection and Training.* Mediums are selected for their roles through spontaneous spirit-possession experiences which involve culturally defined episodes of possession by spirits in which the personality of the practitioner is believed to be replaced by that of a spirit entity. Mediums differ from other shamanistic practitioners in that *initial* ASC episodes leading to the need for training for the practitioner status are thought to be spontaneously induced and outside of the control of intention of the practitioner to-be; the status is not viewed as being sought in a voluntary fashion. Mediums' selection also involves episodes of illness and involuntary dreams or visions, as well as deliberate ASC induction procedures. They may be taught by individual practitioners and/or learn directly from the spirits [Spirit], but are generally trained by groups. (Winkelman's emphasis.)

The fact that Jesus' baptismal possession was spontaneous, i.e., not planned by either Jesus or John and so far as we know unparalleled in John's baptismal practice, is a particularly telling point. The story of the baptism is an account of the standard initial experience of a spirit-possessed healer and prophet.

We have no reports one way or the other of "episodes of illness and involuntary dreams," but the report of Jesus' involuntary vision of the heavens opening and a dove appearing is credible. Jesus was taught by the prophet John the Baptist, but probably only in the weak sense of his being receptive to John's call for repentance. We have no evidence of any value that Jesus was trained by any group (e.g., Essenes). Accordingly, it is best to go with the evidence of the gospels that he learned directly from the Spirit.

---

16 Crossan, *Historical Jesus*, 422.

Motive and Context. The Medium's activities are generally carried out at the request of a client group; their activities may occur in the setting of the client's family group, or may be public ceremonies in which the practitioner's activities are observed or participated in by the local community.

What can one say here but . . . yes, of course. It has often been noted that Jesus healed upon request and that there are no reports that he ever volunteered or offered healing. He did heal at the request of family groups and he did heal publicly and was observed by considerable numbers of people from the local communities.

Supernatural power. Relations with spirits [Spirit] is the primary source of their power for these practitioners. The Mediums are associated with superior spirits and gods [God], and generally did not have evidence of an impersonal source of power. The Medium's power is thought to be based in spirits [Spirit], who are thought to possess the Medium and act independently of the Medium's control, and occasionally without the Medium's awareness. There is the general belief that the Medium is not in control of what happens during the ASC, and may experience amnesia for all that transpired during that time. The Mediums have low control of their power and occasionally low or no awareness of its application, for instance when the spirits act outside of the Medium's consciousness.

The expectation of amnesia has been proven to be a culture-bound syndrome; if amnesia is not expected a spirit-possessed person will probably remember much of what happened during ASC. Given Winkelman's analysis, the case of the woman with a flow of blood (Mark 5:25-34) where Jesus felt power flow from him without his intention is more likely to be a case of "low control of . . . power" than of "an impersonal source of power."

Techniques. Generally the Mediums do not use magical technique, but instead rely upon their propitiation and ASC relationship with spirits [Spirit] as a means of manipulating the supernatural. However, sacrifice, particularly sacrifice consumed by the attending group, is also frequently employed.

Jesus' reported use of evidently ad hoc placebo devices such as spitting and the application of mud is not magic. The total monopoly of sacrifice by the Jerusalem Temple priesthood ruled out the possibility of sacrificial practice by any Palestinian Jewish healer.

Conclusion

Jesus was a "Medium" according to Winkelman's classificatory system; he was a spirit-possessed healer to use my vocabulary. The overall parameters of his role in first-century Palestine are nothing unusual. Indeed, from Winkelman's analysis one would expect to find such healers in a culture like Palestine's, an agricultural society with social stratification and political integration. It would be suprising if there were no spirit-possessed healers there.

This is not to say, however, that Jesus' particular style and technique and alter-persona identification were anything other than unique. He was the only Palestinian healer possessed by the spirit of God of whom we know, he was the only Son of the Most High.[17]

The account of Jesus' baptism is inversely correlative to accounts of Jesus' exorcisms. In the former case spirit-possession was initiated, in the latter cases demon-possession was eliminated. In some of the latter cases it seems reasonable to surmise that exorcised and healed individuals joined Jesus' retinue. In other words, those who came to him were those who went with him.

---

17 In light of the foregoing analysis, and taking Mk. 13:11 to apply to the case of Jesus, the identity of the persona in Mk. 14:61-65 who says "I am," calling forth the demand "Prophesy!" becomes an interesting question.

8

JESUS AND HIS ASSOCIATES

It is customary to call the set of individuals who traveled with Jesus his "disciples" a term drawn from the New Testament. But that term has two drawbacks. First, it implies that Jesus' associates were students of his and so he ought primarily to be regarded as having been a teacher, a view that I believe is mistaken.[1] Second, the term "disciples," has come to imply the set of male individuals celebrated in later Christian art and story to the general exclusion of the women who accompanied Jesus. But Mark informs us that after Jesus' execution, "there were also women looking on from afar, among whom were Mary Magdalene, and Mary the mother of James the younger and of Joses, and Salome, who, when he was in Galilee, followed him, and ministered to him;

---

1 Cf. Martin Hengel, *The Charismatic Leader and His Followers* (New York: Crossroad, 1981). Hengel does well to show that certain common perspectives on Jesus' career are invalid, in particular the view that Jesus was a rabbi with a circle of students, and the view that Jesus was an eschatological prophet along the lines of Theudas, or the Egyptian, or Judas ben Hananiah.
But his own perspective is founded on principles of Christian theology. Jesus, he believes, ailed his disciples "to participate in his mission and authority, in the eschatological event which, taking its beginning in him, was moving powerfully towards the complete dawn of he ride of God *en dynamei* [in power] (Mk 9.1, cf. 13.26//s); that he called them to participate by confronting the whole people, along with him, with the offer of approaching salvation and with the proclamation of the final judgment," 73.
Perhaps so, but if he thus called them why did they come? If you or I call disciples in this way no one will come.

and also many other women who came up with him to Jerusalem" (15:40-41). Luke independently reports that "he went on through cities and villages, preaching and bringing the good news of the kingdom of God. And the twelve were with him, and also some women who had been healed of evil spirits and infirmities: Mary, called Magdalene, from whom seven demons had gone out, and Joanna the wife of Chuza, Herod's steward, and Susanna, *and many others,* who provided for them out of their means" (8:1-3). So to discuss Jesus' "disciples" would suggest, almost inevitably, discussion of "Jesus and the Twelve" to the implicit exclusion of Jesus' female associates. I shall usually refer to Jesus' entourage of followers as his "associates," or "followers."

Many people assume that Jesus' circle of associates had a rather clear internal social structure. Peter, the rest of the Twelve, and then everybody else. This may well have been how the synoptic authors viewed the situation, but it is not at all clear that their reports are accurate portrayals of the circumstances of ca. 28-30 C.E.

The evidence is inconsistent. Matthew tells us that Peter was first among all Jesus' associates; the Gospel of Thomas gives that role first to James (saying 12) and then to Thomas, while subordinating Matthew and Peter (saying 13); John's gospel puts the Beloved Disciple in the primary role and he, whoever he may have been, was not Peter (20:2). Mark indicates that there were three whom Jesus sometimes separated from the other nine: Peter, James, and John, with Andrew added once to that assemblage (13:3), but also would deny that Jesus approved of James and John seeking personal places of prominence (10:35-45) and even, at a crucial point, shows Jesus calling Peter "Satan" (8:33). Paul informs us sarcastically that Peter, James, and John were thought to be pillars of the church in Jerusalem (Gal. 2:9) but his James is Jesus' brother and Mark's James is another person altogether.

The gospels agree that there were twelve men who formed an inner circle but lists of the names of those twelve vary and Luke, rather casually, informs us that Jesus expanded the circle of the twelve up to the number of eighty-two (10:1). The number twelve may be simple fact: Jesus had that many male associates, not eight and not fourteen. It may refer to the complete count of signs of the zodiac, it may refer to the twelve tribes of Israel as they were many centuries before his time; this latter interpretation, almost universally assumed, is nevertheless supported only by QLk 22:28, and there only by inference from the report that since there are twelve tribes to be judged there must(?) be twelve judges. The presumption that there were twelve men who were associates of Jesus is based on historical tradition; that those twelve men were deliberately intended to symbolize, to teach about, twelve of something else (zodiacal signs, early Israelite tribes) is based on rather little.

I am not sure what to make of all this except to suspect, with the majority of scholars, that claims of Jesus' preferring this or that man among his followers are claims that arose rather late in Christian tradition as different Christian groups traced their origins to different men. The precise parameters of power and special status within Jesus' immediate entourage are matters of considerable interest to the evangelists, but the facts of the matter seem to be lost to history. Indeed, Mark informs us that Jesus condemned efforts among his followers to determine who among them is greatest (9:34-37, 10:42-45). Accordingly, I will discuss Jesus' associates generally and not in reference to possible intragroup power or prestige rankings.

The Old and New Family

My analysis of the nature and purpose of Jesus' relationships with his associates begins with an assumption: most of Jesus' associates, male and female, became "followers" after he had cured them of demons and/or illness, i.e., those who came to him were those who went with him. It stands to reason that those who based their adherence to him on his success in healing or exorcising them would have had some motivation to remain in his company—as I will discuss at more length below. It does not stand to reason that Jesus could simply "call" and, by virtue of that fact alone, men would follow, leave their homes, jobs, families to live indigently and itinerantly in his company.

Assuming, then, that some of those who came to Jesus in order to be exorcised and healed were people who subsequently went with Jesus, we can make rather strong inferences about their motivations to be his associates. Recall, if you will, that the primary causal factor in cases of demon-possession is intrafamily conflict wherein subordinate family members, finding themselves to have no other alternative, adopt a demon persona so as to respond and cope with their familial superiors. It can be said rather confidently that a person exorcised of such a demon persona who returns to his or her family situation with the situation unchanged will sooner or later, probably sooner, again respond to the unchanged stresses by the same coping mechanism he or she previously used. Exorcism that does not change the causal circumstances that led to a demon-coping response cannot hope to have long-term success.

We have no reports that Jesus worked as a family therapist to restructure the hierarchical affairs of families. Far from it. But we do have reports that Jesus offered a method by which the formerly demon-possessed might avoid further instances of demon possession. He advocated that individuals leave their families entirely and offered those who did so and became his associates a surrogate family headed by God the Father. If Elisabeth Schüssler Fiorenza's reconstruction of Mt. 23:8-11 is correct, Jesus once said "Call no one father for you have one father (and you are all siblings)."[2]

A brief story in Thomas (99) and Mark 3:32-35 testifies to the fact that Jesus would have his associates become a surrogate family:

> And a crowd was sitting about him; and they said to him, "Your mother and your brothers are outside, asking for you." And he replied, "Who are my mother and my brothers?" And looking around on those who sat about him, he said, "Here are my mother and my brothers. Whoever does the will of God is my brother, and sister, and mother."

This story implies both a repudiation of the standard family and its replacement by the circle of Jesus' associates defined to be a family. It is a well-known fact that Jesus advocated that his followers leave their families. QLk 9:59-62 reports that

> To another he said, "Follow me." But he said, "Lord, let me first go and bury my father." But he said to him, "Leave the dead to bury their own dead; but as for you, go and proclaim the kingdom of God." Another said, "I will follow you, Lord; but let me first say farewell to those at my home." Jesus said to him, "No one who puts his hand to the plow and looks back is fit for the kingdom of God."

In Thomas 16 and QLk 12:51-53 we hear that Jesus said,

---

2 Schüssler Fiorenza, Elisabeth, *In Memory of Her* (New York: Crossroad, 1983), 150.

Do you think that I have come to give peace on earth? No, I tell you, but rather division; for henceforth in one house there will be five divided three against two and two against three; they will be divided, father against son and son against father, mother against daughter and daughter against her mother, mother-in-law against her daughter-in-law and daughter-in-law against her mother-in-law.

Thomas 55 and 101 are paralleled in QLk 14:26-27:

If any one comes to me and does not hate his own father and mother and wife and children and brothers and sisters, yes, and even his own life, he cannot be my disciple. Whoever does not bear his own cross and come after me, cannot be my disciple.[3]

Mark's 10:28-30 reflects this same theme:

Peter began to say to him, "Lo, we have left everything and followed you." Jesus said, "Truly, I say to you, there is no one who has left house or brothers or sisters or mother or father or children or lands, for my sake and for the gospel, who will not receive a hundredfold now in this time, houses and brothers and sisters and mothers and children and lands, with persecutions, and in the age to come eternal life."

I do not intend to produce any detailed exegesis of these passages which, as they stand, include editorial elements added by later tradition and interpretation. But the nucleus of these sayings testifies to a fact, that Jesus did advocate that people leave their families. That fact is understandable in light of the circumstances that caused those people to come to Jesus for exorcism and healing in the first place.

Sayings of Jesus

Due to their use in Christian homiletics, it is very easy to fall into the trap of regarding each of Jesus' sayings as assertions that have uni-

---

[3] Thomas 55 and Ql.k 14:27 are the *only* places in the Gospel of Thomas or in Q where the term "cross" is used. Accordingly, one may not read a cross-resurrection message into this passage. Rather, "cross" is being used here metaphorically for a dreadful burden.

versal application to all of the human race for all time. But a moment's reflection will reveal that when Jesus spoke he spoke to a particular person, perhaps a particular audience, within a particular context for particular reasons. As every contemporary scholar knows, it is dangerous to construct a situation in the life of Jesus for which a saying might have been appropriate and then to proceed to interpret the saying in light of that imagined situation. But that is what I am doing, dangerous or not. My defense is to point out that the situation I imagine is the situation most firmly established in the gospel evidence: Jesus healed and exorcised and therefore Jesus had a circle of associates.

Thus, I do infer that the circle of associates was largely drawn from those whom Jesus healed and exorcised. I note as well that the sayings of Jesus were passed down by the circle of associates, not by outsiders, and so the sayings of Jesus that appealed to them are the sayings we have available to us. And this, to close the circle, supports the presumption that the sayings given above can be understood best by the presumption that they were addressed to Jesus' previously exorcised followers, people who were persecuted within their families and so within themselves. Certain sayings make good sense only when addressed to such an audience, i.e., Gospel of Thomas 68-69a:

> Jesus said, "Blessed are you when they hate you and persecute you; no place will be found where you have been persecuted."
> Jesus said, "Blessed are those who are persecuted within themselves. They have come to know the Father."

The persecutions mentioned there probably did not arise from communities' resentments of early Christians on doctrinal grounds; the persecutions probably occurred within families and so in consequence also within the individuals' psyches prior to their acquaintance with Jesus.

When Jesus advocated leaving and hating families he most probably did so in response to the fact that those whom he addressed were facing serious problems arising from their family circumstances. Therefore he spoke to people who *already* hated their mothers, fathers, mothers-in-law, etc. He is not so much advocating familial hatred as approving it, forgiving it as it were. I should point out that "familial" here includes both biological families and marriage relationships. The sayings of Jesus that supposedly speak against divorce (Mk 10:11-12 // Mt 19:9, QLk 16:18 // QMt. 5:32) are specifically directed against remarriage after separation and are consistent with Jesus' requirement that his associates leave their wives or husbands and with Luke's report that Joanna, wife of Chuza, did just that.

It seems to have been the case that Jesus regarded his circle of associates as a family and advocated that they love one another. And, although approving hatred in some cases, he advocated that in place of it his followers should love their enemies and be kind to those who persecute them.

As for the social formation and social structure of Jesus' entourage we know quite little. They were itinerant. They were under considerable pressure to obtain food and shelter and clothing, as seems evident from the Q material. Sayings of Jesus advocating passive resistence, "turn the other cheek," for example, are probably just good advice. The same sort of advice is given novice bank tellers and visitors to areas where muggings are common: do not resist evil, give in, give them what they want. Much of what is recorded that Jesus said was undoubtedly said to that group and not to humanity at large. Jesus may have sent some of his followers, perhaps the twelve men among them, out on missions of healing and exorcism "in his name;" their effectiveness would have been directly proportional to Jesus' own reputation as a healer. At that point in history the name *Jesus* (as common then as Bob is now) would not have had "magical" efficacy; if he had a powerful reputation as a healer and exorcist, it is not impossible to imagine that his representatives could have worked under the umbrella of that reputation to heal and exorcise on his behalf. One must bear in mind that this group (a much more apt word than "society," or "movement") existed for no more than two years: ca. 28 C.E. to 30 C.E.[4] Detailed inquiry into its social structures is simply impossible and, for such an evanescent assemblage, probably a misguided effort.

I mean to suggest here that various of Jesus' sayings ought to be understood in light of the probable fact that Jesus' associates were, most of them, formerly members of poorly functioning families and that these sayings should be understood to have been addressed for the most part to those people who were formed into a surrogate family under Jesus'

---

4 Its reformulation into the nascent Christian movement and Christian society is the subject of Chapters Twelve and Thirteen below.

leadership. Our understanding of such sayings will be furthered if their context is no longer thought always to be social and political persecution, or family renunciation in light of the coming end of this world.

People look at a random collection of stars and see constellations, people look at ink blots and see pictures, people look at the tradition of Jesus' sayings and find an ideology. But just as different peoples have discovered different constellations, and different individuals see different pictures in blots of ink, so different scholars and theologians find different ideologies in Jesus' sayings. This was true then and it is true now. Each evangelist then and each scholar of the sayings traditions now comes up with something new. But it should not have been so hard then to figure out Jesus' message and it should not be so hard now. If Jesus had an ideology or program that he communicated by means of sayings, whether rabbinic, educational, sapiential, philosophical, cynic or all these at once, it should be knowable with reasonable ease. But it is not. If Jesus intended to communicate a comprehensible message by means of the sort of representative sayings we have he did it very poorly indeed.

In the section above I have tried to point out that some, at least, of Jesus' sayings make sense if they are understood to apply to the particular circumstances of his associates, assuming them to have originally come to him for healing and exorcism. Other sayings are good counsel given to his indigent and itinerant entourage. Such sayings do not constitute an ideology or program so much as situational advice. But many other sayings cannot be understood this way. Jesus' parables, whatever they were, are not simply advice; Jesus' parables, and other elements of his recorded discourse, can best be understood as means by which Jesus enabled his associates to experience the kingdom of God, as I shall proceed to show.

The Kingdoms of God and Satan

To summarize Jesus' career Mark wrote that Jesus proclaimed "the kingdom of God is at hand. Repent [*metanoeite*] and believe in the good news. . . . He cured many who were sick with various diseases, and he drove out many demons" (Mark 1:15, 34). These activities, proclaiming the kingdom of God, *metanoia*, curing, exorcising, are more closely interrelated than is sometimes thought.

It seems to be the case that Jesus, like many others of his time, saw the world as an arena of conflict between divine and demonic powers. In terms of the worldview of Jesus and those whom Jesus healed, Reginald Hiers's observations are probably close to the mark:

> New Testament writings attest to Satan's present rule on earth. In the temptation scene, the devil declares that he has authority over "all the kingdoms of the world" (Luke 4:5-6). Satan's minions, the demons, still afflict humankind. Paul understood that the world was subjugated to Satan or evil powers (1 Cor. 2:8; 15:24-27; 2 Cor. 4:4), while the Fourth Gospel considers Satan "the ruler of this world" (John 12:31; 14:30). The most explicit expression of this understanding is in 1 John 5:19: "the whole world is in the power of the evil one."[5]

These metaphysical perspectives both grow out of and give meaning to the individual experiences of people who believe themselves to be under demonic control.[6] Such control can be either somatic or psychological; in the first case it is manifested by illness, in the second by demonic possession. Illness was normally understood to derive from sin, alienation from the divine, and such alienation put one under the control of the demonic. Given these perspectives, Jesus as a healer and an exorcist would have been thought to free people from demonic rule.

If Jesus believed himself able to free people from an experience of demonic rule, it would follow that he sought to enable people to experience divine rule. "Divine rule" translates the Greek *basileia tou theou* which is usually translated "kingdom of God." As Crossan puts it, when using the term kingdom of God "what we are actually talking about is power and rule, a state much more than a place, or, if you will, a place only because of a state. And, lest one ambiguity replace another, state means way of life or mode of being, not nation or empire."[7]

People who had faith in Jesus' ability to heal were people who took the categories divine and demonic seriously. For such people the world was a place of conflict. Norman Perrin writes of this conflict

> we are here moving in the world of a holy-war theology such as

---

5 Hiers, Reginald, "Kingdom of God," in *Harper's Bible Dictionary*, 528.
6 Horsley, *Jesus and the Spiral of Violence*, 184-86.
7 Crossan, *Historical Jesus*, 266.

we find at Qumran, where references to God and his Kingdom are to be found in the context of the eschatological conflict of the "War of the Sons of Light against the Sons of Darkness". When an exorcism is a manifestation of the kingdom of God, then that rule is manifested in terms of a conflict between good and evil, between God and Satan, between the Sons of Light and the Sons of Darkness. The Kingdom is not only God acting; it is God acting in a situation of conflict.[8]

The kingdom of God is, then, an alternative mode of being to the rule of Satan. The latter is manifested by illness and demon-possession, but the signs of the former are more difficult to pin down. It should be noted that between the kingdom of God and the rule of Satan there may be a neutral category, but it is evidently unstable and prone to revert to the rule of Satan rather quickly; one New Testament passage testifies to this: we are told that an unclean spirit may go out of a person, travel around for a while, and then return with seven other spirits more wicked than itself to make the person's condition worse than it was at first (Lk. 11:2426). One must assume that for a person to be permanently exorcised he or she must not only physically leave a bad family situation, he or she should also enter the category kingdom of God. This seems to be the point of Jesus' saying, "If it is by the spirit of God that I cast out demons, then the kingdom of Heaven is upon you."

I am suggesting, then, that the general ideological outline of Galilean thought on the subject of possession had this simple structure:

Kingdom of God   —Neutral   Kingdom of Satan
possession by spirit   —Neutral   possession by demons

The category "neutral" is more toward the side of the kingdom of Satan than toward the kingdom of God because it was evidently believed that Satan had been allowed considerable control over this world during the present time and, insofar as the arrival of the kingdom of God was conceived to be a future event it was not considered to be in place during the present.

---

8 Perrin, Norman, *Rediscovering the Teaching of Jesus* (San Francisco: Harper and Row, 1976), 67.

It might follow from the outline above that a healer would seek to replace a "possession by demons" modality with a "possession by spirit" modality. And, while I intuit that this is the underlying logic of the situation, *there is no evidence whatsoever that Jesus sought to bring his associates into states of spirit-possession.*[9]

John Dominic Crossan, in line with practically all contemporary scholarship, offers two alternative ways to understand the kingdom of God: apocalyptic and sapiential.[10] The *apocalyptic idea of the kingdom is a future kingdom objectively visible* to every human being; its arrival brings an end to the world as it is at present. The *sapiential kingdom looks to the present and is actualized through a lifestyle* of wisdom, goodness, virtue, justice or freedom. Crossan defends the idea of a present sapiential kingdom and his book details just what sort of lifestyle is in question; it is the lifestyle of the Jewish peasant cynic. But I argue that there is a third alternative: *the kingdom of God is a form of experience,* an altered state of consciousness directly related to Jesus' career as a healer. It is not, first and foremost, a social condition or way of life.

These three alternatives are not mutually exclusive and many scholars, probably the majority, have held that Jesus taught that the kingdom of God was both present and future. While I emphasize that the kingdom was made present by Jesus in the sense of a form of dissociative religious experience, I do not intend to deny either that it entailed a form of life in the present nor to deny that Jesus announced that an objective kingdom of God would arrive in the future.

C. H. Dodd was one of the first to argue strongly that the kingdom Jesus proclaimed was a present reality: "passages in our oldest gospel sources . . . help to make it clear that Jesus intended to proclaim the Kingdom of God not as something to come in the near future, but as a matter of present experience."[11] Today, the idea that the kingdom of God is a present experience is increasingly widespread in scholarship and some note the relationship between healing and kingdom. Perrin observes,

---

9 The fact that spirit-possession occurred among Jesus' associates after his death is profoundly relevant to the present study, but it is a fact that testifies against any thesis that Jesus brought that state about during his lifetime.
10 He separates the two one step further, discussing each in terms of elite or peasant understanding. *Historical Jesus*, 265-302.
11 Dodd, C. H., *The Parables of the Kingdom* (Glasgow: Collins, 1961), 37-38.

Exorcism may be a manifestation of a victory of God in an eschatological-conflict situation, but it is also the experience of an individual. . . . The experience of the individual, rather than that of the people as a whole, has become the focal point of the eschatological activity of God. . . . This concentration upon the individual and his experience is a striking feature of the teaching of Jesus, historically considered, and full justice must be done to it in any interpretation of that teaching.[12]

But "teaching" is probably the wrong idea to have of what Jesus was primarily about.

The Experience of the Kingdom of God

If the kingdom of God was an experience enjoyed by people who were more often than not relieved of what they conceived to be problematic experience of the rule of Satan, the kingdom of God is probably in some sense experientially analogous to the rule of Satan. It would have been an inverse opposite to be sure, but not some wholly different sort of thing. To put it another way, those who brought themselves into states of somatic conversion disorder or states of negative alternate persona consciousness (i.e., demon-possession) were seeking however dysfunctionally to cope with otherwise unmanageable stresses through psychological dissociation. The kingdom of God may have been, therefore, a kind of experience that was an analogous but more functional coping mechanism.

Erika Bourguignon has differentiated "possession belief" from both "possession trance" and "trance."[13] The former two categories have been the subject of discussion in most of this book to this point. Now we shall turn to consideration of "trance" in the life and times of Jesus.

Religious "trance" is an altered state of consciousness where an individual experiences what he or she believes to be supernatural places, beings, and/or knowledge. The individual experiences his or her perceptual and cognitive field as temporarily altered in a significant way, but retains the same ego identity as in his or her ordinary state of consciousness, and accordingly religious trance is differentiated from reli-

---

12 Perrin, *Rediscovering*, 67.
13 Bourguignon, *Possession*, 7-9.

gious possession. Possession is an alteration in identity; religious trance is an alteration in perception. Religious trance perception may be understood to be the perception of some other supernatural place beyond this world or, much more probably for the case of Jesus and his associates, it may be understood to be a radically revised mode of perception of this world. The Gospel of Thomas (113) gives this account: His disciples asked him, "On what day will the Kingdom come?" [Jesus] said, "It will not come by your expecting it. They will not say, 'Look here' or 'Look I here,' but *the Kingdom of the Father is spread out on the earth* and people do not see it."

Leaving aside understandings of trance as glimpses into the realm of the supernatural, we can understand trance to entail glimpses into or, rather, differential access to, creative powers of an individual's own unconscious functioning. And Jesus seems to have understood that the power of the "kingdom" occurs within people. Luke (17:20-21) writes that Jesus said, "The kingdom of God is not coming with signs that can be observed; nor will they say, 'Here it or 'There it is!' Rather, *the kingdom of God is within you.*"[14] The Gospel of Thomas (3a) claims that Jesus said: "If the ones who 1(.1(1 you say, 'There is the kingdom in heaven,' then the birds will go before you into heaven, if they say to you, 'It is in the sea,' then the fish will go before you. Rather, *the kingdom is both within you and outside you.*" I will discuss this matter in more detail in the next chapter.

The induction of trance in the process of healing is both an ancient and a modern technique. Arnold Ludwig writes that

> the shaman, hungan, medicine man, priest, preacher, physician or psychotherapist may regard the production of an Altered State of Consciousness in the patient as a crucial prerequisite for healing and an essential prelude to treatment. There are countless instances of healing practices designed to take advantage of the heightened suggestibility, the tendency to attribute increased meaning to ideas, the propensity for emotional ca-

---

14 On the fact that the translation "within you" is preferable to the translation "among you" cf. Robinson, James, "The Study of the Historical Jesus After Nag Hammadi," in *Semeia 44: The Historical Jesus and the Rejected Gospels* (Atlanta: Scholars Press, 1988), 50-53.

tharsis, and the feelings of rejuvenation associated with ASC's.[15]

Bourguignon concludes that "induced trance is then part of the cure, where trance need not have taken place during the illness. The induction of such states helps the patient to alleviate his (or her) condition, and in some cases, to become a curer, making use of controlled trance in the performance of the curer's role."[16] Similarly, the cross-cultural psychologists Frecska and Kulcsar note that "Recent studies in medical anthropology have pointed out that the ritual therapeutic experience relies on the patients' own healing processes by means of various altered states of consciousness that healers are able to control. Ritual trance invariably occurs in social context and the healer's personality and the expectation of community are profoundly involved in the induction of altered states of consciousness."[17]

In a highly sophisticated statistical analysis of factors present in the healing techniques of twenty-three premodern societies, Shaara and Strathern report that *"the strongest relationship appears to be between possession trance healer behavior and patients using altered states of consciousness behavior in the course of treatment."*[18] They conclude that since the healer's belief system structures the healing event, if the belief system of the healer indicates that external agencies possess the healer to perform a cure, those agencies can also work through a passive patient.[19]

In effect Shaara and Strathern permit us to form a predictive hypothesis: it is predictable and likely that Jesus made use of altered states of consciousness among his healed and exorcised associates in the process of effecting their full cure. This hypothesis from cross-cultural anthropology is backed up by logical inference from psychology. Individuals who have made use of dissociation in the forms of conversion disorder,

---

15 Ludwig, Arnold, "Altered States of Consciousness," in Prince, *Trance and Possession States*, 87.
16 Bourguignon, Erika, "Self, the Behavioral Environment, and the Theory of Spirit Possession," in Spiro, Melford, (ed.) *Context and Meaning in Cultural Anthropology* (New York, Free Press, 1965), 43. Her remarks may be relevant to an interpretation of the reports that Jesus sent some of his associates out to heal and exorcise.
17 Frecska, Ede, and Zsuzsanna Kulcsar, "Social Bonding in the Modulation of the Physiology of Ritual Trance," *Ethos*, Vol. 17, 1989: 84.
18 Shaara, Lila, and Andrew Strathern, "A Preliminary Analysis of the Relationship between Altered States of Consciousness, Healing, and Social Structure," *American Anthropologist* 94, 1992: 153 (emphasis added).
19 Ibid., 156-57.

of somatizing disorder, of alter-persona demon-possession are people experienced in and prone to achieve dissociative states. It should follow that the process of their cure would include the reorientation of dissociative states away from personally and socially unacceptable manifestations toward acceptable manifestations, and so to include the use of ASC's in curing. It does not follow well that individuals prone to use dissociative states as coping and defense mechanisms will simply stop doing so with the assistance of a healer; it does follow well that such individuals will continue to enter dissociative states through the assistance of a healer, but will learn to do so in more socially and personally beneficial fashions. In the next chapter I will argue that we have records of Jesus' discourse that indicate that he did induce healing religious trance and that from those reports we can make reasonable inferences as to the nature and efficacy of the state known as "the kingdom of God."

9

THE FUNCTION OF JESUS' PARABLES

I would imagine, not having tried it, that I could type out the entire corpus of Jesus' parables single-spaced on about four sheets of paper. There are dozens and dozens of homiletic and scholarly books devoted exclusively to those parables, for they arouse a continuing fascination. I will not survey scholarship on the subject but immediately and unapologetically take a side. I adopt the views of the scholars quoted in the paragraphs below.[1] These men and women have come, generally by lines of reasoning independent of each other, to a very similar set of conclusions. I intend to take their set of conclusions and move from it to show the parables' function in the career of the historical Jesus.

The idea of Jesus the Teacher long had a controlling influence on studies of Jesus' parables. The presumption was that they served as means by which Jesus taught certain comprehensible and understandable lessons and that they could be decoded by finding proper allegorical equivalents to terms in the parables.[2] Through this process many people found the parables to be allegorical to matters of importance to many Christian theologies and to diverse Christian views of proper moral behavior. Any number of allegorical interpretations of parables are potentially possible, and indeed, any number have been offered

---
1 There are some wheels one does not need to reinvent.
2 The allegorical interpretation of Jesus' parables is defended by Blomberg, Craig, "Interpreting the Parables of Jesus: Where Are We and Where Do We Go From Here?" *Catholic Biblical Quarterly*, No. 1, Vol. 53, 1991.

over the past two millennia.

But Jesus' parables do not look very much like ancient Jewish or Greek allegories, if only because the latter allegories usually leave little room for doubt as to the way readers should decode them. Jesus' parables leave enormous room for doubt.

The Uniqueness of Jesus' Parables

In recent years several scholars have sought to determine to what extent Jesus' parables fit ancient categories of allegory, or story, or tale, or moral case study, etc. Interestingly, surprisingly, Jesus' parables do not seem to fit any ancient category very well at all. Even more oddly, Jesus' parables do not seem to be like any other form of discourse recorded anywhere in the ancient world.

Bernard Brandon Scott has compared the parables of Jesus in considerable detail to other apparently similar forms found in the ancient world and has drawn several conclusions. In regard to the Hebrew Bible he finds that

> No *mashal* in the Hebrew Bible directly parallels parable as a short narrative. We begin to see the development toward parable in the Ezekiel tale of the eagle and perhaps in Nathan's allegorical warning to David, but parable has not yet emerged as a genre in the Hebrew Bible.[3]

Therefore it would follow that as a speaker of parables Jesus was following no canonical model. Nor does it seem that religious leaders of his time were given to parables. In the records that remain Scott finds that

> A survey of the rabbinic materials turns up a curious anomaly. In those layers of the tradition that can be isolated as belonging to the Pharisees there are no parables. Jacob Neusner in his survey of Pharisaic traditions concludes that there are wisdom sentences, which he does not see as developing on the patterns found in Proverbs. "As to other sorts of Wisdom literature,

---

3 Scott, Bernard Brandon, *Hear Then the Parable: A Commentary on the Parables of Jesus* (Fortress Press: Minneapolis, 1990), 17

such as riddles, parables, fables of animals or trees, and allegories, we find nothing comparable in the materials before us."[1234]

Neusner concludes that specific characteristics of Jesus' parables are missing in early rabbinic writings,

> As to such similitudes as master/servant, tower/war, lost sheep/lost coin, the thief, faithful servant, children at play, leaven, seed growing of itself, treasure in the field, pearl of great price, fish net, house builder, fig tree, returning householder, prodigal son, unjust steward, two sons, and the like—we have nothing of the sort.[5]

Even in Christian materials, where one might assume Jesus' followers would have carried on his parabolic tradition, "Outside these texts [Synoptic Gospels, the Gospel of Thomas, and the Apocryphon of James] no parables occur. The tradition was not as creative in regard to parables as it was with other elements of the Jesus tradition."[6]

James Breech directed a project that collected *all* the extant stories of late Western antiquity from the death of Alexander to the accession of Constantine. From this research, he writes,

> I discovered that there are hundreds of stories about fathers with two sons, hundreds of stories about travelers in distress helped or not helped by passers-by, and so on. There are hundreds of parallels to each of the parables of Jesus. However, of several thousand stories collected, using the criteria of narrative theory *not one* of these stories is similar to any of the core parables of Jesus, though there are similarities to early Christian parables. Jesus' parables were dissimilar from all those extant to three hundred years before his time and three hundred years after him.[7]

He observes that "There is a permanent gap where the ending should

---

4 Ibid.; cf. Neusner, Jacob, "Types and Forms in Ancient Jewish Literature: Some Comparisons," *History of Religions,* Vol. 11 (1972): 360, and Neusner, Jacob, *Rabbinic Traditions About the Pharisees before 70* (Leiden: E. J. Brill, 1971).
5 Neusner, "Types and Forms," 376.
6 Scott, *Hear Then the Parable,* 64.
7 Breech, James, *Jesus and Postmodernism* (Fortress Press: Minnesota, 1989), 25.

be in all of the stories Jesus narrated."[8] However, every single extant story, Greek, Roman, or Jewish, exhibits closure, or if closure is lacking in the events of the story, the narrator intervenes to award approbation or reprobation to the characters.[9]

He concludes that "Jesus' parables are utterly dissimilar from any other stories known in Hellenistic and Greco-Roman antiquity, including Rabbinic parables."[10]

Jesus' parables are sui generis, a form of discourse unique to our knowledge from the places and centuries contiguous to him. In accord with Sullivan's adage: form follows function, *the function of Jesus' parables was quite different from the function of the stories, allegories, similes, moral tales, etc. found elsewhere in ancient Jewish and Greek texts.*

The function of the parables may have been what C. H. Dodd said it was: to bring about the experience of the kingdom of God. In his words, "It appears that while Jesus employed the traditional symbolism of apocalypse to indicate the 'other worldly' or absolute character of the Kingdom of God, He used parables to enforce and illustrate the idea that the Kingdom of God had come upon men there and then."[11]

Jesus' Parables as Metanoia Discourse

When James Breech conducts his own analysis of Jesus' parables he reaches the conclusion that

> The voice of each [parable] makes the characters present to the maximum degree possible in the narrative. Each is real in that sense. Moreover, each addresses a situation in which his previously closed temporal sequence has been brought into contiguity with another temporal sequence and so opened up. *In place of closure, ending, or finality, at the end of these stories we have opening and complexity, a sudden revelation of the genuine ambiguity* that occurs when the consequences of actions are seen in terms of the way they penetrate the lives of others.[12]

---

8 Ibid., 29.
9 Ibid., 41.
10 Ibid., 64.
11 Dodd, C. H., *The Parables of the Kingdom*, 147
12 Ibid., 74 (emphasis added).

The Function of Jesus' Parables

Some years earlier, Robert Funk discovered much the same thing:

> [At first] I dimly perceived the major parables as double paradigms or declensions of reality. The first paradigm brings the logic of everydayness to the surface and confirms that logic as self-evident or self-validating. *The first paradigm is shattered on the second, which disrupts the order of everydayness by reversing certainties or turning things upside down.* This analysis confirmed by the structure of the narrative parables as sketched in [this analysis].[13]

In Funk's opinion the purpose of this odd and surprising discourse is to change the consciousness of those who sympathetically heard it. He writes:

> It would not be incorrect to say *that Jesus, as a maker of parables, invites his hearers, by means of his tales or riddles, to pass over from the attenuated world of jaded sense to some fabulous yonder he sees before him. He calls this fabulous yonder the Kingdom of God,* and he wonders why others about him cannot see what is so evident to him. He admonishes them: you cannot point to the Kingdom here or there, as though it were an object among other objects; rather, the Kingdom is in your midst, if you would but look. . . . If the parable is a threat to the habituated, crystallized world, it is full of promise for those who are ready to quit that world. One could even say: *the kingdom for Jesus is the invitation to quit the received world.*[14]

Funk summarizes his contribution to the study of parables in these words:

> As a metaphor, parable does not merely illustrate some other point. Rather, the parable as metaphor confronts listeners with the reality of another world. Although it draws its imagery from the world of ordinary, everyday life, *parable incorporates* an *unexpected turn that looks through this commonplace existence*

---

13 Funk, Robert W., *Parables and Presence: Forms of the New Testament Tradition* (Fortress Press: Philadelphia, 1982), 52 (emphasis added).
14 Ibid., 17-18 (emphasis added).

> *to a new view of reality and actually presents that new reality to a listener as a potential to be grasped* in *the present.*[15]

Marcus Borg contends that Jesus

> used the forms of wisdom to subvert conventional ways of seeing. His proverbs and *parables often reversed ordinary perception, functioning to jolt his hearers out of their present "world," their present way of seeing reality.*[16]

Werner Kelber, taking the parables: Sower, Wicked Tenants, and Mustard Seed as his examples, writes

> The impression of realism is thus deceiving in all three parables. In each case elements of logical unlikeliness impinge upon the realism of the story, and *credibility is stretched to its limits. Elements of surprise, hyperbole, and paradox are lodged* in *these stories.* The proposition is now widely entertained that in the world of parables not all is "true to life."[17]

Kelber concludes that "the 'oddness' of the [parabolic] narrative *serves to disconfirm conventional expectations and encourages experimentation with a new logic in defiance of common sense."*[18]

The same line of thought is found in the writing of Bernard Brandon Scott who insists that

> The Jesus parables are not myth; *they are antimyth. Because they disorder the mythical world, they are world-shattering.* But their relation to mythemes is important to observe, for parables take up mythical elements and usually block their mediating function.[19]

John Meier similarly writes that Jesus

---

15 Funk, Robert, et. al. (eds.) *The Parables of Jesus: Red Letter Edition* (Sonoma: Polebridge Press. 1988), 87 (emphasis added).
16 Borg, Marcus, *Jesus: A New Vision*, 115 (emphasis added).
17 Kelber, Werner, The Oral and Written Gospel (Philadelphia: Fortress Press, 1976), 67 (emphasis added).
18 Ibid. (emphasis added).
19 Scott, *Hear Then the Parable*, 39 (emphasis added).

employs these mysterious sayings and stories *to tease the minds of his audience, to knock his cocky hearers off balance, destroying false security and opening their eyes.* . . . Far from pleasant stories, *Jesus' parables were at times violent verbal attacks on the whole religious world presumed by his audience. They promised a radical reversal of values, bringing in a new world*, in a revolution wrought by God, not humans. Indeed, the parables did not simply speak about this new world of the kingdom, they already communicated something of the kingdom to those who allowed themselves to be challenged by and drawn into Jesus' parabolic message. *This "turnaround" or conversion in people's lives was jarring yet salvific.*[20]

Bernard Brandon Scott believes that the parables' frequent focus, the rule of God, has been thoroughly misunderstood by scholars who have failed to realize that it is not supposed to be understood.

"Kingdom of God" is a symbol because its content is nebula, it cannot be coded with specificity. Recent scholarship has tried without noticeable success to code the symbol by historical backgrounding in order to control its meaning. That it is "preached," "announced," and "revealed," and that it "comes," indicate that its structural network is discongruent with kingship, since these are not terms identified with kings. *When we consider the rhetoric of the usage of the symbol, it appears like the Zen master's symbol. That much of this language rhetorically is no longer dissonant to us only shows how we have domesticated it* or overcoded it, as when we identify it with church or some other activity.[21]

Mary Ann Tolbert concludes that parables straddle the border between the illustrative and the representational.

Blending the mimetic and the symbolic, *the fractured realism of the parables encourages the interpreter to search for other levels of reference,* to search, in terms of our two models, for the second-order signified or the unexpressed tenor of the epiphoric-type

---

20 Meier, "Jesus," 1320 (emphasis added).
21 Scott, *Hear Then the Parable*, 57 (emphasis added).

movement. The presence of the extraordinary within the ordinary, the typicality of the characters, and the indefinite tone of the stories together develop that puzzling, teasing quality that marks the parables as polyvalent forms eliciting multiple interpretations.[22]

Frederick Borsch makes an analogy between the response of those who heard the parables of Jesus and students of quantum mechanics:

> Their world has had to undergo paradigm shifts for them to be able even to imagine what is happening. With the right paradigm or metaphor, however, they are able to redefine reality. A number of the Gospel parables seem also to be trying to shift perception. The Gospels speak of people having eyes and not seeing and ears and not hearing, and then of new sight and new hearing. At times a kind of riddling goes on as striking reversals are said to take place in the way people think things were meant to be. *What happens has been called* [by Paul Ricoeur] *"reorientation by disorientation." First, hearers have their ways of seeing the moral and spiritual order challenged and disrupted. They are made to see their blindness in order that there can be the possibility of new vision. Or, as is more appropriate to the hearing of parables, they are made to hear dissonance in order that they can discover a new way of hearing.* Things have first to be seen and heard to make no sense, so that another sense can be appreciated. In the terms of Jesus' essential proclamation this reorientation is *metanoia*. The Greek word is usually translated "repentance," but in its basic meaning *metanoia* calls for a changed mind and heart. It is a turning-about—a conversion to a new way of thinking and hoping. "Repent, the kingdom of heaven is at hand" (Matt 4:17).[23]

In evident agreement with the ideas set forth by Breech, Scott contends Jesus' parables were intended to produce a result, a *metanoia*, rather than to communicate an ideology: "We are not looking for a

---

22 Tolbert, Mary Ann, *Perspectives on the Parables* (Fortress: Philadelphia, 1979), 91 (emphasis added).
23 Borsch, Frederick, *Many Things in Parables* (Fortress: Philadelphia, 1988), 13-14 (emphasis added).

single meaning hidden in or behind the text. Rather, meaning is here understood as a performative act."[24] A performative act, in turn, is a speech event that has an effective outcome independent of any meaning or interpretation. We are a long way from Jesus the Teacher here. Jesus spoke and, for comprehensible reasons, understandable psychological effects occurred in members of his audience.

The Function of Jesus' Parables

Please recall that I concluded my previous chapter with the hypothesis that Jesus, a spirit-possessed healer effective in alleviating the immediate difficulties of a dissociative clientele (i.e., the demon-possessed, those with conversion disorders) would probably have sought to make use of altered states of consciousness [ASC's] in the process of assisting them to full cure. Further, I surmised that the kingdom of God was a label he used for a state of religious trance that functioned as an alternative dissociative modality to the benefit of his clientele. I remind readers of the universally attested fact that many, perhaps most, of Jesus' parables were spoken in reference to, most often as similes for, the kingdom of God. Perhaps, then, the parables of Jesus were means to a *metanoia:* a change in mind and a turning-about to achieve a state (not primarily a lifestyle or an eschatological prediction); an ASC trance state of the kingdom of God.

Pursuant to this line of thought it may seem reasonable to suspect that some healers today, in our society, might use trance states for purposes of healing and that they might also use discourse somewhat analogous to Jesus' parables for the purpose of inducing healing trances in their clientele. There is a school of psychotherapy that does exactly that. It is a school founded by and focused on the hyponotherapeutic techniques of Milton Erickson.[25]

---

24 Ibid., 76.
25 Kamila Blessing has independently discovered the utility of Ericksonian theory for understanding the parables of Jesus. Cf. her "Luke's Unjust Steward Viewed from the Window Milton Erickson," an unpublished paper delivered at the Annual Convention of the Society of Biblical Literature, November, 1993. She recommended "greater general familiarity with Milton Erickson. It will be noticed that his approach supports the best NT work; e.g., John Dominic Crossan's work on parable and paradox is supported by Erickson. Crossan appeals to our instinctive sense of human nature. But Erickson tells us why."

Erickson himself was not a man of theory. His therapeutic approach was to do what he found would work and to reformulate his ideas of what might work in light of the situation of each different client. From his lectures, and from the writings of his followers, a psychotherapeutic theory has emerged, one I will proceed to summarize.

Each person's mind has both conscious and unconscious components. The unconscious can be a source of learning and creativity, of ideas and memories that can be therapeutically helpful. A therapist should enable a client to gain access to his or her own unconscious functioning so that the client can thereby work to resolve his or her own difficulties. As the conscious ego structure has limited access to the unconscious (practically by definition) the therapist should enable the client to put aside his or her conscious ego structure so that access to the unconscious is made possible. The way to do this is to place the client into trance and to make nondirective suggestions to the client to facilitate him or her in making use of already present unconscious potentials. Thus trance facilitates resolution of the client's problems with the assistance, but not the direct advice of the therapist.

Ericksonian theory involves what Ernest Rossi describes as "that therapeutic aspect of trance wherein the limitations of one's usual conscious sets and belief systems are temporarily altered so that one can be receptive to an experience of other patterns and modes of mental functioning."[26] Successful clinical trance experience is, he observes, "one in which trance alters habitual attitudes and 'modes of functioning so that carefully formulated hypnotic suggestions can evoke and utilize other patterns of associations and potentials within the patient to implement certain therapeutic goals."[27] He notes that "Erickson frequently utilizes 'surprise' to shake people out of their habitual patterns of association in an effort to facilitate their natural patterns of unconscious creativity.[28] Erickson in almost all his trance induction techniques used confusion to break up clients' ordinary reality orientation.[29]

Erickson carefully used inductive discourse designed to turn clients'

---

26 Rossi, Ernest, Sheila Rossi, and Milton Erickson, *Hypnotic Realities* (New York: Irvington, 1976), 20.
27 Ibid.
28 Ibid., 142.
29 Ibid., 106.

minds away from conventional wisdom:

> *Turns of phrase that are shocking, surprising, mystifying, non sequiturs, too difficult or incomprehensible for the general conscious context, for example, all tend momentarily to depotentiate the patient's conscious sets and to activate a search on the unconscious level that will turn up the literal and individual associations that were previously suppressed.* When Erickson overloads the general context with many words, phrases, or sentences that have common individual associations, those associations (the interspersed suggestion) gain ascendancy in the unconscious until they finally spill over into responsive behavior that the conscious mind now registers with a sense of surprise. *The conscious mind is surprised because it is presented with a response within itself that it cannot account for. The response is then described as having occurred "all by itself" without the intervention of the subject's conscious intention; the response appears to be autonomous or "hypnotic."*[30]

In premodern Palestine an autonomous response would have seemed supernatural in origin; dissociative states were understood to have supernatural causes. Rossi summarizes the process required for the acceptance of suggestions by what he calls the confusion-restructuring approach:

> CONFUSION due to [verbal] shock, stress, uncertainty, etc. [leads to]
> UNSTRUCTURING of usual frames of reference [leads to]
> RESTRUCTURING needed [leads to]
> RECEPTIVITY to therapeutic suggestions.[31]

If we take seriously what specialists in the study of Jesus' parables tell us over and over again, we see that they conclude, with lines of reasoning wholly unrelated to considerations of Ericksonian therapy, that Jesus used parables to produce confusion, unstructuring, restructuring, receptivity. Given that his parables were spoken in reference to the

---

30 Ibid., 226 (emphasis added).
31 Ibid., 145 (capitalization in original, "[leads to] replaces printed arrows in original).

reiterated metaphor "kingdom of God," they can best be understood to comprise part of a technique to enable his associates to attain and experience a state called the kingdom of God and not to communicate to them an ideology *about* the kingdom of God.

Ericksonian trance therapy is founded on the view that all human beings have unconscious knowledge, creativity, memory, and learning potential. From this perspective the unconscious is not considered a place of repressed horrors and uncontrollable drives. Rather, it is a resource that all people may tap into on occasion, but that people in a trance state may access with much greater ease and facility. Trance, then, does not have value in and of itself. Rather, trance allows natural and creative unconscious thought to take place in respect to whatever problems indivduals present to the therapist.

Trance is experientially contrary to standard consciousness, which is to say that both states cannot simultaneously fully exist (although, as with the experientially contrary states of waking and sleeping, they are on a continuum so that as the one state is more present, the other is less present). An Ericksonian therapist does not intend directly to force a client to change in ways the therapist advocates, rather he or she intends to facilitate the client to take advantage of unconscious potentials for learning and creativity and so to take charge of his or her own propensity to change.

Access to unconscious potentials cannot be reached by processes of reasoning or conscious reflection. Reasoning and conscious reflection are built upon personal and cultural axioms, perspectives, consciously accessible memories and strategies, etc. If these are sufficiently functional to insure a fulfilling life, then the client would not need to come to a therapist at all. But when the client's conscious "sets" are inadequate to his or her situation, they can be temporarily supplanted by trance-enabled unconscious potentials. Accordingly, to faciliate trance and concomitant access to the unconscious, Ericksonian therapists find it fruitful to undercut, surprise, and contradict conscious sets through inductive discourse. The fundamental logic (or, perhaps better, illogic) of this discourse is paradox.

> A paradoxical intervention then may be used to help produce several results that can be of value in treatment. It symbolizes the natural wisdom of impermanence; it captures attention and

may provoke new thought. Most of all, it illustrates a line of reasoning to reach its conclusion. *Therefore, it arrests attention, overloads consciousness, and causes the listener to question axioms, postulates, beliefs, reasoning, facts, memory, congruity checking, and so on.* In short, it stimulates thinking in general, and elicits responses that are exactly the social and psychological results sought for and created by paradox.[32]

The results paradox seeks and creates are, fundamentally, for the client to search internally, within his or her unconscious creative potential, for new solutions and perspectives. The therapist can then utilize those solutions and perspectives to facilitate the client's changing so as to alleviate whatever problem brought the client to the therapist.

The logic of presenting a paradox at the beginning of a therapeutic sequence has probably become apparent from the preceding discussion which emphasized that delivering a paradoxical intervention will cause the client to shift frames of reference and initiate an internal search. When this searching does not result in a readily understandable meaning for the client, search phenomena increase and the client displays signs of light trance. Receptivity to additional direction from the therapist is increased at that point; thus it is an optimal time for the therapist to present a series of therapeutic metaphors. *These metaphors may also contain elements of paradox and confusion to overload the conscious mind and allow the client to entertain novel experiences.*[33]

Paradox, the logic of the illogical, demands rational response that cannot occur. This can empower an individual to seek a response from nonrational unconscious thought processes. This can open the way to whole new perspectives.

Rather than teaching specific guidelines or language to clients, Ericksonian therapists attempt to have clients discover

---

32 Lankton, Stephen, and Carol Lankton, "Ericksonian Styles of Paradoxical Treatment," in Weeks, Gerald, (ed.), *Promoting Change Through Paradoxical Therapy* (Brunner/Mazel: New York, 1991), 137 (emphasis added).
33 Ibid., 144 (emphasis added).

their own solutions. *By using such strategies as deliberately vague language with multiple meanings, implied suggestions, and metaphorical references,* clients can, through an internal search, select their own "best" associations and responses. This approach appreciates that many important associations may often be outside of conscious awareness.[34]

Stephen Lankton describes the process of therapeutic trance induction and associated creative work on the part of the client in words that remind one very much of the parables of Jesus:

> We have mentioned that the paradox provides a stimulus that reminds the listener of certain philosophical wisdom and possibilities of applying something previously unconsidered to the solution of a problem or completion of a task. Simultaneously, the paradox enters a slight confusion when a paradoxical situation is posed or paradoxical logic or directives are given. The rules of experience and combining experience that once applied no longer apply. Logic is arrested and unconscious process and search are stimulated. Presenting paradoxes designed to stimulate unconscious search without directing or stimulating that search in some manner would be similar to planting seeds in an area where they do not receive sunshine. Therefore it shouldn't be surprising to find here a discussion of another important technique to be used along with Ericksonian paradox: metaphor. Aristotle said this about metaphor: "The greatest thing by far is to be a master of metaphor . . . and it is also a sign of genius, since a good metaphor implies an intuitive perception of the similarity in dissimilars." Metaphor provided a means by which Erickson could gently guide the growing seed-ideas. More technically, we might say that metaphor provides *controlled elaboration* of ideas that are the subject of unconscious search.[35]

---

34 34 Phelps, Maggie, "Changing Early Life Decisions Using Ericksonian Hypnosis," in Lanloon, Stephen, and Jeffrey Zeig, (eds.) *Research, Comparisons and Medical Applications of Eriksonian Techniques* (New York. Briumer/Mazel, 198H), H2 (emphasis added).
35 Lankton, "Ericksonian Styles," 145-46 (author's emphasis).

The Function of Jesus' Parables

Mark's fourth chapter, his discussion of Jesus' parables, coincidentally makes some of these same points in practically the same language, e.g., the metaphor "seed" for "therapeutic words."

Assuming both that the principal metaphoric directive Jesus gave for his clients' unconscious search is that his audience should find the kingdom of God, and that paradoxical logic is crucial for this endeavor, it should follow that for Jesus' audience "everything is in parables; so that they may indeed see but not perceive, and may indeed hear but not understand; lest they should turn again, and be forgiven" (Mk. 4:11b-12). To his disciples Jesus *gives* the kingdom of God (4:11a) but they do not understand (4:13); he speaks in parables to the crowds, but *explains* everything to the disciples privately (4:34), but they never understand (8:21). It may be pressing a point too far to believe that the evangelist Mark was insisting, in a psychologically sophisticated way, that explanations of inductive discourse led necessarily to misunderstanding while parables, deliberately made incomprehensible, did lead to understanding or, better, apprehension of the kingdom of God. But it can be fairly said that Mark believed that Jesus made his parables rationally incomprehensible, and that Jesus' supposed rational explanations of parables generated no understanding in those who received the explanations.

Jesus seems to have spoken in a way that was intended to allow individuals access to unconscious functioning. But he certainly was not a protomodern psychologist. His perspective is given clearly in diverse texts: people should have access, in the present, to the kingdom of God. The kingdom of God, as a present experience, is left essentially undefined in our texts. But an experience of access to unconscious affirmative personal resources *must* be left undefined for it will vary with the individual concerned and if defined it will become a rational construct and defeat its very purpose.

Jeffrey Feldman distinguishes between Ericksonian views of the power of the unconscious and the views of cognitive therapy. The latter defines and specifies, the former is deliberately vague.

> An Ericksonian approach often uses trance or indirect suggestion to bypass the limitations of the conscious mind and access unconscious resources. In Ericksonian hypnotherapy trance is viewed as a context for change, and it is believed that

therapeutic change can occur without conscious awareness. A fundamental difference between cognitive and Ericksonian therapies, therefore, is that cognitive therapy focuses upon and tries to change conscious thought processes, while Ericksonian therapy often attempts to access and utilize unconscious processes.[36]

Cognitive therapy focuses on the conscious mind and uses the inductive method to generate change in conscious patterns of thinking. This is a direct approach, and from changes in cognitive functioning, changes in perceptions, behavior and affect follow. In Ericksonian hypnotherapy one often bypasses limited cognitive sets and conscious processes and utilizes the unconscious mind, which is thought to provide vast resources for change.

The argument I have been making in this chapter is a very simple one. From cross-cultural anthropology one can predict that a spirit-possessed healer and exorcist would probably use trance as an important part of his or her therapeutic technique. Those whom Jesus healed and exorcised were experienced in (dysfunctional) psychological dissociation and so were highly prone to be enabled to enter dissociative trance states. Scholars of Jesus' parables note that they are an essentially unique form of discourse, substantially different in form and so probably also different in function from the stories and teaching allegories used by anyone known from the Greco-Roman or Jewish world. Parable scholars observe that, in Robert Funk's words, "parable incorporates an unexpected turn that looks through this commonplace existence to a new view of reality and actually presents that new reality to a listener as a potential to be grasped in the present."[37] We find in Ericksonian psychotherapy a present-day theory that incorporates the use of paradoxical "parable" discourse for the induction and utilization of trance for purposes of psychological healing. If we simply put together the evidence in regard to Jesus with the evidence in regard to Ericksonian therapy, we arrive at a contextually located and intellectually

---

36 Feldman, Jeffrey, "The Utilization of Cognition in Psychotherapy: A Comparison of Ericksonian and Cognitive Therapies," in Lankton, *Research, Comparisons and Medical Applications*, 64.
37 Funk, Robert, et. al. (eds.), *The Parables of Jesus: Red Letter Edition*, 87.

comprehensible theory of the nature and function of Jesus' parabolic discourse. The theory fits what we know of his career and practices and what we know of the backgrounds of his audiences and associates. And it allows us to take the concept "kingdom of God" and remove it from the realm of the supernatural and sheer belief to the realm of the psychological and historical fact. For some who associated with Jesus, the state "kingdom of God" was an understandable experienced reality.

We can say little about the nature and parameters of the altered state of consciousness labeled "kingdom of God" because our sources tell us practically nothing and, indeed, there may be nothing that could have been told. The state was experienced by unique individuals uniquely. One may guess that Jesus' entourage were enabled to experience the kingdom and not those people who occasionally happened to hear him speak. Those of Jesus' followers who were faciliated into a state called *kingdom of God* had the benefit of new insight and new vision into the nature of their realities. The fact of that matter is historical, based on analogous reasoning from Ericksonian theory; the idea that their insights arose from the activity of God ruling is a supernatural explanation.

10

Jesus' Therapeutic Speech

Throughout this book I have tried to show that our "bedrock" knowledge of Jesus, that he was considered a *prophet* and that he was a *healer* and an *exorcist*, can be expanded by use of the intellectual resources of cross-cultural anthropology and of psychology to produce a coherent and cogent portrait of the historical Jesus. Although I have insisted that the paradigm "Jesus the Teacher" has sometimes misled scholars into asking the wrong questions it is certain that, just as every Jew and every Christian today occasionally expresses his or her views on society, economics, philosophy, religious belief, and religious law, so undoubtedly Jesus expressed his views on such subjects. We do have some historical records that allow scholars to try and reconstruct Jesus' views. But the expression of those views was not the primary purpose of his career.

Because Jesus was a spirit-possessed healer, the best assumption to make about many of the obscure or paradoxical things that he said is that he spoke in the context of his activity as a healer. Since he principally healed people with various forms of dissociative disorders, we might more precisely say that he spoke in the course of his activity as a therapist. I will give a series of examples of Jesus' sayings that may profitably be understood from this perspective.[1]

---

1 In the context of the thesis of this book I must specify that I believe that the sayings discussed in this chapter, like Jesus' parables, should be attributed to Jesus of Nazareth and not to the spirit of God.

Inductive Speech

Milton Erickson's hypnotherapeutic technique is known for its use of "indirect suggestions." Because "the hypnotic state is nothing more than entering into one's own 'self' so that unconscious phenomena appear in the foreground due to a temporary dissociation from the realities of the surrounding world," Erickson believed that the subject would bring forth already existing unconscious possibilities or potentials.[2] Should a therapist make direct suggestions and clear recommendations to a client, he or she may circumvent the subject's own creative potential and so contradict the principal goal of the therapeutic process. Thus, Erickson used indirect suggestions that were "evocative, invisible, permissive, free in reference to response, and mediated unconsciously."[3]

And Jesus too made use of indirect suggestions. Consider the following: "seek, and you will find"; "whatever is hidden will be made manifest, whatever is covered up will be uncovered"; "ask, and it will be given to you, knock, and it will be opened for you." Thomas 24b tells us that Jesus said, "He who has ears to hear let him hear. There is light within a man of light and it lights the whole world. When it does not shine, there is darkness."[4] Luke 17:21 tells us that Jesus said, "The kingdom of God is not coming with signs to be observed; nor will they say, 'Here it is!' or 'There it is!' for the kingdom of God is within you." Such promises and injunctions are devoid of specifiable content. Assuming that these indirect suggestions were made to a clientele in specific reference to their dissociative experiences of the kingdom of God, what they will find, manifest, uncover, receive, open, illumine, and so forth, will arise from the unconscious of the individuals concerned. Jesus is not directing his associates as to what they will find or uncover; his associates are enjoined to discover buried potentials in a wholly nondirective fashion.

Some of the sayings attributed to Jesus are very similar to forms of speech used for hypnotherapeutic trance induction. Induction tech-

---

2 Jean Godin, "Evocation and Indirect Suggestion in the Communication Patterns of Milton H. Erickson," in Lankton, *Research, Comparison and Medical Applications of Ericksonian Techniques*, 6-7.
3 Ibid., 9.
4 Thomas uses the terms "kingdom of heaven" and "light" interchangeably, e.g., in sayings 49 and 50.

niques often include dissociational injunctions for the separation of the conscious ego from normal body control. Separating the self-concept from the body-image serves to confuse subjects' conscious minds and thus depotentiate their habitual sets, biases, and learned limitations.[12345] Such separation is conceptually similar to the conversion form of spontaneous dissociation that causes a person to experience paralysis of the legs or of a hand when the ego suspends its ability to control those limbs. When used therapeutically a dissociative change in body control or body image can lead to trance. In light of these observations, Jesus' famous but enigmatic injunction: "Do not let your left hand know what your right hand is doing," (Mt. 6:3b) makes sense.[6] It might remind one of a suggestion so frequently encountered in literature on hypnotic induction as to be of cliché status; there it is called "hand levitation." The therapist tells a client that his or her hand is so light it will float into the air without any effort by the client, or the therapist may suggest to the client "your right hand will move but you will not be moving it."[7] If it can be attributed to Jesus, the saying found in the Gospel of Thomas (22): "Make a hand in place of a hand, an eye in place of an eye, a foot in place of a foot, an image in place of an image," similarly requires radical alteration of one's body-image.

"The first will be last and the last first"; "to save your life is to lose it; to lose your life is to save it"; "exalt yourself and you will be humbled; humble yourself and you will be exalted"; "whoever would be great must be a servant." These are antiegocentric injunctions: be last; lose your life; humble yourself. If obeyed they would have led to an attitude of submissiveness and a willingness to let go of ego defenses, which attitude is essential for receptivity to trance. In turn, those who respond with submissiveness are promised that they will be first, be great, be exalted.

We may find early in the Gospel of Thomas (2-3a) remnants of discourse that enabled some to experience the kingdom. We hear that

> Jesus said, "The one who seeks must not cease seeking until

---

5 Rossi, Hypnotic Realities, 69-71.
6 It appears in Thomas 62b without reference to almsgiving. Matthew's use of the phrase to refer to generosity is Matthew's own interpretation.
7 Cf., e.g., Haley, Jay, *Uncommon Therapy: The Psychiatric Techniques of Milton H. Erickson, M.D.* (Norton: New York, 1986), 22.

he finds, and when he finds, he shall be troubled and if he is troubled, he will marvel, and he will reign over all things [and after he has reigned, he will rest]"; Jesus said, "If the ones who lead you say, 'There is the kingdom in the heavens,' then the birds will go first before you into heaven, if they say to you, 'It is in the sea,' then the fish shall go before you. Rather, the kingdom is within you and outside you."

Here we may perhaps see that Jesus gave indirect suggestions leading to a certain confusion that culminated in an exalted experience of reign and the kingdom [or, "reign of God"] within and outside.

In practically all our texts the state Christians must attain is said to be the state of a child. One widely attested saying in the tradition, hence one with a good claim to go back to Jesus himself, speaks of the necessity of age regression: "Truly, I say to you, unless you turn and become like children, you will never enter the kingdom of heaven" (Matt 18:4, Mark 10:15, Luke 18:17, Thomas 22a [21, 37]). We read in Luke 10:21 (from Q): "Jesus rejoiced in the Holy Spirit and said, 'I thank you, Father, Lord of heaven and earth, for hiding these things from the learned and wise, and revealing them to babes."

The expectation of becoming like little children, in terms of hypnotic induction, is the expectation of age regression, which is of such importance in psychotherapy that it is partially definitive of the hypnotic state; almost any book on hypnotherapy discusses the subject. By its very nature trance may be a reversion to more primitive modes of thinking, more concrete thinking, that dominated individuals' conscious lives during their earlier years. Such modes of thought are superseded by more complex adult modes of thought. Erika Bourguignon comments that possession trance is well defined as "regression in the service of the self," a phrase she borrowed from Ernest Kris.[8]

---

[8] Bourguignon, *Possession*, 34 (Kris, Ernest, *On Inspiration: Psychoanalytic Explorations in Art*. New York: International Universities Press, 1952). The psychiatric theorists Merton Gill and Margaret Brenman have constructed what they call a "metapsychological theory of hypnosis as regression," and specify that hypnosis is distinguished from regression proper by being "regression in the service of the ego," a phrase they may have adopted from Carl Jung. "The Metapsychology of Regression and Hypnosis," in Gordon, Jesse, (ed.) *Handbook of Clinical and Experimental Hypnosis* (New York: Macmillan: 1967) 291-318. For a thorough discussion cf. Gill and Brenman *Hypnosis and Related States* (New York: International Universities Press, 1959). Re-

There is a whole literature analyzing the age regression that spontaneously occurs, or can be easily brought about, in trance. Ernest Hilgard summarizes various theories as follows:

The *ablation theory* "interprets extreme hypnotic regression to mean that all habits and learning that took place after the age to which the person has been regressed are so extremely inhibited that they may be considered functionally ablated—functional only because they can be restored when regression is terminated."[9]

Age consistency theory believes that age regression has to do with the appropriateness of abilities associated with the regressed age and not necessarily with particular experiences on the part of the subject.[10]

Role enactment theory argues that age regression occurs more through the effort to pretend to be at an earlier age than from essential elements of dissociative trance experience.[11]

Contemporary psychoanalytic therapy, focusing as it often does on the emotionally charged reenactment of events in the patient's earlier years, finds the age regression possibilities of hypnotherapy particularly useful. But different people do respond in different ways. Sometimes age regression after trance induction results in full "revivification," when the patient talks and acts like a child; sometimes age regression will result only in the patient's apparent memory of events that were previously repressed.[12]

Religious trance can be investigated in the laboratory. Felicitas Goodman acquired electroencephalogram tracings of people in a state of religious trance that showed a surprising result. Adults in a calm wakeful state normally have EEG tracings in the alpha range (7-10 cycles per second), but those tested while in religious trance had readings in the lower theta range (6-7 cycles per second), at which time other frequency bands were unusually quiet. EEG tracings in the theta range are "not seen in normal adults during an awake state, which the religious trance

---

gression in their technical vocabulary does not necessarily require age-regression, but often age-regression occurs. They mean by regression the return to more primitive levels of mental functioning as understood in psychoanalytic theory.
9 Hilgard, Ernest, *Divided Consciousness: Multiple Controls in Human Thought and Action* (New York: John Wiley and Sons, 1977), 53.
10 Ibid., 54.
11 Ibid., 57-58.
12 Edelstien, Gerald, "Age Regression," in Zilbergeld, B., et al (eds.) *Hypnosis: Questions and Answers* (New York W W. Norton, 1986), 159.

is phenomenologically, i.e., from the point of view of experience."[13] If it is the case that in religious trance theta rhythms predominate, it is interesting that while theta rhythms are "prominent and normal components of the EEG of children, they diminish in amplitude and amount throughout the second decade."[14] In young adults theta rhythms are few and small, and in adults rare, but in young children they are diffusely present.[15] Thus individuals in religious trance will re-experience states of consciousness they will be able easily to associate with the states of consciousness they had as young children.

It is not my purpose here to discuss hypnotic age regression in further detail but to emphasize that Jesus' statement "unless you turn and become like children, you will never enter the kingdom of heaven," is a statement entirely in accord with an understanding of the "kingdom of heaven" as an induced dissociative trance state. In fact, the following sequence from the Gospel of Thomas 22 could make more sense to a hypnotherapist as an inductive sequence than it makes to specialists in the sayings of Jesus:[16]

> Jesus saw children being suckled. He said to his disciples, "These children who are being suckled are like those who enter the Kingdom." They said to him, "We are children, shall we enter the Kingdom?" Jesus said to them, "When you make the two one, and when you make the inner as the outer and the outer as the inner and the upper as the lower, so that you will make the male and the female into a single one, so that the male will not be male and the female not be female, when you make eyes in the place of an eye, and hand in place of a hand, and a foot in the place of a foot, and an image in the place of an image, then you shall enter the Kingdom."

---

13 Goodman, Felicitas, *Ecstacy, Ritual and Alternate Reality*, 39.
14 Shagass, Charles, "Electrical Activity of the Brain," Greenfield, in Sternbach, Richard, (ed.) *Handbook of Psychophysiology* (New York: Holt Rinehart and Winston, 1972), 280.
15 Ibid.
16 There is no consensus among specialists that Jesus did say this. But, then, specialists' judgments have not been informed by consideration of Jesus' discourse as therapeutically intended. For a similarly uninformed approach to this saying see Davies, Stevan, "The Christology and Protology of the Gospel of Thomas," *Journal of Biblical Literature*, Vol. 111, No. 4, 1992: 663-82.

Here the expectation of age regression is coupled with paradoxical injunctions and body-image dissociation, all of which can combine to induce therapeutic trance.[17]

Paradoxical Therapy

The use of paradox is such an important aspect of psychotherapeutic practice that it has been argued that "paradoxical strategies are present in all systems of therapy. These strategies share the common element of defying the clients' expectations and involve some form of reframing and/or symptom prescription."[18] In other words, the therapist does not conform to the client's expectations by condemning the client's symptoms. Rather, paradoxically, *the therapist affirms and prescribes the symptoms.*

Gerald Weeks offers a "metatheory" which is that "paradoxical strategies change the meaning of the symptom from that which is uncontrollable to that which is controllable."[19] If the client is disturbed by what he or she believes to be uncontrollable impulses or behaviors or reactions, the goal of the therapist is to return control to the client. Thus the client should be advised to choose consciously the impulses, behaviors or reactions he or she came to the therapist to eliminate.

Jesus seems to have made use of a similar therapeutic method. On occasion he seems to have affirmed a symptom, i.e., the injunction for someone to "hate your mother and father and sisters and brothers and even your own life," but, more commonly (in surviving records at least) he seems to have affirmed, paradoxically, the causes of the symptoms he intended to alleviate. Many of Jesus' injunctions have always been regarded as paradoxical: "humble yourself to be exalted"; "those who

---

17 It is possible that Jesus' use of proverbs, commonsense sayings that seem to have no purpose other than to elicit agreement, were used analogously to what Ericksonian therapy terms a "Yes set." The "Yes set" are statements and questions, usually invented on the spot, that are unquestionably true and completely unobjectionable. They are used at the beginning of an inductive sequence to accustom a client to agreeing with the therapist. But I am so little certain of this that I bury the suggestion in this footnote.

18 Gerald R. Weeks, "A Metatheory of Paradox," in his *Promoting Change Through Paradoxical Therapy: Revised Edition* (New York: Brunner/Mazel, 1991), 303, quoting Seltzer, L., *Paradoxical Strategies in Psychotherapy: A Comprehensive Overview and Guidebook* (New York: Wiley, 1986).

19 Ibid., 304.

are first will be last, and the last will be first"; "blessed are the poor"; "blessed are the hungry"; "blessed are those who weep," and so forth. Injunctions delivered to the poor to "lend without expectation of return," "give all you have in charity," will have the effect of placing the disturbed individual in charge of his or her own situation of stress.

It is nonsense to believe that Jesus intended the blessing and prescription of poverty to be universally applicable to all people. Rather, in the context of his activities as a therapist, healer, and exorcist, he prescribed poverty in cases where the symptomotology he sought to relieve was caused in part by the inability to cope with the condition of poverty. If an individual is unable to eliminate his or her poverty it will do no good for a therapist to prescribe wealth. But to prescribe poverty reframes the problem.

Perhaps the single most common paradoxical strategy used in psychotherapy is "reframing." Reframing can be defined as "changing the conceptual and/or emotional meaning attributed to a situation. The behavior that is reframed is the behavior that has been defined or framed as being symptomatic by the client."[20] Jesus seems to have done this in two ways. First, as discussed immediately above, he reframed the causal conditions contributory to clients' symptoms by paradoxically affirming conditions that produced stresses with which his clients could not effectively cope. Second, as discussed at length in the preceding chapter, Jesus re-framed clients' dissociative symptomatologies by advocating dissociative trance under the rubric of the kingdom of God.

James Dow has proposed a universal structure for what he calls "symbolic healing," drawing insights from religious healing, shamanism, and Western psychotherapy. He writes that "they seem to be versions of the same thing, but what is that thing of which they are all versions?"[21] His analysis reveals that these apparently divergent therapeutic systems have essentially the same structure. It is as follows:[22]

1. "A generalized cultural mythic world is established by universal-

---

[20] Watzlawick, P., J. Weakland, and R. Fisch, *Change: Principles of Problem Formation and Problem Resolution* (New York: W. W. Norton, 1974), quoted in Weeks, ibid., 310.
[21] Dow, James, "Universal Aspects of Symbolic Healing: A Theoretical Synthesis," *American Anthropologist* Vol. 88, 1986: 56.
[22] Ibid., 66.

izing the experiences of healers, initiates, or prophets, or by otherwise generalizing emotional experiences."

In the present case it appears that Jesus generalized his own dissociative experience of spirit-possession such that he believed he could induce others into a related "kingdom of God" ASC.

2. "A healer persuades the patient that it is possible to define the patient's relationship to a particularized part of the mythic world, and makes the definition."

And so Jesus reframed his clients' presumed sinful condition as a condition of forgiveness and encouraged their *metanoia*.

3. "The healer attaches the patient's emotions to transactional symbols in this particularized mythic world."

Of course, in reference to Jesus and his associates, the principal transactional symbol was the kingdom of God.

4. "The healer manipulates the transactional symbols to assist the transaction of emotion."

How Jesus did this has been the subject of my last two chapters. Dow concludes with the observation that

> All symbolic healing methods involve an ontological shift for the patient into a particularized mythic world. Symbolic healing becomes possible when a particularized mythic world exists for both the therapist and the patient and when the patient accepts the power of the therapist to define the patient's relationship to it.[23]

In the earlier chapters of this book I tried to show why it was that Jesus was thought by many to have the power to define relationships to the mythic world of Judaism. Through possession-trance he became, as he and they understood it, the embodiment of the spirit of God. In the course of his relationships with his clientele, some of whom literally followed him as his associates, he encouraged an ontological shift into a particularized mythic world, the kingdom of God, experienced as a religious trance reality. Obviously, neither Jesus nor his clientele thought in the categories of contemporary psychology. The kingdom of God, the spirit of God, the power of sin and forgiveness from God, the existence of demons and demonic possession were real for them, facts

---

23 Ibid.

of the way things are in the world.

The question could be asked: to what extent were these therapeutic methodologies consciously understood by Jesus? There can be no answer. A healer does what works, and a healer works within a system of healing methods established by his or her culture. Of course, Jesus understood nothing whatsoever of our present set of therapeutic paradigms. But we may glimpse his paradigm by analogy to ours, for the two are different not in essence or fundamental methodology but in their vocabularies and worldviews. Jesus did not decide "I will do thus and so, for this or that psychotherapeutic reason"; he did thus and so, one can but assume, because he found that it worked and because it fit the worldview of his own time.[24] My argument is a simple one: if we map a worldview of healing of our time onto the worldview of healing that is dimly evident from the New Testament and so, presumptively, of Jesus' time, we can understand what was going on. As it happens, that worldview of healing seems to be, in Dow's phrase, one example out of countless examples of "universal aspects of symbolic healing."

Jesus' Teachings, Messiahship, and Execution

The subjects I will discuss in the following short section have been the topics of many full-length books. I do not mean to imply, by treating them briefly, that they are not important matters; rather they are simply not the main areas of concern of this book. Nevertheless, they will receive some consideration here.

While I believe that the prevailing metaphor in Jesus research, "Jesus the Teacher," is inadequate, I have mentioned several times that Jesus certainly did offer advice and give opinions on various subjects. I have nothing to say against propositions drawn from the sayings traditions that Jesus advocated payment of taxes, suggested that people settle disputes out of court, thought that his itinerant followers would be wise not to resist attack, believed in the possibility of forgiveness, encouraged justice, mercy, and the love of God, and so forth. But these matters are not what I am concerned with here. I see no significant dif-

---

[24] The writings of Ericksonian therapists do not reveal them to be sophisticated theorists; they too are doing what they find to work. Erickson himself was not at all a theorist but a practitioner who prided himself on doing what worked and who modified his approach for each of his clients.

ference between Jesus' opinions on such subjects and the opinions one would presume any thoughtful Palestinian would have held.[25] The view that Jesus offered God's forgiveness to the poor, to women, to those who were socially marginal is true, but *the interesting fact is that Jesus was thought able to offer forgiveness* not that God would forgive such people should they repent; that was common knowledge. Those who came to Jesus were not sinful people per se but people with physical and mental symptoms for which the announcement of forgiveness by God's spirit was a helpful therapeutic intervention.

Jesus' views on the question of Torah obedience appear to have been rather casual, more in the manner of a Galilean peasant than that of a sophisticated liberal rabbinical theorist. In short: keep the Sabbath but do not be fanatical about it; eat the foods that are set before you; do not worry much about details of purity restrictions, and so forth. These are not a set of complex theories about Torah law but were, probably, the general practices of peasant Jews of Jesus' time. Scholars do not always pause to consider the fact that the intense concern for detailed Torah obedience found in many Jewish texts surviving from his time (e.g., the earlier Mishnaic materials and the Qumran documents) cannot be generalized to apply to the Jewish peasantry.

Although there are good reasons to doubt the narrative historicity of Luke's account of Jesus' initial sermon in Nazareth, the report does give us an accurate view of Luke's thoughts on the matter. In the context of Jesus' healing career, Luke was quite possibly correct. His account is as follows:

> There was given to him the book of the prophet Isaiah. He opened the book and found the place where it was written, *"The Spirit of the Lord is upon me, because he has anointed me* to preach good news to the poor. He has sent me to proclaim release to the captives and recovering of sight to the blind, to set at liberty those who are oppressed, to proclaim the acceptable year of the Lord." (4:17-19, Isaiah 61:1-2)

This account is supplemented by Luke's assessment of Jesus' career,

---

[25] As E. P. Sanders, Jacob Neusner, and many others have maintained, the idea that the Judaisms of Jesus' day opposed or ignored forgiveness, justice, mercy, and the love of God is theological antisemitism and historical nonsense.

put into the mouth of Peter:

> You know . . . beginning from Galilee after the baptism which John preached: how *God anointed Jesus of Nazareth with the Holy Spirit* and with power; how he went about doing good and healing all that were oppressed by the devil, for God was with him. (Acts 10:37-38)

The second passage indicates that the first passage's references to "release to the captives" and the setting at liberty of "those who are oppressed" should be understood in terms of captivity and oppression in the sense of demonic possession.

As nearly everyone knows, "Christ" is the Greek translation of the Hebrew "Messiah." These terms mean, of course, "the anointed one." If Jesus believed himself to be one who was anointed, and so to have had a special role to which he was appointed by God, it is anything but unlikely that the anointing in question was his initial possession experience, his prophetic anointing by the Spirit.[26] The First Letter of John testifies to the fact that the equation of "anointing" with "spirit reception" is *not* an idiosyncratic idea of Luke's. If Jesus labeled the Spirit "the Son," as I will contend in the following chapter, then he was both the Son of God (in the sense of possession by the spirit-Son) and the Christ (in the sense of possession as anointing).

Nothing in the arguments I have made contradicts the idea that the kingdom of God was *also* believed by Jesus and his associates to be a future objective condition of this world. In other words, the idea that Jesus announced the imminent arrival of the eschatological and apocalyptic kingdom of God can easily coexist with the realization that the kingdom of God should be understood as a form of dissociative trance access to unconscious creative functioning. Indeed, as the idea that Jesus was possessed by the spirit of God might be taken to support predictions that in the near future all of God's people might be so possessed, so the present experience labeled kingdom of God might have

---

26 Similarly, it might be suggested that another principal Christological title arose from consideration of Ezekiel 2:1-3: "When I saw this I threw myself on my face, and heard a voice speaking to me: '*Son of Man*, he said, stand up, and let me talk with you.' *As he spoke, a spirit came into me* and stood me on my feet, and I listened to him speaking. He said, '*Son of Man*, I am sending you to the Israelites, a nation of rebels who have rebelled against me.'"

been taken to support predictions that the kingdom would arrive on earth, visible to all, in the near future. Many, perhaps the majority, of New Testament scholars agree that Jesus spoke of both a present and a future kingdom.

But, on the other hand, one influential branch of biblical scholarship has argued that the idea of the future kingdom of God arose in its entirety in the decades after Jesus' death. Marcus Borg even goes so far (perhaps too far) as to declare that "the old consensus that Jesus was an eschatological prophet who proclaimed the imminent end of the world has disappeared. Though some still affirm it, [that] central conviction . . . is no longer held by the majority of North American scholars actively engaged in Jesus research."[27] The scholars of whom Borg speaks conclude that Jesus spoke only of a kingdom to be attained in the present and not of a kingdom to come to earth in the future. This view, too, is consistent with the argument I have made above, although I do not presently endorse such a view.

It seems to be the case that John the Baptist spoke of an impending apocalyptic climax to human history; it is certainly the case that Paul and Q (in the version used by Matthew and Luke) affirmed that this world would soon come to an end with the arrival of the kingdom of God. Mark, Matthew, and Luke agree, earlier stages of John's gospel evidence that point of view, and the Gospel of Thomas, while disapproving of that point of view, attributes it to Jesus' disciples. One can best get from John the Baptist to every known ancient Christian text and movement by postulating that there was continuity between John the Baptist and Christianity and that that continuity was the eschatological prediction of Jesus. Thus I take the side of those who believe Jesus also spoke of a coming future objective kingdom of God. But I have little of my own to add to scholarship on the question, and so refer readers to existing studies.[28]

There is no good evidence that Jesus believed himself to have been the King of Israel or that he sought to organize an uprising against Ro-

---

[27] Borg, Marcus, "A Renaissance in Jesus Studies," Theology Today, Vol. 45, Oct. 1988: 285; cf., e.g., Kloppenborg, John, *The Formation of Q* (Philadelphia: Fortress, 1987); Funk, *Five Gospels*; Mack, *The Lost Gospel*.
[28] Cf. classically, Schweitzer, *Quest of the Historical Jesus*; more recently, Sanders, *Jesus and Judaism*.

man occupation. The three terms: Messiah (Christ), Son of God, kingdom of God, fit together well in reference to his career as an anointed-by-the-spirit and thereby spirit-Son possessed healer who induced his clientele into trance-healing experiences of God's kingdom. However, the same terms are consonant with the claims of an anti-Roman revolutionary leader. To predict the arrival of an objective kingdom of God was to predict either the overthrow of the whole Roman empire or, at the minimum, the end of Roman control of Palestine. These considerations are sufficient to account for his execution. Pilate, hearing of the presence of a Messiah, a Son of God, one who spoke of entering the kingdom of God and, perhaps, the immediate coming of an objective kingdom of God, would understand (mistakenly) that Jesus was an anti—imperial claimant to the throne of Israel and perhaps one who predicted the overthrow of the emperor Tiberias and, in accordance with Roman law, Pilate would have ordered his execution.

11

THE SAYINGS OF THE SPIRIT

In this chapter I will argue that some of the "Johannine style" sayings attributed to Jesus are as historically authentic as are some of the "synoptic style" sayings attributed to him. That conclusion follows rather easily, but not necessarily, from the likelihood that Jesus was a spirit-possessed healer and prophet, as I will demonstrate below.

There are three principal theories about the origin of the sayings, or discourses, of Jesus in John's Gospel. The first arises from Christian faith, beginning and ending with the supposition that Jesus' sayings in John are historically reliable because they appear in inspired scriptures. A second, not often stated clearly by its adherents, is that most of the Johannine sayings were fictions created orally (through the "preaching of the Johannine community") or literarily (by the authorship of John) to serve didactic and missionary purposes. The third is that many of those sayings arose from the utterances of spirit-possessed Christian prophets.[1]

Options two and three are not mutually exclusive. Probably some of the Johannine material arose from the utterances of spirit-possessed Christian prophets. Equally probably, such material was reworked in a literary fashion as it was incorporated into the Gospel of John. The thesis I shall offer is supplemental to these two options; it is not intended wholly to replace them. Indeed, in Chapter Thirteen below I present

---

1 C.f. Boring, Eugene, *The Continuing Voice of Jesus*, 77-79.

a theory of the utility of Johannine sayings based on the presumption that many of them derive from the words of Christian prophets. In the present chapter, however, I argue that some, perhaps not a great many, but *some* Johannine-style sayings arose from the utterances of a particular prophet whose name is known to us: Jesus. It is not unlikely that the style of discourse of the Johannine prophets who subsequently spoke in Jesus' name, and thus elements of the literary style of the authorship of the Gospel of John, derived from a discourse style of the man to whom later Johannine sayings were attributed.

While in an altered state of consciousness Jesus certainly said some things that were to be attributed not to him but to the spirit speaking through him. As we have seen, the Jewish prophetic paradigm practically demands this. His sayings in the synoptic style, proverbs and parables, responses to arguments and to questions, show little sign of having been uttered by a person in an altered state of consciousness. The synoptic-style sayings that scholarship has concluded derive from Jesus were, I presume, spoken by Jesus of Nazareth. What then would God's spirit possessing Jesus have said?

In this chapter I will suggest that we know some sayings that may have been spoken by Jesus himself when he was in a state of spirit-possession. These sayings refer not to Jesus, nor to social or moral issues, but to the spirit's nature and origin, the spirit's powers and relationship to God. The following may be examples; all are taken from the Gospel of John. The attribution I give them will be discussed shortly.

8:23. The spirit of God said, "You are from below, I am from above; you are of this world, I am not of this world."

6:38. The spirit of God said, "I have come down from heaven, not to do my own will, but the will of him who sent me."

3:31-34. The spirit of God said, "He who comes from above is above all; he who is of the earth belongs to the earth, and of the earth he speaks; he who comes from heaven is above all. He bears witness to what he has seen and heard, yet no one receives his testimony; he who receives his testimony sets his seal to this, that God is true. For *he whom God has sent utters the words of God, for it is not by measure that he gives the Spirit."*

16:28. The spirit of God said, "I came from the Father and have come into the world; again, I am leaving the world and going to the Father."

9:5. The spirit of God said, "As long as I am in the world, I am the light of the world."

10:30. The spirit of God said, "I and the Father are one."

14:6-7. The spirit of God said, "I am the way, and the truth, and the life; no one comes to the Father, but by me."

Each of these sayings, when attributed to God's holy spirit, would be little more than Jewish common sense. Of course the spirit of God and God are one; of course the spirit of God comes from God; of course the spirit of God does the will of God; of course the spirit of God is not of this world; of course the spirit of God is the light of the world, the way to God, the truth, and the life. We might hear the spirit of God speaking in these sayings and, if the spirit of God spoke, it spoke through a human voice, through the voice of a person possessed by God's spirit. Jesus was one such person.

In any case of spirit-possession (and in most cases of demonic possession and multiple personality disorder) the following will be true:

1. A second persona will be considered a different person from the first persona.

2. A second persona will have an identity (a categorical label or a name) different from that of the first persona.

3. The speech of the second persona will be different from that of the first persona.

These principles are not modern theories, they govern how oracles were understood in the greater Greco-Roman culture. These principles govern how Philo of Alexandria understood prophetic spirit-possession. These principles are how the evangelist Mark understood the situation, for Mark in 13:11 testifies to the fact that Mark took for granted that Christians could expect, under traumatic circumstances, to be possessed. When possessed, as Mark understands the matter:

1. "It is not you that speaks . . ." and so a second and different persona arises.

2. "but the spirit . . ." and so a different identity is labeled.

3. "speaks;" and by virtue of the fact that this is "not you who speaks, the speaking is recognizably different than it would otherwise be if it were "you" speaking.

Mark's view is in accord with contemporary anthropological concepts of possession and psychological understandings of multiple personality phenomena.

It should follow from all of the above, that if Jesus became possessed by God's spirit at the time of his baptism, then an understanding of the *historical* Jesus, from psychological and anthropological considerations, and from the theory of possession attested in Greco-Roman, Jewish, and early Christian sources, must take the following into account:

1. He had a second persona different from the persona "Jesus of Nazareth."
2. That second persona had a name or label different than "Jesus of Nazareth."
3. That second persona spoke in a manner different than "Jesus of Nazareth."

If Jesus had a second persona different from that of "Jesus of Nazareth" how did anyone know this? They could only have known it if the second persona told them about it; this is what normally happens in conversation between a spirit-possessed persona and an audience: the spirit announces its presence by speech.[2]

Sayings of the Spirit

The spirit persona of a Jewish spirit-possessed healer would have had to inform audiences who it was, where it came from, what it could do. In the case of Jesus, it would have had to do so repeatedly in front of different audiences. This follows from the fact of the itinerancy of Jesus and his entourage.

If Jesus was possessed, then he was possessed by the spirit of God. It follows that when his alternate persona spoke explaining who it was, where it was from, and what it could do, it used self-affirmations appropriate to the spirit of God. This point is nearly tautological: "If there are characteristics of the spirit of God then the spirit of God will have those characteristics," but lists of such characteristics will vary, at least slightly, from person to person. Nevertheless, some of these characteristics are definitive of

---

[2] In very well-established cultic settings, sometimes a spirit will make its particular presence known simply by appropriate symbolic behavior. But Jesus did not operate within an established cultic setting.

the spirit of God from the perspective of any of the ancient Judaisms.

The fundamental characteristics of the spirit of God (or, for the matter, its equivalent, the spirit of prophecy) when present in a human body are, at the minimum, these:

1. The spirit of God comes from God.
2. The spirit of God knows things of God.
3. The spirit of God reveals what God wishes to have revealed.
4. The spirit of God speaks the words of God.
5. The spirit of God returns to God.

Its "coming and returning" are the way the "arising and ceasing" of an alternate persona possession-state will be described given the assumption that the spirit is an external entity.

The five propositions above would occur when a spirit of God possessed person introduced himself. If I am the spirit of God, then if I am to present myself thusly to an audience, I will inform the audience that:

1. I have come from God.
2. I know things of God.
3. I reveal what God wishes to have revealed.
4. I speak the words of God.
5. I will return to God.

So far as I know every Jesus researcher concedes that Jesus referred to God as "Father"—which would generate this sequence:

1. I have come from the Father.
2. I know things of the Father.
3. I reveal what the Father wishes to have revealed.
4. I speak the words of the Father.
5. I will return to the Father.

Was it or was it not the case that Jesus referred to himself, or rather the spirit referred to itself, as "the Son?"

Some of the evidence is as follows:

a. Mark constructs, or reports, two instances of a *bat kol* explaining the origin of that term in Jesus' discourse (1:11, 9:7: "This is my beloved Son; *listen to him"*).

b. Mark 13:32 is a saying wherein Jesus uses "the Son" as a self-reference implying that supernatural knowledge is the Son's usual, but not invariable, characteristic. Meier takes this saying to be probably authentic on the grounds of embarrassment; it attributes ignorance to Jesus in a manner unlikely to have arisen in the early church.[3]

c. Q attributes the usage of "the Son" to Jesus as a self-reference in a passage beginning, *"He rejoiced in the Spirit and said. . . ."* (Q Luke 10:21-22). This passage does not definitively say, but may say (it is certainly an odd usage), that the speech following is to be attributed to Jesus' alter-persona the spirit. According to David Hill, "The unparalleled statement in Luke 10:21 that Jesus 'rejoiced in the Holy Spirit' must mean that the evangelist regarded the sayings which follow as an inspired or even ecstatic prophecy of peculiar significance."[4] In the sayings that follow we are told, "All things have been delivered to me by my Father; and no one knows who the Son is except the Father, or who the Father is except the Son and any one to whom the Son chooses to reveal him."

d. The usage "the Son" is common in John. The idea that this is some sort of Johannine idiosyncracy is belied by points b. and c. above. These points also testify against the thesis that since we know that "the Son" is a Johannine idiosyncracy, whenever else the usage occurs we have traces of Johannine influence. On the contrary, those other occurrences testify against an idiosyncracy thesis.

e. According to Mark, individuals (in a state of demon-possession) identified Jesus (in a state of spirit-possession) as "the Son of the Most High," as discussed in Chapter Seven above.

f. An individual who, it is universally assumed, believed himself to have some sort of special relationship with "the Father" might well have referred to himself as "the Son."

g. Paul regards those possessed by the spirit as having been, by virtue of their possession, transformed into Sons.

Let me expand on the last observation. We know that as of ca. 50 C.E. one Christian apostle took it for granted that spirit-possession entailed the reception of the spirit identified as Son and thus entailed the identity of possessed persons as Sons (Gal. 4:6-7). He seems to take it

---

3 Meier, "Jesus," 1324.
4 Hill, *New Testament Prophecy*, 59.

for granted that the Roman Christian community, which he had never visited, knew of and was in agreement with that idea (Rom. 8:14-19). Where did that idea come from? It is possible that Paul made it up, possible that the problem of the origin of the motif should be attributed to the hypothetical "primitive kerygma,"[5] but it is also possible that the identity of possessed persons as "Sons" twenty years after Jesus' death arose from the fact that those persons were modeling themselves on Jesus who, when possessed, was possessed by the spirit labeled the Son.

We know that the idea of people becoming able, through possession, to identify themselves as Son of God had arisen and become established in the Christian community within only a decade or two after Jesus' death. Further, the idea arose in the mind of somebody who had sufficient authority to make that usage normative; Romans 8 gives us reason to presume that this was not Paul himself. I argue, simply, that the idea is not roughly ten years older than the time of the writing of Galatians but roughly twenty years older than that time. In other words, Jesus was the authority who initiated that usage and it arose about twenty years before the writing of Galatians. This is not particularly difficult to accept from the historiographical viewpoint and the fact that it is of significance to theological Christology does not make it false!

This line of thought is supported by the fact that the Johannine sayings had to arise somewhere or other. To say, as some do, that they arose from the preaching of the Johannine community is simply to move the problem back a stage. Let us follow the problem back into that stage. It does not seem at all likely that Johannine preachers spoke, in the first person, Jesus' side of controversies in words they would have their audience believe Jesus had once spoken. No such preaching is otherwise known from the history of Christendom. No coherent *Sitzen im Leben* for the supposed Johannine preaching that resulted in the sayings of Jesus in John's Gospel have ever been advanced.[6] Much more

---

5 Liberal theologians speak disdainfully of a "God of the gaps" who serves to answer questions that science has not yet managed to answer. New Testament scholarship uses "the primitive kerygma" in a similar way. There may well have been such a thing, hut its explanatory value in and of itself is nil.

6 Rather than a coherent theory of the origin of the Johannine discourses, one finds in scholarship simple assertions such as that the discourse material arose from reflection and from preaching. This is not so much a theory that I can seek to refute as an

likely, Johannine preachers spoke in the voice of the Son in the sense of prophecy, i.e., it was supposedly not they who spoke but the spirit, or the Son.[7] But where did they get that idea, that those possessed by the spirit were able to identify themselves as Sons? They didn't get it from Paul, nor Paul from them. The idea probably arose from a common source. It can be argued that some Pauline Christians and some Johannine Christians were prophets who spoke in the spirit and so in the voice of the Son; that is the precise point made in Gal. 4:6-7 and Rom. 8:15-16. Where did they get the idea that this is an appropriate thing for a spirit-possessed follower of Jesus to do? Most probably these trajectories trace back to Jesus himself.

The most economic explanation for the practice of labeling the spirit as "Son" is that Jesus initiated the practice of doing so just as our evidence says or implies that he did. If we substitute Son for "I" in five presumably unquestionable assertions the spirit of God might make to identify itself we have, at last:

1. The Son comes from the Father.
2. The Son knows things of the Father.
3. The Son reveals what the Father wishes to have revealed.
4. The Son speaks the words of the Father.
5. The Son will return to the Father.

And, of course, we have here the fundamental principles reiterated by the Johannine sayings as well as Lk 10:22 // Mt 11:27. To progress from Jesus of Nazareth, who comes to be baptized repenting his sins, to "I (= spirit of God, = Son) come from the Father, I (= spirit of God, = Son) will return to the Father," one need only acknowledge the historicity of these things:

a. Jesus received the spirit of God at his baptism (understood through the anthropology and psychology of spirit-possession).
b. Subsequently Jesus sometimes spoke in the identity of the spirit.
c. The spirit would have had to identify itself, its origin, and its na-

---

axiom, an act of scholarly faith. Although the theory that the discourses are no more or less than literary fictions is not one I accept, it is coherent and such a procedure for the construction of first-person materials is otherwise attested in the corpus of gnostic writings.
7 Boring, Ibid.

ture to any new audience and the itinerancy of Jesus meant that such self-identification would have had to be done repeatedly.

d. Jesus labeled God "Father."

e. Jesus labeled God's spirit "Son" (or, more precisely, he labeled his alter-persona, identified as spirit, "Son").

Accordingly, when Jesus "rejoiced in the spirit" or, to put it more mundanely, spoke in the voice of the spirit, he may well have spoken in the fashion known to us through sayings preserved for the most part in the Gospel of John. He certainly spoke in some fashion or other that was distinguishable from his standard modes of speech.

All of this has been said in reference to third person self-referential "Son" sayings. First person self-referential "I" sayings by the voice of the spirit were doubtless even more common. "I come from the Father, I know the things of the Father," and so forth. There is no distance from sayings of this sort to self-referential spirit sayings such as "I (the spirit of God) am the way to God, I am the truth, I am the life, I am the light of the world, I and the Father are one."

The Language of the Spirit

It makes a considerable difference for my argument whether all the discourses in John's gospel were or were not composed in Greek. If so, then none of them were spoken by Jesus, who was a speaker of Aramaic. Rudolf Bultmann, although critical of attempts to show that John's gospel was translated in its entirety from Aramaic to Greek, did conclude that both the source behind the Prologue and also the Johannine discourses of Jesus were most probably translated from Aramaic into Greek.[8] Until recently that question has been discussed primarily from the perspective of scholars' personal intuitions based on their understanding of the structures of semitic languages and of Greek.

Most specialists confirm that it is at least theoretically and probably also practically possible to tell "translation Greek" texts—behind which lie semitic original texts—from texts written in Greek from the start. The Septuagint provides a wealth of texts known to be translation Greek. Raymond Martin has constructed a methodology for determining which documents and elements within documents are, and are not,

---

8 Bultmann, Rudolf, *The Gospel of John* (Philadelphia: Fortress, 1971), 18; cf. Burney, C. F., The Aramaic Origin of the Fourth Gospel (Oxford: Clarendon, 1922).

translated from semitic originals.[9] He uses sophisticated statistical tests, with controls both from original Greek texts and translation Greek texts, which reveal that on the whole the Gospel of John is probably a translation from a semitic language, although elements of it were written originally in Greek. He did not expect to find this; "this result was not anticipated and is in sharp contrast with the book of Acts and the Synoptic Gospels which do not show up as translations of entire Semitic documents, but rather only give evidence of Aramaic *sources* lying behind some of their smaller units of tradition."[10]

For our purposes it is particularly interesting that by his tests John's discourse material seems, on the whole, to be more evidently and demonstrably material translated from a semitic language than any other type of material in the gospel. By his criteria, chapters fourteen through seventeen (with the exception of 17:1-5) and such passages as 5:30-40, 8:39-59, 10:22-30, among others, are not probably but *certainly* derived from material, written or oral (he does not distinguish) that was first produced in a semitic language.[11]

Martin seeks to prove by detailed technical analysis what Bultmann intuited from experience and skill; much of John's discourse material was first written (and before that some of it was spoken) in Aramaic.

In the opinion of Matthew Black,

> An inspired "targumizing" of an Aramaic sayings tradition, early committed to a Greek form, is the most likely explanation of the Johannine speeches, but, in that case, it is no different in character from the literary process which gave us the Synoptic *verba Christi*. For the extent of this process of "transformation" we must await the results of further study, but in the light of

---

9 Martin, Raymond, *Syntax Criticism of Johannine Literature, the Catholic Epistles, and the Gospel Passion Accounts*, (Lewiston N.Y.: Edwin Mellen Press, 1989). Readers familiar with his earlier work will be interested to note that he includes in this volume an appendix discussing and defending his methodology in light of critical appraisals.
10 Ibid., 6; cf. Martin, Raymond, Syntax Criticism of the Synoptic Gospels (Lewiston N.Y.: Edwin Mellen Press, 1987).
11 Ibid., 10, 45, 172; "certainty of judgment that a document is translation Greek is claimed only for [those] texts of more than 50 lines in length showing net frequencies of -4 or lower" 172 (his emphasis). I cannot in this space discuss the syntactic frequencies to which he refers; suffice it to say that the net frequencies found for John 14-17 come in at -9. For a fuller explication of these matters one should, of course, turn to Martin's works on the subject.

recent work it would appear to be becoming a gradually diminishing area: the rabbinical character of the discourses and their predominantly poetic form certainly do not discourage the belief that much more of the *verba ipsissima* of Jesus may have been preserved in the Fourth Gospel—with John the Apostle as inspired "author"—than we have dared believe possible for many years.[12]

The likelihood that much of the Johannine sayings material was early and Aramaic in origin does not prove that it derives from Jesus himself. But my thesis that at least a fraction of it does is thereby given some support. If there were Aramaic originals of several Johannine sayings that were first targumized and then put through the processes of editorial revision Raymond Brown and others discern beneath the text of our present edition of John's gospel—then those Aramaic originals were certainly of a very considerably earlier date than John's gospel.[13]

John's sayings demonstrate that there was at least one Jewish person recorded in the first century, a Palestinian speaker of Aramaic who, when possessed and speaking as the spirit, identified himself as Son. But we do know of a Jewish person in the first century, a Palestinian speaker of Aramaic, of whom it is claimed that he spoke of himself as Son: Jesus. It is a very odd hypothesis to ignore the evidence of our sources that Jesus spoke as Son and spirit, and thus to postulate that it was always the case that others, some of whom were Jewish Palestinian Aramaic speakers living at roughly the same time, who similarly spoke in a state of possession by the spirit, did say, e.g., "I come from the Father," and that, for reasons we do not know, within decades such speech became normative in Paul's and John's Christian communities. By far the simplest hypothesis is that Jesus spoke sometimes as Son and also in the first person as God's spirit. Subsequently the substance and style of his practice became standard in some of the communities his adherents founded.

---

12 Black, Matthew, *An Aramaic Approach to the Gospels and Acts*, Third Edition (Oxford: Clarendon Press, 1967), 151.
13 Brown, Raymond, *The Gospel According to John: Two Volumes* (New York: Doubleday, 1966, 1970).

Jesus said—Spirit said

Sometimes a point is so obvious that it becomes lost in the ever-growing library of scholarly theory and speculation. An affirmation that the historical Jesus said such things as "I and the Father are one," or "I come from the Father and I will return to the Father," may seem at this stage of scholarship to be little more than a statement of personal faith by anyone making that assertion. This is to lose sight of the obvious point: near contemporaries of Jesus of Nazareth contend, in no uncertain terms, that he did in fact say that sort of thing during his lifetime: QLuke 10:22, QMatthew 11:26-27, Mark 13:32, Thomas 28a, 77a,[14] and the Gospel of John throughout. The question then is not whether there is any evidence to support the view that Jesus did sometimes speak in the voice of the spirit, but whether or not elements of the body of evidence *that contend he did exactly that* should or should not be considered reliable.

The perspective that this evidence is not reliable in its depiction of a style of Jesus' speech is standard in scholarship. It derives from two supposed facts. First, due to their difference in style and content it is agreed that the Johannine style of Jesus' sayings and the synoptic style of Jesus' sayings were spoken by different persons. Second, the identification of Jesus of Nazareth with God's spirit is said to reflect a "high incarnationalist" Christian theology and so to be a later development of the Christian movement.

Both of these pillars rest on the seemingly commonsense foundation that Jesus of Nazareth was a human being who spoke, as most human beings do, with his own voice to convey his own convictions. That common sense does not always apply here; it is applicable to the worldview of contemporary scholars, but it is not applicable to the presuppositions of the myriad cultures and persons who accept the possibility of spirit-possession, and it is not applicable to the prophets of Judaism.[15] By its very definition, spirit-possession is a state where a

---

14 Thomas 28a: Jesus said, "I stood in the midst of the world, and I appeared to them in the flesh. I found all of them drunk; I did not find any of them thirsting." Thomas 77a: Jesus said, "I am the light that is above all things. I am all things. All things came forth from me and all things extended to me."
15 Cf. Geertz, Clifford, "Common Sense as a Cultural System," in his *Local Knowledge: Further Essays in Interpretive Anthropology* (New York: Basic Books, 1983), 73-93.

voice that normally speaks from the persona of a human, e.g., Jesus of Nazareth, can alternatively speak from the persona of a divinity, e.g., the spirit of God. The speech forms of the two personae should differ in tone or style or diction. The speech content of the latter persona, in this case the spirit of God, will be referential to the nature and knowledge and intentions of the spirit of God. It follows, then, that the synoptic speech style of Jesus of Nazareth and the Johannine speech style of the spirit of God could both have been utilized by Jesus. This point is substantiated by the scholars who contend that Johannine speech elements were uttered by Christian "prophets." They spoke as prophets in one way, identifying themselves with the spirit (or the spirit of the "risen Jesus"); when at home or in the marketplace they spoke in quite different ways. If some of their comments in the marketplace on current topics of interest had been recorded they would seem to us to be the speech of other individuals altogether. What is true for such Christian prophets and, for that matter, prophets in the Hebrew Bible, is also true for Jesus. As I have been at pains to emphasize, Jesus himself spoke as a prophet. A case in point is the clear separation by early Muslims of God's revelations through the prophet Mohammed, the Quran, from the recorded sayings of Mohammed himself, the Hadith.

I regret that I cannot continue to the end of this line of thought. While I am rather confident that it is possible to construct a list of spirit-referential sayings that are most probably from Jesus, just as John Dominic Crossan constructed a list of the sayings of Jesus of Nazareth of the synoptic type that are most probably authentic, I do not have in hand a methodology to do that for the Johannine style sayings. Martin's methodology can only give us good reasons to exclude some material in John's gospel on the grounds that it was written originally in Greek. Still, the discovery of Jesus' own "Johannine" sayings, or at least the establishment of a set of affirmations he most probably made that subsequently led to prophetic Johannine imitations, should be technically possible.

In respect to the first-person spirit utterances (and to the Son self-references) of later Christian prophets the thesis: Jesus did that, thus they did that, is the simplest hypothesis. The alternative is that all of Jesus' spirit-possession utterances were lost and, at a slightly later date, they (we know not who) spoke in a Johannine way (for obscure reasons) and they then retrojected their novel practice back onto Jesus.

This creates a set of unnecessary complications. Most probably the origin of that set of complications is the ubiquitous notion that the proposition "Jesus is the Son of God" arose as an intellectual *belief* an ideological *construct,* a consciously worked-out *theory* of theological Christology. It was originally no such thing; it was an assertion of an alter-persona identity of the sort that is always a necessary element of spirit-possession.

I concur with the nearly unanimous judgment of scholarship that the idea, belief, ideology that Jesus of Nazareth was himself, from birth, by his own nature the Son of God is a development of early Christian speculation. That is a different proposition from the proposition that a person possessed by the spirit of God might declare himself to be Son of God simply by substituting the word *Son* for the word *spirit.* This, I conclude from the various lines of evidence given above, is what Jesus did and it is what John certainly and Matthew, Mark, Luke, and Q occasionally say or imply he did.

The rise of the high Christology that identifies Jesus of Nazareth (i.e., his primary persona) with the Son of God is surprisingly easily explicable. All that had to happen is that introductory "Jesus said" clauses prefacing prophetically uttered spirit or Son self-affirmations be taken to mean what they manifestly *seem* to say, that the self-affirmations refer to Jesus himself and not to the spirit of God.

The fact that Jesus said things that were spirit of God referential at times when he was not to be understood to be Jesus of Nazareth speaking but, rather, the spirit of God speaking seems quickly to have been forgotten. It survives only in Q's "He rejoiced in the spirit and said. . . ." The problem of reference is implicit in the utterances of Hebrew Bible prophets as well, and a solution was found that Christians rarely adopted. In some of the books of the Hebrew Bible prophets we find a device used to avoid identification of the prophet with the voice speaking through him: "thus saith the Lord." The early Christian tradition did not use this device, with the consequence that high Christology arose.

Jesus was possessed by the spirit of God, not by the Father. This is a system of single mediation. The human persona is not the spirit of God and the spirit of God persona is not synonymous with God. Systems of possession that postulate a mediating spirit (or angel) correlate with monotheistic theologies. Single mediation possession systems will separate first the possessed human and, second, the supposed possessing entity from identification with the One God Himself.

The often attested passage "He who receives any one whom I send receives me; and he who receives me receives him who sent me" (Jn. 13:20, QMt. 10:40, QLk. 10:16, cf. Mk. 9:37, Jn. 12:4445) may not refer to Jesus of Nazareth's relationship to his followers in the sense of agency. Rather, it may refer to the spirit's relationship to possessed Christians.[16] One who receives a person whom the spirit sends receives the spirit; one who receives the spirit of God receives God. To receive a person possessed by the spirit of God is not to receive the spirit's representative, it is to receive the persona spirit itself; that is a fundamental principal of spirit-possession in any culture.

The pronoun structure of ordinary grammar is really not set up to handle circumstances wherein the normal persona does not speak but a second supernatural persona speaks, and the words of a third supernatural mind are heard! However, that is what is happening according to sentences of the Gospel of John. There are several instances in John where the spirit persona distances itself from its own utterances. Johannine Christology emerges from these as soon as the ascription of the utterances is to the persona of Jesus of Nazareth himself. But, as I argue, the original ascription of the utterances was to the spirit of God.[17] To exemplify the point I am trying to make, I will shift the ascription:

5:30. The spirit of God said, "I can do nothing by myself; I can only judge as I am told to judge, and my judging is just, because my aim is to do not my own will, but the will of him who sent me."

7:16. The spirit of God said, "My teaching is not from myself; it comes from the one who sent me; and if anyone is prepared to do his will, he will know whether my teaching is from God or whether my doctrine is my own."

14:24. The spirit of God said, "My word is not my own, it is the word of the one who sent me."

The "I" of these passages is *not* that of a primary persona but the "I" of an alternate persona. That is the point such passages make over and over again. To acknowledge the truth of the statements is to acknowledge that a person is in an altered state and (simultaneously) that the

---

16 If the saying is "authentic," as its multiple attestation indicates it is, then the one who is sent is Jesus himself speaking in the voice of the spirit.

17 Whether or not this was normally labeled "Paraclete" in Johannine usage and, if so, why, is not significant to this line of reasoning.

altered state is the spirit come from the Father. An "I" is subordinated or superseded by another "I," so what "I" have said "does not come from myself." From a perspective outside the social paradigms of the premodern world, the "I that is not myself" is an alternative persona (by definition) to be understood in light of the psychological and anthropological discussions of possession-trance states discussed earlier.

Conclusion

Some readers may suspect that this is all just speculation. It is not. I am presenting an interpretation and defense of the historicity of at least some of the elements of a considerable body of first-century textual evidence. I argue from the perspective that conceiving Jesus to have been a spirit-possessed prophet renders that evidence more comprehensible than does any other mode of approach. I must acknowledge with regret that I do not know how to construct a methodology to separate the specific units of Johannine-style sayings that can be reliably attributed to Jesus from units spoken by Christian prophets who believed that Jesus' own words were recalled to them by the spirit (cf. John 14:26). Their supposed imitation of Jesus' spirit discourse does, however, provide support for the thesis that Jesus did indeed use that style of discourse, even if little of it is preserved for us.

My line of reasoning leads to interesting consequences. For example, the historical Jesus, speaking in the voice of the spirit, may well have said such things as "I and the Father are one." If the spirit of God and God are one, and the spirit of God speaks of itself through a human voice, that is the sort of thing it might well say; it is a commonsense assertion grounded in unexceptionable Jewish theory. Place a "Jesus said of himself" presumption in front of that utterance and you have Johannine Christology. *All it takes to move from early first-century Palestinian Judaism to high Christology is a simple shift in the concept of reference vis-à-vis a certain set of Jesus' sayings.* To shift from "the spirit of God said this," to "Jesus said this" is enough.

The nearly universal opinion of scholarship in Jesus research is that Jesus never said what John affirms Jesus said except in the few instances where John is apparently revising a synoptic saying.[18] The reason for

---

18 An admixture of the phraseology of the persona Jesus of Nazareth with the utterances of an alter persona spirit of God is to be expected.

this is a simple one; it is evident from style and content that whoever it was who spoke the parables and proverbs and enigmas attributable to Jesus from synoptic sources, a different person spoke the Johannine discourse sayings. As I have tried to show, and as anthropological reports attest by the hundreds, there is such a thing as one person having two different psychologically and socially defined personae. We have reliable historical evidence that Jesus was such a person. The hypothesis of spirit-possession gives us a Jesus of Nazareth who spoke one way (in the synoptic style) and a Jesus possessed by God's spirit who *necessarily* spoke another way. The scholarly consensus that Jesus of Nazareth did not say "I have come from the Father and I will return to the Father" is quite reliable, but those words may well have come out of Jesus' mouth when, to paraphrase Mark 13:11, "it was not Jesus of Nazareth who spoke but the spirit."

I realize that this thesis will sound far-fetched to some, but I urge them to reflect upon the fact that it is a thesis with both explanatory value and textual evidence in its support.

It is generally assumed that Johannine Christianity was a comparatively late development within the first-century Christian movement. Yet a fundamental principle of the Johannine circle, that Jesus and the spirit of God can be identified and considered fundamentally synonymous, may have arisen quite early.[19] While this principle is not entailed in the practice of prophetic spirit-possession, it can easily be understood to have arisen from that practice. It could not have arisen easily if Jesus was a rabbi, a cynic philosopher, a social critic, etc.

If some of the Gospel of John's special sayings are "authentic," i.e., spoken by Jesus, yet do not appear in the synoptic tradition, there necessarily must have been a decoupling of the two sayings styles early in the development of Christianity. The separation by Jesus' own followers of his synoptic-style sayings from his Johannine-style sayings does logically follow from the presumption that the former were spoken by Jesus of Nazareth and the latter by the spirit of God through Jesus' mouth. The principles of spirit-possession would naturally lead to the collection of the sayings of Jesus' supposedly supernatural persona that would be recognizably different from collections of the sayings of Je-

---

19 The theory presented here supports, but does not confirm, John A.T. Robinson's thesis that John's gospel should be dated considerably more early than it usually is; cf. *The Priority of John* (Oak Park III: Meyer-Stone, 1987).

sus of Nazareth himself. The books of Jewish prophets and the collections of pagan oracles are examples of compilations of the former type. On the history of traditions level there certainly should have been two different forms of sayings traditions, the one synoptic and the other perhaps Johannine, the one from Jesus of Nazareth, the other from the spirit of God spoken through Jesus. If the sayings in the latter collection were introduced by "Jesus said," a practice used throughout the Gospel of Thomas, then one can see clearly how high Christology might have arisen.

The mists of history hide the process by which there came to be Christian communities with very different perspectives about the nature of Jesus. When they are lifted we find two principal schools of thought. The sayings of Jesus of Nazareth, the synoptic style of sayings, were incorporated into the texts of the authors who considered Jesus to have been one who suffered, died, and rose again, one who taught his disciples either as a principal task (e.g., Matthew) or as an incidental practice (e.g., Mark). The recorded traditions of the sayings of the spirit of God were retained by the Johannine school, where Christian prophets probably continued to speak in the self-referential voice of the spirit, and where Jesus was identified with the spirit of God. It is possible that both traditions could have traced their origin to Jesus with equal validity.

Jesus and his associates believed that a persona known to them as the spirit or Son of God alternated with Jesus' primary persona, and they believed that it originated externally to Jesus' own mind. But I am assuming it arose from within him. This brings into question the "reality" of a spirit-persona. One who adopts a normative realist perspective will assert that unless a spirit-persona exists externally to the mind it possesses, then it is not a reality at all but a mental condition. A perspective conditioned by idealism will answer that a mental condition, in this case a functioning personality, is itself a reality, an alter-persona is just as "real" as a primary persona. An argument that a primary persona is a reality while a possession persona is not a reality may not be philosophically coherent. So, if an alter-persona is understood to be "spirit" the reality of "spirit" is of the same order as the reality of a human person.

This whole line of thought leads to a historical Jesus who not only claimed to be the Son of God, but who really was the Son of God (depending on the philosophical perspective one takes toward the reality of an alter-persona). The New Testament evidence is reliable that he was taken to be the spirit or Son of God by at least some of the peasant Jewish people to whom he spoke. And this, in turn, nicely explains how Jesus was an effective healer and exorcist.

12

THE CHRISTIAN CULT

According to John Meier, Jesus died on April 7, 30 C. E.[1] All the gospels report that some of Jesus' associates were present in Jerusalem at the time; others may have fled. Their group organization had been shattered by the death of their focal leader; their own lives were perhaps in judicial jeopardy as followers of a supposed anti-Roman activist, or so the story of Peter's triple denial testifies. They no longer had access to a man who became possessed by God's spirit. Jesus' unique talent for inductive discourse about the kingdom of God was no longer at their service. For many of these people the choice of giving up and going home was not available; bridges had been burned.

A Christianity premised on the induced emergence of the religious trance state "kingdom of God" would have inevitably declined in the absence of the talented inducer of that state. However, a Christianity premised on the reception of an alternative persona state of possession might have prospered. In most of the world's cultures a spirit-possession state, when expected, can be brought about fairly easily in a cultic setting. Cult organization based on nonpossession trance experiences are rare (in the Western world) and usually require single-minded dedication and self-discipline on the part of adherents: Hindu and Buddhist meditation-trance groups are examples. Cult organizations based

---

[1] Meier does not give this as an established fact but as the most likely date. *Marginal Jew*, 402.

on possession trance are quite common (both in the Western world and elsewhere). Drawn primarily from the lower socioeconomic orders of society, their members usually live conventional familial and occupational lives outside of the cult environment.

It is historical *bedrock* that the first Christians formed a cult oriented to experience of the spirit. In the words of C. K. Barrett, *"No more certain statement can be made* about the Christians of the first generation than this: they believed themselves to be living under the immediate government of the Spirit of God."[2] What occurred to Jesus' followers after his death is practically predictable; it certainly is explicable. This group, some of whom, probably most of whom, were prone to dissociative experiences continued to experience dissociation but in, for them, a novel form. Under conditions of social stress arising from factors both external to and internal to their social group (their surrogate family), they spontaneously became spirit-possessed and from that point on formed themselves into a missionary spirit-possession cult. When I consult scholarship on "the social world" of formative Christianity, however, I find no discussion of the role of spirit-possession at all. I am as baffled by this as if I were to discover that scholarship on Afro-Catholic religions (e.g., Santeria, Vodou, Macumba) had managed to overlook altogether the fact that the central and defining feature of those religions is that adherents either become possessed themselves or interact with those who do.

The Pentecost Experience

The foundational event of the Christian religion was the mass spirit-possession of Jesus' followers (just as Jesus' own initial possession experience, at his baptism, was the foundational event of his career). Thanks to Luke we call this foundational event Pentecost.[3]

> When the time of Pentecost was fulfilled, they were all in one place together. And suddenly there came from the sky a noise like a strong driving wind, and it filled the entire house in which they were. Then there appeared to them tongues as of fire, which parted and came to rest on each one of them. And

---

2 Barrett, *Holy Spirit and the Gospel Tradition*, 1 (emphasis added).
3 Whether it happened on the specific day "Pentecost" we cannot know for certain, but there is no particular reason to deny it.

they were all filled with the holy Spirit and began to speak in different tongues, as the Spirit enabled them to proclaim." (Acts 2:1-4)

John reports that on the sabbath after Jesus' death

> The disciples rejoiced when they saw the Lord. Jesus said to them again, "Peace be with you. As the Father has sent me, so I send you." And when he had said this, he breathed on them and said to them, *"Receive the holy Spirit.* Whose sins you forgive are forgiven them, and whose sins you retain are not forgiven." (20:19-23)

The two accounts are, of course, entirely different in detail. But on a higher level of generality, they agree. Within weeks of Jesus' death his followers received the spirit.

For Luke and for Paul and for John, receiving the spirit is the sine qua non requirement for membership in the Christian movement.[4] Luke writes in regard to Samaritans who heard apostles favorably that

> When the apostles at Jerusalem heard that Samaria had received the word of God, they sent to them Peter and John, who came down and prayed for them that they might receive the Holy Spirit; for it had not yet fallen on any of them, but they had only been baptized in the name of the Lord Jesus. Then *they laid their hands on them and they received the Holy Spirit.* (Acts 8:14-17)

Here the initiation ceremony of baptism in Jesus' name precedes reception of the Holy Spirit. But Luke relates that in Caesarea, as Peter spoke,

> the Holy Spirit fell on all who heard the word. And the believers from among the circumcised who came with Peter were amazed, because the gift of *the Holy Spirit had been poured out even on the gentiles. For they heard them speaking in tongues and*

---

4 Mark (13:11) takes it completely for granted that Christians may be spirit-possessed, as does Matthew (10:20). The author of the First Letter of John takes it for granted that all Christians are possessed by the spirit; his Christian opponents too are possessed, but supposedly by a false spirit.

> *extolling God.* Then Peter declared, "Can any one forbid water for baptizing these people who have received the Holy Spirit just as we have?" And he commanded them to be baptized in the name of Jesus Christ. (Acts 10:44-48)

And so, here, the experience of the spirit precedes initiation by baptism. We hear of the arrival in Ephesus of Apollos of Alexandria who

> had been instructed in the way of the Lord; and being fervent in [his own] spirit he spoke and taught accurately the things concerning Jesus, though he knew only the baptism of John. . . . He powerfully confuted the Jews in public, showing by the scriptures that the Christ was Jesus. (Acts 18:25, 27-28)

And Luke tells us that Paul then came to Ephesus, found disciples there, and asked them

> "Did you receive the Holy Spirit when you believed?" And they said, "No, we have never even heard that there is a Holy Spirit." And he said, "Into what then were you baptized?" They said, "Into John's baptism. And Paul said, "John baptized with the baptism of repentance, telling the people to believe in the one who was to come after him, that is, Jesus." On hearing this, they were baptized in the name of the Lord Jesus. And when Paul had laid his hands upon them, *the Holy Spirit came on them; and they spoke with tongues and prophesied.* (Acts 19:2-6)

From this it is clear that believing, accurate knowledge of the way of the Lord, knowledge of Christian midrash, and so forth are not sufficient for full membership in the Christian movement, at least as Luke understands the matter. One *must,* before or after baptism, experience the Holy Spirit. Accordingly, the single most important element, the defining factor, in being a member of the Christian movement is to have received the Holy Spirit; without that even one who has belief, knowledge, missionary zeal, remains outside.

Whether there should be any distinction drawn between spirit-possession and speaking in tongues is debatable. Paul certainly did not make any such distinction (Rom 8:14-16, Gal 4:6-7). Even if the two states are distinguishable they are certainly of the same dissociative type. John Kildahl, who has analyzed contemporary glossolalia from a psychological perspective, writes:

> The deep subordination to an authority figure required for learning to speak in tongues involves a type of speech regression. The ego is partially abandoned; that is, the ego ceases its conscious direction of speech. Subordination also involves emotional regression; without it there cannot be the unconscious, automatic, and fluent selection of audible syllables which constitutes glossolalia.[5]

I do not intend to use Luke's own opinion of the nature of holy spirit's influences on human behavior as determinative for the situation in the years from 30 to 60 C.E. when Christianity formed. It seems to me very clear that Luke wrote during a time when the initial spirit-possession phenomena of formative Christianity were beginning to die down and the theory that has been with us ever since, that the spirit is an "inspiration," a useful additive to individuals' primary-persona activities, began to arise. And this historical sequence is to be expected.

Luke and the Rise of Spirit "Inspiration"

Luke wrote at least sixty years after Pentecost and perhaps closer to a century after that event. Scholarship on the subject presently vacillates between a late first century and an early second-century date for Luke's writings. The spirit-possession cult of formative Christianity probably lasted only for one or perhaps two generations. I. M. Lewis concludes that

> If certain exotic religions thus allow ecstasy to rule most aspects of their adherents' lives, all the evidence indicates that the more strongly-based and entrenched religious authority becomes, the more hostile it is towards haphazard inspiration. New faiths may announce their advent with a flourish of ecstatic revelations, but once they become securely established they have little time or tolerance for enthusiasm. For the religious enthusiast, with his direct claim to divine knowledge, is always a threat to the established order. What then are the fac-

---

5 Kildahl, *The Psychology of Speaking in Tongues*, 52.

tors which inhibit the growth of this attitude towards ecstacy . . . ? The empirical evidence, which we review, suggests that part at least of the answer lies in acute and constantly recurring social and environmental pressures which militate against the formation of large, secure social groups.[6]

Although the early Christian movement certainly had its troubles and difficulties, by the beginning of the second century there appear to have been stable Christian communities scattered throughout the Roman empire. The occasional persecution of Christianity by Roman authorities offers no evidence of the acute social pressures that would have facilitated retention of spirit-possession activity but the opposite; Christianity's success in forming large secure social groups was so great that their society, their religion, was conceived to be a threat to the empire itself.

Study of Massachusetts Puritanism, Wesleyanism, the Quaker movement, and so forth, will show that over a few generations such initially ecstatic movements can gain elite adherents, seek social respectability, bring about the upgrading of members' socioeconomic status (through mutual assistance and self-discipline), develop patterns of institutionalized group leadership, revise entry requirements to focus on adherence to doctrinal and moral norms, and allow for "birthright" membership. These social changes, in practically all cases, bring about a decline in focus on psychophysiological possession experiences and can rather quickly lead to the marginalization of the spirit-possessed prophets and "ecstatics" who formed the group's initial membership.

The *Didache is* a text that gives instruction on how a Christian community should treat itinerant Christian prophets. It was written sometime in the late first or early second century and gives good evidence for a structured church's shift in orientation away from spirit-possession. The *Didache* is written from the view point of a community leadership that distrusts, and yet respects, Christian prophets, one that wishes the prophets to leave town as quickly as possible, yet would have them welcomed in town when they arrive. The Pastoral and Petrine epistles stem from a slightly later time, when authority in the Christian movement was based on the prerogatives of office rather than on prophetic

---

6 Lewis, *Ecstatic Religion*, 29.

powers.

Luke believes that the spirit inspires people to speak well (Acts 4:8), and boldly (4:31), that the spirit is akin to wisdom (6:3,10), that it grants visions (7:55), and predicts things (11:28, 21:11), that it tells people to do things and go places (11:12, 13:2, 13:4, 19:21) and not to do things and go places (16:6-7, 21:4). But the concepts of the activities of the spirit one finds in Acts are, by and large, more of the nature of spirit inspiration than of spirit-possession. In other words, there is indeed communication between an alter-persona labeled spirit and a primary persona, but in Luke's opinion, the latter is not replaced by the former.[7] When one hears of speaking in tongues, one hears of a spirit-possession phenomenon. But even as Luke's own account moves from ca. 30 to ca. 60 C.E., one hears less and less of that sort of thing, in fact less and less of the spirit. Luke's focus on the importance of the spirit in the first chapters of his book, and decline in attention to the spirit in the latter chapters, is probably indicative of accurate historical insight.

Spirit-related phenomena did decline rapidly, and predictably, through the first decades of Christianity. The novelty wore off, the initial members grew older, the intracult social circumstances changed. The historian Luke is not a representative of a spirit-possession cult, he and his Christianity are a few decades removed from that. But in the first chapters of Acts, Luke does report on a spirit-possession cult, one enrolling Jesus' own associates as members. Presumably he does so as best he can within the limitations of his own later perspective.

Paul the Apostle

We can move at least forty, maybe closer to one hundred, years back in time from Luke to a much better, first person, on-the-scene witness. Paul too believed that without the experience of the Holy Spirit a person was simply not a Christian at all; for him, too, spirit-possession was the sine qua non. And Paul was there.

He insists that spirit-possession is the determining factor of mem-

---

[7] An interesting essay on the subject of Luke's theory of the spirit is that of Max 'Rimer, "The Spirit of Prophecy and the Power of Authoritative Preaching in Luke-Acts: A Question of Origins," *New Testament Studies*, Vol. 38, 1992: 66-88. He categorizes and comments on Luke's particular perspectives quite well, but his presupposition that there is a *typically Jewish* (his emphasis) notion of the Spirit of prophecy, one that he observes is not that of Josephus or Philo, weakens his study.

bership in the Christian movement. It is the defining Christian experience; without possession, one is outside the movement altogether. In Romans Paul makes this absolutely clear: "Whoever does not have the Spirit of Christ does not belong to him" (Rom. 8:9). Of his own so-called conversion experience Paul writes that God "was pleased to reveal his Son *in* me" (Gal. 1:2). Henceforth, apparently, Paul could affirm that "it is not I who live, but Christ who lives in me" (Gal. 2:20). Though a genius, Paul is not a solitary figure cut off from those who are Christians with him. Paul wrote Romans to a church he did not found and had not yet visited, but he assumes his audience is entirely in agreement that the spirit is crucial to Christian life.

In none of Paul's conflicts with his Christian opponents does he ever accuse them of lacking the spirit of Christ. From his perspective, and the perspective of his congregations, that would have been a devastating accusation. Even in Galatians he does not argue that he and his Galatian Christians have the spirit, while his opponents do not. Rather, he argues that his opponents' insistence that Christians follow Torah will not cause spirit-possession, while faith in his discourse will. In the course of that argument he makes it clear that the initial experience of Christians is possession (3:2-4). In Second Corinthians he objects to other apostles who too dramatically demonstrate their "gifts of the spirit." The idea that spirit-possession is a crucial factor in Christian life is not Paul's invention; he assumes he shares that idea with all other Christians.

Paul writes in Romans 8:9-14 that:

> For you are not in the flesh, you are in the Spirit, *if the Spirit of God really dwells in you.* Any one who does not have the Spirit of Christ does not belong to him. But *if Christ is in you,* although your bodies are dead because of sin, your spirits are alive because of righteousness. If *the Spirit of him who raised Jesus from the dead dwells in you,* he who raised Christ Jesus from the dead will give life to your mortal bodies also *through his Spirit which dwells in you.*

The equation of the Spirit of God and the Spirit of Christ is to be found also in John's Gospel where there seems to be no essential difference between the spirit-Paraclete and Jesus. But it is by no means immediately obvious that the spirit of an executed Palestinian healer and the Spirit of God are the same thing!

In the ancient world, indeed, throughout the world, it was and is believed that the spirits of human beings who were executed or who otherwise died violent, inappropriate, untimely deaths might possess the living. We know, of course, that in Judaism the idea of a prophet often entailed a human being possessed by the spirit of God. Given that Jesus was a human being possessed by the spirit of God, then Jesus had two personae, one of Jesus of Nazareth, one of the spirit of God. The second persona, then, was simultaneously Jesus Christ (Jesus anointed) and the spirit of God, and it was by that alter-persona that Christians believed themselves possessed. Accordingly, the motifs of the spirit of the executed man and the spirit of God do come together in Christian theory. And the convergence of those two in that later theory arises from and supports the contention that Jesus was regarded as the spirit-possessed son of God during his lifetime.

Christian interpretations of spirit-possession, arising from a monotheistic religious base, insisted that there was only one spirit. The one spirit supposedly manifested both demonstrable and non-demonstrable qualities. By demonstrable qualities I mean the sort of things Paul lists in 1 Cor. 12:8-11: wisdom, knowledge, faith, power to heal, power to do mighty deeds, prophecy, discernment of spirits, glossolalia, interpretation of glossolalia. These are demonstrable because they are experienced by an individual or by the group. Nondemonstrable qualities are ideological assumptions made about the consequences of the possession state, e.g., that individuals are saved, made righteous, granted eternal life.

If the demonstrable qualities of the possessing spirit are distributed variously, as Paul concedes, the nondemonstrable qualities such as "righteousness" or "eternal life" are the same for all. Insofar as it is affirmed that the spirit of God is justified, immortal, without sin, which undoubtedly was universally affirmed, it could also be affirmed that those whose persona identities are transformed into the persona-identity of the spirit by possession will be justified, immortal, and without sin.

There are two evidentiary loops at work here. First, if Paul could induce possession through his oral gospel then when that induction was effective and individuals experienced dissociative spirit-possession, his gospel's assertions would be validated. The truth of the gospel was demonstrated by its experiential effectiveness. Second, the demonstrable manifestations of spirit power would provide evidence for the truth of the asserted nondemonstrable manifestations. Thus, for example, power to heal, or to utter prophetic speech, or to produce glossolalia would confirm in the minds of the group that they were justified and that they would not spiritually die.

Social Roles

In literature on Paul one sometimes finds the strange notion that he is somehow opposed to such "ecstatic" phenomena as prophecy and glossolalia, and is opposed to a group some scholars label the "Corinthian ecstatics." This is almost nonsense. Paul writes to the Corinthians "I thank God that I speak in tongues more than you all" (1 Cor. 14:18), and commands that they "earnestly desire to prophesy, and do not forbid speaking in tongues" (1 Cor. 14:39) just as he had instructed his Thessalonian Christians "do not quench the Spirit, do not despise prophesying" (1 Thess. 3:19-20). Paul created a series of local spirit-possession cults where such phenomena were conditions for entry and proofs of salvation and he was proud of it, numbering himself among the most fervent experiencers of possession's effects. But, for good and comprehensible reasons, he does indeed wish that prophets and tongues speakers would restrain themselves within the context of community meetings (1 Cor. 12:2-14:40). Any survey of anthropological reports of spirit-possession cults will reveal that there are conditions and controls in place to render participants' experiences useful for the benefit of other members of the group. Spirit-possession is a social phenomenon and its use within the cultic society is of paramount importance; this is not just a Pauline principle, it is a universal principle within established possession cults.

Paul's community was evidently composed of people who enacted community leadership roles in accordance with what they took their possession experience to be. He writes, "Within our community God has appointed, in the first place apostles, in the second place prophets, thirdly teachers, then miracle-workers, then those who have gifts of healing, or ability to help others or power to guide them, or the gift of ecstatic utterance of various kinds" (1 Cor. 12:28). Prophecy and ecstatic utterance are possession phenomena practically by definition. Healing, the power to guide others, and so forth are tasks spirit-possessed persons have in nearly all the possession cults known cross-culturally. Only the "apostle" role might be uniquely Christian.

Within the bounds of the community, the members could enact social roles of supernatural importance. Studies of spirit-possession groups in the present day frequently remark on the fact that through possession-experience, and possession induced role enactments, people of low or marginal social positions are able temporarily to experience very high status within their groups. This is often one of the principal motivating factors for the successful recruitment of members into those groups.[8] Bourguignon writes of possession experience in Haitian society that

> discontinuity in personal identity, the temporary substitution of other "selves" in the context of a belief in ritual possession by spirits, cannot be considered deviant in the reference system of Haitian culture. While such discontinuity surely does not represent the statistical norm, it does represent the opportunity for acting out certain positively evaluated social roles, and does provide the individual with a wider field for social action and social effectiveness. It lends the individual support for varieties of actions and enhances his self-esteem.[9]

She argues that "ritualized dissociation provides the self with an alternate set of roles, in addition to his everyday inventory of roles, in which unfulfilled desires, 'unrealistic' in the context of the workaday world, get a second chance at fulfillment, a fulfillment which is surely not merely vicarious because the glory goes to the possessing spirit."[10] Paul's Christianity, and doubtless other forms, offered Christians both possession-related social roles (prophet, teacher, miracle worker, healer, etc.) and, at the same time, elevated supernatural identities (Christ, Son of God, heir of God, etc.). Bourguignon writes that

> Possession trance offers alternative roles, which satisfy certain

---
8 Lewis, *Ecstatic Religion*, passim.
9 Bourguignon, Erika, "The Self, the Behavioral Environment, and the Theory Of Spirit Possession," 56.
10 Ibid., 57.

individual needs, and it does so by providing the alibi that the behavior is that of spirits and not of the human beings themselves. And furthermore, *in order for human beings to play such assertive roles, they must be totally passive*, giving over their bodies to what are ego-alien forces. In a hierarchical society, demanding submission to those in authority, one acquires authority by identification with symbols of powers, identification which goes as far as *the total assumption of the other's identity, total loss of one's own*. In this authoritarian society, *it is possible to act out dominance fantasies by pretending, to self as well as others, total passivity and subjection.*"[11]

Paul emphasizes the shift of social self-definition that takes place in possession when he writes "to prove that you are sons, God sent the spirit of his son, crying 'Abba! Father!' You are therefore no longer a slave but a son, and if a son, then also by God's own act an heir" (Gal 4:6-7). Similarly, from Rom. 8:15-16, "All who are led by the Spirit of God are sons of God. For you did not receive the spirit of slavery to fall back into fear, but you have received the spirit of sonship. When we cry, 'Abba! Father!' it is the Spirit himself bearing witness with our spirit that we are children of God."[12] Those who find in these accounts solid supporting evidence of Jesus' own use of the word "Abba" for "father" may wish to reflect on the following observation by William Samarin:

> We have seen that although glossolalia seems to come easily to some people, others—by their own report—begin speaking tongues by stammering, babbling, or uttering syllables repetitiously. One man reported that his first words were ab, ab, abba, abba; another, that his first utterance consisted of "only two words or sounds." So common is "abortive" glossolalia (statements about it are made by writers in the beginning of this century), that some people make a distinction between what they call "evidential glossolalia" that reveals the arrival of the Holy Spirit and fluent glossolalia that is used as a means of

---

11 Bourguignon, *Possession*, 40 (emphasis added).
12 Readers should be reminded that the distinctions in capitalization for "son" and "Son" are not in the original Greek but are translators' interpretations.

grace.[13]

In a similar report, Kildahl tells of a man earnestly desiring to speak in tongues who hears that he is to say whatever

> "the Lord gives you to say, and I will move your mouth." Abadaba abadaba abadaba rahbadaba rmanama . . . and the syllables started to come smoothly. Tears flowed down his cheeks as strange words issued from his mouth. He was speaking in tongues.[14]

Paul tells us that by receiving the spirit of the Son individuals become that by which they are possessed and become Sons of God. There is here, to say the least, a considerable elevation in social status for those who may regard themselves as Sons and heirs of God. These claims for elevations in status, and such assertions as Paul's "Not I live but Christ lives in me" (Gal. 2:20) are, in Bourguignon's terms, "dominance fantasies."

Her conclusions might lead one to reflect on Mark's central section: 8:27-10:45 where the issue of power and authority in the Christian movement is repeatedly raised only, paradoxically, to be answered by the principle that authority comes from passivity and subjection. Thus ego-denying submissiveness has social consequences, exalted intragroup social roles for persons who have been successfully inducted into possession trance. And so the meek inherit the earth.

Death and Resurrection

I see no reason to doubt that Jesus was seen by some of his followers after his death.[15] Equally surely, the sight of a ghost would have impressed very few of those who were told about it; most would have stories of their own to tell of ghosts they or their friends had seen. The puzzle in the "kerygma" of Jesus' death and resurrection appearances is *not* that a "risen" Jesus was seen, but in the development of the thesis that his death and subsequent appearances had vital importance to

---

13 Samarin, William, *Tongues of Men and Angels: The Religious Language of Pentecostalism*, (New York: Macmillan, 1972), 74.
14 Kildahl, *The Psychology of Speaking in Tongues*, 74.
15 But I am puzzled by the fact that Paul's, Matthew's, Luke's, and John's reports of resurrection appearances are so hopelessly at odds with each other and so internally inconsistent.

other individuals. The explanation I offer below is that the *importance* of his death and subsequent appearances derived from the *experience* of later Christians that they too had died and subsequently arisen to new lives as persons possessed by his spirit.

The experience of spirit-possession is cognate to an experience of death and resurrection. For example, Alex Wayman reports that when Tibetan mediums first enter possession trance, "when such seizures are imbued with religious significance, they are interpreted as death of the old personality . . . followed by rebirth in a changed mode of being."[16] Similarly, the anthropologist Larry Peters informs us that Tamang shamanism considers possession to be the result of successful initiation and that it is controlled, remembered, and nonpathological; in the process of initiation, "the Tamang shaman," he reports, "must confront death and be reborn."[17] Such an interpretation of the possession experience is known from the ancient world. For example, in the so-called Mithras Liturgy, which is a systematic exercise designed to culminate in an individual's possession by a god who will then speak oracles through the individual's mouth, the practitioner is to say just prior to the moment when the god comes to dwell in him:

While being born again,
I am passing away;
While growing and having grown;
I am dying;
While being born from a life-generating birth;
I am passing on, released to death. (710-40)[18]

The onset of possession experience, particularly initial experience, often has striking physiological effects. Those effects can occasionally be so overwhelming as to cause unconsciousness, a seeming death that pentecostal Christians call being "slain in the spirit."

The experience of possession is, by definition, an experience of one's

---

16 Alex Wayman, "The Religious Meaning of Possession States," in Prince, *Trance and Possession States*, 172.
17 Peters, Larry, "Trance, Initiation, and Psychotherapy in Tamang Shamanism," *American Ethnologist*, Vol. 9, 1982: 30-32.
18 Betz, Hans Dieter, *The Greek Magical Papyri in translation* (Marvin Meyer, transl. the passage) (Chicago: University of Chicago Press, 1984), 52.

primary-persona exiting and of another persona entering. Diverse metaphors might be used for this, for example to cease and then be born again. Paul does not use "born again" as a principal metaphor. Rather, he uses the formulation to die and to rise again (Rom 6:1-11). In Paul's "gospel" the primary-persona identity declines and a second persona, the spirit of Christ, arises.

Persons possessed by the spirit of Christ the Son of God are, of course, acting out dominance fantasies. Becoming possessed by Christ the Lord is correlated by Paul with the absolute submissiveness of dying with Christ. From both psychological and anthropological perspectives, to die, submit one's own ego, and thus to live, through possession trance as Christ's persona, makes sense.

The "kerygma" arose from Christian experience. The profound importance for the Christian movement of the death and resurrection of Jesus Christ arose from the retrojection of the psychologically understandable death/resurrection experiences of formative Christians. Those who had "died and risen" conceived themselves to have died and risen with Christ, the mythic paradigm of the spirit by whom they were newly possessed. The significance of Christians' experience of death/resurrection was retrojected biographically back to the mythic occasion of Jesus' death/resurrection giving personal and mythic significance to reports that some of Jesus' followers had seen him after he died. When this first occurred we do not know; but it could have happened not long after the Pentecost event.

In turn, we may infer from Paul's letters that the discourse he used to induce the experience of the spirit made use of the kerygmatic paradigm in order to encourage and define that experience.[19] And, to close the circle, Paul's converts' experience of death/resurrection would have validated for them the mythos of Christ's death/resurrection. The foregoing factors allow us to understand how it came to be that the reports by some of Jesus' followers that they had seen him after his death took on such great significance in the formative Christian movement.

---

19 Paul's techniques for the induction of spirit experience are discussed in more detail in the following chapter.

The United Community

The logic of Paul's paradigm for possession is based on two axioms. First, from monotheism: there is only one spirit, i.e., one alter-persona identity. Second, from possession theory generally: a person possessed acquires the identity of the possessing entity or, to put it differently, the alter-persona. The logic of these axioms leads Paul to insist that in a group possessed by the same spirit, all who are possessed necessarily have an identical new persona identity and so are metaphorically one body and, in theory, psychologically one person; all are one person in Christ Jesus. Distinctions in the manifestations of the possession experience that would be understood in other cultures to imply a plurality of possessing entities are, according to Paul, distinctions in "gifts" of one spirit. He argues that in their single new spirit-persona identity there cannot be grounds for distinction on the basis of ethnic (neither Jew nor Greek), gender (neither male nor female), or class (neither slave nor free) distinctions (Gal.3:26-28). Unpossessed people are individuated; individuals possessed by one spirit are one person. This line of reasoning is not born of some mystical insight on Paul's part; it is a simple and logical consequence of the idea that the sine qua non for group membership was possession by a single supernatural person's spirit and so the group ought to be considered one alter-persona. Paul writes that this "one person in Christ Jesus" may profitably be considered, metaphorically, to be the body of Christ (1 Cor. 12:1-31) within which, as Paul puts it, "we have the mind of Christ" (1 Cor 2:16). The possession experience should, as Paul understands it, dissolve the boundaries of ego individuality.

Frecska and Kulcsar point out what Paul, in his own quite different way, emphasizes on various occasions: "Ritual trance invariably occurs in social context and the healer's personality and the expectation of community are profoundly involved in the induction of altered states of consciousness."[20] They write, rather technically, about trance states that "the need for and the possibility of identification are interwoven at a psychobiological level: regression promotes endogenous opioid mediation while endogenous opioids mediate affiliation, and help deper-

---

[20] Frecska and Kulcsar, "Social Bonding in the Modulation of the Physiology of Ritual Trance," 84.

sonalization by loss of ego boundaries."²¹ Arnold Ludwig similarly says of altered states of consciousness that they have "a common propensity for individuals to experience a profound sense of depersonalization, a schism between body and mind, feelings of derealization, or a dissolution of boundaries between self and others, the world, or the universe."²² He quotes Davidson, who points out that during such experiences "for a short time the painfully isolated individual merges himself into the ecstatic group and achieves forgetfulness of his limitations and the boundary lines of self."²³ One should expect, then, that when group formation is founded on the basis of possession experience, the ego boundaries of the individuals involved will be reduced and group affiliation will be exceptionally strong. Christian group cohesion did not arise only from mutual affirmations of theological principles and mutual social assistance; it was built into the psycho-physiological nature of the group's defining experience.

Paul's successful missionary activity led to community formation partially by means of the sort of psychophysiological mechanisms discussed above. His new Christians did not only believe they were one person in the spirit, they sometimes actually experienced this, and their experience can be understood, to some degree, even on the biochemical level. The logic of Paul's position, that all are one in Christ and so social differentiations no longer apply, accords with the nature of the possession experience itself.

Conclusion

The status of the self-identity of spirit-possessed Christians necessarily would have been a central issue in the formative Christian movement, stemming from the fact that spirit-possession was the defining characteristic of movement members. The idea that the mythic and Christological reflections of the early church were primarily the result of intellectual theorizing about Jesus' nature and history is simply wrong. *Christology grew out of pneumatology. Pneumatology originated from possession experience.* Possession experience can be analyzed for the individual by means of psychological theory and for the group by an-

---

21 Ibid., 79.
22 Ludwig, "Altered States of Consciousness," 78.
23 Ibid., 89.

thropological theory.

In this chapter I have briefly surveyed lines of reasoning that could easily be discussed, exemplified, and explicated in another whole book altogether. But for present purposes my principal points are two. First, it was the case that the associates of Jesus founded a spirit-possession cult shortly after his death. Second, it is the case that analysis of texts in the New Testament (Paul's and others), and of the theories and social structures within those texts, should be done in the light of anthropological and psychological information concerning spirit-possession.

The Christian movement arose from the spontaneous "Pentecost" event and spread rapidly and successfully. But *how* did it spread? Why did the dissociation prone Christians of Pentecost not simply live out their lives and disappear from history? I turn now to the question of the necessary techniques and the accompanying theories that led to the establishment of a social world of Christian churches.

13

MISSIONARY INDUCTIVE DISCOURSE

The spread of a religious movement premised on spirit-possession necessarily entails the development of successful techniques designed to induce the experience of possession. As the sine qua non of Christianity was possession by the spirit of Jesus Christ (according to Paul, Luke, John, etc.) then the sine qua non of apostolic missionary discourse must have been speech designed to, or found to, cause people to have the experience of possession by that spirit. I call such modes of speech "inductive discourse."

Possession experience could not possibly have been induced by the sort of apostolic sermons Luke places in the mouths of the apostles in Acts. Whether or not the logic of those sermons would have actually convinced anyone not already convinced is irrelevant; the very fact that those sermons are supposed to be logically and intellectually convincing means they were operating on psychological levels far removed from dissociative experience. People cannot be convinced, reasoned, or argued into a state of dissociative spirit-possession.

In this chapter I will suggest two modes of early Christian inductive discourse. The first I discuss in reference to Paul; it concerns the manifest confusing content and dissociative rhetoric of his (inferred) discourse. The second I discuss in reference to sayings in John's Gospel; it concerns the factor of "modeling" as part of inductive technique. These are not mutually exclusive, in fact "modeling" is discernable from what we can infer of Paul's technique, and the confusion and dissociative elements I discuss in reference to Paul may be found in the Johannine sayings material. Jesus' parables too should be included in the category "inductive discourse." In reference to the development of the formative Christian possession cult, Jesus' behavior was "modeling."

Pauline Inductive Discourse

It is all very well to observe that the Christians of Galatia believed themselves possessed by the spirit of the Son of God and to observe that Paul credits himself for having brought this about. It did not just happen; he *caused* it. But how did he cause it to happen? Having no transcripts of his discourse, we may never know how he did it. But, if we can make the assumption that in some respects the "gospel" he relates in his letters is the "gospel" he delivered orally in order to effect the induction of spirit-possession in susceptible listeners, then perhaps we can discern something of his technique.

In Galatians Paul writes to an audience who, through his induction, became possessed by the spirit, "I want to learn only this from you: did you receive the spirit from works of the law, or from hearing with faith?" The answer, of course, is that because of their hearing, with faith, their initial spirit experiences occurred. Faith here means receptivity to Paul's discourse in such a fashion that spirit-possession occurs. Similarly, in Romans 11:17, he writes that "faith comes from what is heard, and what is heard comes through the word of Christ." The word of Christ sometimes comes through the mouth of Paul who writes of "the Christ who speaks through me" (2 Cor. 13:3).

Many scholars and theologians have spent their lives trying to make rational sense of Paul's letters. Yet, after centuries of effort on their part one cannot say that they have been entirely successful. It seems improbable that Paul's gospel made good rational sense to Galatian gentiles, and more improbable that it made good rational sense to Galatian Jews. It is more likely that the effect of his oral gospel was not coherently rational. It seems to have fit the Ericksonian "confusion-restructuring" paradigm:

CONFUSION due to [verbal] shock, stress, uncertainty, etc. [leads to]

UNSTRUCTURING of usual frames of reference [leads to]

RESTRUCTURING needed [leads to]

RECEPTIVITY to therapeutic suggestions.[1]

In other words, Paul was inducing trance, here possession trance, by means that are analogous to, and comprehensible in terms of, contemporary psychotherapeutic theory. Suffice it to say that the proclamation of a crucified Messiah, to an audience of gentiles, who are all to be one offspring of Abraham, but who should have no concern for the Torah obedience definitive of Jews, who are not really the offspring of Abraham, unless they have faith in Christ, because the sacrifice of the Jewish God's incarnate son, brought an end to death—is going to have a thoroughly confusing effect. Paul's restructuring is his vision of a transformed "Judaism" available to those who receive the spirit by faith in his discourse.

I am here, and below, arguing from analogy, i.e., that discourse productive of spirit-possession states can be understood in reference to discourse productive of hypnotic states. The two states are not the same, but they are related by the fact that they are dissociative in nature. This relationship can be seen in the following comments by Nicholas Spanos:

Under some circumstances hypnotic subjects interpret their actions as stemming from the activities of multiple indwelling selves and present themselves in a manner consistent with this interpretation. Kampman, for example, found that forty one percent of highly susceptible subjects manifested evidence of a new identity and called themselves by a different name when given hypnotic suggestions to regress beyond their birth and become a different person. Watkins and Watkins found that 60% of highly susceptible hypnotic subjects indicated that they possessed a hidden part and called themselves by a new name while enacting the role of this "part" in a study of suggested deafness.[2]

From the perspective of a premodern culture a trance state wherein

---

[1] Rossi, *Hypnotic Realities*, 145.
[2] Spanos, Nicholas, "Hypnosis, Demonic Possession, and Multiple Personality," 99; cf. Kampman, R., "Hypnotically Induced Multiple Personality," *International Journal of Clinical and Experimental Hypnosis*, Vol. 24, 1976: 215-27.

an individual has a different name would commonly be presumed to be a state of possession.

In addition to discourse that can be understood in reference to the "confusion-restructuring" paradigm, Paul used discourse that emphasized the conceptual severing of the spirit of the individual from the body of the individual. In other words, he insisted that people must renounce the flesh to live in the spirit, e.g.,

> For the law of the Spirit of life in Christ Jesus has set me free from the law of sin and death. For God has done what the law, weakened by the flesh, could not do: sending his own Son in the likeness of sinful flesh and for sin, he condemned sin in the flesh, in order that the just requirement of the law might be fulfilled in us, who walk not according to the flesh but according to the Spirit. For those who live according to the flesh set their minds on the things of the flesh, but those who live according to the Spirit set their minds on the things of the Spirit. (Rom 8:3-8, etc.)

Paul insists that those who hear him create within themselves a dual consciousness that repudiates the old self, the flesh, and establishes a new self, the Spirit.

In addition to confusion-restructuring discourse, to "facilitate dissociation" Erickson utilized a technique designed to cause a person conceptually to sever himself from his body. Rossi quotes some of Erickson's discourse: "You can as a person awaken but you do not need to awaken as a body"; "You can awaken when your body awakes but without a recognition of your body." [3] Thus, "awakening as a person is dissociated from awakening as a body," and "awakening as a person and body are dissociated from a recognition of the body."[3] Sayings of this sort serve to "confuse subjects' conscious minds and thus depotentiate their habitual sets, biases, and learned limitations; under these circumstances the field is cleared for the possibility of creative processes to express themselves in a more autonomous and unconscious manner."[4] The kind of depotentiating intended here is remarkably similar to Paul's comments on the necessary separation between an individual's "flesh"

---

3 Ibid., 69-70.
4 Ibid., 70.

and an individual's new divine "spirit." The new divine "spirit" is a set of psychological capacities that arise from within the individual. The idea that they come from outside the individual, i.e., the possession paradigm, is a culturally established explanation, not a fact.

Using terminology coincidentally (but significantly) similar to psychological terminology, the theorist of rhetoric Chaim Perelman believes an argumentative pattern he calls, "the dissociation of ideas" is "the classical solution for incompatibilities that call for an alteration of conventional ways of thinking."[5] He notes that

> By processes of *dissociation* we mean techniques of separation which have the purpose of dissociating, separating, disuniting elements which are regarded as forming a whole or at least a unified group within some system of thought: dissociation modifies such a system by modifying certain concepts which make up its essential parts.[6]

Further, "The dissociation results in a depreciation of what had until then been an accepted value and in its replacement by another conception to which is accorded the original value."[7] This is what Paul does with the dichotomy spirit/flesh.

Antoinette Wire has applied Perelman's theory of rhetoric to Paul's discourse in 1 Corinthians. She concludes that Paul argues, in part, by dissociation of ideas: "Paul's rhetoric in Corinthians again and again stresses the dissociation of divine and human, spirit and flesh. . . . Whatever is not of the spirit is of the flesh and antithetical to it."[8] "To participate in Christ excludes pirticipating in anything human or fleshly."[9] The dissociation between spirit/ Christ and humanity/flesh is the dissociation between a supposedly supernatural persona and a normal persona that is equated with the physical body. Accordingly, one characteristic of Paul's inductive technique may have been the separation of normal persona consciousness from an alternative persona consciousness with access to the creative and affirmative powers of the

---

5 Perelman, Chaim, The New Rhetoric and The Humanities (Boston: Reidel, 1979), 23.
6 Ibid., 190 (emphasis in original).
7 Ibid., 24.
8 Wire, Antoinette, *Corinthian Women Prophets* (Minneapolis: Fortress, 1990), 22.
9 Ibid.

unconscious.

Both in Erickson's hypnotic technique and in Paul's induction of the spirit experience, dissociation between body and self facilitates the emergence of another aspect of the self. Paul assumes this arrives from outside the individual, Erickson that it emerges from within the individual. But the facilitation of access to the creative unconscious through discourse of dissociation is similar for each man. Paul writes, for example:

> But, as it is written, "What no eye has seen, nor ear heard, nor the heart of man conceived, what God has prepared for those who love him," God has revealed to us through the Spirit. For the Spirit searches everything, even the depths of God. For what person knows a man's thoughts except the spirit of the man which is in him? So also no one comprehends the thoughts of God except the Spirit of God. And we impart this in words not taught by human wisdom but taught by the Spirit, interpreting spiritual truths to those who possess the spirit. . . . "For who has known the mind of the Lord so as to instruct him?" But we have the mind of Christ. (1 Cor 9-13, 16)

While Erickson and his followers use the modern dichotomy "conscious/unconscious," rather than the antique "flesh/spirit," the underlying presumptions are the same.

Erickson's method "facilitated an experiential distinction between the recognizable operations of conscious and unconscious functioning."[10] Conscious functioning "operates linearly, and often with qualities that might be called doubt, ambition, pride, confusion, and so on," which are qualities Paul associates with "flesh."[11] Erickson insisted that trance induction could and should place individuals in an altered state of consciousness wherein their unconscious knowledge and creativity could function somewhat independently of the constraints usually imposed by their conscious modes of processing. The different "person" induced by Erickson was the unconscious of the original person. One must bear in mind that the same is true for Paul: the different "person" induced

---

10 Lankton, Stephen, and Carol Latikton, *The Answer Within: A Clinical Framework of Ericksonian Hypnotherapy* (New York: Brunner/Maiel, 1983), 141.
11 Ibid.

by Paul was also the unconscious of the original person.

When Paul insists that people must dissociate themselves as flesh from themselves as Spirit he is doing almost exactly the same thing Erickson is doing. In both cases individuals' unconscious minds are enabled to gain primacy. When this happens, as Ericksonian psychology has it, the unconscious "thinks globally; has its own idea of what you need; holds a vast storehouse of learning, dreams, and potentials; makes things happen in your best interest."[12] These claims are similar to those Paul makes about the spirit.

Rossi argues that patients do not know how to use their own potential different frames of reference.[13] Consciousness, he believes, is constrained to remain within the limitations of whatever belief system a person has. However, the unconscious is more free and more open to the reinvention of frames of reference. The induction of trance is, then, a way to permit the reinvention of belief systems especially for those people whose belief systems are no longer functioning well. For both modern and ancient therapists it is obvious that people satisfied with themselves and their condition in society will not become clients. As Jesus supposedly said, it is the sick who need the physician. By the induction of the trance state labeled "spirit," Paul offers a means by which individuals can reinvent their frames of reference through access to their own unconscious functioning (i.e., the spirit) in general accord with the reframing ideas of Paul's gospel.

Johannine Spirit Theory

The Gospel of John presents itself as the account of a unique person speaking on behalf of God who promises that another person, another Paraclete, or spirit, will replace him and will dwell within people. Those in the audience who are sympathetic may become children of God (1:12), born of the spirit (3:05), born from above (3:03), sent into the world (17:18), to which they do not belong (17:16), as sons of light (12:36), who will do the same works he does himself (14:12).

The Gospel quotes Jesus as saying:

Whoever loves me will keep my word and my father will love

---
12 Ibid., 147.
13 Erickson, Milton H., and Ernest Rossi, *Experiencing Hypnosis: Therapeutic Approaches to Altered States* (New York: Irvington Publishers, 1981), 256.

him, and we shall come to him and make our dwelling with him. Whoever does not love me does not keep my words; yet my word is not my own, it is the word of the one who sent me. I have told you this while I am with you. The advocate, the holy spirit, whom the father will send in my name, will teach you everything and remind you of all I have said to you. (14.23-26)

Thus, according to John, Christians are to receive the spirit and so we have here further evidence of the importance of spirit-possession in formative Christianity.

I am not here discussing the Gospel of John per se but, rather, the implications of some of its sayings. As it stands the Gospel of John identifies Jesus and the spirit *not* in the sense of spirit-possession but more in the sense of synonyms. Raymond Brown puts it this way, "virtually everything that has been said about the Paraclete [spirit] has been said elsewhere in the Gospel about Jesus."[14] He concludes that, in many ways, "the Paraclete is to Jesus as Jesus is to the Father."[15] But perhaps another formulation is better: The spirit is to the Father as Jesus is to the Father. This equation perhaps arose when sayings of the Holy Spirit that were attributed secondarily to Jesus (i.e., they came through his voice while he was in a state of possession by the Holy Spirit), became attributed primarily to Jesus so that one no longer heard the Holy Spirit describing itself, its supernatural origin, its relationship to God but one heard Jesus describing himself, his supernatural origin, his relationship to God.

Even though spirit-possession does not describe the Christology of John's gospel itself, the idea of spirit-possession is present throughout that gospel in reference to Christians. For example, Jesus supposedly said, "I shall ask the father, and he will give you another advocate to be with you for ever, that spirit of truth whom the world can never receive since it neither sees nor knows him; but you know him because he is with you, he is *in* you" (14:16-17), and "On that day you will understand that I am in my father and you in me and I *in* you" (14:20). Again, "I have yet many things to say to you, but you cannot bear them

---

14 Brown, Raymond, *The Gospel According to John: XIII—XXI* (New York, Doubleday, 1970), 1140.
15 Ibid.

now. When the Spirit of Truth comes, he will guide you into all the truth; for he will not speak on his own authority, but whatever he hears he will speak, and he will declare to you the things that are to come" (16:13). Individuals who have so received the Spirit were labeled, in Christian communities, prophets.

Eugene Boring notes that

> John's prophetic "I am" is a dominant feature of the discourses of the Fourth Gospel. This is to be expected, in view of the identification of Jesus and the Paraclete-prophet who will not speak "on his own authority" (16:13). The many "I-sayings" of the Fourth Gospel should not be accounted for as simply literary fiction, the retrojection into the mouth of the historical Jesus of traditional Christological statements about Jesus that he could not have said. They are rather to be seen as prophetic utterance in which the risen Lord speaks through the prophet in the first person.[16]

Boring is almost entirely right, but it is not the "risen Jesus" who speaks but the spirit of God.[17] Regarding the origin of Johannine sayings, John Neumann summarizes Hans Windisch's view that they came from

> a man of strong prophetic, Spirit-filled consciousness, like the *Pneumatiker* who produced the Apocalypse. The "new" sayings of Jesus and the revelation discourses in John are to be explained as arising out of the Spirit-filled Christian community. John's is the Gospel of the Spirit, *the* Gospel, produced under the Spirit, to replace all others.[18]

Similarly, Gary Burge writes that Christ's

> experience of the Spirit could become paradigmatic for the

---

16 Boring, Eugene, *Continuing Voice of Jesus*, 160-61.
17 I see nowhere in the Gospel of John any indication that the present activity of the "risen Jesus" is a concept of which that community was aware. It can well be argued that the Paraclete/Spirit is equated with Jesus. But this does not mean the best phrase for that circumstance is "risen Jesus."
18 Neumann, John, "Introduction," in Hans Windisch, *The Spirit Paraclete in the Fourth Gospel* (Fortress Press: Philadelphia, 1968), x.

community. . . . Thus in Jesus' death/glorification we find the notion that here the Spirit is released (7:37; 19:30,34). In fact, it is within the process of glorification that the disciples are anointed (20:22). This relationship explains the full adjustment of Johannine eschatology. If Spirit and Christ were one, to experience the eschatological Spirit was to experience the eschaton and Christ.[19]

Following these authors we may conclude that some if not most of the sayings attributed to Jesus in John's gospel arose from the sayings of Johannine prophets. But not all. I have argued not only that the historical Jesus set the pattern and style for Johannine sayings but also that some of them are authentically his sayings.

A classic passage in John, formative for later Christian theology:

The word was made flesh, he lived *among/in* us and we saw his glory, the glory that is his as the only Son of the father (1:14)

hinges on a single word: "among." It is not illegitimate to translate the Greek word *"en"* as "among" but the word may, of course, be translated "in." And if "in," then the passage will read "the word became flesh and lived in us. . . ." and "he" will refer not to Jesus personally but to the mediating word and spirit dwelling in a multiplicity of individuals. Looked at in this way, the word and the spirit are alternative paradigms for the possession experience along with a third paradigm: the "son." The "spirit," "word," "son" paradigms are synonymous in John. To claim "I am possessed by the Spirit of God," "I am possessed by the Word of God," "I am possessed by the Son of God," are the same thing. As discussed above, Paul also testifies that Christians experienced the spirit of the Son and so became Sons who could then speak prophetic words.

John's gospel appears complex because it uses a multiplicity of terms for exactly the same thing. Take for example John 4:34, "He whom God has sent speaks God's own words: God gives him the spirit without reserve. The father loves the Son and has entrusted everything to him." The categories "He whom God sent," "speaker of God's words,"

---

19 Burge, Gary, *The Anointed Community: The Holy Spirit in the Johanninr Tradition* (Grand Rapids, MI: Eerdmans, 1987), 223.

"receiver of Spirit," "the Son," are synonymous here. The key is the idea of reception of "spirit," which we know was a condition available to people in general, and not a condition unique to Jesus. But if "spirit" is an available condition, then being "the Son" is, equivalently, an available condition, as is being "He whom God sent," or "speaker of God's words." The latter is obvious, for it is a principal function of the condition called "spirit" to produce utterances attributable to God. The ancient Jewish paradigm for this condition is prophecy.

Johannine Inductive Discourse

Given the sine qua non character of both the dissociative possession experience and the acceptance of the Christian possession paradigm, formative missionaries either were in, or could on occasion attain, the state they sought to induce. Some spoke with the persona of the possessing spirit: John discourses are examples, as are Paul's statements that it is not he who lives but Christ who lives in him (Gal. 2:20) and that to hear him is to hear Christ (2 Cor. 13:3).

The discourse of spirit-possessed people that produced successful induction into that state must have contained, or have been followed by, the delivery of an explanatory paradigm that depicted the possession state as both beneficial and possible.

So an inductive sequence would have been:

A. A person presented himself by intonation, gesture, or other means as being in a state of dissociative possession. That presentation may often have included the performance of diverse "signs and wonders," which functioned within the culture to affirm the claim to be possessed.

B. The speaker defined his present identity to be the Spirit of God/Son of God, and so he orally presented the movement's explanatory paradigm of the dissociative possession.

C. The benefits of this nominal identity would have been asserted. These benefits were of three varieties. First, the externally verifiable claim to be able to perform "signs and wonders." Second, the internally verifiable claim to enjoy supernatural experiences including access to hidden truths and revelations; such claims are psychologically self-validating. Third, nonverifiable claims including such constructs as forgiveness of sins, and eternal life.

The externally verifiable claims would serve to support the explanatory paradigm presented and show the desirability of the state. When the state was attained by others, the internally verifiable claims would serve to affirm the paradigm, for predicted and powerful psychophysiological experiences would occur and, therefore, the nonverifiable claims would seem to be confirmed.

The original setting of the sayings in John was a performance of spirit-possession. Lambek writes of this aspect of possession:

> To view possession as performance is to focus upon the relatively formal enactments in which it is realized. The model focuses on the experience of the participants, whether those actually entering trance (the "performers") or those observing it (the "audience") who must be *moved* in some way. This movement may refer to a submission to authority, a transcending of unconscious conflict, an enlargement of the self, a deeper understanding of the cosmos, or merely a resituation of participants in their social context. This is to view possession as ritual, but ritual that does not merely speak, in symbolic language, about society, but actively constructs it.[20]

Some discourses' manifest point, apart from the spirit's self-affirmations, is to invite hearers into a community apart from the "world":

> If you were of the world, the world would love its own; but because you are not of the world, but I chose you out of the world, therefore the world hates you. (15:18-19)

Thus the possessed Christian's discourse invites the hearer to enter the possession state and to become a member of the society of the possessed, the society of those not of this present, standard, social world. Lambek quotes Boddy as arguing that "possession is, among other things, a vehicle for the expression of otherness, not only an objective, if symbolically embellished, catalog of its varieties . . . but an embracing of it, in order to reflect upon and transform the self."[21] Whoever can say "I am not of this world," in the voice of the spirit, is someone who has transformed the self to embrace and express otherness.

---

20 Lambek, "From Disease to Discourse," 55.
21 Ibid., 57.

The discourses in the gospel of John are almost entirely without information. Their point is not to reveal information derived from spirit-possession but to declare, over and over again, that spirit-possession is a possibility. They arose from the speech of individuals who presented themselves as models for an attainable possession state.

Bultmann summarizes discourses in John:

> In the discourses a pattern can be more or less plainly discerned that advances in three motifs.
> *First* the Revealer presents himself and his significance;
> *then* follows the invitation to come to him;
> *lastly* the consequence of the acceptance or rejection of the Revealer is made known in promise and threat.[22]

I understand "Revealer" here to mean spirit-possessed Christians of the Johannine community. Assuming that "come to him" is an invitation to receive the spirit, the sequence would motivate and facilitate entry into possession trance. One must bear in mind, of course, that inductive discourse is effective only for those people for whom it is effective; a tautology, of course, but not insignificant. It stands to reason that Pauline and Johannine induction was effective only for a few people, *but* they were the people who formed Christian churches.

> People who become possessed today, in the sense of dissociative speaking in tongues, have certain common characteristics. Kildahl concludes that they are neither more or less emotionally disturbed than equally religious non-tongue speakers. Nevertheless, pronounced dependence on an authority figure regarded as benevolent, and prior need for acceptance by a group and by God, were characteristic of the tongue-speakers we interviewed. Once the ability had been achieved, a feeling of relaxation and euphoria followed, together with that of having found oneself and of having found a home in the company of other tongue-speakers. All the glossolalists we interrogated reported this to be the most exciting and thrilling experience of their lives.[23]

---

22 Bultmann, Rudolf, *The Gospel of John*, 7 (emphasis and indentation added).
23 Kildahl, Psychology of Speaking in Tongues, 65.

He also discovered that

> the principal difference between tongue-speakers and non-tongue-speakers was that the glossolalists developed deeply trusting and submissive relationships to the authority figures who introduced them to the practice of glossolalia. Without complete submission to the leader, speaking in tongues was not initiated.[24]

As noted in the previous chapter Luke informs us that at the outset Christian apostolic missionaries brought about glossolalia in some who heard them speak.[25] It is not hard to see the immediate applicability of Kildahl's conclusions to the case of Paul, who certainly does expect (and probably received when physically present in a community) trusting and submissive relationships to himself, the one who introduced them to the experience of the spirit (e.g., Gal 3:1-5). The origin of the Corinthian Christians' parties of adherence to different apostles arises from the factors Kildahl analyzes (cf. 1 Cor. 1:12).

The missionary prophets who spoke some of the Johannine sayings as inductive technique presumably found a receptive audience in those who needed "pronounced dependence on an authority figure regarded as benevolent, and who had a prior need for acceptance by a group and by God." These people were presented with an authority figure who was, through possession, the embodiment and voice of the spirit of God. And so divine authority, invitation to membership in a group, acceptance by God, and the offer of experience of the spirit were combined.

Imitability and Modeling

Bultmann emphasizes the contentless content of Jesus' discourse in John:

> But the astonishing thing about it is that Jesus' words never convey anything specific or concrete that he has seen with the Father. Not once does he communicate matters or events to which he had been a witness by either eye or ear. Never is the

---
24 Ibid., 50.
25 Whether Johannine Christians spoke in tongues is unknown.

heavenly world the theme of his words. Nor does he communicate cosmogonic or soteriological mysteries like the Gnostic Redeemer. His theme is always just this one thing: that the Father sent him, that he came as the light, the bread of life, witness for the truth, etc.; that he will go again, and that one must believe in him.[26]

And again, "Jesus' words communicate no definable content at all except that they are words of life, words of God."[27] These contentless revelations are purely self-referential, what counts is not *what* is said but *that* it is said.

Given that possession by the spirit is a possibility, the point of what is said is not simply to gain an acknowledgment that some person is possessed but to present the possibility that the beholder too may become spirit-possessed. The words in John's gospel that "communicate no definable content at all" are, then, not utterances of propositions that one must accept as true but utterances that derive from a state that one must acknowledge as attainable. John offers as the "content" of the spirit's seemingly contentless discourses the present fact that the utterance of such discourses is an available possibility.

It stands to reason that anyone commending a particular state would be capable of entering that state; it stands to reason that since the state is imitable, imitation of the speaker would be commended, the speaker being the local model. Through acknowledgment of the explanatory paradigm of the speaker's state, and thus, necessarily, acknowledgment of the statements made by the speaker regarding the benefits of the state, some people may become open to attaining the state. This is well exemplified in Gospel of Thomas 108. [In the voice of the spirit] Jesus said, "He who will drink from my mouth will become like me. I myself shall become he, and the things that are hidden will be revealed to him."[28]

Revelations of the Johannine revealer have practically no other purpose than having the audience acknowledge the revealer as a revealer. This makes good sense if the point of the discourses is to model an

---

26 Bultmann, Rudolf, *Theology of the New Testament: Volume Two* (New York: Scribner's, 1955), 62.
27 Ibid., 63.
28 The motif of the Spirit as a distributed liquid is quite common cf., particularly, Jn. 7:37-39, Acts 2:17-18.

imitable state. *Should the hearer attain the state, he or she will also be the revealer and have the revelations and, accordingly, details of the revelations never need to be verbalized.* That such a dissociative state would lead to hidden things (from the unconscious of the individual) being revealed is fundamental to theories of hypnotic induction in psychotherapy, and is assumed in early Christianity under the paradigm that the hidden things are revealed by the spirit or, as Paul puts it, the mind of Christ. The proverb, "don't give a man a fish, teach him to fish," is applicable here and so is the adage, "the medium is the message."

14

Conclusion

I have tried to present a comprehensive causal system whereby reported New Testament events hold together and lead from one to the other, from Jesus' baptism, to healing, to exorcism, to group formation, to antifamily strictures, to speech in parables and advice for itinerants, to execution, to Pentecost, to Pauline theory and discourse, to Johannine theory and discourse, to later Christian spirit-inspiration theory and the authoritarian churches of the Pastoral and Petrine epistles. I have sought in every instance not only to show what happened but why it happened.

One key to discovering the systemic and comprehensible sense to all these events is that, rather than thinking in terms of different intellectual belief systems, one should think in terms of different manifestations of a single underlying genetic potential, the ability of minds to experience dissociation. Dissociation can manifest as alter-persona consciousness of an affirmative or negative sort, and it can manifest itself in trance states. Some members of the earliest church progressed during a period of only two years from the forms of dissociation we might call conversion disorder or negative possession, *to* a dissociative trance state they were encouraged to know as the kingdom of God, *into* a dissociative affirmative state of possession that they understood to be possession by the spirit of Jesus Christ. The healings and exorcisms and parables of Jesus, the "I am" and "Son" and rebirth discourse in John, the spirit/flesh, death/new-life dichotomies of Paul are all ways of inducing and defining and redefining those dissociative states.

It seems virtually certain that one aspect of Paul's experience on the road to Damascus was his initial experience of possession by the spirit (cf. Gal. 1:2: "God revealed his Son in me"). Accordingly, a principal element of the initiatory events of Jesus' career, Paul's career, and the careers of the Christians present at Pentecost appears to have been fundamentally the same. In texts concerned with the activities of these persons: Mark (et al.), Galatians, Acts, those events are presented as the cause and explanation for all that follows.

The Gospel of John and the Epistles of Paul are not as unrelated as they seem to be—the former, say, a gnosticized Christianity, the latter a Christ cult. John and Paul, and for that matter Mark, are theorizing about states of possession. Their writings are anomalies in world literature because "theorizing about" possession states is *not* typical of members of possession-cults, the membership of which is normally drawn from nonliterate and semiliterate segments of society.

So it fits together: You can travel from the sinful Nazarene come to receive baptism to the Johannine "I and the Father are one," from Jesus the itinerant exorcist and healer to Paul's insistence that "we are all one person in Christ Jesus," from a peasant Galilean casual about the Torah to Q's "No one knows the Father but the Son." These things are not due to the fits and starts of inexplicable creative impulses on the part of various individuals; they are due to a reasonable sequence of events, mainly relating to various dissociative states and the subsequent theorizing that took place about them.

When we theorize about such states in the formative Christian period we should, I believe, keep in mind the following. Pneumatology was an explanatory paradigm for altered states of consciousness. Christology was often an explanatory paradigm for pneumatology. Anthropology can provide explanations for the social relationships among persons who experienced the states in question. Psychology can help us understand those states apart from the Christian language by which they are described in our texts.

Realism and Idealism

Jesus' presentation of the kingdom of God as within, a form of present experience, and his concurrent announcement or the kingdom as a future objective geopolitical event, was bifurcated after his death. His personal talent for induction of the kingdom of God, a religious trance experience, was not available after his death. The kingdom therefore became for most a matter of theory, a belief rather than an experience.

From that bifurcation we have, on the one hand the Q perspective, one that is both "realist" and future oriented. By "realist" I mean that it was conceived that the kingdom of God will actually be visibly out there in the external world on some future date. On the other hand, we have the perspective of the Gospel of Thomas, both "idealist" and present oriented. By "idealist" I mean that the kingdom of God is now potentially (for all) and now actually (for some) within the minds and experiences of people.

From the latter point of view, Jesus' sayings that refer to a future kingdom might have been understood to refer to the potential for the kingdom to occur in the immediate future for those individuals who might separately come to experience it. For the Gospel of Thomas, the kingdom is not to be imagined in reference to an eschatological and apocalyptic future but conceived in terms of the initial conditions of the world in the mythic primordial past of Genesis' chapter one.[1] From an idealist perspective the kingdom is a form of experience and, in theory, it has always been potentially available. The potential for experience logically precedes the actualization of experience.

On the other hand, from a realist perspective the kingdom is the perception of an externally existing state of affairs, one which does not yet exist in the present. And so the logic of realism places the kingdom in the future. If Jesus brought about, induced, a dissociative religious trance experience called "kingdom of God," and also announced the imminent arrival of an objectively observable kingdom of God (for which the induced experience of kingdom served as foretaste and supporting evidence) then Jesus combined in his own discourse both idealist and realist perspectives—indeed, New Testament evidence tells us he did.[2]

Conceptions of the realist and future-eschatological kingdom, such as are found in Q, became normative for orthodox Christianity. Con-

---

1 Davies, Stevan, "Christology and Protology," passim.
2 My sentences are an unpacking of the scholarly-theological phrases "realized eschatology," "proleptic apprehension of the kingdom," "the already but not-yet elements in Jesus' discourse," and so forth.

ceptions of the idealist and past-primordial kingdom, such as are found in Thomas, allowed for a subsequent syncretism of Christianity and gnostic mythemes.[3]

A realist view of divine spirit as an external divine person who comes into the minds of human persons became normative for orthodox Christianity. An idealist view of divine spirit as a potential that has always been present within the minds of human persons by their nature became normative for gnostic Christianity.[4] Both streams of tradition can claim with some justification to derive from the historical Jesus. However, along with most scholars, I doubt that Jesus himself would have understood anything of what either second century orthodox (e.g., Tertullian) or gnostic (e.g., Valentinus) Christians were talking about.

As one must bear in mind the idealist and realist dimensions of Jesus' presentations of the kingdom of God, so one must bear in mind the idealist and realist dimensions of the present book. I have, of necessity, jumped from, first, discussing spirit-possession from a seemingly realist perspective (there is a real spirit of God out there in the external world who sometimes comes into human bodies and speaks and acts through them) to, second, an idealist perspective (the spirit of God is a label put upon a form of dissociative experience and the words and actions of that spirit are actually words and actions that arise from the unconscious of the individual supposedly possessed). The first is a level of analysis in accord with the belief structures of the people concerned. The second is a level of analysis in accord with the belief structures of contemporary anthropology, psychology, and secular scholarship generally. The difference is not in the description of the phenomena in question but in the explanatory paradigm put upon the phenomena. Both the experiences in question, and the explanatory paradigms that cultures place upon them, are historical facts.

To return finally to spirit-Christology, Professor Lampe contended, it seems to me correctly, that:

---

3 Perkins, Pheme, *Gnosticism and the New Testament* (Minneapolis: Augsburg/Fortress, 1993).
4 Cf. Davies, Stevan, "Gnostic Idealism and the Gospel of Truth," in Neusner, Jacob, et al. (eds.) *Religious Writings and Religious Systems: Vol. One*, (Atlanta: Scholars Press, 1989).

The category of Spirit-possession was used to some extent in early Christian thought to interpret not only Christ's present relationship to believers but also his relationship to God. If believers are sons of God through the indwelling of God's Spirit, possessing their souls and reshaping their lives according to the pattern of Christ, can Christ's own sonship be interpreted in the same terms? The gospels suggest this possibility. In the synoptists Spirit-possession and messianic sonship are linked together in the narrative of Christ's baptism. The Spirit descends upon him and he receives the divine assurance that he is Son of God.[5]

Whether what I have written is at all relevant to high Christological theology may depend upon the question of the reality of a person. Possession theories always presuppose a mind—persona duality: this body may have in it persona X most of the time and yet the same body may have in it the supposedly supernatural persona Y some of the time. If we take the persona X to be a reality distinct from the body, as is done naively by most, and philosophically by some, then we must also take the persona Y to be a reality distinct both from the body and from persona X. Thus, if one says, in the case of Jesus, that he is Jesus of Nazareth most of the time and the Son of God some of the time, one can affirm the reality of the persona Son of God. Whether the origin of the Son of God arises from within Jesus' mind, or arrives within him from God, depends on the adoption of an idealist or realist perspective on the situation. Readers should be reminded, though, that from an idealist perspective a mental reality is not a "mere" psychological state, a mental reality is what reality itself is.

From this it follows that the assertion "Jesus was possessed by the Spirit-Son of God" is a way of saying there was a *reality* labeled "Spirit-Son of God," and not just a *theory* or a *belief or* a *hypothesis*. Nor is it an "experience" if that term is more accurately used (and I have not so used it very often) because the term "experience" implies that the primary persona Jesus of Nazareth had a particular sort of experience rather than, as it should properly be put, the primary persona Jesus of

---

[5] Lampe, G. W. H., "The Holy Spirit and the Person of Christ" in Sykes, S. W., and J. P. Clayton, (eds.) *Christ, Faith and History: Cambridge Studies in Christology* (Cambridge: Cambridge University Press, 1972), 117.

Nazareth ceased (as his family is said to have believed, Mk. 3:21), and the persona Son of God came to be.

Christian faith enters the equation in answer to the question of whether Jesus' persona, understood by some at his time to be the Spirit-Son of God, is a matter of particular importance. It is not inherently important; it is a state of consciousness to which a particular label has been applied and which is understood in reference to a particular religious system.[6]

Some Christians may assert that the Spirit-Son of God is best conceived from a realist perspective as an external supernatural persona who came into Jesus; if so then they share the perspective of Jesus and his followers. On the other hand, some Christians might say that when they speak of the Spirit-Son of God and Jesus they speak idealistically, that the reality of Jesus' possession state as an alter-persona known as the Spirit-Son of God is the reality their faith affirms. They may justifiably affirm that Jesus had the potential for the actualization of that state prior to the time that he came for baptism and at all subsequent times. If so, then they speak of a state of affairs that can be confirmed by historical scholarship supported by psychology and by anthropology. The Jesus of history and the Christ of faith are reunited, for the secular historical Jesus is the secular historical Son of God.

---

6 For example, one need not take the experience of possession by the Yoruba deity, Ogun, to be a matter of importance although, to he sure, members of a Santeria group find it very significant that some of their membership are, sometimes, supposedly so possessed.

On the Odes of Solomon as Evidence for a Pre-Christianity

In this essay I will argue that Christianity as we know it, a religion focused on Jesus of Nazareth, arose from an antecedent religion known to us through the Odes of Solomon. In the first part I will show that the general scholarly understanding of the Odes as products of early first century Christianity is mistaken and that they are not demonstrably Christian at all. In the second part I will show that the Odes may represent the religion of the Churches of God that Paul first persecuted and then joined, which I will call "Odes Judaism." I will show that principal ideas in the Odes are also to be found in the Gospel of John and in other ancient Christian writings, and argue that the temporal-causal arrow points from the Odes to the Christian texts, rather than vice versa.

Part One
The Religion of the Odes of Solomon

The Odes of Solomon are a collection of hymns that are generally believed to be Christian even though they represent a very peculiar variety of Christianity, one hard to classify using any of the standard scholarly types. James Charlesworth writes, for example, that "The Odes of Solomon were composed at a time when Gnosticism had not yet developed and when gnosis was a worldwide Spiritual way of thinking. They also come to us from a time when Judaism and Christianity had not yet gone their separate ways." [1] He believes that they derive from a religious group profoundly influenced by the spirituality of the Essenes and yet that the Odes are so similar in ideology to the Gospel and Letters of John that it is even possible "the Odist and John shared the same milieu, and it is not improbable that they lived in the same community." [2]

The Odes of Solomon are not Gnostic insofar as they do not argue for a cosmic dualism separating a perfect One from a fallen world, and they are in agreement with the standard Jewish view that God created this world out of his benevolence; there is no myth of the pre-cosmic fall of God or of God's Sophia, who then needs to be rescued by gnosis from this fallen or illusory world. Despite the absence of Gnostic cosmology, a myth of rescue is clearly present throughout the Odes of Solomon. Human beings are enslaved or enchained in a prison existence wherein they are persecuted and in need of rescue. Rescue comes, at least from one of the Odes' metaphorical perspectives, from gnosis. This is most clear in Ode 17, which shows remarkable kinship to Gnostic ideas, although it does not presuppose a Gnostic myth of origins. Michael Lattke's translation of 17:7-9a reads, "And he who knew me made me great, the Most High in his complete *pleroma*. And he glorified me by his benevolence and lifted up my *gnosis* to the height of Truth. And thence he gave me the way of his steps. And I opened the gates that were shut, and broke the bars of iron."[3] There is a particularly significant connection between one of the greatest Gnostic works, the Gospel of Truth (perhaps written by Valentinus himself) and Ode 7:20-21. In the Ode we hear (Lattke's translation), "hatred will be lifted from the earth and be submerged together with jealousy. For non-*gnosis* has been destroyed, because the *gnosis* of the Lord has come." The fundamental and reiterated theme of the Gospel of Truth is that when gnosis comes, illusion disappears: e.g. "but what comes into existence in him is knowledge, which appeared in order that oblivion might vanish and the Father might be known. Since oblivion came into existence because the Father was not known, then if the Father

---

[1] Charlesworth, James. *Critical Reflections on the Odes of Solomon*, Volume One, Sheffield UK: Sheffield Academic Press, 1998 18.
[2] Ibid. 229.
[3] Lattke, Michael. *The Odes of Solomon* (Hermeneia Series) Philadelphia PA: Fortress Press 2009. Lattke retains the Greek "pleroma" and "gnosis" in his translation.

comes to be known, oblivion will not exist from that moment on."[4] This is a remarkable similarity of ideas. While the problem the Odes of Solomon addresses is not formulated in terms of the Gnostic myth, the solution offered by the Odes is shared with Gnosticism.

The Odes are known today from a variety of manuscripts and citations (all of which are discussed in detail by Lattke in his recent magisterial tome on the Odes) but experts differ on whether they were written originally in Syriac (so Charlesworth) or in Greek (so Lattke).[5] David Aune, having surveyed scholarly opinion, concludes that the Odes most probably were in originally written in Greek, but that there is no consensus.[6] There appears to be a general agreement in scholarship at present that they come from a very early period of Christian history. Lattke concludes that the date of the Odes of Solomon is "the first quarter of the second century C.E." and they represent "the overlap of early Judaism, early Gnosticism, and early Christianity."[7] Charlesworth basically concurs, writing that "the date of the composition is most likely some time before 125 C.E."[8]

Many authorities locate the origin of the Odes somewhere in western Syria which, as Charlesworth points out, includes the region of Galilee. Lattke does not think it is possible to be very specific about the Odes' place of origin, but he does believe that while the affiliations of the Odes with the Letters of Ignatius of Antioch do not prove that they are of Antiochean origin, nevertheless those affiliations "do strongly suggest Syria as the area."[9] Robert Grant concluded that the Odes are most likely "composed in Syriac at Edessa."[10]

---

4 Attridge, Harold and George MacRae translators, in James M. Robinson, ed., *The Nag Hammadi Library*, revised edition. HarperCollins, San Francisco, 1990.
5 Ibid. 11, and Charlesworth 15.
6 Aune, David. *The Cultic Setting of Realized Eschatology in Early Christianity*, Leiden: Brill, 1972: "a majority of scholars concerned agree that Greek was the original language in which the Odes were composed." 167 and n. 5 where Aune lists 16 major scholars who believe that Greek was the original language and 10 who believe that the original language was Syriac.
7 Lattke, 1.
8 Charlesworth, *Critical Reflections* 15.
9 Lattke, 11.
10 Grant, Robert., "The Odes of Solomon and the Church of Antioch," *Journal of Biblical Literature*, Vol. 63, No. 4, Dec., 1944 377.

The Odes Are Not Christian

It is difficult to argue a negative, but I will try to show that the Odes of Solomon are not Christian. In the first place, they never once mention Jesus of Nazareth. Not one sentence of the Odes indicates that they derive from the religion that regards Jesus as its founder. They may be Christian in the sense that they are profoundly concerned with the concept of a human being who becomes Christ, but if this person is not uniquely Jesus, then we need to be careful how the word Christian is being used.[11]

Only if we assume from the outset, by hypothesis, that the Odes are Christian do we have any reason to think that the Odes derive from members of the religion focused on the life, death, resurrection of Jesus. No, in fact the Odes of Solomon are not Christian at all unless we oddly define their Christianity to be a cult unrelated to the religion focused on Jesus of Nazareth. But this might indeed be a way of understanding them, for it might not be absurd to say that they derive from a form of "Christianity" for which Jesus of Nazareth was entirely irrelevant.

The supposed Christianity of the Odes is very hard to define, although in their vocabulary and phraseology they are certainly are similar to what one reads in early Christian writing, especially the writing that comes from the Johannine community. However, while phrases in the Odes may sound familiar, the ideas they communicate are not. As Robert Grant wrote in 1944, "In regard to Christian doctrines inherited from Judaism [the Odes of Solomon] do not mention forgiveness, atonement, or in fact, sin. The only circumcision is that of the heart (Ode 11:1-2), while the offering of the Lord is righteousness and purity of heart and lips (20:5)."[12] Grant continues, "As for doctrines more

---

11 We need to bear in mind that the word "Christ" is the Greek version of the Hebrew term "Messiah" and that both simply mean "an anointed person." However, in Judean religio-political language the words Messiah and Christ came to mean anointed in the sense of being a person ceremonially anointed to be the king of Judea. The last such king in the lineage of David, a man named Zedekiah, died in 586 B.C.E., but some Judeans speculated that God would eventually intervene and install a Davidic descendant as the Judean king, give him supernatural power to liberate the land, and help him to bring an end to wickedness; that man came to be called the Messiah or the Christ. While this is an early Jewish meaning of the term, it is not the way the term is used in the Odes of Solomon or in most of the later Christian texts.
12 Ibid. 364

specifically Christian, they do not speak of resurrection and ascension (though these may be implied in Christ's victory), nor of baptism and the Eucharist."[13] Major themes that are vital to the Christian religion are missing in the Odes of Solomon. Grant quotes a conversation with his friend Arthur Darby Nock: "Professor Nock has observed to me in this connection, we can probably conclude that the Christ of the Odes of Solomon was not really born, did not really live, was not really crucified, did not really die."[14]

One can go further. The Odes do not mention Jesus in any sense. His name is never used, nor do the Odes contain a single one of his sayings, nor do they mention even one event in which the gospels say he participated. The word "cross" supposedly appears twice in the Odes of Solomon (Odes 27 and 42), but only when translators such as Charlesworth take the Syriac (*qaysa*) or Greek (*xylon*), the word for tree or wood and translate it as "cross." Less tendentious translators do not do this. The first English translator, Rendel Harris, used the word "wood." Lattke's recent translation gives, for Ode 27 "I stretched out my hands and hallowed my Lord, because the spreading out of my hands is his sign, and my stretching [up] is the wood, which is upright;" (The passage in Ode 42 is nearly identical). Charlesworth and others have assumed that "wood" must be "the cross" and that the physical position of the one speaking is cruciform. Accordingly, while Charlesworth's version of Ode 27 is "I extended my hands and hallowed my Lord, For the expansion of my hands is His sign. And my extension is the upright cross," Lattke argues that the speaker stands with arms upraised, stretched up and outwards, not in a cruciform shape.[15] This matters a great deal because if Lattke is correct (and his recent tome of commentary makes him the world's leading expert on the Odes) then there is no reference to cross or crucifixion in the Odes anywhere.

On the other hand, arboreal imagery is rather common in the Odes. For example, in Ode 11 the speaker becomes a tree in the garden of God: "Blessed, O Lord, are they who are planted in Your land, and who have a place in Your Paradise; and who grow in the growth of Your trees, and have passed from darkness into light."[16] In Ode 38 the

---

13 Ibid.
14 Ibid. 365.
15 Lattke, 380.
16 Unless specified otherwise in the text, I will use the translation of James Charles-

speaker says he "was established and lived and was redeemed, and my foundations were laid on account of the Lord's hand; because He has planted me, for He set the root, and watered it and endowed it and blessed it, and its fruits will be forever." The speaker standing in a manner that suggests a tree does not in any way require one to presume that the speaker represents the cross of Jesus. One cannot validly conclude from these two instances (Odes 27 // 42) of the term wood (*xylon* / *qaysa*) that the Odes refer to the crucifixion of Jesus of Nazareth.

Some might argue that there are specific references to Christian themes in Ode 19, which discusses a virgin birth, and in Ode 24 where a dove flutters above the Messiah. But in both cases the imagery in the Odes is utterly unlike any that has ever been associated with the Christian idea of Mary or of the Spirit-dove in the story of Jesus' baptism. In Ode 19 we hear that the Father's breasts are full and that He is milked by the Spirit so that his milk runs into the cup which is the Son. The milk from the Father's breasts is the metaphorical semen that "the womb of the Virgin caught, and she conceived and gave birth." This is hardly an expansion of the Matthean or Lukan account! It is something wholly different. While in later centuries some Christians occasionally spoke of the milk of Christ, that is the not the metaphor used here where the Son is the cup receiving the milk of the Father.

The only other reference to a Virgin comes in Ode 33, which is a reference to God's Wisdom; the passage reads "The Perfect Virgin stood up proclaiming and crying out and saying 'Sons of men, turn back, and their daughters, come, and leave the ways of this Corruption and draw near to me....'" (5-7). This is not a reference to Mary but to the female Wisdom who speaks in passages such as this one from Proverbs 8:1-5: "Does not wisdom call out? Does not understanding raise her voice? At the highest point along the way, where the paths meet, she takes her stand; beside the gate leading into the city, at the entrance, she cries aloud: 'To you, O people, I call out; I raise my voice to all mankind. You who are simple, gain prudence; you who are foolish, set your hearts on it.'"

Ode 19 also contains a trinity of terms "Father," and "Son," and "Spirit," that became, of course, crucial to later Christian theology, but the terms are hardly unique to Christianity. The use of the concept

---

worth, found in his work *The Odes of Solomon: Edited, with Translation and Notes* Oxford UK: Clarendon Press, 1973.

"Father" for God, and the discussion of God's Spirit are common in Judaism, only the "Son" is unusual in that theological context. This trinity of terms is unusual in earliest Christianity, occurring only once as such in the New Testament (Matthew 28:19), but it is not a set of concepts that is unique to Matthew. The Spirit of Christ and the Spirit of the Father are conceived synonymously by Paul, who also refers to the Spirit of the Son (Romans 8:9-16, Galatians 4:6)). It is entirely possible, however, that the Odes community preceded and strongly influenced branches of earliest Christianity and so the fact that both communities occasionally utilize seemingly Trinitarian vocabulary indicates ideological connection, but it does not give us evidence of chronological priority. Indeed, when the Trinitarian terms are listed in Ode 23, they may be a later interpolation, for while line 21 refers to a letter entirely written by the finger of God, line 22 lists its authors as the Father and the Son and the Holy Spirit.

As for the dove, we hear in Ode 24:1-2 (Lattke): "The dove flew onto the head of our Lord Messiah, because he was her Head. And she cooed on/over him, and her voice was heard…" This might, at a stretch, appear to have something to do with the account in Mark 1:10 but as the passage continues on we quickly enter wholly alien territory, (3-4) "and the inhabitants were afraid, and the sojourners were disturbed,. The birds gave up their wing [beat], and all creeping things died in their hole," that soon becomes cosmic mythos, (5-6), "and the primal deeps were opened and covered. And they sought the Lord like those who are about to give birth, and/but he was not given to them for food, because he was not their own," One does not have to raise the question of what kind of Christian theology identifies the Messiah as the head of the Spirit (assuming that the Odes' dove is symbolic of the Spirit, which is very far from obvious) to realize that the conjunction of the words "dove" and "Messiah" here have nothing whatsoever to do with Mark's scene of the baptism of Jesus by John.

The Odes of Solomon are an extraordinary mixture of the incomprehensible (e.g. the bizarre accounts of the impregnation of a symbolic virgin with the Father's milk; the fluttering flight of a deadly dove who opens the door to primal deeps) with the platitudinous. The Odes are replete with boilerplate praise formulae that would not be at all out of place in a Christian church today or, for that matter, a synagogue, or a mosque, or a convocation of worshippers of Govinda. To give just one of many possible examples, Ode 40:1-2 reads (Lattke's translation): "As honey drips from the honeycomb of bees, and milk flows from the woman who loves her children, so also my hope is on thee, my God. As a spring gushes out its water, so my heart gushes out praises for the Lord, and my lips bring forth a hymn to him." Nothing about this sort of poetic piety is specific to Christianity.

The Transformation from Human to Divinity

What makes the Odes particularly interesting is their propensity to shift back and forth from poetic speech that seems to emerge from a human worshipper to speech that seems to emerge from a divine being, a Messiah, a Son of God. These speakers are so interwoven within various Odes that translators have added in "ex ore Christi" before some sentences and "ex ore Odist" before others to prompt readers to keep supposedly different characters separate. The original texts, however, see no need to try and separate speakers in this way. In Ode 10, for example, we hear that "The Lord has directed my mouth by His Word, and has opened my heart by His Light. And He has caused to dwell in me His immortal life, and permitted me to proclaim the fruit of His peace. To convert the lives of those who desire to come to Him, and to lead those who are captive into freedom." So far we hear the voice of a human being but the remainder of the Ode appears to be spoken by a divine person: "I took courage and became strong and captured the world, and the captivity became mine for the glory of the Most High, and of God my Father. And the Gentiles who had been dispersed were gathered together, but I was not defiled by my love for them, because they had praised me in high places. And the traces of light were set upon their heart, and they walked according to my life and were saved, and they became my people forever and ever." As is often the case in the Odes, we do not have here two separate people speaking, one human and one divine, but one person speaking who has been transformed from human to divine, a person in whom dwells God's immortal life who becomes a savior with a people whom he has saved. Presumably those who are saved are now in the same condition he is, once captives but now in freedom.

For a similar example we read in Ode 29 at first the words of a human person who has been transformed: "According to His mercies He exalted me, and according to His great honor He lifted me up. And he caused me to ascend from the depths of Sheol, and from the mouth of death He drew me. And I humbled my enemies, and He justified me by His grace. For I believed in the Lord's Messiah, and considered that He is the Lord." This transformed person immediately begins to speak as the one who drew him and transformed him, "He revealed to me His sign, and He led me by His light. And He gave me the scepter of His power, that I might subdue the devices of the people, and humble the power of the mighty. To make war by His Word, and to take victory by His power. And the Lord overthrew my enemy by His Word, and he became like the dust which a breeze carries off." If we do not insert separate speaker categories into the translation, and the originals contain nothing of that sort, then the one who ascends and is justified is also the one who has the scepter of power and who humbles the power of the mighty.

It is important to realize that the Odes are not just the product of speculation, wishful thinking, believer's faith or some other use of poetic imagination. Rather, the Odes, when they reflect a transformation of a human person to a divine person, ultimately derive from a particular type of human experience, one that is documented everywhere and through all times. That experience is a form of psychological dissociation that we can call "Spirit possession," a type of experience that is probably a genetically determined possibility available to anyone with the right cultural conditioning and group expectation. This conclusion follows simply from the observation that spirit possession seems to occur throughout the world in virtually all religious cultures.[17]

The Spirit possession experience is logically prior to any explanation of the experience. The experience can be described in secular terms as follows: one's primary personality is set aside or minimized and a secondary personality occurs. The secondary personality may speak fluently or incoherently and it may control the body well or poorly. Modern psychology will define this experience as a form of dissociation and

---

[17] Cf. for example, Bourguignon, Erika. *A Cross-Cultural Study of Dissociational States*. Columbus: Research Foundation, Ohio State University. 1968.
    Bourguignon, Erika. *Possession*. Chandler & Sharp Series in Cross-cultural Themes. San Francisco: Chandler & Sharp Publishers. 1976.
    Cohen, Emma. "What is Spirit Possession? Defining, Comparing, and Explaining Two Possession Forms" *Ethnos*, Vol. 73 No. 1, March 2008 (1-25).

discuss its origins and nature in reference to states of mind or measure the experience with an electroencephalograph.[18] In religious settings, however, the experience of such personality dissociation will usually be explained as the arrival into a person of an external secondary personality which will be understood to be that of God, a Spirit, an Ancestor and so forth depending on the local theology. Personality dissociation that has negative consequences will be understood to be the result of a demon, positive consequences will be associated with the arrival of a beneficial Spirit. Within a Judaic cultural setting (and within settings historically derived from the Judaic) the Holy Spirit is the term most often used. In secular terms "Holy Spirit" is an explanatory paradigm for positively valued experiences of personality dissociation in Judaic cultural settings.

The experience of Spirit possession is not that of a person experiencing, but rather of a person ceasing to experience while being replaced by another who does experience. A single body alternates persons who inhabit it, there being one person there some of the time and another person there some of the time. In the Odes of Solomon, a single body is transformed by the addition of a second person so that the first person becomes the second person, although presumably the active domination of the second person is occasional and the first person is normally dominant.

If the Odes derive from a kind of possession experience, then the odists will understand themselves sometimes to be speaking as the possessing divine entity and sometimes as themselves. Insofar as they have become a Spirit, they can speak sometimes as themselves transformed and sometimes as the Spirit within them. Speaking as Spirit, for example, the Odist speaks of descent, of arrival in this world from a world beyond this world. Speaking as a human merged with Spirit, the Odist speaks of ascent, of arrival in the paradise beyond this world, of becoming a divine person. Ode 36: (Lattke's translation)

The Spirit of the Lord rested upon me, and she lifted me up to the height and set me on my feet in the height of the Lord before his pleroma/fullness and his glory. While I gave praise by the composition

---

18 Cf. e.g. Oohashi, T., Kawai, N., Honda, M., Nakamura, S., Morimoto, M., Nishina, E., Maekawa, T. 2002. Electroencephalographic measurement of possession trance in the field. *Clinical Neurophysiology*, No. 113, 435-445.

of the odes, she brought me forth before the face of the Lord. And although I was a (son of) man, I was called the Shining One, the Son of God, while I was glorious among the glorious and was great among the great.

For according to the greatness of the Most High, so she made me, and according to his renewal he renewed me. And he anointed me from his perfection, and I was/became one of those beside him. And my mouth was opened like a cloud of dew, and my heart gushed forth a flood of righteousness. And my access was in peace and I was established in the Spirit of the plan of salvation. Hallelujah.

We find the following stages of transformation in Ode 36:

1. The Spirit of the Lord arrives; the speaker has an experience that receives this culturally conditioned explanation.

2. The experience is understood to include ascent to the presence of God, a common theme in Jewish mysticism.

3. The speaker, who is a human, a son of man, becomes a new type of being, here called "the Shining One," and "the Son of God." Charlesworth, assuming that the speaker is Jesus, assumes also that the Christian title "Son of Man" used sometimes in the Gospels for Jesus as a cosmic being should be used in translating this part of the Ode, and so he writes: "because I was the Son of Man, I was named the Light, the Son of God." But Lattke is not so tendentious; the phrase "son of man," is a Semitic language commonplace for any human being. As Lattke translates it, a human person becomes the anointed Son of God; Charlesworth understands the Ode to be about Jesus, the unique Son of Man.[19]

4. The speaker is transformed toward divinity by being remade "according to greatness" and "renewed."

5. The speaker is "anointed," and so is by definition a christ or a messiah, i.e. one who has been anointed.

6. The speaker is located in the heavenly space, "one of those beside him."

Ode 36 describes the speaker's experience as a Spirit-caused ascent resulting in transformation from a human status to a divine or heavenly status as anointed Son of God. There is no reason to doubt that if the

---

19 Translators of ancient Christian texts incorporate a considerable amount of commentary into their translations through their use of capitalization although no ancient language distinguished words in that way.

speaker can experience this one time he can experience it repeatedly. Since many of the Odes speak of what is evidently the same experience understood more or less in the same way, we can assume that this type of experience is available to members of the Odes community generally; it is evidently their prototypical experience and as far as we know the main point of their community life.

The speaker in the Ode becomes the Son of God and, through the Spirit of God, is anointed to become a being in the heavenly world. He takes on the past and the future of the Son of God, as various Odes describe it. To become Son of God or Messiah is to absorb both the Messiah's history and his mission. His history is to have escaped from the shackles and imprisonment of the world below, of Sheol, and his mission is to act as an ideal example for other humans. In more mythological terms, he brings them salvation from above so that they might recapitulate his career by escaping the shackles and imprisonment of the world below, ascending through the Spirit to become Son of God, and then bringing others salvation and so on.

We find an excellent example of such a transformation in Ode 17 where the speaker, having been unchained, becomes the liberator of others whose chains he destroys. Ode 17 begins with a transformation story: "Then I was crowned by my God, and my crown was living. And I was justified by my Lord, for my salvation is incorruptible. I have been freed from vanities, and am not condemned." In this instance the transformation is not described as an ascent but as liberation. "My chains were cut off by His hands, I received the face and likeness of a new person, and I walked in Him and was saved. And the thought of truth led me, and I went after it and wandered not. And all who saw me were amazed, and I seemed to them like a stranger." The speaker is a new person, newly unchained, now a stranger in the world from which he came. The Odes' process of transformation identifies the speaker not only with labeled categories of being (Son of God, Shining One, Anointed) and with categories of religious excellence (saved, renewed) but also with a mythological pattern, here one of bondage and freedom: "And from there He gave me the way of His steps, and I opened the doors which were closed. And I shattered the bars of iron, for my own shackles had grown hot and melted before me. And nothing appeared closed to me, because I was the opening of everything." The speaker, transformed, can now facilitate the transformation of others. As the

Ode begins the speaker's chains are cut off, now the speaker shatters bars and opens doors for others. "And I went towards all my bound ones in order to loose them; that I might not leave anyone bound or binding. And I gave my knowledge generously, and my resurrection through my love. And I sowed my fruits in hearts, and transformed them through myself. Then they received my blessing and lived, and they were gathered to me and were saved because they became my members, and I was their Head. Glory to You, our Head, O Lord Messiah." The Lord Messiah is both the savior and a status that one might strive to attain, the goal and culmination of the Odes religious quest, so that the speaker in the Ode is himself the saved savior.

The Odes of Solomon present a "saved savior" model such that potentially any and all human beings can receive the Spirit, ascend to the place of God, and be transformed into a Son of God to serve as a model so as to facilitate the saving transformation of others. Accordingly, the Odes shift deliberately back and forth between a human speaker and a divine speaker or, as some translators have it, between the Odist and Christ. One must bear in mind, however, that an Ode will be spoken by a single individual and reflect the experience of the person who composed it.

The idea that the Odist and Christ are two separate persons is mistaken. The Odes speak of the transformation of the speaker (the "Odist") into the one spoken about ("Christ"). The mythological career of the Christ was that he was in bondage below but escaped his bonds and soared into heaven, which is also the metaphorical career of the Speaker who was liberated from chains and taken into heaven from here below. There is, in the Odes, a mythological Christ prototype that is assumed by the speaker, the successful human being ("son of man") who becomes the Son of God. If we think about this in terms of the Spirit-possession paradigm common throughout the world, then it is no great surprise that one person can speak as both a human and a divine being.

As discussed above, there is no mention of Jesus in the Odes anywhere, no mention of the crucifixion anywhere, not one saying of Jesus or miracle story about him found in any gospel is referenced in any of the Odes. When the Odes speak of mythological activities of the savior, they are activities that have never been connected with Jesus. For example, the Odes' motif of escaping imprisonment and breaking shackles of iron is not mentioned in any account of Jesus' life. In a manner not characteristic of Christianity the speaker in Ode 22 is given the power to destroy the seven headed serpent, as well as the power to free others from bondage, as we can see in Lattke's translation: "He who brought me down from the high places which are above, and has brought me up from the places in the depth below,"which nicely shows the commensurability of the savior who descends and the saved who ascends, and "He who has scattered my enemies and my adversaries. He who has given me authority over bonds, to release them. He who has smitten the serpent with seven heads by my hands. He has set me up over its root so that I might wipe out its seed." Stories like this are simply not connected to the tradition of Jesus of Nazareth in any way. They are stories where the human speaker and a divine personage shift identities back and forth. The divine person has scattered the enemies and adversaries of the human speaker who then receives authority to release people from bonds (a standard role of the savior in the Odes). The speaker's hands destroy the seven headed serpent, whatever that might be, and the speaker becomes the cosmic warrior who will wipe out the seed of the serpent.

The Odes characteristically blur the distinction between the speaker and the spoken-of, between the son of man and the anointed Son of God. While the Odes share some language and conceptions with the Christianity associated with Jesus of Nazareth, they have nothing to do with him.

In his fascinating book on the New Testament Christological Hymns, which are Philemon 2:6-11, Colossians 1:15-20, Ephesians 2:14-16, 1 Timothy 3:16, 1 Peter 3:18-22, Hebrews 1:3, and the Prologue to the Gospel of John, Jack T. Sanders finds that the hymns "all seem to present generally the same myth of the redeemer, involving his participating in creation, his descent and ascent to and from the world, and his work of redemption."[20] "It may reasonably be assumed that this mythical drama has some background in the history of religions, that the way was already prepared in the general (or in some particular) religious milieu of early Christianity for the formulation of this particular myth – if the myth had not in reality already been formulated."[21]

---

20 Sanders, Jack T. *The New Testament Christological Hymns: Their Historical Background*, Cambridge UK: Cambridge University Press, 1971 24.
21 Ibid. 25.

Sanders argues that the similarities in the Christological hymns and the Prologue to John "necessitate some kind of unified explanation of the historical religious background of all the hymns together, not of any one in isolation."[22] His observation that there is a common redeemer myth embedded in a variety of New Testament hymns leads him to believe that this myth existed before the rise of the Christian religion so that there was, in a sense, a pre-Jesus Christianity in existence, one that was then adapted to the movement that became the Jesus-oriented Christian religion.

Sanders believes that the background to the New Testament Christological hymns "is in all probability to be sought in pre-Christian Judaism," a form of pre-Christian Judaism that spoke of a "divine figure that was in the image (likeness, form) of God, i.e. that it possessed equality with God, that it participated in creation and embodied the All, that it descended from the sphere of the divine to the sphere of the mortal, that it in some way entered into human existence, i.e. became identified with human existence for the sake of the revelatory task."[23]

After having analyzed the canonical New Testament Christological hymns, Sanders takes up the analysis of the Odes of Solomon. He studies the Odes' connection to the themes of the canonical Christological hymns and comes to the strong conclusion that their "parallels with the New Testament Christological hymns are so close as to imply either influence from one to the other, or influence from a common background. Thus one must ask, 'Did these elements come into the Odes of Solomon from Christianity, or from somewhere else?'"[24] After considerable discussion, he concludes that the Odes of Solomon contain only a few, and perhaps no, signs of Christian influence. The few that they do seem to contain probably, in his view, and in the opinion of other scholars whom to whom he refers, derive from later scribal interpolations. In Sanders' opinion, the Odes of Solomon originate from a Jewish group that was in existence shortly before the rise of Christianity.[25]

Sanders notes that "the possibility that the myth in the New Testament Christological hymns was already intact prior to its use by Christianity is still further increased when it is seen that the redeemer myth

---
22 Ibid. 57.
23 Ibid. 96-97.
24 Ibid. 104.
25 Ibid. 113.

of the Odes of Solomon is connected with a stage of hypostatization of divine qualities less developed than the stage present in the New Testament Christological hymns."[26] He argues that the mixture of ideas found in the Odes of Solomon probably arose independently of the New Testament and therefore, "then presumably also prior to it; therefore, the possibility is increased that the element of cosmic reconciliation, which completes the act of redemption, had already become a part of the developing myth lying behind the New Testament Christological hymns prior to its appropriation by Christianity. The redeemer of the Odes of Solomon certainly effects redemption by incorporating the redeemed, as is clear from Ode 17:14f."[27] While a "myth" is known to us only as it is found in ancient texts, it once was the centerpiece of a social movement, of a cult whose practices, whatever they might have been, were far more extensive than simply propagating a myth. Accordingly, when Sanders proposes that there was a myth that preceded the rise of Jesus-oriented Christianity, one that came to be incorporated into that Christianity, he is proposing that a cult, an assembly of like-minded people, existed. This fact is trivially obvious, but it can be overlooked.

Not only does Sanders conclude that the Odes of Solomon are evidence of a pre-Jesus Jewish Christianity that incorporated the main themes of crucially important New Testament Christological hymns, he does something few other scholars ever do: he looks north. It should be, but often is not, obvious that there were cultural influences on Galilee, and Samaria, and even Judea that come from the north, from Syria, Tyre, Sidon, Damascus, Antioch, influences on Judaism that were not Judean in origin. We should especially bear in mind the fact that Paul of Tarsus, when he was first initiated (by God, he would say) into the Christian faith, had an experience that took place near a Christian community in Damascus, and that he spent some of his early years with a Christian community in Antioch, and that he saw no purpose in visiting Jerusalem until three years of his time as a Christian had passed.

There were, of course, religions in the ancient world near Palestine that were not Judaism and Jewish people and Jewish cults were influenced to lesser or greater degrees by those religions. In reading the

---
26 Ibid. 114.
27 Ibid. 113.

Odes of Solomon, Jack T. Sanders is struck by the frequency of their use of the word "Lord." That word leads to some ambiguity for two reasons. First, it is not always clear when the term "Lord" refers to God and when the word "Lord" refers to the secondary figure of the Son or Messiah. Second, influenced by their Christian backgrounds, modern scholars will tend to assume that "Lord" refers to the Lord Jesus Christ even though there is no place in the Odes where this is evident.

Sanders suggests that the word "Lord" in Hebrew, which is "Adon," the plural of which, "Adonai" is commonly used in Judaism as the name or title of the Jewish God, may have entered the community of the Odes of Solomon from another religious tradition than Judaism, the tradition that worshipped Adon, the Lord, as God, the religion of the worship of Adonis. Sanders writes that ," Adonis, it should be remembered, is the western designation of Tammuz (or, viewed otherwise, Tammuz is regularly designated simply 'the Lord'), and his influence was felt on Jewish religion before the time of Ezekiel, as is attested by Ezek. Viii.14: 'Then he brought me to the entrance of the north gate of the house of the Lord; and behold, there sat women weeping for Tammuz.'"[28] Sanders does not push this point of view very far, he writes that "the eclecticism present in the Odes of Solomon prevents a final explanation of the character of the redeemer they present simply in terms of a fusing between concepts from Judaism and from the cult of Adonis; still, the Odes of Solomon seem to attest that Judaism could, under some outside influence, give birth to at least one myth of redemption similar to that displayed in the New Testament Christological humans, and yet apparently independent of the New Testament tradition."[29] Looking to the north, as Sanders did, will remind us of the fact that the people of Judea, and much more so the people of Galilee were influenced by a host of different religious ideas and systems.

Leaving aside possible connections to the religion of Adonis to the north, the Odes do have a strong relationship with the mystical tradition of late second-Temple Judaism to the Judean south. April de Conick writes that "It is apparent that during the Second Temple Period, an esoteric tendency was developing and manifesting itself within different varieties of Judaism including the Philonic corpus, the sectarian communities of the Therapeutae and Qumran, apocalyptic circles,

---
28 Ibid. 109-110.
29 Ibid. 113.

and rabbinic teachings. This early Jewish mysticism filtered into Christianity, Gnosticism, and the Hekhalot literature, teaching that, after proper preparations, one could seek to ascend into heaven in order to gain heavenly knowledge and a transforming vision of the deity."[30] This is the background of some of the Odes of Solomon.[31]

From the Dead Sea Scrolls' hymn 4Q491-C we hear of the ascent of a person to the presence of God and of that person's identification with the holy beings who reside there: "I am reckoned with the gods and my abode is in the holy congregation. [My] desi[re] is not according to the flesh, and everything precious to me is in the glory [of] the holy [habit]ation. [Wh]om have I considered contemptible? Who is comparable to me in my glory? Who of those who sail the seas shall return telling [of] my [equa]l? Who shall [experience] troubles like me? And who is like me [in bearing] evil? I have not been taught, but no teaching compares.... [with my teaching]. Who then shall attack me when [I] ope[n my mouth]? Who can endure the utterance of my lips? Who shall arraign me and compare with my judgment [... Fo]r I am reck[oned] with the gods, [and] my glory with that of the sons of the King."[32] The Odes of Solomon too identify the one who ascends with the divine beings who are in God's presence, as we will discuss below.

David Aune writes, in connection to Ode 38:1 specifically, where we hear "I went up to the light of truth as if into a chariot and the truth took me and led me," as well as to Odes 36:1-2, 11:16-17, 20:7, 38:1, 36:1-2, that "the mention of a chariot within a context where a trip to the celestial Paradise is in view calls to mind Gershom Scholem's claim that Paul's use of the term "Paradise" in II Cor. 12:3 together with an experience of mystical transport puts the apostle of the Gentiles in the tradition of Jewish Merkabha ("chariot") mysticism.[33] The Antiquity of this variety of Jewish mysticism is attested by the discovery of the so-called Angelic Liturgy (4QS1) at Qumran, revealing that the Essenes

---

30 De Conick April, *Seek to See Him: Ascent and Vision Mysticism in the Gospel of Thomas*, Leiden: E. J. Brill, 1996. 38.
31 For example, Ode 38: "I went up into the light of Truth as into a chariot, and the Truth led me and caused me to come. And caused me to pass over chasms and gulfs, and saved me from cliffs and valleys. And became for me a haven of salvation, and set me on the place of immortal life."
32 For the full translation refer to http://www.qumran.org/js/qumran/hss/4q491
33 Scholem, Gershom, *Major Trends in Jewish Gnosticism*, New York: Schocken, 1941 16f.

of Qumran were occupied with the Throne or Chariot mysticism so characteristic of medieval Jewish mysticism." [34]

Aune concludes with these remarks: "To summarize, the Odes of Solomon appear to be a collection of prophetic or charismatic hymns of praise and thanksgiving which were of central importance in the cultic worship of Christian communities in Syria. The Spirit of God is the agent who enables the cult leader and the congregation to participate in eschatological salvation through the proleptic experience of participating in the future heavenly worship of God within the setting of an earthly community assembled for worship. The participation of the congregation in this experience is demonstrated by the frequent shift from 'I' to 'we' in the Odes, the characteristic use of plural imperatives, and the final 'Hallelujah.'"[35] This summary characterizes the communitarian setting of the Odes quite well, although I do not believe that "Christian" here should be understood to refer to the religion founded upon Jesus of Nazareth. The religion of the Odes is surely as he describes it, a cult comprised of people who are focused on a mystical prophetic experience closely related to the ascension mysticism of second temple Judaism. As such the religion of the Odes presumably was attractive to intellectuals who appreciated the beauty of the Odists' compositions and who could undergo the spiritual disciplines necessary to the experiences of ascension mysticism.

April DeConick has pointed out significant connections between pre-Christian Jewish ascension mysticism and some of the sayings found in the Gospel of Thomas, particularly the dialogue of saying 50 and the mystical revelation of sayings 83 and 84.[36] She also observes that the Odes of Solomon share motifs with certain Thomasine passages, noting that saying number 108 of the Gospel of Thomas: "Jesus

---

[34] Aune, n.1 186, and cf. Dupont-Sommer, Andre. *The Essene Writings from Qumran*, London: Peter Smith, 1973 332-35.

[35] Aune, 182-183.

[36] 50a Jesus said: If they ask you "Where are you from?" reply to them "We have come from the place where light is produced from itself. It came and revealed itself in their image." 50b. If they ask you "Are you it?" reply to them, "We are his sons. We are chosen ones of the living father." 50c. If they ask you "What is the sign within you of your father?" reply to them, "It is movement. It is rest." 83. Jesus said: The images are revealed to people. The light within them is hidden in the image of the father's light. He will be revealed. His image is hidden in his light. 84. Jesus said: You are pleased when you see your own likeness. When you see your images that came into being before you did, immortal and invisible images, how much can you bear?

said: He who drinks from my mouth will become like I am, and I will become him. And the hidden things will be revealed to him," derives from the same wisdom-based conceptual background as Ode 11:6-9 "And speaking waters touched my lips from the fountain of the Lord generously. And so I drank and became intoxicated, from the living water that does not die. And my intoxication did not cause ignorance, but I abandoned vanity, and turned toward the Most High, my God, and was enriched by His favors. I rejected the folly cast upon the earth, and stripped it off and cast it from me. And the Lord renewed me with His garment, and possessed me by His light." Indeed, the motif of "stripping off" also can be found in Thomas' gospel, for saying 37 says: "His disciples asked him: When will you appear to us? When will we see you? Jesus replied: When you strip naked without shame and trample your clothing underfoot just as little children do then you will look at the son of the living one without being afraid." Motifs such as these probably stem from the Jewish wisdom tradition.

The Odes of Solomon are part of the development of Jewish mysticism in the later second Temple period. Ideas they contain are found also in hymns from the Dead Sea scrolls' Essene community and in sayings attributed at an early time to Jesus of Nazareth. The Odes are ideologically connected with forms of Judaism that preceded Christianity and with forms of Christianity, but nothing they contain requires them to be dated to a time after the lifetime of Jesus of Nazareth.

The Influence of Odes Judaism in the Rise of Christianity
Paul's Religion of Transformation

Before the hardening of Christianity into The Church in the later second century, much of the Christian religion was the same as the Odes religion, although the Odes are not Christian. The fundamental identity of savior and saved that is found in the Odes is also a fundamental idea in the early Christianity oriented to Jesus. I will discuss that theme as it appears in two major sources, the letters of Paul and the Gospel of John, stressing the fact that in both texts the Savior, Son of God, Messiah, whom those texts identify with Jesus, is identified with the individuals who are saved through the experience of the Spirit who enters into and possesses the individuals. I see no reason to doubt that the experiences discussed in John's Gospel under the category "Paraclete," and by Paul of Tarsus under the category "Spirit," are fundamentally the same. Certainly they have been assumed to be the same throughout the history of Christian theological discussion.

Paul's letters are the earliest known Christian documents. Paul identifies himself as the saved savior when he writes in Galatians 2:20: "I have been crucified with Christ and I no longer live, but Christ lives in me." This identification of the saved with the savior is fundamental to Pauline Christianity and not just an idiosyncratic experience of the apostle himself. As he sees it, "God sent his Son, born of a woman, born under the law, to redeem those under the law, that we might receive adoption as Sons. Because you are his Sons, God sent the Spirit of his Son into our hearts, the Spirit who calls out, 'Abba, Father.' So you are no longer a slave, but God's Son; and since you are his Son, God has made you also an heir," Galatians 4:4-7 and cf. Romans 8:14-16). Translators often try to distinguish the Son (capitalized) from the people who have become son (not capitalized) via the Spirit, or even to use "Son" for the one and "child" for the other. But in the Greek they are not distinguished. As Paul can say "I no longer live, but Christ lives in me," so can any Christian transformed by the experience called the Spirit of the Son say, "I am the Son of God," just as he may say "I am Christ" if Christ lives in him.

One must remember that the Spirit is an explanatory hypothesis for certain kinds of experience rather than an entity out there in the external world, and that the Spirit experience is the substitution of one personality for another so that one becomes that which one believes oneself to be possessed by. While these fundamental factors in possession are considered obvious facts when applied to our understanding of demonic possession, or when one discusses possession phenomena in other cultures, it is surprisingly difficult to find this applied to possession in early Christianity. "If you receive the Spirit of Christ you become Christ" sounds preposterous, even though it is a simple restatement of the possession paradigm, and there is every reason to think that when Paul says that Christ lives in him (Gal. 2:20) this is because he has received the Spirit of Christ (Rom. 8:9). It is hard for many to think that receiving the Spirit of the Son means to Paul that you are the Son of God despite the fact that Paul says so. The difficulty arises from the fact that Christianity stopped being a possession-oriented religion in the mid-second century C.E. and henceforth for two thousand years it has been a Christian commonplace that whatever you might say about Christ the Son of God, you are not him and you cannot become him.

David Aune believes that the Odes of Solomon are the sort of hymns Paul describes with the term *odai pneumatikai* or "spiritual songs" in Col. 3:16 and that "a member of the Pauline circle connects this term even more closely with inspired utterance: 'Be filled with the Spirit, addressing one another in psalms and hymns and spiritual odes.'" (Eph. 5:18b-19).[37] He believes that such odes were sung during ecstatic congregational worship "enabling the Christian community assembled for worship to encounter a proleptic experience of worshipping God in the presence of heavenly angelic beings in Paradise.[38] We also find, in Ephesians 2:4-6, a passage that could have come directly from one of the Odes of Solomon describing, in the past tense, heavenly ascent to Paradise: "But because of his great love for us, God, who is rich in mercy, made us alive with Christ even when we were dead in transgressions—it is by grace you have been saved. And God raised us up with Christ and seated us with him in the heavenly realms in Christ Jesus." The religious experiences advocated in Pauline Christianity seem to have been quite similar to those advocated in the Odes of Solomon.

Transformation in the Gospel of John

I won't make many arguments of my own regarding John's Gospel but I will take advantage of the conclusions drawn by the great Johannine scholar Raymond Brown, who recognizes that the Spirit-Paraclete that comes to dwell within Christians transforms them into what Jesus also was. Brown writes of John 17:20-26 that, "from the viewpoint of a later and more precise theology, one might like to have a sharper differentiation than John provides between God's incarnation in Jesus and God's indwelling in the Christian – in other words between natural Sonship and general Christian sonship."[39] Further, Brown concludes that the Spirit "carries on the earthly work of Jesus. The Paraclete/Spirit is not corporeally visible and his presence will only be by indwelling in

---

37 Aune, 177.
38 Ibid., 179.
39 Brown, Raymond. *The Gospel According to John (xiii-xxi)*: Anchor Bible Series, Garden City NY: Doubleday and Company, 1970, 779.

the disciples," and so "the presence of Jesus after his return to the Father is accomplished in and through the Paraclete. Not two presences but the same presence is involved."[40] "It is our contention," Brown writes, "that John presents the Paraclete as the Holy Spirit in a special role, namely, as the personal presence of Jesus in the Christian while Jesus is with the Father."[41] Indeed, "the Paraclete is to Jesus what Jesus is to the Father."[42]

Brown concludes that, "The one whom John calls 'another Paraclete' is another Jesus," and so "Jesus' promises to dwell within his disciples are fulfilled in the Paraclete."[43] Like Paul, John assumes an identity of the Spirit-possessed person that would validate an identity of that person with the Messiah, or the Son of God, or even with Jesus himself. John's Gospel claims that one can learn the teachings of Jesus through the Paraclete, which means in real cultic life that when a person living after the time of Jesus' death who is possessed by the Paraclete speaks, the words will be attributed to Jesus; as Brown translates John 14:26: "the Paraclete, the Holy Spirit, that the Father will send in my name, will remind you of all that I told you [myself]." The sayings of Jesus found in John's Gospel, which are radically different from sayings found in other sources (Mark, Thomas, Q) derive from Jesus, to be sure, but this Jesus is the Paraclete speaking in Greek through the mouths of persons in a state of possession by his Spirit. While the vocabulary is diverse, the underlying assumption is simple: through a particular type of experience understood to be that of an externally existing Spirit entering into him and transforming him, a person becomes another divine person so that, as Brown put it, there is "the personal presence of Jesus in the Christian." [44]

Ode 12:12: "For the dwelling place of the Word is man," is remarkably similar to John 1:14, "the Word became flesh and dwelt in us." While the Greek sentence in John's Gospel (ὁ λόγος σὰρξ ἐγένετο καὶ ἐσκήνωσεν ἐν ἡμῖν,) is usually translated "the word became flesh and dwelt among us," the Greek word ἐν can be translated with either the English preposition "in" or "among." The preposition "in" construes

---

40 Ibid., 644, 645.
41 Ibid., 1139.
42 Ibid., 1140.
43 Ibid., 1141.
44 Brown, 1139.

the passage to refer to the Word potentially dwelling within any human being; the preposition "among" understands the Word to be one unique human being, Jesus. This is something of an archetypal case, for understanding the sentence one way reveals an underlying religion of transformation behind the Johannine prologue where the Word dwells within us, while construing it the other way reveals a religion focused on worshipping a unique divine person, Jesus, who once lived among us. I argue that Christianity did move from the former type of religion, transformative, to the latter type, Jesus-centric, in the course of its first century of existence. The prologue to the Gospel of John may have first expressed a transformative understanding of the Word "in" us only to be incorporated into a biographical narrative where, in that context, it henceforth is to be understood as a reference unique to Jesus dwelling "among" us.

Charlesworth finds the ideas of Johannine Christianity to be so similar to ideas found in the Odes of Solomon that he concludes that the two must arise from a common milieu. "It is improbable that the Odes systematically borrowed from John," he writes, "the most probable solution, at this stage in our research, is that both the author of John and the odist contemporaneously inhabited not only the same milieu but perhaps the same community."[45] If there were, as I argue here, pre-Christian communities of Odes Judaism, the Gospel of John perhaps represents the next stage in the development of those communities themselves as they merge with the cult that arose from the followers of Jesus of Nazareth.

To summarize my observations so far:

1. The Odes of Solomon are not Christian in the sense that they do not show any awareness of the religion that is oriented to Jesus of Nazareth.

2. The Odes of Solomon feature an experience of transformation such that through the experience of Spirit and ascent, individuals identify themselves as Christ or Son of God and their own speech, history and mission can be understood to be those of the Christ or Son of God.

3. Principal texts of the Christian religion oriented to Jesus of Nazareth also speak of an experience of transformation such that through the experience of Spirit, individuals can identify themselves as Christ

---

45 Charlesworth, *Critical Reflections*, 216.

or the Son of God.

It is clear to me, as it has been clear to everyone who has studied the Odes of Solomon, that the ideas and phraseology of the Odes is quite similar to those found in early Christianity. This does not mean that the movement arising from Jesus of Nazareth led to the writing of the Odes of Solomon. Rather, I believe that the temporal arrow, or arrow of causality, should be pointed in the opposite direction. I think it is more likely that the Odes of Solomon existed before Jesus of Nazareth was ever born, than that the Odes of Solomon emerged from the Jesus of Nazareth cult.

Intertextuality of the Odes of Solomon

Evidently, the people who wrote about the Odes in the earliest times for which we have records believed that the Odes were Jewish hymns composed at roughly the same time as the Psalms of Solomon, c. 50 B.C.E.[46]. If we must separate ancient religious writing of the Palestinian region into two great volumes, the Hebrew Bible and the New Testament, then the Odes of Solomon belong in the Hebrew Bible category, to be labeled perhaps Hebrew Bible apocrypha. That is how they were regarded in the ancient world, so far as we know. Both the manuscript evidence and the evidence from lists of ancient religious texts (stichometria – discussed by Lattke) show that the Odes of Solomon were always copied in sequence with the Psalms of Solomon.[47] Further, in ancient stichometria they were included in the category of Hebrew Bible apocrypha along with the Psalms of Solomon, the Wisdom of

---

46 The Psalms of Solomon are eighteen hymns similar in style to the canonical psalms. Today they exist only in Greek but they were originally Hebrew. One of the psalms describes the death of the Roman general Pompey (48 B.C.E.) and they can be dated c. 70 B.C.E. – 40 B.C.E. overall. They defend the legalism of the Pharisees against the supposed immorality of the Saducees and they distain the Hasmonean dynasty and priesthood. Occasionally the Psalms of Solomon discuss "the Lord Messiah" and envision him as a political figure, a human person given special powers by God, who will battle successfully to liberate Israel from foreign occupation and install a reign of righteousness forever. Until that time the Psalms of Solomon believe that God properly allows his people to suffer as punishment for their sins. While these Psalms are bound together with the Odes in ancient text collections, and both may derive from roughly the same time period, they are from two different Jewish communities and reflect quite different ways of thinking even when they refer to the same subject such as the Messiah.

47 Lattke, 1-2.

Solomon and the books of Maccabees.[48] Lattke writes "whether there was ever a collection limited to the Odes of Solomon (i.e., without the Psalms of Solomon) is unknown."[49] He observes that Lactantius, writing in ca. 305 C.E., "doubts neither the (prophetically inspired) authorship of the Odes of Solomon nor their place in the canon of his OT."[50] In ancient times both the Psalms of Solomon and the Odes of Solomon were regarded as Jewish writings, distinct from writings of the Christian religion. As with all of the texts of the Hebrew Bible, Christian authors felt free to make use of them as sacred scripture, but the Christian use of a text does not, of course, make that text a Christian text.

Lattke writes that "the dependence of the Odes of Solomon on – or their relation to – the Johannine corpus (especially John and 1 John) has always been highlighted. But it only became clear with the completion of this commentary that in addition to the pseudo-and deutero-Pauline letters (especially Colossians, Ephesians, and 1 Timothy) Hebrews, and the letters ascribed to Peter (1 Peter), all seven of the authentic Pauline epistles, the Synoptic Gospels (especially Matthew), and possibly Revelation had all exerted a quite surprising influence in the shaping of the Odes of Solomon."[51] All that, and yet there is not one quotation or clear allusion from any of those texts in any of the Odes!

Claims that the Odes of Solomon are dependent on the Johannine corpus requires clear literary proof via cause-and-effect intertextuality. Claims that there is a relation between the Johannine corpus and the Odes corpus means that people sharing ideas interacted with each other, and that is quite a different thing, one having no necessary temporal or causal arrow connected with it. Literary intertextuality means that the one written manuscript pre-existed another that depends on it, while ideological relationships are much more fluid in terms of timelines. So, while one does find similarities between phrases or ideas or vocabulary in the Odes of Solomon and in a wide variety of early Christian writings, there is not thereby any certain arrow of time and causality. Professor Charlesworth and others have found a host of intertextual commonalities between the Essenes' Dead-Sea scrolls and the Odes of

---

48 Ibid.
49 Ibid., 5 n. 32.
50 Ibid., 2.
51 Ibid., 13-14.

Solomon; the Dead-Sea scrolls were completed and hidden away before most of the New Testament authors had written their texts.

Professor Lattke is mistaken when he reasons from the similarities he finds between one set of documents and another that the one set therefore pre-existed and exerted a causal influence on the other. I see no reason to conclude from ideological and phraseological similarities that a whole host of New Testament texts "exerted a quite surprising influence in the shaping of the Odes of Solomon."[52] On the contrary, I think it is much more likely that the Odes of Solomon exerted quite a surprising influence in the shaping of the New Testament. I mean only that ideas and phrases found in the Odes of Solomon were written before the time when similar ideas and phrases were written into the New Testament, and that the community behind the Odes of Solomon was in existence before there were any Christian communities oriented to Jesus of Nazareth. I have no reason to believe that any New Testament author had ever read any of the Odes, or that any author of the Odes had ever read any of the New Testament.

The Odes of Solomon, I believe, came first; the writing in the New Testament was later, perhaps a generation or two later. I believe that the ancients who placed the Odes of Solomon alongside the Psalms of Solomon and who included both texts in their lists of Hebrew Bible apocryphal books had it right. I believe that the reason Jesus of Nazareth is not known by name, or by quotation, or by deed, or by stories of crucifixion and resurrection anywhere in the Odes of Solomon is because they were written before the time of Jesus' ministry. I think that the Odes come from the period 50 B.C.E. – 25 C.E., roughly the time that many of the Dead Sea scrolls were produced and not far from the period that is commonly assigned to the Psalms of Solomon.

Paul of Tarsus and the Odes of Solomon

Earlier in this essay I discussed how Paul (and John, and others, such as the author of Ephesians 2:6) believed, along with the authors of the Odes of Solomon, that a human being could be transformed through the Spirit of the Son into a Son of God, a Christ, and that Paul believed this had occurred to him, for Christ now lives in him – he has had the experience called "the Spirit of Christ." At the beginning of his letter to

---

52 Ibid.

the Galatians Paul tells us how he understands that experience first to have occurred in his own life: Galatians 1:13-2:1a

> For you have heard of my previous way of life in Judaism, how intensely I persecuted the church of God and tried to destroy it. I was advancing in Judaism beyond many of my own age among my people and was extremely zealous for the traditions of my fathers. But when God, who set me apart from my mother's womb and called me by his grace, was pleased to reveal his Son in me so that I might preach him among the Gentiles, my immediate response was not to consult any human being. I did not go up to Jerusalem to see those who were apostles before I was, but I went into Arabia. Later I returned to Damascus. Then after three years, I went up to Jerusalem to get acquainted with Cephas and stayed with him fifteen days. I saw none of the other apostles—only James, the Lord's brother. I assure you before God that what I am writing you is no lie. Then I went to Syria and Cilicia. I was personally unknown to the churches of Judea that are in Christ. They only heard the report: "The man who formerly persecuted us is now preaching the faith he once tried to destroy." And they praised God because of me. Then after fourteen years, I went up again to Jerusalem. (NIV)

This account is supplemented by stories in Luke's Acts of the Apostles and in other letters of Paul's (Acts 9:1-2; 22:4-5; and 26:9-1; 1 Cor 15:9; and Phil 3:6)., but the autobiographical account in Galatians tells us enough.

Paul's conversion takes place about 33 C.E. Udo Schnelle in his recent comprehensive study of Paul dates the conversion to 33 C.E., and Jerome Murphy-O'Connor does so too, but the conversion has been dated as late (!) as 35 C.E.[53] Jesus' crucifixion is dated by some to 30 C.E. but many scholars conclude that 33 C.E. is the correct date. (Raymond Brown says that he cannot decide between 30 and 33.). The period between Jesus' crucifixion and Paul's conversion may have been as much

---

53 Schnelle, Udo. *Apostle Paul: His Life and Theology*, Grand Rapids, MI: Baker Academic, 2005, 87.
Murphy-O'Connor, Jerome. *Paul: A Critical Life*, New York, NY: Oxford University Press, 1998, 7.

as five years or even less than one year if the crucifixion and conversion both occurred in 33 C.E.

Evidently the churches that Paul persecuted covered a remarkably large geographical area. Presumably Paul spent some period of time persecuting them, for he says he intensely persecuted the churches and tried to destroy them. There is no reason at all to believe that such persecution started and ended with Paul himself. Presumably he had associates. It probably preceded his participation, and later on it may have segued as a historical process into the persecution of churches organized by the followers of Jesus of Nazareth.

According to Paul's eyewitness testimony there were churches to be persecuted that extended from Jerusalem through Judea and Galilee at least to Damascus and quite possibly into Arabia, whence Paul traveled immediately after his conversion experience. Given the time frame, as little as one year (33 C.E.) to no more than five (30 C.E. to 35 C.E.) it is impossible that the religion of Jesus of Nazareth the crucified and resurrected Savior managed to begin, then expand, then spread out as a network of church communities from Jerusalem and Judea past Samaria through Galilee and all the way Damascus while engaging activities so nefarious as to spur persecution, and then to suffer the consequent intense and destructive persecution about which Paul reports. I think that it is likely that our assumption that Paul persecutes a network of Christian churches founded through the mission of Jesus of Nazareth and his immediate family (James, Mary, etc.) and disciples (Peter, John, etc.) is wrong. Rather, there was a network of communities oriented to the Judaism of the Odes of Solomon that existed well before c. 33 C.E. stretching at least from Jerusalem to Damascus.

Paul adds some extraordinary information about the situation prior to his conversion when he reports in First Corinthians that he first told the Corinthian Christians something he had himself been told, which is that the risen Jesus appeared, in order, to Cephas, the Twelve, and "to over five hundred brothers at once, of whom the greater part are still alive, although some have died," (1 Cor. 15:6) and after that to James, then to all the apostles and finally to Paul himself. Paul reports that all of this took place in the brief period prior to Paul's conversion in 35 C.E. or before, during the time of Paul's active persecution of the churches. We should not underestimate the fact that Paul finds it reasonable that there would have been more than five hundred Christians gathered in one place all experiencing something they came to regard as an appearance of Jesus. Further, by telling us that many of them are still alive, Paul claims there are eyewitness participants in this event who can confirm it. One might speculate that the number given is exaggerated, but the significant fact for our purpose is that Paul believes such an event could have taken place, which in turn confirms the impression one receives from his reports of persecuting churches from Jerusalem to Damascus that there were an awful lot of Christians at an awfully early time. Presumably the hundreds of people he mentions in 1 Cor. 15:6 had gathered for some purpose other than watching the skies in hopes of seeing Jesus. What actually happened then is a puzzle, to be sure, but the fact is that Paul believes himself supported by hundreds of potential eyewitnesses in reporting that over five hundred people at one time were gathered together pursuant to some sort of Christian activity ca. 30 – 34 C.E. There seems to have been a much more extensive Christian religious movement at that period than is generally assumed.

Paul quotes the churches in Judea as having heard from other churches in the network that "the man who formerly persecuted us is now preaching the faith he once tried to destroy," and Paul regards this as a statement of fact (Gal. 1:23). This is Paul reporting on Paul's own life and experience and so is a uniquely strong piece of evidence that Paul joined a network of churches that taught a Pauline Christianity. If so, then the view commonly held during the past century that Christianity was founded on Jesus' moralistic and apocalyptic teachings only to become a complex soteriological religion through the inventiveness of Paul is quite mistaken. Paul did not join a network of hypothetical Q-sayings oriented communities concerned about the apocalyptic kingdom to come, as Bart Ehrman, Dominic Crossan and others argue arose in Galilee and Judea (if anything did) in response to the teachings of Jesus.[54] The discontinuity between the historical Jesus as he has been constructed by scholars throughout the past century and the form of religion preached by the apostle Paul is so overpowering that some conclude that there was no historical Jesus at all.[55] Some others

---

[54] Crossan, John Dominic. *The Historical Jesus*, New York NY: HarperOne 1993
Ehrman Bart. *Jesus : Apocalyptic Prophet of the New Millennium*, New York NY: Oxford University Press, 1999.
[55] Cf. Doherty, Earl. *The Jesus Puzzle: Did Christianity begin with a mythical Christ?* Ottawa CA: Canadian Humanist Publications 1999.

believe that Paul invented the Christianity he preached ab novo or, as he would say, from divine revelation, but Paul reports to us that he has joined with a group of communities that were preaching the religion that he himself began to preach, and since the religion Paul preaches is one focused largely on the experience of the transformational Spirit of God/Christ/Son it is not difficult to argue that the churches he first persecuted and then joined were also focused largely on the experience of the transformational Spirit of God/Christ/Son, as was the Jewish religion of the Odes of Solomon.

Persecution and the Odes of Solomon

In the Odes of Solomon we may hear the feelings of those who were persecuted by the likes of Paul. For example, in Ode 28 the speaker says,

> I am ready before destruction comes, and have been set on His immortal side. And immortal life embraced me, and kissed me. And from that life is the Spirit which is within me. And it cannot die because it is life. Those who saw me were amazed, because I was persecuted. And they thought that I had been swallowed up, because I seemed to them as one of the lost. But my injustice became my salvation. And I became their abomination, because there was no jealousy in me. Because I continually did good to every man I was hated. And they surrounded me like mad dogs, those who in stupidity attack their masters because their thought is depraved, and their mind is perverted.

This description of the self as a righteous person rescued from entrapment and persecution is part of the Odes' soteriological vision of human beings who are in bondage and rescued by a savior whom they themselves become, but it also may also reflect their social reality as a Jewish community persecuted by Jewish authority. In Ode 5 we hear the speaker declare: "My persecutors will come but let them not see me. Let a cloud of darkness fall upon their eyes; and let an air of thick darkness obscure them. And let them have no light to see, so that they cannot seize me. Let their designs become hardened, so that whatever they have conspired shall return upon their own heads." This passage is a curse formulation similar to curses found in ancient magic. It certainly sounds as if it derives from people who are persecuted in reality not just in their mythic self-perceptions. These words may come from the people who lived in communities persecuted by the likes of Paul, and who later came to say "The man who formerly persecuted us is now preaching the faith he once tried to destroy," (Gal. 1: 23).

Paul is a Christian because, he says, the Son of God was revealed in him (ἀποκαλύψαι τὸν υἱὸν αὐτοῦ ἐν ἐμοί,) so that henceforth Christ would live in him (ζῶ δὲ οὐκέτι ἐγώ, ζῇ δὲ ἐν ἐμοὶ Χριστός). Furthermore, Paul believes that the Son of God enters into members of his community so that they too become Sons of God and so forth. In other words, the primary experience of conversion that convinces Paul that the communities he was persecuting had it all right all along is an experience that is central to the Odes of Solomon. I believe that the churches of Christ that existed in c. 33 -35 C.E. of whom Paul speaks, and which Paul joined, the Church of God, or the Churches of Judea that are in Christ, were oriented to the type of Jewish religion manifested by the Odes of Solomon. Presumably some of those churches used the Odes of Solomon in their worship services. Those churches featured the experience of people being possessed by the Spirit of God understood to be the Spirit of the Son or the Spirit of Christ and so, when God revealed his Son in Paul, much to Paul's astonishment Paul experienced what the people whom he had been persecuting also had experienced. Paul claims with no evident doubt in his mind that his gospel, his Christianity, is the same as the Christianity of the network of churches he persecuted and it is not entirely unreasonable to think that Paul might have been right.

When God revealed his son in Paul the first thing Paul did was to go to Arabia. Only after three years did he go to Jerusalem, and then only for a fortnight to speak with no more than two people who had known Jesus. This does not indicate to me that Paul had any significant interest in Jesus' life or teaching, quite the opposite. He seems initially to have joined a religious movement where the historical Jesus of Nazareth was of no particular interest. Bear in mind that all Paul knows of Christianity at this point is antagonistic information that supports the view that it should be persecuted. That is not nothing; people who persecute movements have some idea of what it is they are persecuting. But if the network of churches that Paul persecuted was based on the life and teachings of Jesus of Nazareth and if God revealed His Son in

Paul so that Paul now affirmed that he persecuted the true Churches of God, he would have gone first to Jerusalem, or Capernaum, and not to Arabia. However, if the Odes represent a form of Christianity without a focus on Jesus, then Paul could begin to preach what he formerly condemned without thinking that he needed to find out more about Jesus. In that case, though, what would motivate Paul to speak so fervently about Jesus Christ and him Crucified? Paul clearly separates two things we put together. About the life, personality, miraculous deeds and wise inspired sayings of Jesus he evidently cares nothing at all. He seeks no information about such things and nothing about them is ever mentioned in his letters, but about Jesus the crucified and risen Christ he cares a great deal.

Jesus of Nazareth and the Odes of Solomon

It is clear in the first chapter of Mark's Gospel that Jesus of Nazareth comes repenting his sins to John's baptism rite and has the experience of the Spirit coming into him, (καὶ τὸ πνεῦμα ὡς περιστερὰν καταβαῖνον εἰς αὐτόν). He is henceforth regarded by some as the Christ the Son of God (Mark 1:1). Mark's story of Jesus is transformational, Jesus was an ordinary human being (cf. Mark 6:1-6) who is changed by Spirit possession experience into the Spirit possessing him, which is the Spirit of the Son, or the Spirit of Christ.

If the Odes community existed before the time of Jesus, existing from Judea through Galilee to Damascus, then it may have influenced Jesus' understanding of himself. If he was familiar with a community represented by the Odes he would have anticipated that his experience of possession would be transformation into a Christ, a Son of God, as Mark's Gospel indicates that he did. Evidently he quickly turned this condition into a remarkably successful career as a healer and exorcist, or so all of the synoptic gospels report. When Jesus arrived in Jerusalem for a Passover he was arrested and executed and, his body having been removed from a temporary entombment, stories of his resurrection began to be told.

The Odes are in theory spoken by the Spirit through the mouth of the transformed human odist (e.g. Ode 16:5: "I will open my mouth, and His Spirit will speak through me the glory of the Lord and His beauty,") and so the Spirit speaking through the ones it possesses is a feature of the Odes. I suggest that it is not unreasonable to think that some of the sayings in the Gospel of John, or perhaps the style of some of those sayings, derive from the speech of Jesus of Nazareth when the Spirit was speaking of itself through him. There is even one such saying in Q (Luke 10:22).

Jesus' associates evidently understood him to be Christ or Son of God, but they did not initially regard this condition to be one they might themselves aspire to. To them Jesus was a unique case, the only Christ the only Son of God. But Jesus may not have understood himself that way and so may have suggested that the Spirit might potentially come to all of his associates, a circumstance they came to call "being baptized in the Spirit." We hear that they did become possessed on Pentecost by the Spirit that they believed Jesus had sent to them (cf. Acts of the Apostles 2:1-13, 33, and passim). One finds in Paul's letters and in the Johannine corpus the idea that one can become Christ through the Spirit, but in both cases one specifically becomes Jesus Christ, whom John identifies as Paraclete and whose crucifixion and resurrection were central to Paul's religion. In the cases of Paul and John we have an amalgamation of the ideas found in the Odes, that one can become Christ the Son of God through the Spirit, and an idea not found in the Odes that Jesus of Nazareth was Christ the Son of God in a unique fashion.

If Paul's reports about his own experiences are reliable, and there is no reason to prefer modern interpretations to ancient eyewitness evidence, there was a network of possession oriented churches stretching from Jerusalem to Damascus, one whose realm of influence therefore inevitably passed through Galilee. This network of churches practiced a form of religion that, through Paul's idiosyncratic interpretation, came to be what we call Christianity. Jesus of Nazareth himself may have been affiliated with this movement. If Mark's account is even somewhat reliable, Jesus had an exceptionally successful medical career as an exorcist in Galilee and southern Syria, a career that was founded on his ability as "the Holy One of God" to drive out demons. If Jesus had received the Holy Spirit so that he was identified by some as a Son of God, and then worked to free people from demonic control, he was operating within the realm of ideas found in the Odes of Solomon.

Paul testifies, and the Odes themselves seem to confirm, that Jewish legal authorities, in part consisting of Pharisees like Paul, sought to destroy the religion of the Odes by attacking the members of the Odes communities. If such persecution had been going on for some time we probably should regard the Odes Judaism as a form of Syrian Judaism that was forced to be secretive, hidden away, and defensive. Repeatedly the Odes speak of persecution, e.g. in Ode 28 "Those who saw me were amazed, because I was persecuted. And they thought that I had been swallowed up, because I seemed to them as one of the lost. But my injustice became my salvation," and it stands to reason that the people who found their ecstatic religious transformations an escape from real persecution would keep a low profile in ordinary society. The Odes communities probably kept to themselves and tried to avoid publicly giving their Pharisaic enemies reason to attack.

Jesus, however, acted publicly and attracted a significant number of followers some of whom imitated his practice (cf. e.g. Mark 6:7-13) so that his influence spread rapidly and successfully. The Odes religion regarded the career of the savior as recapitulating the feelings of people transformed by possession, released from imprisonment and bondage into liberation and escape, to ascent and transformation, so that they can now liberate others, break the bonds of prisoners, kill dragons, and so forth. The Odes would have you become a Christ and they speak generally about ascent and descent, bondage and liberation, etc., but the Jesus movement would have you become Jesus Christ and understand yourself to have died and risen with him, or so Paul understood it. Paul evidently joined the Odes Judaism that he had been persecuting, but he had been influenced in Jerusalem by "those who were apostles before he was" who led him to believe that the movement was specifically oriented toward Jesus Christ. The Odes Judaism as Paul understood it was not one offering Christ status to anyone who achieved certain experiences but one that spoke particularly about Jesus Christ crucified.

If the Odes of Solomon are the remnant of a Jewish cult of a Pauline type that existed before Jesus, we might understand what happened way back when. Jesus perhaps became part of the Odes movement but rather than simply practicing within the community he launched a highly public and highly successful career as a Spirit possessed exorcist. People outside the Odes may have thought him to be uniquely the Son of God and Christ but the Odes community had any number of members who also were Son of God and Christ. After his death his associates experienced mass spirit-possession beginning at the event called Pentecost. Their appreciation of this condition and their discovery of means to spread it to others, Jews and gentiles alike, ultimately gave rise to Christianity itself. The Jesus of Nazareth religion featured Jesus as the prototypical Christ who sends the Spirit to possess all of his followers (so the Acts of the Apostles 2:33). But soon, rather than identifying themselves as Sons of God (cf. Galatians 4:6-7 and passim), Christians began to define Jesus alone as the unique Son of God.

Paul persecuted the Odes community itself, one which was rather well established around 33 C.E. As its persecutor, while he knew something of it, he hardly knew it well. Paul conflated the Odes Christianity with the Christianity that identified the Christ with the crucified and risen Jesus to achieve the form of religion evident in his letters. Whether this conflation was his own contribution, or whether it had started within the Odes communities themselves thanks to the missionary efforts of Jesus' associates, I cannot tell.

Subsequently, the Johannine community produced a set of sayings attributed to Jesus some of which had to do with the Paraclete. The Johannine Paraclete sayings retained the Odes' old perspective that everyone who receives the Spirit becomes the Son but added the specification that Jesus Christ is the Son who dwells within his followers via the Paraclete. In-dwelling language for transformation is found in the Odes of Solomon. For example, in Ode 32 we read: "The Lord has directed my mouth by His Word, and has opened my heart by His Light. He has caused to dwell in me His immortal life, and permitted me to proclaim the fruit of His peace, to convert the lives of those who desire to come to Him, and to lead those who are captive into freedom. I took courage and became strong and captured the world, and the captivity became mine for the glory of the Most High, and of God my Father." and in Ode 32: "To the blessed ones the joy is from their heart, and light from Him who dwells in them; And the Word of truth who is self-originate, Because He has been strengthened by the Holy Power of the Most High; and He is unshaken forever and ever." The Johannine idea of Spirit possession speaks of the power of the Spirit and of Jesus coming to dwell within Jesus' followers. As we read in John 17:20-23 "I pray also for those who will believe in me through their message, that all of them may be one, Father, just as you are in me and I am in you. May they also be in us so that the world may believe that you have sent me. I have given them the glory that you gave me, that they may be one as we are one— I in them and you in me—so that they may be brought to complete unity." Raymond Brown wrote of passages such as this one: "The one whom John calls 'another Paraclete' is another Jesus ... Jesus' promises to dwell within his disciples are fulfilled in the Paraclete."[56] To experience, as Ode 32 puts it, "light from Him who dwells in them" or to receive the glory that God gave to Jesus, as John 17:22 phrases it, cannot be two different things from two unrelated forms of first century Judaism. They are, I think, substantially and essentially the same thing. But while the Gospel of John focuses on Jesus of Nazareth, the Odes never do. Therefore, I think, the Odes came first and then Jesus, and then Paul's gospel, John's Gospel, and the religion of Christianity.

The communities behind the Odes were not ordinary folks but people with the special mental dispensations and the time for disciplined reflections that entitle them to be called "mystics." Theirs is not a religion that is likely to spread rapidly into a large semi-literate or illiterate population of relatively poor people, as early Christianity did. But when people associated with Jesus of Nazareth experienced mass possession experiences on the day called Pentecost and they quickly began to enable others to experience Spirit possession experiences, that movement achieved major success and came to incorporate the preexisting mystical cult that produced the Odes of Solomon in part through the conversion of Paul of Tarsus. In essence, a Jewish mystical cult with a limited number of disciplined members became a Gentile-oriented pentecostal cult that spread throughout the ancient world.

Conclusion

I propose that the following occurred:

A: Before 25 C.E. there was a network of communities stretching from Jerusalem to Damascus whose religious ideas are to some degree preserved for us through some of the hymns they chanted, the Odes of Solomon. Those communities believed that humans could be transformed into Christ or the Son of God through an experience understood in terms of the Spirit that we can understand in terms of the generic category of spirit possession.

---

56 Brown, 1141.

B: Jesus of Nazareth was affiliated with or influenced by one of those communities. He came to understand himself as one transformed into Son of God and Christ through an experience understood in terms of the Spirit. He was rather widely regarded as one transformed into Son of God or the Holy One of God and thereby was able to have a brief but very successful career as an exorcist-healer and to gather a cadre of associates who regarded him as being, uniquely, Christ and Son of God.

C: The communities of Odes Judaism were persecuted through Judean police power and Paul carried out such persecution. However, Paul, to his surprise, spontaneously experienced what those communities advocated, believed that the Son of God had been revealed in him, and he began to spread their form of religion into Gentile areas. Paul understood the Odes religion in reference to the much more public career of Jesus of Nazareth, whose associates identified him as crucified and risen Christ. Paul conflated the Odes religion with the idea that Jesus is Christ to produce a form of Christianity that offered people the possibility of identification through the Spirit with Jesus Christ crucified.

D: Jesus' associates, who eventually came to understand him to have been the unique Son of God and to have been the only Christ, initially had "pentecostal" experiences of Spirit possession that were thought to derive from Jesus Christ now in heaven with God. The success of Christianity in spreading throughout the Roman Empire was based largely on the success of Christian missionaries in inducing Spirit possession in people in diverse areas, presumably through methods similar to those that are utilized by Pentecostal missionaries today.

E: Johannine Christians believed that possession by the spirit Paraclete would transform them so that they might believe that Jesus dwells in them and that they can speak words of the Spirit, understood to be Jesus' words recalled to them. Their experiences meant to them that they are now the presence of the Son of God, Jesus, on the earth; it is possible that some of the communities of Odes Judaism became Johannine Christian churches. The Johannine community may be the principal form in which Odes Judaism continued to exist after the rise of Christianity oriented to Jesus of Nazareth.

F. By the mid-second century Jesus the Christ came to be regarded as a separate divine being to be worshipped as God. The Spirit was separated out to be an independent divine Person. The Christian religion ceased to be fundamentally concerned with Spirit-possession, which was left to fringe groups and heretical cults.

I suggest that we should reverse Professor Lattke's observation that the Johannine Gospel and Letters, the epistles of Paul both authentic and pseudepigraphal, the Synoptic Gospels, the letter ascribed to Peter and even Revelation "exerted a quite surprising influence in the shaping of the Odes of Solomon."[57] It is more likely that the influence went the other way, that the Odes represent the Jewish religious movement out of which Christianity arose so that the Judaism of the Odes (not the specific texts of the Odes themselves) lies at the root of Pauline Christianity and Johannine Christianity and possibly even the Christianity of Jesus of Nazareth. Accordingly, the influence of that kind of religion is to be found practically everywhere, from the Letter to the Galatians to the speech of Jesus in John 17 to the Gospel of Thomas.

The arrow of temporal-causal influence should be reversed. The Odes of Solomon are not influenced by virtually all varieties of early Christianity but the religion and phraseology of the Odes of Solomon preceded and influenced virtually all those varieties. The Syrian Odes' form of Judaism may have been more influential on the Galilean Jesus of Nazareth than Judean Temple Judaism was. The religion of the Odes, coupled with the idea of a Jesus Christ crucified, was substantially the Gospel of Paul and, in quite a different way, is at the root of the Gospel of John. To see that these are not idle speculations you need only realize that it is a relatively recent idea that the Odes are Christian and c. 125 C.E. in date. People of ancient times thought the Odes of Solomon were as Jewish as the Psalms of Solomon and of roughly the same date. I think they were right.

---

57 Lattke, 13-14.

The Odes of Solomon

The Odes And Psalms Of Solomon Vol. II: The Translation with Introduction And Notes By Rendel Harris and Alphonse Mingana, London : Longmans, Green & Company. 1920.

[I have changed this translation by revising archaic or awkward English usage and by removing many of the theological capitalizations. — Stevan Davies]

ODE I
1 The Lord is upon my head like a crown and I shall not be without him.
2 The crown of truth was woven for me, and it caused your branches to bud in me;
3 For it is not like a withered crown that does not bud
4 But you live upon my head and you have blossomed upon my head.
5 Your fruits are full-grown and perfect. They are full of your salvation.
(Hallelujah.)

ODE II
This Ode is missing.

ODE III

1 . . . .
2 And (his) members are with him, and on them I depend, and he loves me.
3 For I should not have known how to love the Lord, if he had not loved me.
4 For who is able to distinguish love, except one that is loved. Where his rest is, there also am I.
For with the Lord Most High and Merciful there is no jealousy.
7 I have been united (to Him), for the lover has found the beloved. In order that I may love him that is the son, I shall become a son.
9 And he that has pleasure in the living one, will become living.
10 This is the Spirit of the Lord, which does not lie,
Which teaches the sons of men to know his ways.
11 Be wise and understanding and vigilant.
Hallelujah.

ODE IV

1 No one, O my God, changes your holy place, nor can one alter it, and put it in another place.
2 Because he has no power over it, for you designed your sanctuary before you made other places.
3 That which is the elder shall not be changed by those who are younger; you have given your heart, O Lord, to your believers.
4 you will never fail, nor will you be without fruits;
5 For one hour of your faith is more precious than all days and years.
6 For who shall put on your grace, and be injured?
7 Your seal is known, and your creatures are known to it.
8 The hosts possess it, and the elect archangels are clad with it.
9 You have given us your fellowship; it was not that you were in need of us, but that we are in need of you.
10 Rain your dews upon us, and open your rich fountains to pour forth milk and honey to us.
11 For you do not repent and you should not repent of anything that you have promised.
12 And the end was known to you;
13 For what you gave, you gave freely so that you may not draw back and take them in again.

14 For all was known to you as God and set in order from the beginning before you.
15 And you, O Lord, have made all things.
Hallelujah.

ODE V
1 I will give thanks to you O Lord because I love you;
2 O Most High, do not you forsake me, for you are my hope.
3 I have received your grace freely and I shall live thereby.
4 My persecutors will come but let them not see me.
5 Let a cloud of darkness fall on their eyes, and let an air of thick gloom darken them.
6 Let them have no light to see so that they may not grab hold of me.
7 Let their plans become thick darkness, and make what they have cunningly devised return upon
their own heads.
8. For they have devised a plan and it has come to nought.
9 They have prepared themselves maliciously, but they were ineffective.
10 My hope is upon the Lord and I will not fear.
12 He is as a garland on my head, And I shall not be moved ;
14 And if (all) things visible should perish, I shall not die
15 Because the Lord is with me, and I am with him.
Hallelujah.

ODE VI
1 As (the hand) moves over the harp and the strings speak,
2 So speaks in my members the Spirit of the Lord, and I speak by his love.
3 For he destroys what is foreign to him, and everything is of the Lord.
4 For thus he was from the beginning, and (shall be) to the end.
5 Nothing should be his adversary, and nothing should stand up against him.
8 For there went forth a stream, and it became a river great and broad. It swept away everything, and broke up and carried away the Temple.
9 And the restraints (made) by men were not able to restrain it, nor

the arts of those whose (business it is to) restrain water.
10 It spread over the face of the whole earth and it filled everything.
11 All the thirsty upon earth were given to drink (of it) and thirst was done away and quenched
12 For from the Most High the drink was given.
13 Blessed then are the ministers of that drink, who have been entrusted with his water,
14 They have moistened the dry lips, and the will that had fainted they have raised up
15 And souls that were nearly departed they have held back from death,
] 6 And limbs that had fallen they have straightened and set up.
17 They gave strength to their coming and light to their eyes.
18 For everyone knew them in the Lord, and because of the water they lived an eternal life.
Hallelujah.

ODE VII

1 As is the motion of anger over evil, so is the motion of joy over the beloved, and it brings in its fruits without restraint.
2 My joy is the Lord, and my motion is towards Him; this path of mine is excellent.
3 For I have a helper, to the Lord. He has shown himself to me generously in his simplicity
because his kindness diminished his awesomeness.
4 He became like me that I might receive him. He took on a form like mine, that I might put him on.
5 I did not tremble when I saw him because he was gracious to me.
6 Like my nature he became, that I might learn him, and like my form, that I might not turn away from him.
7 The Father of knowledge is the word of knowledge;
8 He who created wisdom is wiser than his works.
9 He who created me when I was not yet existing knew what I should do when I came into being;
10 Wherefore he pitied me in His abundant grace and permitted me to ask from him and to receive from his sacrifice
11 For he is incorrupt. He is the perfection of the worlds and the Father of them.

12 He has permitted those who are his to appear to them so that they may recognize him that made them and that they might not suppose that they came of themselves.
13 For he has appointed the way to knowledge; he has widened it and extended it and brought it to
perfection.
14 He set the traces of his light over it and it proceeded from the beginning to the end.
15 For by him he was served. And he was pleased with the son.
16 And because of his salvation he will take possession of everything. And the Most High shall be known in his saints
17 To announce, to those who have songs, the coming of the Lord so that they may go forth to meet him and sing to him with joy and with the harp of many tones.
18 The seers shall go before him and they shall be seen before him
19 And they shall praise the Lord in his love because he is near and sees.
20 And hatred will be taken from the earth. Along with jealousy it will be drowned
21 Ignorance has been destroyed because the knowledge of the Lord has arrived.
22 Let the singers sing the grace of the Lord Most High and let them bring their songs
23 And let their hearts be like the day, and let their harmonies be like the excellent beauty of the Lord, and let there be nothing without life, nor without knowledge, nor mute.
24 For (the Lord) has given a mouth to his creation to open a voice towards him and to praise him,
25 Confess his power, and show forth his grace.
Hallelujah.

ODE VIII
1 Open yourselves, open your hearts to the exultation of the Lord
2 Let your love abound from the heart to the lips
3 To bring forth fruits to the Lord: a holy life and to talk watchfully in his light.
4 Rise up and stand erect, you who were sometimes brought low
5 You who were in silence, speak out, (Now) that your mouth has

been opened.
6 You who were despised be lifted up now that your righteousness has been lifted up,
7 For the right hand of the Lord is with you and he will be your helper.
8 And peace has been prepared for you, before your war happened.
9 Hear the word of truth and receive the knowledge of the Most High
10 Your flesh does not know what I am saying to you, nor your raiment what I am showing to you;
11 Keep my secret, you who are kept by it. Keep my faith, you who are kept by it.
12 Understand my knowledge, you who truly know me.
13 Love me with affection, you who love,
14 For I do not turn away my face from those who are mine, for I know them.
15 I knew them before they came into being and I set my seal onto their.
16 I fashioned their members; I prepared my own breasts for them so that they might drink my holy milk and live through it.
17 I took pleasure in them, and I am not ashamed of them.
18 They are workmanship and the strength of my thoughts.
19 Who will stand up against my handywork? Who is there that is not subject to them?
20 I willed, and fashioned mind and heart, and they are mine, and by my own right hand I set up my elect ones.
21 My righteousness goes before them and they shall not be detached from my name, for it is with them.
22 Pray and abide continually in the love of the Lord. You beloved ones, abide in the beloved. And you who are kept, in him who lives, and you that are saved, in him that was saved.
23 And you shall be found incorrupt in all ages through the name of your Father.
Hallelujah.

ODE IX
1. Open your ears and I will speak to you.
2. Give me your souls, that I may also give you my soul,
3. The Word of the Lord and his good pleasures, the holy thought

that he has thought concerning his Messiah.
4. For in the will of the Lord is your life, and his intention is (your) everlasting life, and your end is incorruptible.
5 Be enriched in God the Father, and receive the intention of the Most High. Be strong and be redeemed by his grace.
6 For I announce peace to you his saints that none of those who hear may fall in war
7 And that those who have known him may not perish, and that those who receive (Him) may not be ashamed.
8 An everlasting crown is Truth. Blessed are those who set it on their heads.
9 A stone of great price (it is). Wars occurred on account of the crown.
10 Righteousness took it and has given it to you.
11 Put on the crown in the true covenant of the Lord and all those who have conquered shall be inscribed in his book.
12 Their inscription is the victory, which is yours, and she (victory) sees you before her, and wills that you shall be saved.
Hallelujah.

ODE X
1. The Lord has directed my mouth by his word, and he has opened my heart by his light.
2. He has caused deathless life to dwell in me and has allowed me to speak the fruit of his peace
3. To convert the souls of those who are willing to come to him and to lead the captives to freedom.
4. I was strengthened and made mighty and took the world captive, and (the captivity) became to me for the praise of the Most High and of God my Father.
5 The gentiles were gathered together who had been scattered abroad, and I was unpolluted by my love (for them) because they confessed me in high places.
6 Traces of the light were set in their hearts, and they walked in my life and were saved, and they became my people forever and ever.
Hallelujah.

ODE XI

1. My heart was opened and its flower appeared; grace sprang up in it and it brought forth fruit to the Lord.
2. For the Most High circumcised (my heart) by his Holy Spirit, and turned my affection towards him and filled me with his love.
3 And his circumcising of (my heart) became my salvation, and I ran in the way, in his peace, in the way of truth.
4 From the beginning to the end I received his knowledge.
5 I was established upon the rock of truth; there he set me up.
6 Abundant speaking waters drew near my lips from the fountain of the Lord.
7 I drank and was inebriated with the living water that does not die, and my inebriation was not ignorance,
8 But I forsook vanity
9 And turned to the Most High my God, and was enriched by his bounty.
10 I forsook folly thrown over the earth; I stripped it off and cast it away.
II The Lord renewed me in his raiment, and possessed me by his light,
12 And from above he gave me rest without corruption. I became like the land which blossoms and rejoices in its fruits.
13 The Lord (was) like the sun (shining) upon the face of the land.
14 My eyes were enlightened, and my face received the dew
15 And my nostrils had the pleasure of the odor of the Lord.
16 He carried me into his Paradise, where the abundance of the pleasure of the Lord is
17 And I worshipped the Lord on account of his glory.
18 I said: Blessed, O Lord, are those who are planted in your land and who have a place in your p;aradise,
19 And that grow in the growth of your trees, and have changed from darkness to light.
20 Behold! All your servants are fair, they who do good works and turn away from wickedness to your pleasantness.
21 And they have turned away from themselves the bitterness of the trees, when they were planted in your land.
22 And everything became like a remembrance of yourself, and a memorial forever of your faithful servants.

23 For there is abundant room in your paradise and nothing there is useless; everything is filled with fruit.
24 Glory be to you, O Lord, the delight of paradise forever. Hallelujah.
[Note, in line two and three I replaced "clave" and "cleaving" with "circumcised" in accordance with Charlesworth and Lattke's translations. -- S.D,]

ODE XII

1. He filled me with words of truth so that I might speak the same.
2 And like the flow of waters, truth flows from my mouth, and my lips produce its fruits.
3. Truth caused knowledge to abound in me, because the mouth of the Lord is the true word, and the door of his light.
4 The Most High has given him to his worlds. (Worlds) which are the interpreters of his own beauty and the repeaters of his praise and the confessors of his thought and the heralds of his mind and the instructors of his works.
5 For the swiftness of the word is inexpressible, and like his expression is his swiftness and his sharpness, and his course has no limit.
6 Never (does the word) fall for it stands forever.
8. His descent and his way are incomprehensible.
7 For as his work is, so is his limit.
9. He is the light and the dawn of thought
8 And by him the worlds spoke one to the other, and those who were silent acquired speech.
9 From him came love and concord and they spoke one to the other what they had (to tell)
10 They were stimulated by the word, and they knew him that made them because they came into agreement.
11 For the mouth of the Most High spoke to them and gave them his interpretation of himself.
12 The dwelling-place of the word is man, and his truth is love.
13 Blessed are those who have comprehended everything by it, and who have known the Lord by his truth.
Hallelujah.

ODE XIII
1 Behold! The Lord is our mirror; open your eyes and see them in him
2. And learn the manner of your face, and give praises to his Spirit.
3 Wipe off the filth from your face, love his holiness and clothe yourselves with it
4 And you will be unstained at all times with him.
Hallelujah.

ODE XIV
1 As the eyes of a son to his father, so are my eyes at all time towards you, O Lord.
2 My consolations and my delights are with you.
3 Do not turn your mercy from me, O Lord, and do not take your kindness from me.
4 Stretch out to me your right hand at all times, my Lord, and be my guide up to the end, according to your good pleasure.
5 Let me be well-pleasing before you. Let me be saved from the Evil One because of your glory and because of your name.
6 Let your gentleness, O Lord, abide with me, and the fruits of your love.
7 Teach me the Odes of your truth that I may bring forth fruit in you
8 Open to me the harp of your Holy Spirit, that I may praise you with all (its) notes, O Lord.
9 Give to me in accordance with your many mercies and hurry to grant our petitions;
10 You suffice for all our needs.
Hallelujah.

ODE XV
1 As the sun is joy to them that seek daybreak, so is my joy the Lord
2 Because he is my sun. His rays have lifted me up; his light has removed all darkness from my face.
3 I have acquired eyes from him and have seen his holy day.
4 I have acquired ears and have heard his truth.
5 I have acquired the thought of knowledge and have been delighted by him.
6 I left the way of error and I went towards him, and I have received abundant salvation from him.

7 According to his bounty he has given to me, and according to his excellent beauty he has made me.
8 I have put on incorruption through his name, and I have put off corruption by his grace.
9 Death has been destroyed before my face, and Sheol has been abolished by my word.
10 Deathless life has arrived in the Lord's land, and it has been made known to his faithful ones, and has been given without stint to all those who trust in him.
Hallelujah.

ODE XVI

1 As the work of the husbandman is plowing, and the work of the steersman is in guiding the ship, so also my work is praising the Lord in his psalms.
2 My craft and my occupation are in praising him because his love has nourished my heart. He poured out his fruits to my lips.
3 For my love is the Lord and therefore I will sing unto him,
4 For I am made strong in his praise, and I have faith in him.
5 I will open my mouth, and his spirit will utter in me the glory of the Lord and his beauty,
6 The work of his hands and the fabric of his fingers,
7 The multitude of his mercies, and the strength of his word.
8 For the word of the Lord searches out the unseen thing, and scrutinizes his thought.
9 The eye sees his works, and the ear hears his thought.
10 It is he who spread out the earth, and settled the waters in the sea;
11 He expanded the heavens, and fixed the stars
12 And he fixed the creation and set it up, and he rested from his works
13 And created things run in their courses, and work their works and they know not how to stand (still) and to be idle.
14 And the hosts are subject to his word.
15 The treasury of the light is the sun, and the treasury of the darkness is the night.
16 And he made the sun for the day that it might be bright, but night brings darkness over the face of the earth
17 And (by) their reception one from the other they speak the beauty

of God.
18 And there is nothing that is without the Lord, for he was before anything came into being.
19 And the worlds were made by his word and by the thought of his heart.
20 Glory and Honor to his name.
Hallelujah.

ODE XVII

1 I was crowned by my God, and my crown is living
2 I was justified by my Lord, and my salvation is incorruptible.
3 I was loosed from vanities, and I am not condemned. The choking bonds were cut off by his hand.
4 I received the face and the fashion of a new person, and I walked in him and was redeemed.
5 The thought of truth led me, and I walked after it and did not wander,
6 And all that have seen me were amazed, and I was supposed by them to be a strange person.
7 And he who knew and brought me up, is the Most High in all his perfection. He glorified me by his kindness, and raised my thought to the height of truth.
8 And from there he gave me the way of his steps, and I opened the doors that were closed
9 And I broke in pieces the bars of iron. My own iron (bonds) melted and dissolved before me.
10 Nothing appeared closed to me, because I was the opening of everything.
11 I went towards all the bound people to free, that I might not leave anyone bound.
12 I imparted my knowledge without grudging, and their requests to me with my love.
13 And I sowed my fruits in hearts, and transformed them through myself,
14 And they received my blessing and lived. They were gathered to me and were saved
15 Because they became to me as my own members and I was their head

16 Glory to you our Head, the Lord Messiah.
Hallelujah.

ODE XVIII
1 My heart was lifted up and enriched in the love of the Most High so that I might praise him by my name.
2 My members were strengthened so that they might not fall from his power.
3 Sickness left my body, and it stood for the Lord by his will, for his kingdom is firm.
4 O Lord, for the sake of them that are deficient, do not deprive me of your word,
5 Nor, for the sake of their works, keep your perfection from me.
6 Do not let the luminary be conquered by the darkness, nor let truth flee away from falsehood.
7 Let your right hand bring our salvation to victory, and receive from all quarters, and preserve whomever is affected by ills.
8 Falsehood and death are not in your mouth, my God, but your will is perfection.
9 And vanity you do not know, neither does it know you.
10 And error you do not know, neither does it know you.
11 And ignorance appeared like dust, and like the scum of the sea.
11 Vain people supposed that it was (something) great, and they came to resemble it and became vain
13 And the wise understood and meditated (thereon) and were unpolluted in their meditations for such were in the mind of the Lord.
14 And they mocked at those who were walking in error
15 And on their part they spoke truth, from the inspiration which the Most High breathed into them.
16 Praise and great beauty to his name.
Hallelujah.

ODE XIX
1. A cup of milk was offered to me and I drank it in the sweetness of the delight of the Lord.
2. The son is the cup, and he who was milked is the Father, and he who milked him is the Holy Spirit
3. Because his breasts were full, and it was not desirable that his milk

should be spilt to no purpose.
4 The Holy Spirit opened his bosom and mingled the milk of the two breasts of the Father,
5 And gave the mixture to the world without their knowing, and those who take (it) are in the fullness of the right hand.
6 The womb of the virgin took (it) And she received conception and brought forth
7 And the virgin became a mother with great mercy.
8 She was in labor and brought forth a Son without incurring pain, for it did not happen without purpose.
9 She had not required a midwife, for he delivered her.
10 And she brought forth, as a man, by (God's) will, and she brought (him) forth with demonstration and acquired (him) with great dignity;
11 And loved (him) in redemption, and guarded (him) kindly, and showed (him) in majesty.
Hallelujah.

ODE XX
1 I am a priest of the Lord, and to him I do priestly service
2 And to him I offer the offering of his thought.
3 For his thought is not like (the thought of) the world, nor (like the thought of) the flesh nor like them that serve carnally.
4 The offering of the Lord is righteousness and purity of heart and lips,
5 Offer yourself (before Him) blamelessly, and let not your heart do violence to heart
nor your soul do violence to soul.
6 You shall not acquire a stranger . . . neither shall you seek to deal guilefully with your neighbor,
7. Nor shall you deprive him of the covering of his nakedness.
7 But put on the grace of the Lord without stint, and come into his paradise and make yourself a garland from his tree
8 And put it on your head and be glad, and recline on his rest
9 And his glory shall go before you, and you shall receive his kindness and his grace and you shall be fat in truth in the praise of his holiness.
10 Praise and honor to his name.
Hallelujah.

ODE XXI

1 My arms I lifted up on high, even to the grace of the Lord
2 Because he cast off my bonds from me and my helper lifted me up to his grace and his salvation.
3 And I put off darkness, and clothed myself with light
4 And my soul acquired members free from sorrow or affliction or pain.
5 Increasingly helpful to me was the thought of the Lord, and his incorruptible fellowship.
6 I was lifted up in the light, and I passed before Him and I became near to him, praising and confessing him.
8 He made my heart overflow, and it was found in my mouth, and it shone upon my lips.
9 And upon my face the exultation of the Lord increased, and his praise likewise.
Hallelujah.

ODE XXII

1 He who brings me down from on high, and brings me up from the regions below,
2 Who gathers the things that are between, and throws them to me,
3 Scattered my enemies and my adversaries,
4 Gave me authority over bonds, that I might loosen them.
5 He who overthrew by my hands the dragon with seven heads, and set me at his roots that I might destroy his seed —
6 You were there and helped me, and in every place your name was round about me.
7 Your right hand destroyed his wicked venom and your hand leveled the way for those who believe in you.
8 It chose them from the graves, and separated them from the dead, and covered them with bodies.
10 They were motionless, and it gave (them) energy - for life.
11 Your way was without corruption and your face; you brought your world to corruption, that everything might be dissolved and renewed,
12 So that the foundation for everything might be your rock. On it you built your kingdom and you became the dwelling-place of the saints.
Hallelujah.

ODE XXIII

1 Joy is of the saints! Who shall put it on but they alone?
2 Grace is of the elect! Who shall receive it but those who trust in it from the beginning?
3 Love is of the elect! Who shall put it on, but those who have possessed it from the beginning?
4 Walk in the knowledge of the Most High and you shall know the grace of the Lord plentifully and his exultation and the perfection of his knowledge.
5 His thought was like a letter, and his will descended from on high;
6 It was sent like an arrow violently shot from the bow.
7 Many hands rushed to the letter, to seize it and to take it and to read it.
8 It escaped from their fingers; they were frightened by it and by the seal that was on it.
9 They were not permitted to loosen the seal as the power that was over the seal was greater than they.
10 But those who saw it went after the letter, so that they could know where it would alight, and who should read it, and who should hear it.
11 But a wheel received it, and (the letter) came over it
12 And there was with it, a sign of the kingdom and of the government.
13 The wheel mowed and cut down everything that was moving;
14 It destroyed many things that were adverse, and it spanned the rivers
15 And crossed over and rooted up many forests, and made a broad path.
16 The head went down to the feet for down to the feet ran the wheel, and that which had come upon it.
17 The letter was one of recommendation and all districts were included it.
18 And there was seen at its head, a head which was revealed, the son of truth from the Most High Father;
19 And he inherited and took possession of everything, and the thought of the many was brought to nothing,
20 And all of the apostates became bold and fled away, and the persecutors were blotted out and became extinct.

21 The letter became a great tablet that was wholly written by the finger of God.
22 The name of the Father was upon it, and of the Son, and of the Holy Spirit, to rule forever and ever.
Hallelujah.

ODE XXIV

1 The dove flew over the head of our Lord the Messiah, because he was her head
1 And she sang over him, and her voice was heard,
3 And the inhabitants were afraid, and the sojourners trembled.
4 Birds took to flight, and all creeping things died in their holes.
5 The abysses were opened and closed. They were seeking for the Lord, like (women) in labor.
6 He was not given to them for food because he did not belong to them,
7 and the abysses were submerged in the submersion of the Lord, and they perished in the thought which they had existed in from the beginning.
8 For they labored from the beginning, and the end of their labor was life.
9 Every one of them who was defective perished, for it was not permitted to them to make a defense for themselves that they might remain;
10 And the Lord destroyed the imaginations of all them that did not have the truth with them regarding the Messiah.
11 For they were defective in wisdom, those who were lifted up in their hearts,
12 And they were rejected, because the truth was not with them.
13 For the Lord disclosed his way, and spread abroad his grace
14 And those who understood it know his holiness.
Hallelujah.

ODE XXV

1 I was rescued from my bonds, and unto you, my God, I fled,
2 For you were the right hand of my salvation, and my helper.
3 You have restrained them that rise up against me; they were seen no more

4 Because your face was with me, which saved me by your grace.
5 But I was despised and rejected in the eyes of many, and I was in their eyes like lead
6 And I acquired strength from your, and help.
7 You set me a lamp at my right hand and at my left so that in me there might be nothing that is not bright.
8 I was covered with the covering of your spirit, and I removed the raiment of skins,
9 For your right hand lifted me up, and removed sickness from me.
10 I became mighty in your truth and holy by your righteousness.
11 All my adversaries were afraid of me. I became the Lord's by the name of the Lord
12 And I was justified by his gentleness, and his rest is forever and ever.
Hallelujah.

ODE XXVI

1 I poured out praise to the Lord for I am his
2 And I will speak his holy song, for my heart is with him.
3 His harp is in my hands, and the Odes of his rest shall not be silent.
4 I will cry unto him from my whole heart;
I will praise and exalt him with all my members.
5 For from the East and the West is his praise,
6 And from the South and the North is his confession.
7 From the top of the hills to their utmost limit is his perfection.
8 Who can write the Odes of the Lord, or who can read them?
9 Who can train his soul for life, that his soul may be saved?
10 Who can rest on the Most High, that from his mouth he may speak?
11 Who is able to interpret the wonders of the Lord?
He who interprets would be dissolved, but that which was interpreted will remain.
12 It is enough to know and to rest, for in the rest the singers stand,
13 It is like a river that has an abundant fountain and flows to the help of them that seek it.
Hallelujah.

ODE XXVII
1 I expanded my hands, and I sanctified (them) to my Lord. For the expansion of my hands is his sign.
2 And my expansion is the upright wood.

ODE XXVIII
1 As the wings of doves over their nestlings and the mouths of their nestlings towards their parents mouths, so also are the wings of the Spirit over my heart.
2 My heart is delighted and leaps up, like the babe who leaps up in the womb of his mother.
3 I believed; therefore I was at rest, for faithful is he in whom I have believed.
He has richly blessed me, and my head is with him.
4 Neither the sword nor the scimitar will divide me from him.
5 I was ready before destruction came, and I have been set on his immortal pinions.
6 Deathless life embraced me and kissed me.
7 And from that (life) is the spirit within me, and it cannot die; it lives.
8 Those who saw me marveled at me because I was persecuted,
9 And they supposed that I was swallowed up for I seemed to them as one of the lost.
10 But my oppression became my salvation.
11 They scorned me because there was no wrath in me.
12 Because I did good to every man I was hated.
13 They circled round me like mad dogs who ignorantly attack their masters,
14 For their thought is corrupt and their understanding perverted.
15 But I was carrying water in my right hand, and their bitterness I endured by my sweetness.
16 And I did not perish, for I was not their brother, nor was my birth like theirs.
17 They sought for my death and could not (accomplish it) for I was older than they could remember.
Vainly did they cast lots against me.
18 Those who came after me sought without cause to destroy the memorial of him who was before them.

19 For the thought of the Most High cannot be anticipated, and his heart is superior to all wisdom.
Hallelujah.

ODE XXIX

1. The Lord is my hope. In him I shall not be confounded.
2 For according to his praise he made me, and according to his goodness he gave unto me.
3 According to his mercies he exalted me. According to his excellent beauty he set me on high.
4 And he brought me up out of the depths of Sheol; from the mouth of death he drew me.
5 And I laid my enemies low and he justified me by his grace,
6 For I believed in the Lord's Messiah, and he appeared to me that he is the Lord.
7 He showed me his sign, and led me by his light.
8 He gave me the rod of his power so that I might subdue the imaginations of the people
and bring down the power of the men of might,
9 And make war by his word, and take victory by his power.
10 The Lord overthrew my enemy by his word, and he became like the stubble which the wind carries away.
11 And I gave praise to the Most High because he exalted his servant and the Son of his handmaid.
Hallelujah.

ODE XXX

1 Fill yourselves with water from the living fountain of the Lord for it has been opened to you,
2 And come all you thirsty and take a drink, and rest by the fountain of the Lord.
3 Fair it is and pure, and it gives rest to the soul.
4 Much sweeter is its water than honey, and the honeycomb of bees is not to be compared with it.
5. It flows from the lips of the Lord, and from the heart of the Lord comes its name.
6. It came unlimited and invisible, and until it was set in the midst they did not know it.

7 Blessed are those who have drunk from it, and rested thereby.
Hallelujah.

ODE XXXI
1 The abysses were dissolved before the Lord, and darkness was destroyed by his appearance.
2 Error went astray and disappeared from him, and I gave no pathway to falsehood;
it was submerged by the truth of the Lord.
3 He opened his mouth and spoke grace and joy, and he spoke a new (song of) praise to his name.
4 He lifted up his voice to the Most High, and offered him the sons that were in his hands.
5 And his face was justified; for thus his Holy Father had given to him.
6 Come forth, you that have been afflicted, and receive joy.
7 Possess your souls by grace, and take immortal life.
8 They condemned me when I rose up, I who had not been condemned.
9 They divided my spoil, though nothing was due to them.
10 But I endured and held my peace and was silent, that I might not be moved by them.
11. I stood unshaken like a firm rock beaten by the waves that yet endures.
12 And I bore their bitterness for humility's sake, that I might redeem my people and inherit it,
13 And so that I might not make void the promises to the patriarchs to whom I was promised for the salvation of their seed.
Hallelujah.

ODE XXXII
1 To the blessed the joy is from their hearts, and light from him that dwells in them,
2 And the word from the truth who is self-originate.
3 For he has been strengthened by the holy power of the Most High, and he is unperturbed forever and ever.
Hallelujah.

ODE XXXIII

1 Grace ran again and left the corruptor and came down upon him to bring him to naught.
2 He brought about utter destruction and devastated all his array,
3 He stood on a lofty summit and cried aloud from one end of the earth to the other.
4 He drew to him all those who obeyed him, and he did not appear as an evil one.
5 A perfect virgin stood proclaiming and crying and saying,
6 "O you sons of men, return, and you their daughters, come;
7 Leave the ways of that corruptor, and draw near to me
8 And I will enter into you and bring you forth from destruction, and I will make you wise in the ways of truth.
9 Be not destroyed nor perish.
10. Hear me and be saved for the grace of God I proclaim among you.
11 By my means you shall be redeemed and become blessed; I am your judge.
12 Those who have put me on shall not be injured but they shall possess incorruption in the new world.
13 My chosen ones have walked in me, and I will make known my ways to them that seek me, and I will make them trust in my name.
Hallelujah.

ODE XXXIV

1 There is no hard way where there is a simple heart
nor is there any barrier where the thoughts are upright,
2 Nor is there any storm in the depth of the illuminated thought.
3 One who is surrounded on every side by open country is freed from doubts.
4 The likeness of that which is below is that which is above,
5 For everything is above, and below there is nothing, even if it is believed to be so by the ignorant.
6 Grace has been revealed for your salvation. Believe and live and be saved.
Hallelujah.

ODE XXXV

1 The dew of the Lord brought me rest and caused a cloud of peace to rise over me
2 So that it might guard me continually. It became salvation to me.
3 Everyone was shaken and frightened and there came forth from them smoke and judgment,
4 But I was keeping quiet in the ranks of the Lord. More than shadow was he to me, and more than support.
5 I was carried like a child by its mother, and he gave me milk, the dew of the Lord.
6 I grew great by his bounty, and I rested in his perfection,
7 And I spread out my hands in the lifting up of my soul, and I directed myself towards the Most High,
And I was redeemed with him.
Hallelujah.

ODE XXXVI

1 The Spirit of the Lord rested on me, and (the Spirit) raised me on high
2 And made me stand on my feet in the high place of the Lord, before his perfection and his glory while I was praising (him) by the composition of his Odes.
3 (The Spirit) brought me forth before the face of the Lord, and although a son of man, I was named the luminary, the son of god, and the greatest among the great ones.
5 For according to the greatness of the Most High, so she made me, and like his own newness he renewed me
6 And he anointed me from his own perfection, and I became one of those who are near to him.
7 And my mouth was opened like a cloud of dew, and my heart gushed out, as it were, a rush of righteousness;
8 And my access (to Him) was in peace, and I was established in the Spirit of Providence.
Hallelujah.

[Note: in line 1 I adopted Lattke's emendation of "I rested in the Spirit of the Lord" -- SD]

ODE XXXVII

1 I stretched out my hands to the Lord and to the Most High I lifted my voice
and I spoke with the lips of my heart.
2. He heard me when my voice reached him.
3 His word came to me, and gave me the fruits of my labors,
4 And gave me rest by the grace of the Lord.
Hallelujah.

ODE XXXVIII

1 I went up into the light of truth as into a chariot, and the truth led me and brought me
2 And carried me across hollows and gulfs. From the cliffs and reefs it preserved me
3. And became haven of salvation for me, and it set me on the place of immortal life.
4 It went with me and made me rest and caused me not to err, because it was and is the truth.
5 I ran no risk because I walked with him, and I made no error in anything, because I obeyed him,
6 For error fled away from him, and would not meet him.
7 Truth proceeded in the right way, and whatever I did not know he made clear to me,
8 Such as all the drugs of error and plagues of death that are considered to be sweet (beverages).
9 I saw the destroyer of the corrupter when the bride who was being corrupted was adorned, along with the bridegroom who corrupts and is corrupted.
10 And I asked the truth, "Who are these?" and he said to me, "This is the deceiver and error.
11 And they imitate the beloved and his bride, and they lead astray and corrupt the world.
12 They invite many to the banquet, and let them drink of the wine of their intoxication.
13 They make them vomit up their wisdom and intelligence, and they deprive them of understanding.
14 Then they leave them behind and so they go about like corrupted madmen."

15 And I was made wise so as not to fall into the hands of the deceiver and I congratulated myself that the truth had gone with me.
16 I was established and lived and I was redeemed
My foundations were laid by the Lord, for he planted me.
17 He set the root, and watered it and fixed it and blessed it, and its fruits will be forever;
18 It grew deep down and sprang up and spread wide, and it was full and was enlarged.
19 And the Lord alone was glorified, in his planting and his husbandry,
20 In his care and in the blessing of his lips, in the beautiful planting of his right hand,
21 And in the splendor of his planting, and in the thought of his mind.
Hallelujah.

ODE XXXIX
1 Mighty rivers are the power of the Lord that carry headlong those who despise him
3 And entangle their paths, and sweep away their fords,
3 And carry off their bodies and destroy their souls.
4 They are more swift than lightning, and more rapid.
5 But those who cross them in faith shall not be moved,
6 And those who walk by them without blemish shall not be afraid.
7 For the sign in them is the Lord and the sign becomes the way of those who cross in the name of the Lord.
8 Put on, therefore, the name of the Most High and know him, and you shall cross without danger, while the rivers shall be subject to you.
9 The Lord has bridged them by his word, and he walked and crossed them on foot.
10 His footsteps stand (firm) on the waters, and were not erased. They are as a beam that is firmly fixed.
11 The waves were lifted up on this side and on that, and the footsteps of our Lord Messiah stand (firm),
12 And are not obliterated, and are not defaced.
13 A way has been appointed for those who cross after him, and for those who agree to the course of his faith and for those who adore his name.

Hallelujah.

ODE XL

1 As the honey distils from the comb of the bees, and the milk flows from the woman that loves her children, so also is my hope on you, my God.
2 As the fountain gushes out its water, so my heart gushes out the praise of the Lord, and my lips utter praises to him.
3 And my tongue is sweet in his intimate converse and my limbs are made fat by the sweetness of his
Odes.
4 My face is glad with his exultation, and my spirit exults in his love, and my soul shines in him.
5 The fearful one shall confide in him, and in him redemption stands assured.
6 His gift is immortal life and those who participate in it are incorruptible.
Hallelujah.

ODE XLI

1 Let all the Lord's infants praise him; let us appropriate the truth of his faith so that his children will be acknowledged by him.
3 We live in the Lord by his grace, and we receive life in his Messiah,
4 For a great day shone upon us. Marvelous is he who has given us of his glory.
5 Let us, therefore, all of us unite together in the name of the Lord, and let us honor him in his goodness,
6 And let our faces shine in his light, and let our hearts meditate in his love by night and by day.
7 Let us exult with the joy of the Lord.
8 All those who see me will be astonished, for I am from another race.
9 The Father of Truth remembered me, he who possessed me from the beginning;
10 His riches begat me, and the thought of his heart.
11 His word is with us in all our way,
the savior who makes us live and does not reject our souls.
12 The man who was humbled and was exalted by his own righteousness,

13 The son of the Most High appeared in the perfection of his Father
14 And light dawned from the word that was previously in him.
15 The Messiah is truly one and he was known before the foundations of the world so that he might save souls forever by the truth of his name.
16 Let a new song arise to the Lord from them that love him. Hallelujah.

ODE XLII
1 I stretched out my hands and approached my Lord, for the stretching out of my hands is his sign
2 And my expansion is the outspread wood that was set up on the way of the righteous one.
3 I became of no use to those who knew me, for I hide myself from those who did not take hold of me,
4 But I will be with those who love me.
5 All my persecutors have died, those who sought after me and who proclaimed about me, because I am alive.
6 I rose up and am with them and I will speak by their mouths
7 For they have despised those who persecute them.
I threw over them the yoke of my love.
Like the arm of the bridegroom over the bride, so is my yoke over those who know me.
9 As the couch that is spread in the chambers of the bridegroom and the bride, so is my love over those who believe in me.
10 I was not rejected, though I was reckoned to be so, and I did not perish though they thought it of me.
11 Sheol saw me and was in distress; death cast me up and many along with me.
12 I have been gall and bitterness to it and I went down with it to the extreme of its depth,
13 And the feet and the head it let go for it was a not able to endure my face.
14 I made a congregation of living men among his dead men and
I spoke with them by living lips in order that my word may not be void.
15 Those who had died ran towards me and they cried out, "son of God, have pity on us,

16 And treat us in accordance with your kindness, and bring us out from the bonds of darkness,
17 And open the door by which we shall come out to you, for we know that our death does not touch you.
18 Let us also be saved with you, for you are our savior."
19 And I heard their voice and I laid up their faith in my heart
20 And I set my name upon their heads for they are free men and they are mine.
Hallelujah.

Afterword: The Two Most Important Events in Western History

This book has been about the rise of the Christian movement from the beginning of Jesus' ongoing spirit experience through his career as an exorcist empowered, so he would say, by the Spirit of God. It has focused much attention on the subsequent event called Pentecost, which initiated the spread of the Christian movement throughout the Mediterranean world. In this Afterword I will briefly argue that the Pentecost event was not just important (I think everyone will acknowledge that) but that it is one of the two most important events in Western history.

The religions of Judaism, Christianity and Islam come from the same historical root both in terms of their mythic story of origination via Abraham, and in terms of the historical events I will discuss below. These three religions are the underpinning of Western civilization and to this day they can claim to rule the lives of two billion people. Judaism, Christianity and Islam underlie the philosophical, economic, military and artistic factors that have had enormous importance in the Western world. They are the Western world's predominant nature.

Western religion began on a particular day. We don't know the exact date but it was roughly in 627 B.C.E., eighteen years into the reign of King Josiah of Judea whose reign began when he was only eight years old. On that day the twenty-six year old king was informed that a book entitled "the book of the law of Yahweh by the hand of Moses" (2 Chronicles 34:14) had been discovered in the main Jerusalem temple by priests of the god Yahweh. The subsequent events suggest that Josiah had been raised and educated to a considerable degree by priests of the god Yahweh. For example, while he was a very young king Yahweh priests had convinced Josiah to use tax money to construct and restore their areas of the temple. "The book of the law of Yahweh by the hand of Moses" was written to instruct Josiah not just to favor the priests of Yahweh of the Jerusalem temple, but to destroy all forms of religion except theirs. And Josiah did just that. He bought the story; he conceded the authority of the priests' book; he destroyed all forms of religion except theirs.

The account in 2 Kings 22 and 23 is quite thorough. All forms of religious practice were to be outlawed except for the worship of Yahweh in the Jerusalem temple:

> And the king commanded Hilkiah the high priest, and the priests of the second order, and the keepers of the door, to bring forth out of the temple of the Lord all the vessels that were made for Baal, and for the grove, and for all the host of heaven: and he burned them without Jerusalem in the fields of Kidron, and carried the ashes of them unto Bethel. And he put down the idolatrous priests, whom the kings of Judah had ordained to burn incense in the high places in the cities of Judah, and in the places round about Jerusalem; them also that burned incense unto Baal, to the sun, and to the moon, and to the planets, and to all the host of heaven. ....
>
> And he took away the horses that the kings of Judah had given to the sun, at the entering in of the house of the Lord, by the chamber of Nathanmelech the chamberlain, which was in the suburbs, and burned the chariots of the sun with fire. And the altars that were on the top of the upper chamber of Ahaz, which the kings of Judah had made, and the altars which Manasseh had made in the two courts of the house of the Lord, did the king beat down, and brake them down from thence, and cast the dust of them into the brook Kidron. And the high places that were before Jerusalem, which were on the right hand of the mount of corruption, which Solomon the king of Israel had builded for Ashtoreth the abomination of the Zidonians, and for Chemosh the abomination of the Moabites,

and for Milcom the abomination of the children of Ammon, did the king defile. (2 Kings 23:4-5, 11-13 KVJ)

That's a lot. Included in the purge were the Levite priests of cult sites outside of Jerusalem. They were permitted to continue as priests only by accepting subordination to the Jerusalem priesthood. Even the folk religious practices of the peasantry were condemned:

> "Moreover the workers with familiar spirits, and the wizards, and the images, and the idols, and all the abominations that were spied in the land of Judah and in Jerusalem, did Josiah put away, that he might perform the words of the law which were written in the book that Hilkiah the priest found in the house of the Lord." (2 Kings 23:24).

Evidently the worship of all manner of gods had been practiced in Judea since days immemorial, or as the account tells us, for at least three centuries, from the days of Solomon down to Josiah. The main Jerusalem temple had been the place for worship of the sun and of Baal and the host of heaven. Ashtoreh, Chrmosh, Milcom had their temples just outside the city. The kings of Judea had enthusiastically supported this polytheistic melange.[1] Now Judea was to have but one cult, one priesthood, one God only. Josiah learned that from the document presented to him by the Yahweh priests and Josiah accepted the document's authority.

Religions hate novelty. All the various religious truths have supposedly been with us since the primordial mythic time. From claims that our sect alone follows the original teachings of the Buddha, to claims that all other teachings than ours are innovative blasphemy against Allah's Quran, religions can be seen to presume original perfection from which changes can only be devolution toward error. Accordingly, if in fact one is engaged in changing the original pattern of a religion, one must insist that one's changes are actually the divinely commanded restoration of the original pattern, and that the pattern now in effect is a catastrophic deviation from the ideal original.

In Christianity, for example, we discover that the teachings of the

---

[1] King Hezekiah is reported to have sought the destruction of non-Yahweh religion in Judea ca. 700 B.C.E., but his efforts were unsuccessful.

Prophet Smith were not novelties but were in fact returning the church to its condition before the great apostasy of ca. 150 C.E. Hence, only the Latter Day Saints practice the religion of the Former Day Saints, one that ceased to be for centuries. Similarly, we hear, and it is the main thing we hear in much of the Hebrew Bible, that the religion established through the police power of King Josiah, the monotheistic religion of Jerusalem Temple Yahweh worship, had since time immemorial been the only permissible religion of Judea, one that ceased to be for centuries, while other forms of religion were allowed to thrive. This is nonsense, although it is almost universally believed to be the Truth. To this day scholars do not hesitate to speak of Josiah's "reforms" as if the destruction of cult activities that had admittedly been practiced for at least three centuries, if not back beyond into the mists of time, was simply returning Judean religion to its normal and natural state. Or, returning to my analogy, as if the reforms of Christianity revealed by the Prophet Smith simply brought back to our day the practices of the church of Jesus and Paul and the apostles, practices unknown to any Catholic or Orthodox or Protestant church.

After Josiah came the Babylonian Exile, after that the restoration of Judean government and religion, this time following the new pattern. According to that pattern a holy book has authority over the governing authorities, the Judean people, and the priests of Yahweh. The holy book is to be interpreted by legal authorities answerable to the priests of Yahweh. The police power of the state is to be utilized to insure that no worship takes place except for the worship conducted by priests of Yahweh in the Jerusalem temple. This is police-enforced scriptural monotheism.

For the next six hundred years or so police-enforced scriptural monotheism held sway in Judea. Except insofar as Judeans emigrated to other places, e.g. Alexandria and Rome, Judean religion was of no particular significance to anyone outside of Judea any more than Judea itself was of any particular significance. I recall being at a conference on the Etruscan civilization where one presenter displayed a huge map of the Roman Empire with dozens of its provinces, regions and rivals labeled and I thought: "Judea isn't even labeled on this map. And yet after a few hundred more years, all of these regions and places and powers were dominated by Judean ideology. How did that happen?" It's astonishing that the religious culture of Judea, its clerical elite, its foundational scriptures and its police-enforcement of monotheism, had remained isolated in poor, upland, politically insignificant, and economically trivial Judea for six hundred and more years, and then rather rapidly that culture became dominant in the Western world. For, after all, Judean religious culture is the foundation of Islam and of Christianity.

We take for granted that it is not unreasonable to have a Christian Western Europe for a dozen centuries where the Bible is in theory an authority above kings and potentates and where the promotion of the worship of gods other than Yahweh, in all of his trinitarian monotheistic glory, is a capital crime. For nearly fourteen centuries the Quran has dominated the rest of the Western world and a great deal of the East in its role as an authority above kings and potentates where promotion of the worship of gods other than Yahweh, there called Allah, was and in places still is a capital crime. Judean religion, reinterpreted to define Christians or Muslims as Yahweh's chosen people, became the foundation for all Western religion.

There is nothing logically or socially or psychologically or economically compelling about police-enforced scriptural monotheism. The cultures of East Asia and South Asia have gotten along quite nicely without it. While it held sway in Judea for six or seven centuries as Judea shifted from Babylonian to Persian to Greek to Roman control, none of those occupying empires adopted Judean religion. Indeed it was not adopted anywhere, nor was it influential in revising the religious or political cultures of Greece, or Rome, or Egypt, or Gaul.

What caused the break-out of a particular insignificant region's religious style so that it came to dominate the Roman world? It was not some set of teachings attributed to Jesus, nor the notion that Jesus had risen from the grave, it was Pentecost, May 27, 33 C.E.[2] The explosive spread of Christianity, based on the new potential for anyone anywhere to experience the Holy Spirit of Yahweh, brought about the rapid dispersion of Christian communities throughout the Roman Empire. With the wide dispersion of Christian communities came the dispersion of what they adopted as their holy scripture, the Hebrew Bible. The Hebrew Bible, written to mandate and defend Josiah's po-

---

2 Assuming a date of April 7, 30 for Easter. Perhaps the date is wrong, perhaps the Pentecost event is an invention of Luke's. Be that as it may, the cult of mass spirit possession called Christianity did begin around that time.

lice-enforced monotheism, stands on the foundation of "The book of the law of Yahweh by the hand of Moses" mandating the destruction of all rivals of the Yahweh priests of Jerusalem.[3]

The spirit-experience-initiated spread of Christianity throughout the Roman Empire carried with it the spread of the Hebrew Bible, understood to speak prophetically of Christ Jesus and understood to define the chosen people of God as those of Christian faith (Galatians 3:6-9) and so forth. After Constantine's adoption of the Christian religion, the biblical injunctions to eliminate all cults except for the cult of Yahweh in Jerusalem came to be understood to be injunctions to eliminate all cults except for that of the Catholic Christian church. And, a bit later on, they were understood to be injunctions to replace all polytheistic religions with Islam. These injunctions still dominate Western political and military conflicts in the twenty-first century, and the work of Josiah in ca 627 B.C.E. is still being done in the Islamic world by what American media call "Jihadis."

Without the events of ca. 627 B.C.E., spread into the wider world by the events of ca. 30 C.E., Western religion and culture would probably look much like Chinese or Indian or Greco-Roman religion and culture. But not so. The Western world is based on police-enforced scriptural monotheism and it is so because of two specific historical events. This book has largely been about the origin and nature of the second of them.

---

3 The book found "accidentally" by the Yahweh priests of Jerusalem, is today understood to be principal sections of the book of Deuteronomy. Further, the vision of Josiah's destruction of all rival cults being the desired outcome of all Judean history was written in narratives we now know as "the Deuteronomic History," i.e. Joshua, Judges, First Samuel, Second Samuel, 1 Kings, 2 Kings. This narrative was originally composed during the time of Josiah. Eventually the dominant view of the Judean religion as a police-enforced scriptural monotheism was ultimately encoded into a Hebrew Bible tracing that cultic point of view back to the very creation of the universe. Cf., e.g., Richard Elliot Friedman, *Who Wrote the Bible*, HarperOne 1987.

BIBLIOGRAPHY

Adityanjee, M. D., G. S. P. Raju, and S. K. Khandelwal, "Current Status of Multiple Personality Disorder in India," *American Journal of Psychiatry*, Vol. 146, No. 12, 1989.

Aune, David, *Prophecy in Early Christianity and the Mediterranean World*. Grand Rapids: Eerdmans, 1983.

———, *The Cultic Setting of Realized Eschatology in Early Christianity*. Leiden: Brill, 1972.

Barrett, C. K., *The Holy Spirit and the Gospel Tradition*. London: S.P.C.K, 1947, reprinted 1966.

Betz, Hans Dieter, *The Greek Magical Papyri in Translation*. Chicago: University of Chicago Press, 1986.

———, "Jesus and the Cynics: Survey and Analysis of a Hypothesis," *The Journal of Religion*, Vol. 74. No. 4, October, 1994.

Black, Matthew, *An Aramaic Approach to the Gospels and Acts*, Third Edition. Oxford: Clarendon Press, 1967.

Blessing, Kamila, "Luke's Unjust Steward Viewed from the Window of Milton Erickson," unpublished paper delivered at the Annual Convention of the Society of Biblical Literature, Fall, 1993.

Blomberg, Craig, "Interpreting the Parables of Jesus: Where Are We and Where Do We Go From Here?" *Catholic Biblical Quarterly*, Vol. 53, No. 1, 1991.

Borg, Marcus, "A Renaissance in Jesus Studies," *Theology Today*, Vol. 45, Oct. 1988.

———, *Jesus: A New Vision.* San Francisco: Harper, 1987.
Boring, Eugene, *The Continuing Voice of Jesus.* Louisville: John Knox Press, 1991.
Borsch, Frederick, *Many Things in Parables.* Fortress: Philadelphia, 1988.
Bourguignon, Erika, *A Cross-Cultural Study of Dissociational States.* Columbus: Research Foundation, Ohio State University, 1968.
———, *Possession.* San Francisco: Chandler and Sharp, 1976.
———, *Religion, Altered States of Consciousness, and Social Change.* Columbus: Ohio State University Press, 1973.
———, "Self, the Behavioral Environment, and the Theory of Spirit Possession," in *Context and Meaning in Cultural Anthropology,* ed. Melford Spiro. New York: Free Press, 1965.
———,"World Distribution and Patterns of Possession States," in Raymond Prince, *Trance and Possession States.*
Brandon, S. G. F., *Jesus and the Zealots.* Manchester: Manchester University Press, 1967.
Breech, James, *Jesus and Postmodernism.* Fortress Press: Minnesota, 1989.
Brown, Karen McCarthy, *Mama Lola: A Vodou Priestess in Brooklyn.* Berkeley: University of California Press, 1991.
Brown, Raymond, *The Gospel According to John: Two Volumes.* New York: Doubleday, 1966, 1970.
———, "The burial of Jesus (Mark 15:42-47)," *Catholic Biblical Quarterly* Vol. 50, 1988.
Bultmann, Rudolf, *Theology of the New Testament: Volume Two.* New York: Scribner's, 1955.
———, *The Gospel of John.* Philadelphia: Fortress, 1971.
Burge, Gary, *The Anointed Community: The Holy Spirit in the Johannine Tradition.* Grand Rapids: Eerdmans, 1987.
Burney, C. F., *The Aramaic Origin of the Fourth Gospel.* Oxford: Clarendon, 1922.
Cadbury, Henry J., *The Peril of Modernizing Jesus.* New York: Macmillan, 1937.
Carrier, Richard ed., *Bart Ehrman and the Quest of the Historical Jesus of Nazareth: An Evaluation of Ehrman's Did Jesus Exist?*, Parsippany, NJ: American Atheist Press, 2013.
Charlesworth, James, *Critical Reflections on the Odes of Solomon, Vol-*

ume One. Sheffield UK: Sheffield Academic Press, 1998.

———, The Odes of Solomon: Edited, with Translation and Notes Oxford UK: Clarendon Press, 1973.

Cohen, Emma, "What is Spirit Possession? Defining, Comparing, and Explaining Two Possession Forms" *Ethnos*. No.73, March, 2008.

Crapanzano, Vincent and Vivian Garrison, eds., *Case Studies in Spirit Possession*. New York: John Wiley and Sons, 1977.

Crapanzano, Vincent, "Mohammed and Dawia: Possession in Morocco," in *Case Studies in Spirit Possession*.

Crossan, John Dominic, *The Historical Jesus*. San Francisco: Harper and Row, 1991.

Crossley, James, "Writing about the Historical Jesus: Historical Explanation and 'the Big *Why* Questions', or Antiquarian Empiricism and Victorian Tomes?" [sic] in *Journal for the Study of the Historical Jesus* Vol. 7, 2009.

Davies, Stevan, "Afterword" in The Revolt of the Widows: The Social World of the Apocryphal Acts, Second Edition. Dublin: Bardic Press, 2012.

———, "The Christology and Protology of the Gospel of Thomas," *Journal of Biblical Literature*, Vol. 111, No. 4, 1992.

———, "Gnostic Idealism and the Gospel of Truth," in *Religious Writings and Religious Systems: Vol. One*, eds. Jacob Neusner et al. Atlanta: Scholars Press, 1989.

———, *The Gospel of Thomas and Christian Wisdom*. Second Edition. Dublin: Bardic Press, 2004.

De Conick April, *Seek to See Him: Ascent and Vision Mysticism in the Gospel of Thomas*. Leiden: E, J, Brill, 1996.

Depue, R. A. and S. M. Monroe, "Conceptualization and Measurement of Human Disorder in Life Stress Research: The Problem of Chronic Disturbance," *Psychological Bulletin*, Vol. 99, 1986.

Dewey, Joanna, "Jesus' Healings of Women: Conformity and Non-Conformity to Dominant Cultural Values as Clues for Historical Reconstruction," *SBL Seminar Papers 1993*. Scholars' Press: Atlanta, 1993.

Diagnostic and Statistical Manual of Mental Disorders, Revised Edition. Washington, D.C.: American Psychiatric Association, 1987.

Dodd, C. H., *The Interpretation of the Fourth Gospel*. Cambridge: Cambridge University Press, 1953.

———, *The Parables of the Kingdom*. Glasgow: Collins, 1961.
Doherty, Earl, *Jesus: Neither God Nor Man - The Case for a Mythical Jesus*. Ottawa: Age of Reason Publications, 2009.
Dow, James, "Universal Aspects of Symbolic I sealing: A Theoretical Synthesis," *American Anthropologist*, Vol. H8, 19146.
Downing, F. Gerald, *Christ and the Cynics*. Sheffield: Sheffield Academic Press, 1988.
Dunn, James D. G., *Jesus and the Spirit*. Philadelphia: Westminster, 1975.
Dupont-Sommer, Andre, *The Essene Writings from Qumran*. London: Peter Smith, 1973.
Edelstien, Gerald, "Age Regression," in *Hypnosis: Questions and Answers*, B. Zilbergeld, ed. New York: W. W. Norton, 1986.
Ehrman, Bart, *Did Jesus Exist? The Historical Argument for Jesus of Nazareth*. San Francisco CA: HarperOne, 2013.
Erickson, Milton H. and Ernest Rossi, *Experiencing Hypnosis: Therapeutic Approaches to Altered States*. New York: Irvington Publishers, 1981.
Evans, Craig, *Life of Jesus Research: An Annotated Bibliography*. Leiden: Brill, 1989.
Falk, Harvey, *Jesus the Pharisee*. New York: Paulist Press, 1985.
Feldman, Jeffrey, "The Utilization of Cognition in Psychotherapy: A Comparison of Ericksonian and Cognitive Therapies," in Stephen Lankton, *Research, Comparisons and Medical Applications*.
Field, M. J., "Spirit Possession in Ghana," in *Spirit Mediumship and Society in Africa*, John Beattie and J. Middleton, eds. London: Routledge, 1969.
Frecska, Ede, and Zsuzsanna Kulczar, "Social Bonding in the Modulation of the Physiology of Ritual Trance," *Ethos*, Vol. 17, 1989.
Fredriksen, Paula, *From Jesus to Christ*. New Haven: Yale University Press, 1988.
Freed, Stanley and Ruth Freed, "Spirit Possession as Illness in a North Indian Village," in John Middleton, *Magic, Witchcraft*, and Curing. Garden City: The Natural History Press, 1967.
Friedman, Richard Elliot, *Who Wrote the Bible*. San Francisco CA: HarperOne, 1987.
Funk, Robert, *Parables and Presence: Forms of the New Testament Tradition*. Philadelphia: Fortress Press, 1982.

Funk, Robert, et al. eds., *The Five Gospels*. Sonoma: Polebridge, 1994.
———, *The Parables of Jesus: Red Letter Edition*. Sonoma: Polebridge Press, 1988.
Geertz, Clifford, "Common Sense as a Cultural System," in his *Local Knowledge: Further Essays in Interpretive Anthropology*. New York: Basic Books, 1983.
Gill, Merton, and Margaret Brenman, *Hypnosis and Related States*. New York: International Universities Press, 1959.
———, "The Metapsychology of Regression and Hypnosis," in *Handbook of Clinical and Experimental Hypnosis*, ed. Jesse Gordon, New York: Macmillan, 1967.
Godin, Jean, "Evocation and Indirect Suggestion in the Communication Patterns of Milton H. Erickson," in Stephen Lankton, *Research, Comparison and Medical Applications of Ericksonian Techniques*.
Goodman, Felicitas, *Ecstasy, Ritual, and Alternate Reality*. Bloomington: Indiana University Press, 1988.
Grant, Robert, "The Odes of Solomon and the Church of Antioch," *Journal of Biblical Literature*, Vol, 63, 1944.
Gray, Rebecca, *Prophetic Figures in Late Second Temple Palestine: The Evidence from Josephus*. New York: Oxford University Press, 1993.
Greenbaum, Leonora, "Social Correlates of Possession Trance in Sub-Saharan Africa," in Erika Bourguignon, *Religion, Altered States of Consciousness and Social Change*.
Haley, Jay, *Uncommon Therapy: The Psychiatric Techniques of Milton H. Erickson, M.D.* Norton: New York, 1986.
Hamerton-Kelly, Robert, "Note on Matthew 12:28 par. Luke 11:20," *New Testament Studies*, Vol. 11, 1965.
Harmon, A. M., *Lucian*, Loeb Classical Library. New York: MacMillan, 1961.
Hamilton, William, *A Quest for the Post-Historical Jesus*. New York: Continuum, 1994.
Helms, Randal, *Who Wrote the Gospels*. Agawam MA: Millenium Press, 1997.
Hengel, Martin, *The Charismatic Leader and His Followers*. New York: Crossroad, 1981.
Hiers, Richard H., "Kingdom of God," *in Harper's Bible Dictionary*. San Francisco: Harper and Row, 1985.
Hilgard, Ernest, *Divided Consciousness: Multiple Controls in Human*

Thought and Action. New York: John Wiley and Sons, 1977.
Hill, David, *New Testament Prophecy*. Atlanta: John Knox, 1979.
Hollenbach, Paul, "Help for Interpreting Jesus' Exorcisms," *SBL Seminar Papers 1993*. Scholars Press: Atlanta, 1993.
——, "Jesus, Demoniacs and Public Authorities: A Socio-Historical Study," *Journal of the American Academy of Religion*, Vol. 99, 1981.
Horsley, Richard, "'Like One of the Prophets of Old': Two Types of Popular Prophets at the Time of Jesus," *Catholic Biblical Quarterly*, Vol. 47, 1985.
——, *Jesus and the Spiral of Violence*. San Francisco: Harper and Row, 1987. "Q and Jesus: Asumptions, Approaches, and Analyses," in *Semeia: 55, Early Christianity, Q and Jesus*. Atlanta: Scholars Press, 1991.
Hulse, E. V., "The Nature of Biblical 'Leprosy' and the Use of Alternative Medical Terms in Modern Translations of the Bible," *Palestine Exploration Quarterly*, Vol. 107, 1975.
Kampman, R., "Hypnotically Induced Multiple Personality," *International Journal of Clinical and Experimental Hypnosis*, Vol. 24, 1976.
Alice Kehoe, and Dody Giletti, "Women's Preponderance in Possession Cults: The Calcium Deficiency Hypothesis Extended," *American Anthropologist*, Vol. 83, 1981.
Kelber, Werner, *The Oral and Written Gospel*. Philadelphia: Fortress Press, 1976.
Kessler, C., "Conflict and Sovereignty in Kelatanese Malay Spirit Seances," in Vincent Crapanzano, *Case Studies in Spirit Possession*.
Kiev, Ari, "The Psychotherapeutic Value of Spirit-Possession in Haiti," in Raymond Prince, *Trance and Possession States*.
Kildahl, John, *The Psychology of Speaking in Tongues*. New York: Harper and Row, 1972.
Kloppenborg, John, *Excavating Q: The History and Setting of the Sayings Gospel. Philadelphia: Philadelphia PA: Fortress Press*, 2000.
——, *Q, The Earliest Gospel: An Introduction to the Original Stories and Sayings of Jesus*. Louisville KY: Westminster - John Knox Press, 2008.
——, *The Formation of Q*. Philadelphia: Fortress, 1987.
Kloppenborg, John, et al. eds., Q *Thomas Reader*. Sonoma: Polebridge, 1990.
Kluft, Richard P., "An Update on Multiple Personality Disorder," *Hospital and Community Psychiatry*, Vol. 38, No. 4, 1987.

Koester, Helmut, "Jesus the Victim," Journal *of Biblical Literature,* Vol. 111, 1992.

Lambek, Michael, "From Disease to Discourse," in Colleen Ward, *Altered States of Consciousness.*

Lampe, G. W. H., "The Holy Spirit and the Person of Christ," in *Christ, Faith and History: Cambridge Studies in Christology,* eds. S. W. Sykes and J. P. Clayton. Cambridge: Cambridge University Press, 1972.

Lankton, Stephen, and Carol Lankton, *The Answer within: A Clinical Framework of Ericksonian Hypnotherapy.* New York: Brunner/Mazel, 1983.

———, "Ericksonian Styles of Paradoxical Treatment," *in Promoting Change through Paradoxical Therapy,* Gerald Weeks, ed. New York: Brunner/Mazel, 1991.

Lankton, Stephen, and Jeffrey Zeig, *Research, Comparisons and Medical Applications of Ericksonian Techniques.* New York: Brunner/Mazel, 1988.

Lattke, Michael, *The Odes of Solomon,* Hermeneia Series, Philadelphia PA: Fortress Press 2009.

Lewis, I. M., *Religion in Context.* Cambridge: Cambridge University Press, 1985.

———, *Ecstatic Religion: A Study of Shamanism and Spirit Possession.* London: Penguin Books, 1971.

———, *Ecstatic Religion: Second Edition.* London: Routledge, 1989.

Ludwig, Arnold, "Altered States of Consciousness," in Raymond Prince, *Trance and Possession States.*

Mack, Burton, A *Myth of Innocence.* Philadelphia: Fortress, 1988.

———, *The Lost Gospel: The Book of Q and Christian Origins.* San Francisco: Harper, 1993.

Martin, Raymond, *Syntax Criticism of Johannine Literature, the Catholic Epistles, and the Gospel Passion Accounts.* Lewiston, N.Y.: Edwin Mellen Press, 1989.

———, *Syntax Criticism of the Synoptic Gospels.* Lewiston, N.Y.: Edwin Mellen Press, 1987.

Meier, John P., "Jesus" in the *Jerome Biblical Commentary. Revised.* New York: Doubleday, 1986.

———, A *Marginal Jew: Rethinking the Historical Jesus.* New York: Doubleday, 1991.

Michaelsen, Peter, "Ecstasy and Possession in Ancient Israel: A Review of Some Recent Contributions," *Scandinavian Journal of the Old Testament*, No. 2, 1989. Middleton, John, *Magic, Witchcraft, and Curing*. Garden City: The Natural History Press, 1967.

Mischel, W. and F. Mischel, "Psychological Aspects of Spirit Possession," *American Anthropologist*, Vol. 60, 1958.

Murphy-O'Connor, Jerome, *Paul: A Critical Life*. New York, NY: Oxford University Press, 1998.

Neumann, John, "Introduction," in Hans Windisch, *The Spirit Paraclete in the Fourth Gospel*. Fortress Press: Philadelphia, 1968.

Neusner, Jacob, *From Politics to Piety: The Emergence of Pharisaic Judaism*. New York: KTAV, 1979.

——, *Judaism: Practice and Belief 63 BCE-66 CE*. Philadelphia: Trinity Press International, 1992.

——, *Rabbinic Traditions about the Pharisees before 70*. Leiden: E. J. Brill, 1971.

——, "Types and Forms in Ancient Jewish Literature: Some Comparisons," *History of Religions*, Vol. 11, 1972.

——, "Who Needs 'the Historical Jesus'? Two Elegant Works Rehabilitate a Field Disgraced by Fraud," in his *Ancient Judaism: Debates and Disputes*, Third Series, Number 83. Atlanta: Scholars Press, 1993.

O'Collins, Gerald, "What They Are Saying About Jesus Now," *America*, Vol. 171, August 27, 1994.

Oesterreich, Traugott, *Possession: Demoniacal and Other*. London: Kegan Paul, 1930.

Oohashi, T., Kawai, N., Honda, M., Nakamura, S., Morimoto, M., Nishina, E., Maekawa, T., "Electroencephalographic Measurement of Possession trance in the Field," *Clinical Neurophysiology*. No. 113, 2002, pp, 435-445.

Patterson, Stephen, *The Gospel of Thomas and Christian Origins*. Leiden: Brill 2013.

——, *The Gospel of Thomas and Jesus*. Sonoma: Polebridge, 1993.

Pattison, E. M., "Trance Possession States," in *Handbook of States of Consciousness*, Benjamin Wolman and Montague Ullman, eds. New York: Van Nostrand, 1986.

Perelman, Chaim, *The New Rhetoric and The Humanities*. Boston: Reidel, 1979.

Perkins, Pheme, *Gnosticism and the New Testament*. Minneapolis: Augsburg Fortress, 1993.

Perrin, Norman, *Rediscovering the Teaching of Jesus*. San Francisco: Harper and Row, 1976.
Persinger, M. A., "Striking EEG profiles from single episodes of glossolalia and transcendental meditation," *Perceptual and Motor Skills*. No. 58 Vol. 1, 1984.
Peters, Larry, "Trance, Initiation, and Psychotherapy in Tamang Shamanism," *American Ethnologist*, Vol. 9, 1982.
Phelps, Maggie, "Changing Early Life Decisions Using Ericksonian Hypnosis" in Stephen Lankton and Jeffrey Zeig, *Research, Comparisons and Medical Applications of Ericksonian Techniques*.
Price, Robert M, *Deconstructing Jesus*. Amherst NY: Prometheus, 2000.
Prince, Raymond, *Trance and Possession States*. Montreal: R. M. Bucke Memorial Society, 1966.
———, "Shamans and Endorphins," *Ethos*, Vol. 10, 1982.
Robinson, James M., *A New Quest of the Historical Jesus and Other Essays*. Philadelphia: Fortress, 1983.
———, *The Problem of History in Mark*. Philadelphia: Fortress, 1982.
———, "The Study of the Historical Jesus After Nag Hammadi," in *Semeia 44: The Historical Jesus and the Rejected Gospels*. Atlanta: Scholars Press, 1988.
Robinson, John A. T., *The Priority of John*. Oak Park Ill: Meyer-Stone, 1987.
Rodd, C. S., "Spirit or Finger," *Expository Times*, Vol. 72, 1961.
Rossi, Ernest, Sheila Rossi, and Milton Erickson, *Hypnotic Realities*. New York: Irvington, 1976.
Rousseau, John J., "Jesus, an Exorcist of a Kind," *SBL Seminar Papers 1993*. Scholars Press: Atlanta, 1993.
Samarin, William, *Tongues of Men and Angels: The Religious Language of Pentecostalism*. New York: Macmillan, 1972.
Sanders, E. P., "Jesus in Historical Context," *Theology Today*, Vol. 50, 1993. Sanders E. P., *Jesus and Judaism*. Fortress: Philadelphia, 1985.
Saunders E., "Variants in Zar Experience in an Egyptian Village," in Vincent Crapanzano, *Case Studies in Spirit Possession*.
Sanders, Jack T, *The New Testament Christological Hymns: Their Historical Background*. Cambridge UK: Cambridge University Press, 1971.
Schnelle, Udo, *Apostle Paul: His Life and Theology*. Grand Rapids, MI: Baker Academic, 2005.
Scholem, Gershom, *Major Trends in Jewish Gnosticism*. New York, NY:

Schocken, 1941.
Schüssler Fiorenza, Elisabeth, *In Memory of Her*. New York: Crossroad: 1983.
Schweitzer, Albert, *The Quest of the Historical Jesus: A Critical Study of Its Progress from Reimarus to Wrede*, transl. William Montgomery. New York: Macmillan, 1968, first published 1906.
Scobie, Charles H. H., *John the Baptist*. Philadelphia: Fortress Press, 1964.
Scott, Bernard Brandon, *Hear Then the Parable: A Commentary on the Parables of Jesus*. Fortress Press: Minneapolis, 1990.
Seltzer, L., *Paradoxical Strategies in Psychotherapy: A Comprehensive Overview and Guidebook*. New York: Wiley, 1986.
Shaara, Lila, and Andrew Strathern, "A Preliminary Analysis of the Relationship between Altered States of Consciousness, Healing, and Social Structure," *American Anthropologist*, Vol. 94, 1992.
Shagass, Charles, "Electrical Activity of the Brain," in Richard Sternbach, *Handbook of Psychophysiology*.
Shekar, C. R. Chandra, "Possession Syndrome in India," in Collcen W.11-(1, *Altered States of Consciousness and Mental 1 Was*.
Smith, Morton, *Jesus the Magician*. San Francisco: Harper and Row, 1978.
Spanos, Nicholas, "Hypnosis, Demonic Possession, and Multiple Personality," in Colleen Ward, *Altered States of Consciousness*.
Spiegel, David, and Etzel Cardena, "Disintegrated Experience: The Dissociative Disorders Revisited," *Journal of Abnormal Psychology*, Vol. 100, No. 3, 1991.
Sternbach, Richard, ed., *Handbook of Psychophysiology*. New York: Holt Rinehart and Winston, 1972.
Tolbert, Mary Ann, *Perspectives on the Parables*. Fortress: Philadelphia, 1979.
Turner, Max, "The Spirit of Prophecy and the Power of Authoritative Preaching in Luke-Acts: A Question of Origins," *New Testament Studies*, Vol. 38, 1992.
Van Cangh, Jean-Marie, "Par L'Esprit De Dieu—Par Le Doigt De Dieu,"337-42, in *Logia: Le Paroles De Jesus—The Sayings of Jesus*, ed. Joel Delobel, Leuven: Leuven University Press, 1982.
Vermes, Geza, *The Dead Sea Scrolls in English*. Sheffield: JSOT Press, 1987.

———, *Jesus the Jew*. Philadelphia: Fortress, 1973.
Ward, Colleen, *Altered States of Consciousness and Mental Health: A Cross-Cultural Perspective*. Newbury Park: Sage Publications, 1989.
———, "Possession and Exorcism," in *Altered States of Consciousness and Mental Health*.
———, "Spirit Possession and Mental Health: A Psycho-anthropological Perspective," in *Human Relations*, Vol. 33, 1980.
Watzlawick, P., J. Weakland, and R. Fisch, *Change: Principles of Problem Formation and Problem Resolution*. New York: W. W. Norton, 1974.
Wayman, Alex, "The Religious Meaning of Possession States," in Raymond Prince, *Trance and Possession States*.
Webb, Robert, *John the Baptizer and Prophet: A Socio-Historical Study*; Journal for the Study of the New Testament Supplement Series Number 62. Sheffield: JSOT Press, 1991.
Weeden, Theodore, *Mark: Traditions in Conflict*. Minneapolis MN: Augsburg-Fortress, 1979.
Weeks, Gerald, "A Metatheory of Paradox," in his *Promoting Change Through Paradoxical Therapy: Revised Edition*. New York: Brunner/Mazel, 1991.
Wells, George A, *The Jesus Legend*. Chicago IL:Open Court Publishing Company 1996.
Wilson, R. R., "Prophecy and Ecstasy: A Reexamination," *Journal of Biblical Literature*, Vol. 98, 1979.
———, "Prophet," in *Harper's Bible Dictionary*. San Francisco: Harper and Row, 1985.
Winkelman, Michael, *Shamans, Priests and Witches: A Cross-Cultural Study of Magico Religious Practitioners*, Anthropological Research Papers: Number 44. Tempe: Arizona State University, 1992.
Winston, David, *Philo of Alexandria: The Contemplative Life, the Giants, and Selections*. New York: Paulist Press, 1981.
Wire, Antoinette, *Corinthian Women Prophets*. Minneapolis: Fortress, 1990.
Wolman, Benjamin and Montague Ullman, eds., *Handbook of States of Consciousness*. New York: Van Nostrand, 1986.
Yap, P. M., "The Possession Syndrome—A Comparison of Hong Kong and French Findings," *Journal of Mental Science*, 1960.

www.ingramcontent.com/pod-product-compliance
Lightning Source LLC
Chambersburg PA
CBHW060107230426
43661CB00033B/1427/J